MFC
Developer's
Workshop

Frank Crockett,
with Jocelyn Garner

Microsoft Press

PUBLISHED BY
Microsoft Press
A Division of Microsoft Corporation
One Microsoft Way
Redmond, Washington 98052-6399

Library of Congress Cataloging-in-Publication Data
Crockett, Frank, 1968-
   MFC Developer's Workshop / Frank Crockett.
      p.   cm.
   Includes index.
   ISBN 1-57231-511-3
   1. Application software–Development. 2. Microsoft foundation
class library. 3. Microsoft Visual C++. I. Title.
QA76.76.A65C76   1997
0005.26'8--dc21   97-7751
                                               CIP

Printed and bound in the United States of America.

1 2 3 4 5 6 7 8 9   MLML   2 1 0 9 8 7

Distributed to the book trade in Canada by Macmillan of Canada, a division of Canada Publishing Corporation.

A CIP catalogue record for this book is available from the British Library.

Microsoft Press books are available through booksellers and distributors worldwide. For further information about international editions, contact your local Microsoft Corporation office. Or contact Microsoft Press.International directly at fax (206) 936-7329.

Acquisitions Editor: Eric Stroo
Project Editor: Sigrid Anne Strom
Technical Editor: Jim Fuchs

CONTENTS

PART I: WORKSHOP

CHAPTER ONE

AppWizard and the MFC Library **3**

CHAPTER TWO

Application and Frame Window Architecture **45**

CHAPTER THREE

Document Templates **75**

PART II: REFERENCE SECTION

Knowledge Base Articles **325**

APPENDIX

Searching for Articles in
the Microsoft Knowledge Base **413**

ACKNOWLEDGMENTS

Without contributions and support from the following people, you would not be holding this book. My sincere thanks to all of them.

To Grandfather for his support and gifts.

To Kathy Swihart, who was always there to support me, even when everything else seemed to be spinning out of control.

To the excellent people who make up the Microsoft Technical Support teams for Visual C++ for their technical expertise and advice, with special thanks to Dan Kirby, Joel Krist, Joe Massoni, Ed Dore, and Kelly Ward.

To Mike Blaszczak (did I spell it right?), John Elsbree (a man who doesn't have to drink to have a good time!), and Michael Malone (a pretty good pilot and sorcerer) for their advice and assistance in some of the more technical areas of MFC.

To Chuck Sphar, an excellent mentor who was always there (sort of <g>) to keep me writing.

To Jocelyn Garner, who rounded out this book nicely with a chapter on database classes and MFC.

And finally, to my parents for letting me read my books, instead of making me go out and play (like "normal" kids).

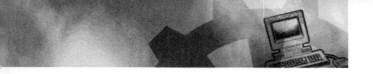

INTRODUCTION

MFC Developer's Workshop is part of a series of task-centered books that focus on solutions to common programming tasks. The purpose of this book is to assist developers in quickly implementing common features found in Microsoft Foundation Class (MFC) applications. It is intended as a solution set for intermediate developers, not as an introduction to the MFC library.

What's in This Book

This book consists of a collection of programming tasks that center around the MFC library. The tasks presented in the collection are problems commonly encountered during the development of Microsoft Windows applications using Microsoft Visual C++ and their solutions. Each task presents the steps and information needed to implement a particular feature or behavior.

How This Book Is Organized

This book is designed to demonstrate the modularity of the MFC library through a series of focused programming tasks. The structure of the book is itself modular; each chapter includes a discussion of the general topic to be covered (usually an area of program functionality or an area of the MFC library) and several common tasks that illustrate various details of the topic being discussed (for instance, document-view architecture, dialog boxes, and menus and controls). Each chapter (and each task within the chapter) is self-contained. The only common thread from one task to another is that all tasks implement a solution to a problem using components of the MFC library. Having said this, however, I recommend you read Chapter 1 before jumping into the rest of the book because it introduces the modular approach that clarifies the relationships among the various components of the MFC library.

Is This Book for You?

This book is intended for people who have had at least one year of experience developing MFC applications for Windows or who have developed one or two small applications using MFC. It will also be helpful if you understand the basic concepts of C++ programming, such as class inheritance and over-riding member functions.

What You Need to Use This Book

To use this book, you will need version 2 or later of the MFC library. The contents of the book are based on the MFC library and not on the development interface, so you don't have to have Visual C++ or Microsoft Developer Studio. However, I recommend using either Visual C++ version 2 or later or Developer Studio because they are tightly integrated with the MFC library and greatly simplify programming for Windows.

Overview of Chapters

Chapter 1

In Chapter 1, I demonstrate the functionality of AppWizard and the modularity of the MFC library through a series of five tasks. Each task addresses the addition of a specific feature (available via AppWizard) to an existing MFC application—a good introduction to using the class.

Chapter 2

In Chapter 2, I focus on MFC tasks from an application-wide perspective. Each of the seven tasks demonstrates a feature that affects the entire application, such as customizing the system menu or implementing tooltips for various types of tools.

Chapter 3

In Chapter 3, the life cycle of a document-view pair in an MFC application is discussed in detail. In the discussion, I walk you through the steps to create the document, frame, and view elements and discuss the various points at which you can customize the process. The three tasks in the chapter demonstrate creating multiple views on a single document, creating switchable views, and customizing the interface for choosing a new document.

Chapter 4

The four tasks of Chapter 4 address the topic of dialog boxes and illustrate the techniques you can use to implement various features for them. Among the topics discussed are customizing the background of a dialog box, customizing common dialog boxes, and implementing custom DDX functions.

Chapter 5

The five tasks included in Chapter 5 address the use of various Windows controls in your application—for example, modifying the application menu that is based on the current open child window, moving list box data to and from a *CStringArray* object, and implementing tooltips for dialog controls.

Chapter 6

The four tasks in this chapter deal with various aspects of using Microsoft ActiveX controls and implementing OLE in MFC applications. Some of the issues I address include marking a control as safe for scripting and initializing when used in Microsoft Internet Explorer, implementing a custom OLE interface, and loading an ActiveX control property asynchronously.

Chapter 7

This chapter consists of a group of miscellaneous tasks related to MFC applications, their components, and their interactions with the system. Some examples include saving the system state from one program session to the next, implementing resource-only DLLs, and implementing drag and drop support for an MDI application.

Chapter 8

Six of the eight tasks presented in this chapter address using DAO database classes and sample databases to link data sources to Microsoft Access, to open data sources directly, and to mix static and dynamic binding in an application. The remaining two tasks address using output parameters with the ODBC API and using ODBC database classes to open a recordset on a stored procedure. Nondatabase techniques that are discussed within these tasks include using Developer Studio components from the Gallery and using ActiveX controls.

Comments and Questions

If you have comments or questions regarding this book or ideas for other tasks you would like to see addressed in future editions, contact me at the address provided below:

http://mspress.microsoft.com/mspress/products/1066

PART I

WORKSHOP

AppWizard and the MFC Library

AppWizard was developed by the same people who developed the Microsoft Foundation Class (MFC) library, for which reason it's the best and most efficient starting place for your MFC development. AppWizard is like the framer of a new house; it knows its materials (the elements of the MFC library) and what's needed to set up the basic structure (in this case, an MFC application).

AppWizard initially uses a series of six dialog boxes to create a blueprint for your project. The first dialog box helps you set up your application framework (single document interface or multiple document interface), set up several basic features whose scope is application-wide (such as OLE abilities and Data Access Objects), and set up several common features (such as print preview and context-sensitive help). After you have made your choices, AppWizard shows you the current plan. Unlike designing a house, where you must pay an architect for every change to the initial plan, you can jump back and forth at will between pages and change options until you're satisfied. Once you are satisfied, you can examine the framework objects (each represented by a class) and modify basic features (such as derivation from a certain parent class, filename, and so forth). AppWizard designs the pad (the underlying architecture) and the frame (OLE or database) on the basis of your choices.

After you click OK, AppWizard builds the application framework using various objects from the MFC library, such as frame windows, documents, control bars, and views. When it is finished, you have a fully functioning framework application, that is, you can build and execute the project without errors and without crashing. Granted, its functionality is limited, but how many people build just the frame of their new home and then move in? At this point, you start adding the floors, windows, doors, and siding.

This chapter is not intended either as a tutorial for using AppWizard or as a broad overview of the library. I focus on the modularity of the MFC library and how AppWizard uses it to generate a framework application. We will break down a project that has been created with AppWizard in a modular fashion instead of breaking it down exclusively by classes or files.

Background

One of the primary purposes of this discussion, and of the book in general, is to describe the way components implemented by MFC classes are put together, pulled apart, or customized with relative ease by AppWizard or by you. In the tasks that are included in this chapter, I will demonstrate this modularity by customizing several common features offered by AppWizard and then show exactly what AppWizard creates to implement your project's desired features. The discussion covers the following major topics:

- General architecture of a framework application

    The general framework components of an MFC application generated by AppWizard are described, using a model of layering to discuss each basic type of MFC application: dialog box–based, single document interface (SDI), and multiple document interface (MDI).

- Application types created by AppWizard

    The concept of modularity is used to describe the three types of basic applications created by AppWizard: dialog box–based, SDI, and MDI. Each type of application is described and broken into its respective elements; the classes that AppWizard generated are then used to implement the elements of the framework.

- Application-wide options provided by AppWizard

    This is a brief discussion of how OLE compound document and database support options affect the basic application framework.

- Customizing application features

    This is a brief discussion of the ways an application created with AppWizard can be customized.

General Architecture of a Framework Application

The typical MFC application consists of three layers (Figure 1-1): primary, secondary, and tertiary.

The Primary Layer

The primary (or innermost) application layer contains objects that make up the framework of the application (Figure 1-2 on page 6). In most cases, this layer is created solely by AppWizard. Using your input, AppWizard creates a project that contains classes that implement the four base elements of your application:

- **An application element** An element that is implemented by a *CWin-App*-derived class. The application element is the first thing created

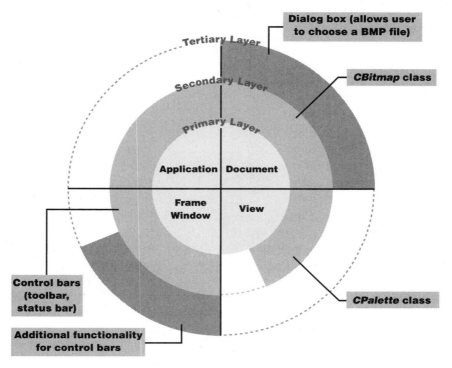

Figure 1-1.
The three layers of a typical MFC application.

when your application executes. It is responsible for initializing the application data and creating the remaining application framework elements.

■ **A frame window element** An element that is commonly implemented by a *CFrameWnd*-derived (or *CMDIFrameWnd*-derived) class. The frame window element acts as the container for the interface elements of the application: the windows and the controls of your application. The frame window element is the second thing that is created when your application executes. This element is primarily responsible for creating the document and view elements of the application and managing the control bars of the window object. Sometimes the frame window element is referred to as the glue of the application because it creates and links the other application framework elements together. However, it is also one of the least often modified elements of an MFC application.

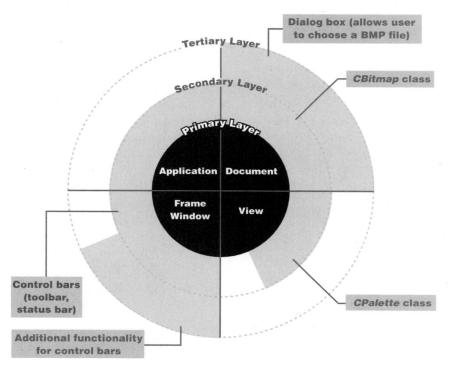

Figure 1-2.
The primary layer of a typical MFC application.

- **A document element** An element that is commonly implemented by a *CDocument*-derived class. The document element contains the data of the application and is half of a document-view pair. It is responsible for storing and retrieving data from external sources, modifying application data, and notifying all view objects related to the document when changes have occurred. It is one of the most misunderstood elements of the MFC application. (For more details on the document-view pair, see the discussion in Chapter 3, "Document Templates."

- **A view element** An element that is implemented by a *CView*-derived class. This element implements the graphical side of the document-view relationship. It is responsible for rendering a graphical representation of the document element and the state of the document or application. Because MFC applications run on the Microsoft Windows operating system, the "view" is the workhorse of an MFC application and the most heavily modified element. Like the document element, the view element is often misunderstood.

These four elements are the "parents" of the second and third application layers. For example, if you want an application with a single document interface that can display bitmaps, AppWizard generates an application framework consisting of these four basic elements, on which you later build.

Note that not all applications created with AppWizard have these four elements of the primary layer. Dialog box–based applications have only an application element and a dialog box element. The dialog box element takes the place of the frame window, document, and view elements.

The Secondary Layer

The secondary application layer (Figure 1-3) includes additional application elements that represent the data or items used by the application. These elements are the objects with which an element of the primary layer, such as the document element, interacts closely.

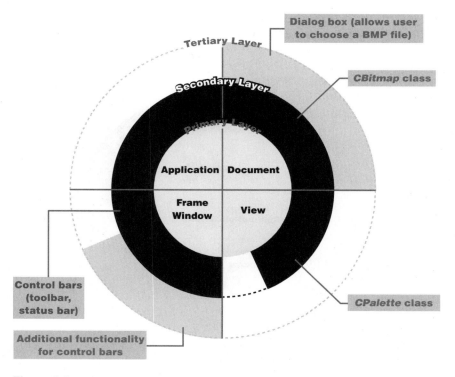

Figure 1-3.
The secondary layer of a typical MFC application.

The elements can be implemented by classes created with ClassWizard or added from other projects. The secondary layer is usually where the bulk of the implementation code can be found whether it is added manually or with ClassWizard. In an application that displays bitmaps, for example, this layer might consist of an element class of type *CBitmap* that stores the bitmap currently being displayed. Another class derived from *CPalette* might store the bitmap's palette. In most cases, this layer is implemented after you have created the application framework using AppWizard but before you implement the tertiary layer. However, at other times the secondary and tertiary layers are implemented simultaneously.

The Tertiary Layer

The final, or tertiary, application layer (Figure 1-4) provides the final touches and specific details of the application—that is, the items that are manipulated by elements of the secondary layer. Because the tertiary layer interacts with the application to varying degrees, depending on the application, it is not considered a "true" framework layer.

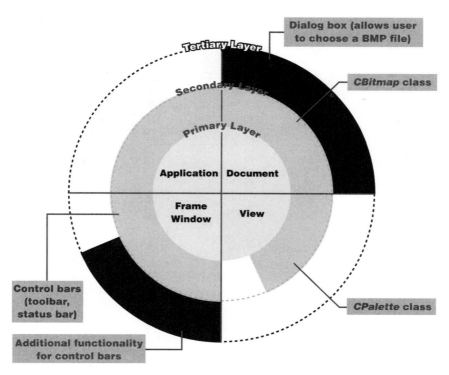

Figure 1-4.

The tertiary layer of a typical MFC application.

In an application that displays bitmaps, the tertiary layer might provide functionality for control bars beyond the functionality provided by AppWizard; or it might provide a dialog box that shows the statistics of the current bitmap in graphical form. In some cases, these details can be provided by overriding a function of an existing parent class or by adding a new data member to track a common value. In other cases, such as when you add a new dialog box, this layer might consist of an entire class that is used by the view element to display bitmap information. Implementation of the tertiary layer is usually the last thing completed before testing or release. Sometimes the layer is not completed. After all, you must have something for the next release!

Application Types Created by AppWizard

AppWizard can build three "houses": dialog box–based, SDI-based, and MDI-based. Using a modular method of development, you can build on these frameworks with little modification to the underlying code. To use the house-building analogy again, not using a modular approach would be like hacking holes in interior walls and putting in windows for quick access, putting doors on the second floor because the existing doors just don't work, or..., well, you get the idea. If you don't have a solid understanding of the underlying architecture, you will have problems adding elements without damaging the existing framework. Keeping the modular method of development in mind, let's look at the three possible types of applications AppWizard can build for us.

> **N O T E :** If you choose OLE compound document support or database support when using AppWizard to create an application, the primary and secondary layers of your application will be modified. These changes consist mainly of the addition of elements that implement either OLE or database support and changes in the derivation of some classes. For more information, see "OLE Options" on page 14.

Dialog Box–Based Applications

The dialog box–based application is the simplest of the three types of applications to create because it only takes two classes to implement all four primary elements. The application element is still the core of the application. However, the framework, document, and view elements are replaced by a dialog box element. Because the dialog box class, which implements the dialog box element, is derived from *CWnd*, the dialog box object inherits the functionality of a window object. In addition, the dialog box object takes the place of a document-view pair by storing both the data and the graphical interface in the dialog box class. Therefore, in this element model the application element is implemented with a *CWinApp*-derived class and the other three elements with a *CDialog*-derived class. You might have to add another class or two for additional functionality, but most of your work will be contained within the dialog box element. Figure 1-5 illustrates the primary layer of the framework created by AppWizard for a dialog box–based application.

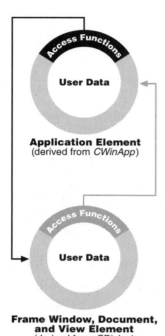

Figure 1-5.
The framework of a typical MFC dialog box–based application.

The table on the next page relates each application framework element to its respective MFC class.

SDI Applications

The SDI application is a more modularized version of the application framework created by AppWizard (Figure 1-6 on page 13). In an SDI application, the application element handles the initialization of the other primary elements and interacts with the system. The application uses just one frame window

Element	Class	Comments
Application	*CWinApp*-derived	The application element initializes any application data and performs any actions before the application becomes visible.
Frame window	*CDialog*-derived	The frame window element manipulates and displays data using a dialog box. Other elements can be added as members to the dialog box class.
Document	*CDialog*-derived and also other classes	Dialog box controls are the main interface, and they handle the majority of the work. Data members can be added to store information from the user.
View	*CDialog*-derived	Controls are the main interface, and they handle the majority of the work.

element that contains the document and view elements and that is the glue of the document-view pair. In an SDI application, the majority of code creates and manages any control bars of the frame window. Because this is an SDI application, all application control bars are managed by the frame window. More code can be added for initialization purposes. And you can also have the frame window store application data that directly affects both the document and the view elements.

However, the real workers in the application are the document and view elements. In the MFC library, these two elements are implemented by two closely related classes derived from *CDocument* and *CView*. These classes can access each other with pre-implemented member functions. (For more information on the mechanics of documents, views, and document templates, see the discussion in Chapter 3, "Document Templates.")

In the SDI element model, the application element is implemented once again with a *CWinApp*-derived class. The frame window element is implemented with a *CFrameWnd*-derived class, and the document and view elements are implemented with *CDocument*-derived and *CView*-derived classes, respectively. Figure 1-6 on the following page illustrates the primary and secondary layers of the framework created by AppWizard for an SDI-based application. The table on the following page relates each framework element to its respective MFC class.

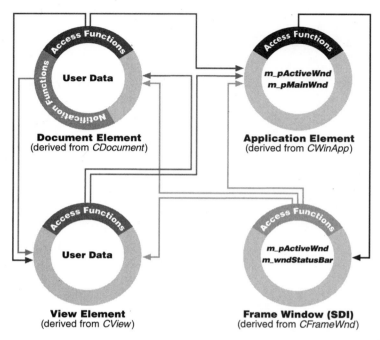

Figure 1-6.
The framework of a typical MFC SDI application.

Element	Class	Comments
Application	*CWinApp*-derived	Initializes any application data and performs any actions before the application becomes visible.
Frame window	*CFrameWnd*-derived	Manages the creation of the application's control bars and some message handling.
Document	*CDocument*-derived and also other classes	Contains the application's data in the form of data members or pointers to user-derived classes. Closely tied to the view element through member functions.
View	*CView*-derived and also other classes	Graphically displays the state of the document data and of the application. Closely tied to the document element through member functions.

MDI Applications

The primary layer of an MDI application is exactly the same as the primary layer of an SDI framework except for the presence of an additional frame window object. This additional object contains the document-view pairs of the MDI application. Figure 1-7 illustrates the primary and secondary layers of the framework created by AppWizard for an MDI application.

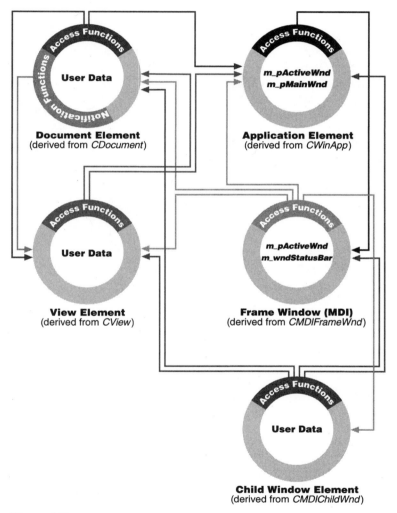

Figure 1-7.
The framework of a typical MFC MDI application.

In an MDI application, unlike an SDI application, you can have multiple child windows open, each of which contains a different view of the same document or which contain views of different documents. If you look at the MDI application as an element framework, this ability adds an extra object between the main application frame window and the view. Instead of the main frame window having direct access to the view, it must now query for the active child window of the application and then, with that object, query for the attached view. Within an MDI application, you can almost think of each child window as a mini-application.

In the MDI element model, the application element is implemented the same way as an SDI application except that the main frame window element is implemented with a *CMDIFrameWnd*-derived class, which contains additional code for handling MDI child windows within the application. The additional frame window object for the MDI application, the child window, is implemented with a *CMDIChildWnd*-derived class. Once again, code was added to function properly in an MDI environment. The document and view elements are implemented with *CDocument*-derived and *CView*-derived classes, respectively.

As the name suggests, an MDI application can contain multiple documents. Each document is part of a document template that contains a frame window, a document, and a view object. If the application has more than one document template and the user wants to create a new document, a dialog box displays the available document types to the user. The table on the next page relates each application framework element to its respective MFC class.

Application-Wide Options Provided by AppWizard

When we create an application with AppWizard, there are two steps that affect the structure of the application framework. The effects include the addition of classes that provide OLE compound document support and database support. In addition, the parents of some application framework elements can change, depending on what options are selected.

OLE Options

By default, AppWizard does not automatically include OLE compound document or database support. If you choose to include these (which are found on the second and third steps of AppWizard), the primary and secondary layers of the application will change significantly. There are four possible variations of OLE compound document support: container, mini-server (for SDI

Element	Class	Comments
Application	*CWinApp*-derived	Initializes any application data and performs any actions before the application becomes visible.
Application's frame window	*CMDIFrameWnd*-derived	Manages the creation of the application's control bars, all MDI child windows, and some message handling.
Child window	*CMDIChildWnd*-derived	Used to manage control bars and to handle certain messages. Like the main frame window, this element is the glue of each document type.
Document	*CDocument*-derived and also other classes	Contains the application's data in the form of data members or pointers to user-derived classes. Closely tied to the view element through member functions.
View	*CView*-derived and also other classes	Graphically displays the state of the document data and the application. Closely tied to the document element through member functions.

applications only), full-server, and container/server. (For a complete description of these types of support, see online documentation for AppWizard.)

Container support   If you choose to include container support, your document class is derived from *COleDocument.* This class includes extra support for the activation of objects called clients in an OLE document. In addition, a new element called a client (or client item) is added to the secondary layer. The client item is implemented using a *COleClientItem*-derived class and acts as an intermediary between the OLE item and the client.

Mini-server support (for SDI applications only)   If you choose to include mini-server support, your document class is derived from *COleServerDoc* instead of *CDocument.* This class includes server support for interaction with server items. Visual editing for the items, within the document-view architecture, is also supported. In addition, two new elements are added to the secondary layer. The first element, implemented with a *COleServerItem*-derived class, represents the server items of your application. The second element, implemented with a *COleIPFrameWnd*-derived class, is the frame window of a server item that has been activated within your application. The following table relates each element to its respective class.

Element	Class	Comments
Server item	*COleServerItem*-derived	Acts as an intermediary between the OLE item and the server.
In-place frame window	*COleIPFrameWnd*-derived	Handles the placement of toolbars within the container's application window. Also handles notifications when the in-place window is resized.

Full-server support If you choose to include full-server support, the same derivation changes and element additions are made that are made for a mini-server. The only difference is in the implementation code.

Container/server support Support for a container/server is basically provided by a combination of the container and server elements. Once again, the derivation of your document class is *COleServer*. The new elements are classes that implement the client item, the server item, and an in-place frame window. This implementation is specified in the following table.

Element	Class	Comments
Client item	*COleClientItem*-derived	Acts as an intermediary between the OLE item and the client.
Server item	*COleServerItem*-derived	Acts as an intermediary between the OLE item and the server.
In-place frame window	*COleIPFrameWnd*-derived	Handles the placement of toolbars within the container's application window. Also handles notifications when the in-place window is resized.

Database Support Options

The database support options are simpler to implement than other options because they require fewer modifications to the primary layer. The first option simply adds the header files to your project. The second and third options change the derivation of the view element from *CView* to *CRecordView*. As I mentioned earlier in the chapter, support is added to the view class for easily displaying database records. A new element, derived from *CRecordSet*, is added to the second layer of the MFC application. This class implements the database query function of your application and stores information about database queries performed in your application. (See Chapter 8 for information about MFC and databases.)

Customizing Application Features

Besides using AppWizard to set up the core elements of your application, you can choose from a variety of application-wide features to customize your framework application. These features range from fundamental application-wide elements to the small user-interface details that always seem to be left until the end of the project. AppWizard, for the most part, plays it safe by using a default customization that includes most of the cooler user interface features (such as control bars, print preview, and so on) and stays away from the more fundamental features (such as OLE compound document support).

To demonstrate the modularity of an application created with AppWizard, I have included five tasks in this chapter that show how to retrofit several of the most common AppWizard features to an existing application.

- Adding a dockable toolbar and a status bar to an existing MFC application

- Adding an MRU list to an existing MFC application

- Adding print preview to an existing MFC application

- Adding MAPI and Windows Sockets support to an existing MFC application

- Converting an existing MFC SDI application to MDI

For a complete discussion of the features of AppWizard, see the AppWizard article family in *Programming with MFC Encyclopedia* and "Creating Applications Using AppWizard" in *VC++ User Guide*.

Adding a Docking Toolbar and a Status Bar to an Existing MFC Application

The purpose of this task is to add a docking toolbar and a status bar to the main frame window of an existing MFC application. A docking toolbar contains buttons for common tasks, such as opening and saving files, editing, and printing. It can be docked on any side of the application's main frame window or can be dismissed, as the user chooses. The status bar, positioned at the bottom of the application's main frame window, displays descriptive text for toolbar buttons and idle-time messages. A status bar requires only a parent class and code that creates and initializes the status bar. An MFC docking toolbar, on the other hand, requires several elements:

- A bitmap that represents the toolbar buttons

- Code that maps each toolbar button to a command ID

- A *CWnd*-derived class in the application that will function as the parent of the toolbar

- Code that creates and initializes the toolbar

The task of adding a docking toolbar and a status bar to an application consists of three steps:

1. Importing a bitmap resource to an application

2. Adding member variables and message map entries

3. Adding initialization and implementation code for the control bars

The requirement for this task is a bitmap resource for the toolbar. (A default toolbar bitmap resource can be found in the DEFAULT.RC file on the companion CD-ROM, located in the \Projects\Default directory.)

After you have completed the task, the application will have a docking toolbar and a status bar exactly as if you had chosen the toolbar and status bar option in AppWizard.

Step 1: Importing a Bitmap Resource into an Application

For simplicity's sake, only the bitmap resources will be added in this step. The status bar code will be added later. There are two methods for creating a bitmap resource for an application: importing a resource from another project and inserting a new toolbar with the Resource editor. Because we will be adding an entire toolbar—a toolbar bitmap and command mappings for each button—it is easier to import an existing bitmap resource. To prevent conflicts as much as possible, we will use the toolbar generated by AppWizard (Figure 1-8).

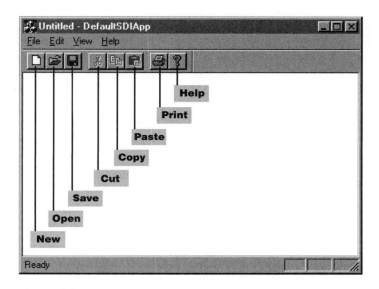

Figure 1-8.
Default toolbar generated by AppWizard.

The default toolbar generated by AppWizard has eight buttons, each mapped to a task. To import an existing toolbar into an application, follow these steps:

1. Load your project into Microsoft Visual C++ and select the Resource-View pane.

2. Open the resource file (with the extension of RC) containing the toolbar you will import. A resource file containing the default toolbar can be found in the DEFAULT.RC file, located in the \PROJECTS\DE-FAULT directory on the companion CD-ROM.

3. Expand the toolbar node by double-clicking the Toolbar folder icon.

4. Drag the IDR_MAINFRAME object to the ResourceView pane, and drop it onto the resource folder object.

5. Save the resource file.

Your project should now have a toolbar folder that contains IDR_MAINFRAME. Your resource script has been modified to include a bitmap resource (the toolbar bitmap) and a toolbar. In addition, the bitmap has been copied into your application's \RES subdirectory.

TIP: If your application does not support Print Preview, be sure you remove the Print Preview button.

Step 2: Adding Member Variables and Message Map Entries

Now you have to modify portions of the application code. The application's main frame window normally is the parent of any control bars, so you will now have to add member variables to the application's main frame window class for both the toolbar and the status bar. Specifically, you need to modify the *CMainFrame* class (derived from *CFrameWnd* or *CMDIFrameWnd*) by adding two protected member variables to the header file of class *CMainFrame* (MAINFRAME.H) as shown below. These two variables contain the toolbar and the status bar objects after the application creates them.

```
protected:  // Control bar embedded members
    CStatusBar  m_wndStatusBar;
    CToolBar    m_wndToolBar;
```

You also need a place to create and initialize the control bars before the application is used. Use the handler for the WM_CREATE message to do this. At this point, just add this handler to your *CMainFrame* class, either manually or using ClassWizard. The new code (in bold) should look similar to the following examples.

■ In the header file:

```
afx_msg int OnCreate(LPCREATESTRUCT lpCreateStruct);
    // NOTE - the ClassWizard will add and remove member
    // functions here.
```

■ In the implementation file:

```
⋮
ON_WM_CREATE()
//}}AFX_MSG_MAP
```

Now modify the *CMainFrame* implementation file to add the status bar. Add the following lines of code immediately after the end of the message map declaration:

```
static UINT indicators[] =
{
    ID_SEPARATOR,              // Status line indicator
    ID_INDICATOR_CAPS,
    ID_INDICATOR_NUM,
    ID_INDICATOR_SCRL,
};
```

This code creates a static array, named *indicators*, that stores a common set of flags. These flags indicate the state of certain keys (such as Scroll Lock) in the status bar. (For more information on status bar indicators, see Technical Note 22 in the Visual C++ online documentation.)

Step 3: Adding Initialization and Implementation Code for the Control Bars

Now create and initialize the control bars in the WM_CREATE handler. To add control bar code, follow this procedure:

1. Add the code below to the WM_CREATE handler after the call to the base class *OnCreate* function:

```
if (!m_wndToolBar.Create(this) ||
    !m_wndToolBar.LoadToolBar(IDR_MAINFRAME))
{
    TRACE0("Failed to create toolbar\n");
    return -1;      // Fail to create
}

if (!m_wndStatusBar.Create(this) ||
    !m_wndStatusBar.SetIndicators(indicators,
        sizeof(indicators)/sizeof(UINT)))
{
    TRACE0("Failed to create status bar\n");
    return -1;      // Fail to create
}
```

2. To display tooltips and make the toolbar resizeable, include the following code lines after the code that creates the control bars in the *OnCreate* function of *CMainFrame*:

```
m_wndToolBar.SetBarStyle(m_wndToolBar.GetBarStyle() |
    CBRS_TOOLTIPS | CBRS_FLYBY | CBRS_SIZE_DYNAMIC);
```

21

3. To make the toolbar dockable, add the following code lines after the code that creates the control bars in the *OnCreate* function of *CMain-Frame*:

```
m_wndToolBar.EnableDocking(CBRS_ALIGN_ANY);
EnableDocking(CBRS_ALIGN_ANY);
DockControlBar(&m_wndToolBar);
```

Your application's main frame window now has a docking toolbar and a status bar.

Additional Information

A common feature of control bars is the ability to determine whether to display them or not. This ability to display or hide the control bars is accomplished by making use of two standard command IDs. To add the ability for users to toggle control bars on and off, follow these steps:

1. Switch to your project's ResourceView pane, and open the main menu resource, commonly named IDR_MAINFRAME.

2. Add a top-level menu named View. (If you already have this menu, skip to the next step.)

3. Add a command named Toolbar to the View menu. This command should have the resource ID ID_VIEW_TOOLBAR.

4. Add a command, named Status Bar, to the View menu. This command should have the resource ID ID_VIEW_STATUS_BAR.

5. Save your project's resource file.

You can also use *CFrameWnd::ShowControlBar* to display or hide your application's control bars. This function can be called from any menu command handler or can be called directly as the result of some action—for example, the appearance of a certain type of window. (For more information on using *CFrameWnd::ShowControlBar*, see the CTRLBARS MFC sample that is located in the Visual C++ section of Books Online.)

The following articles in the Microsoft Knowledge Base contain information related to toolbars and status bars:

- SAMPLE: Adding Control Bars to Dialog Boxes in MFC: Q141751

- Setting First Pane of CStatusBar: Q110505

- Displaying the Current Time in a CStatusBar Pane: Q99198

Adding an MRU List to an Existing MFC Application

The purpose of this task is to enable an existing MFC application to display a most recently used (MRU) list in the File menu. An MRU list is a common feature of most Windows applications, as shown in the example in Figure 1-9. The list, commonly found on the File menu, allows the user to select from the last *n* files accessed. It is enabled by a call to *LoadStdProfileSettings* and modification of the application's menu resource.

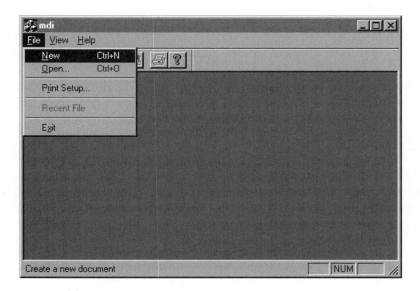

Figure 1-9.
The MRU list of an application created with AppWizard.

The following procedure modifies a menu resource by adding an entry for the MRU list under the File menu. To add a menu entry for an MRU list, follow these steps:

1. Use Visual C++ to open the RC file of the target project.

2. Open the main menu resource of the project, which is commonly named IDR_MAINFRAME.

3. Add a new command named Recent File with the ID ID_FILE_MRU_FILE1 to the File menu, and check the grayed check box in the Properties dialog box for the new menu item. This ID is

predefined by the MFC library, and the command will be disabled until the MRU list has one or more entries. If you want, you can add a separator menu item to differentiate the MRU list from the preceding menu entries.

Once this command has been added, a call to *CWinApp::LoadStdProfileSettings* can be made in the application's *InitInstance* function. The call can be made in the beginning of the function as follows:

```
BOOL CProjNaApp::InitInstance()
{
    ⋮
// Load standard INI file options (including MRU)
    LoadStdProfileSettings();
    ⋮
```

This function loads the default settings for an application of this type and maintains an MRU list for the application. You can disable the MRU list by passing 0 to *LoadStdProfileSettings*.

When you enable the MRU list for your application, you will notice that the file list never exceeds 4 entries. This is the default number of entries specified by the MFC library. However, the framework can handle a list of up to 16 entries. To increase the number of items in the MRU list, pass the number to the application's call to *LoadStdProfileSettings*. For example, for an MRU list that contains ten filenames, make the following call in your application's *InitInstance*:

```
LoadStdProfileSettings(10);  // Load standard INI file options
                             // (including MRU)
```

To learn more about this command handler and other handlers, see Technical Note 22 in the Visual C++ online documentation.

Adding Print Preview to an Existing MFC Application

The purpose of this task is to add print preview to an existing MFC application. When you have completed the task, your application will have a Print Preview menu item and the user will be able to preview the application's current document. The task has two steps:

1. Adding new menu resources to an application

2. Adding handlers for the new print commands

The requirement for this task is a main frame window menu with additional submenus.

Step 1: Adding New Menu Resources to an Application

In this first step, add the Print and Print Preview menu items to the application's File menu. This allows easy access to print preview and printing as well as supporting the code that handles the Print and Print Preview requests. The end result is similar to the menu pictured below in Figure 1-10:

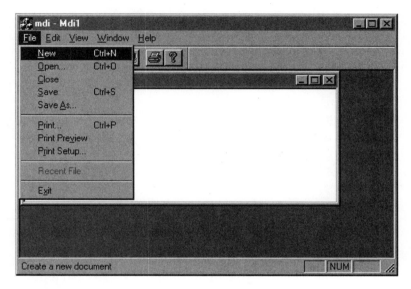

Figure 1-10.
The top-level File menu of a standard MFC application.

In most cases, when an application requires printing resources (such as buttons or views), it gets them from a resource file named AFXPRINT.RC, which contains common MFC printing resources, such as dialog boxes and resource strings. For your application to have access to these resources, you must include this resource file in your project's RC file. This can be done either by adding the RC file manually or by adding the resource file using the Resource Includes dialog box. If you want to add resource files using the Resource Includes dialog box, follow this procedure:

1. Load your project's workspace.

2. Choose Resource Includes from the View menu.

3. In the Compile-Time Directives list box, scroll down until the following line appears:

```
#include afxres.rc // Standard Components
```

4. Enter the code line below immediately after the line in the preceding step.

```
#include afxprint.rc // printing/print preview resources
```

5. Click OK to dismiss the dialog box.

You will get a second dialog box that warns you of dire consequences if you didn't enter the code correctly. This is just one of many instances in which Microsoft Developer Studio is making sure you know what you are doing. Because you are the daring type, go ahead and click OK. Now add the Print, Print Preview, and Print Setup commands to the File menu of your application. I assume that you are familiar with adding menu items, so I will give you just the properties for each item. Be sure you insert a separator item just before the Print menu item.

Print Menu Properties

ID	Caption	Prompt
ID_FILE_PRINT	&Print...\t Ctrl+P	Print the active document\nPrint
ID_FILE_PRINT_PREVIEW	Print Pre&view	Display full pages\n Print Preview
ID_FILE_PRINT_SETUP	P&rint Setup...	Change the printer and printing options\n Print Setup

The last items you need to add to the RC file are two strings that are used as explanatory text on the status bar. Because you are familiar with adding string resources to an application, I will provide you only with the values you need in the table on the next page. The position of the values is not important in the string table.

Once you have made modifications, save the resource file.

Step 2: Adding Handlers for the New Print Commands

Now that you've added the graphic front end for printing to your application, you have to add command handlers for the new commands. You will

String Table Properties

ID	Caption
ID_FILE_PAGE_SETUP	Change the printing options\nPage Setup
AFX_IDS_PREVIEW_CLOSE	Close print preview mode\nCancel Preview

add two standard sets of handlers, which will match the handlers created by AppWizard if Print Preview is chosen. I divided the handlers into two sets because one set must be added by hand, although you can use ClassWizard to add the other. (For more information on these standard command handlers, see Technical Note 22 in the Visual C++ online documentation.)

The first set of handlers, consisting of four print commands, just calls the default command handler of the base class. Of course, because you are working with C++ classes, you can remove the existing handlers and add your own, using ClassWizard, if the default behavior isn't good enough. To add the first set of command handlers, follow these steps:

1. Open the implementation file of the application class.

2. Add the following line of code after the handlers for ID_FILE_NEW and ID_FILE_OPEN:

```
// Standard print setup command
ON_COMMAND(ID_FILE_PRINT_SETUP, CWinApp::OnFilePrintSetup)
```

   This function invokes the standard Print Setup dialog box.

3. Add the remaining handlers—ID_FILE_PRINT, ID_FILE_PRINT _DIRECT, and ID_FILE_PRINT_PREVIEW—to the view class message map. In the implementation file of the view class, add the following lines of code (shown in bold) after the end of the ClassWizard portion of the message map:

```
//}}AFX_MSG_MAP
// Standard printing commands
ON_COMMAND(ID_FILE_PRINT, CView::OnFilePrint)
N_COMMAND(ID_FILE_PRINT_DIRECT, CView::OnFilePrint)
ON_COMMAND(ID_FILE_PRINT_PREVIEW, CView::OnFilePrintPreview)
END_MESSAGE_MAP()
```

   Respectively, these handlers print the current document using the Print dialog box, print the current document bypassing the Print dialog box, and enter Print Preview mode for the current document.

Because the code for handling the next set of commands is implemented in the application's view class, you can use ClassWizard. Follow these steps:

1. Open ClassWizard for your project. From the Message Maps page of ClassWizard, choose the view class.

2. From the listing of messages on the right, add the *OnBeginPrinting*, *OnEndPrinting*, and *OnPreparePrinting* functions.

3. Click OK to exit ClassWizard.

You should end up with three declarations in your view class's header file similar to the ones below:

```
protected:
virtual BOOL OnPreparePrinting(CPrintInfo* pInfo);
virtual void OnBeginPrinting(CDC* pDC, CPrintInfo* pInfo);
virtual void OnEndPrinting(CDC* pDC, CPrintInfo* pInfo);
//}}AFX_VIRTUAL
```

And you should have three function bodies in your view class's implementation file as shown below:

```
// CPPrevView printing
BOOL CPPrevView::OnPreparePrinting(CPrintInfo* pInfo)
{
    // default preparation
    return DoPreparePrinting(pInfo);
}
void CPPrevView::OnBeginPrinting(CDC* pDC, CPrintInfo*pInfo)
{
    // TODO: add extra initialization before printing
}
void CPPrevView::OnEndPrinting(CDC* pDC, CPrintInfo* pInfo
{
    // TODO: add cleanup after printing
}
```

After adding these print handlers, add specific code to each function to fully implement them.

Adding MAPI and Windows Sockets Support to an Existing MFC Application

The purpose of this task is to enable an existing MFC application to support the Microsoft Messaging application programming interface (MAPI) and Windows Sockets. MAPI provides your application with the ability to create, send, and otherwise manipulate mail messages. It is commonly seen in MFC applications as a Send Mail option on the File menu. MFC support for this API is not complete, but the basic functionality is available through the *CDocument* class. Even though the MFC support is incomplete, all MAPI functions can be called directly from a MAPI-enabled application. (For more information about MAPI support and for answers to more MAPI-specific questions, see the articles "MAPI" and "MAPI Support in MFC" in the Visual C++ online documentation.)

Windows Sockets enables an MFC application to support a socket (an end point of communication across a network). Sockets are used to send and receive data. MFC uses two classes to implement support for sockets: *CAsyncSocket* (implemented with minimal wrapping) and *CSocket* (implemented with a "heavier" wrapping for ease of use). (For more information on Windows Sockets, see the articles "Windows Sockets in MFC: Overview" and "Windows Sockets: Background" in the Visual C++ online documentation.)

After you complete this task, your application will have the same support for MAPI and Windows Sockets that it would have had if you had used AppWizard to add it when you created the application. This task has two steps:

1. Adding the Send Mail command and string resources

2. Adding support code

Step 1: Adding a New Menu Item and String Resources

First add a command that allows the user to send mail messages, and also add some strings for informational prompts and error messages to the File menu. I assume that you are familiar with adding menu items, so I will just provide you with the properties and let you do the rest. Be sure you insert a separator item right after the Send menu item.

Send Menu Item Property

ID	Caption	Prompt
ID_FILE_SEND_MAIL	Sen&d Mail...	Send the active document through electronic mail\n Send Mail

Now insert a string that provides explanatory text on the status bar into the application's string table. I assume you are also familiar with adding string resources to an application, so I'll provide you only the values you need. The position of the values is not important in the string table. After you have made these additions, save the resource file.

String Table Properties

ID	Caption
IDP_SOCKETS_INIT_FAILED	Windows Sockets initialization failed.

Step 2: Adding Support Code

Now you have to add code to a few of the project's files. Because the features to be added are related to the document class and the main frame window class, we work mainly with the classes *CProjNameDoc* and *CMainFrame*. To add support code for Windows Sockets, follow this procedure:

1. Add the following include file—which consists of standard code that initializes and implements Windows Sockets support—to the end of your project's STDAFX.H header file:

   ```
   #include <afxsock.h>          // MFC socket extensions
   ```

2. Add the resource symbol IDP_SOCKETS_INIT_FAILED, which tells the framework if the application fails to initialize the Windows Sockets.

Follow the procedure below to add the resource symbol using the Resource Includes dialog box. When you are finished, save the resource file.

1. Load your project's workspace.

2. Choose Resource Symbols from the View menu.

3. Click New.

4. For Name, enter IDP_SOCKETS_INIT_FAILED, and for Value, enter *104.*

5. Click OK to dismiss the New Symbol dialog box, and click Close to dismiss the Resource Symbols dialog box.

The last modification related to MAPI support involves the manual addition of command handlers for the new Send command. You will have to add an ON_COMMAND_UPDATE_UI handler as well as an ON_COMMAND handler. The ON_COMMAND handler sends the current document to a mail application specified by Windows. The ON_COMMAND_UPDATE_UI handler updates the menu item, whether a mail application is available or not. Add the following code immediately after the AFX_MSG_MAP portion map of the document's class. The message map can be found in the document's implementation file:

```
ON_COMMAND(ID_FILE_SEND_MAIL, OnFileSendMail)
ON_UPDATE_COMMAND_UI(ID_FILE_SEND_MAIL, OnUpdateFileSendMail)
```

At this point, you have completed installing MAPI support. To complete the support for Windows Sockets, add initialization code to the application. A good place to do this is in the *InitInstance* function of the *CMainFrame* class, which was derived from *CFrameWnd*. Add the following code to the beginning of *InitInstance*:

```
if (!AfxSocketInit())
{
    AfxMessageBox(IDP_SOCKETS_INIT_FAILED);
    return FALSE;
}
```

Notice that the new resource string displays a message box if the Windows Sockets initialization fails.

Additional Information

Now that you have Windows Sockets support, you might want to read a few articles about implementing a socket client or server. In the Visual C++ online documentation, read the Windows Sockets in MFC family of articles in "Programming with MFC."

Converting an Existing MFC SDI Application to MDI

The purpose of this task is to convert an existing application's interface from SDI to MDI. (This task does not apply to dialog box–based applications.) The task has six steps:

1. Creating a new child frame menu and add resources

2. Modifying the main frame menu

3. Replacing the main frame window

4. Adding child windows to the project

5. Modifying the initialization code of the main frame window

6. Modifying the application's execution

W A R N I N G : This task makes significant structural changes to the SDI application that is being converted. I cannot guarantee that the application will function properly after you make the conversion, so I recommend that a copy of the project be used in case the conversion does not work.

When I refer to a "target project" in this task, I am referring to the project you are converting. When a project name is needed for the examples, the project name PROJNA is used.

Step 1: Creating a New Child Frame Menu and Adding Resources

The main difference between SDI and MDI applications is that MDI applications can support multiple child frame windows. Because of this difference, MDI applications need two menu resources. The first menu, which is often called IDR_MAINFRAME, is used when no child windows are open. The existing menu resource of the target project (Figure 1-11) will be used for this purpose. This menu is basically a shorter version of the standard SDI menu without the Save operations of either the File menu or the Edit menu that are generated by AppWizard.

The second menu, or child frame menu, is used when one or more child windows are open (Figure 1-12). This menu resource (whose ID is often IDR_*<name of project>*TYPE—for example, IDR_PROJNATYPE) has the Edit menu, a Windows menu that can perform common MDI operations (such as creating a new window or arranging multiple child windows) and possibly other commands that are specific to the child windows as well.

To make things as easy as possible, make a copy of the application's existing menu (named IDR_MAINFRAME) and then modify the copy. For this task, the child frame menu resource will have the ID IDR_PROJNATYPE. To create the child frame menu, follow these steps:

1. Go to the target project's Resource pane, and expand the Menu node.

2. Right-click the IDR_MAINFRAME menu, and drag and drop a copy into the same node. You should now have a copy of the IDR_MAIN-FRAME menu named IDR_MAINFRAME1.

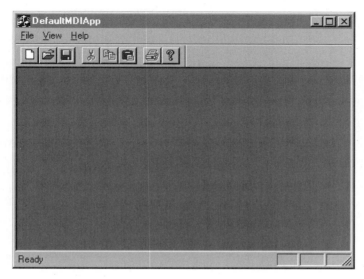

Figure 1-11.
The default main frame window menu of an MDI application.

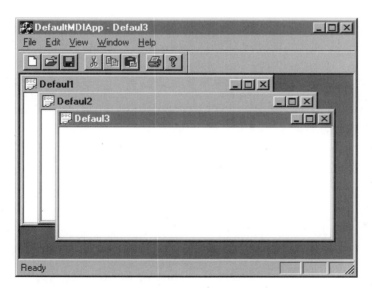

Figure 1-12.
The default child frame menu of an MDI application.

3. Rename the new menu resource IDR_PROJNATYPE.

4. From the File menu of the IDR_MAINFRAME resource, remove the Close, Save, Save As, Print, and Print Preview commands.

5. Remove the entire Edit menu of the IDR_MAINFRAME resource.

6. Confirm the menu changes by saving the resource file of the target project.

7. Add a Window menu between the View and Help menus.
    This menu allows the user to manipulate open child windows in various ways, such as cascading or tiling them. I assume you are familiar with adding menu resources to a project, so I will provide you with just the ID, the caption, and the prompt for each command.

Information for Window Menu Items

Resource ID	Caption	Prompt
ID_WINDOW_NEW	&New Window	Open another window for the active document\nNew Window
ID_WINDOW_CASCADE	&Cascade	Arrange windows so they overlap\nCascade Windows
ID_WINDOW_TILE_HORZ	&Tile	Arrange windows as non-overlapping tiles\nTile Windows
ID_WINDOW_ARRANGE	&Arrange Icon	Arrange icons at the bottom of the window\n Arrange Icons

You can also copy a Windows menu from another project, but be sure it has only the following four commands: New Window, Cascade, Tile, and Arrange Icons.

Adding a String Resource

Because the second menu resource, IDR_PROJNATYPE, requires a resource string of the same name, this resource string must be added to the project. The following string is an example of a new string resource:

```
\nProjna\nProjna\n\n\nProjna.Document\nProjna Document
```

Replace all occurrences of *Projna* with the name of your project. This string will be used in a later piece of code to tie resources to the modified document template that uses the MDI child window class.

Adding Other Child Frame Icons

The child frame window also needs an icon resource. This icon can be copied from another source or created. However, for the icon to be used for the appropriate child frame window, it must have the same ID as the child window menu and string resource. In this case, the ID is IDR_PROJNATYPE.

Step 2: Modifying the Main Frame Menu

The purpose of this step is to modify the main frame menu so that all commands that depend on an open document or an active window are moved to the child frame menu IDR_PROJNATYPE. This ensures that any commands of this type are available only when a child window is open.

In this step, if the target project's main frame menu has changed significantly from the standard version generated by AppWizard, the potential exists for resource ID conflicts and confusion. For the purposes of this discussion at this point, I will assume that the existing main frame menu has not changed significantly from the standard generated by AppWizard. If the menu does not have the commands being discussed, skip to the next step. Once again, it is a good idea to back up the project you are converting in case you have to restore the project to its initial state. To modify the main frame menu, follow this procedure:

1. Open your menu resource, and remove the Save and Save As commands from the File menu.

2. Move any other commands that require an open document or an active window from the File menu to a corresponding place on your child frame menu resource. You can move these items to a corresponding place in the IDR_PROJNATYPE menu by cutting and pasting each menu item to the child frame menu. A quick way to move these menu items is to drag each (while holding down the right mouse button) to the proper place on the child frame and drop it. A context menu should appear when the command is dropped. To move the menu item, choose the Move option.

3. If the main frame menu has an Edit menu, expand it.

4. If the Edit menu contains only the Undo, Cut, Copy, and Paste commands, remove the entire menu. If the Edit menu contains more

than these four commands, remove the Undo, Cut, Copy, and Paste commands and also all other commands that require an open document or an active window. Commands that do not fall under this category can remain.

5. For each remaining menu, move any commands that require an open document or an active window to their corresponding location on the child frame menu. These menu items depend on a window (such as a child window) being open; if you don't move them, they will be available when the application has no child windows open. Thus, if the user chooses menu items that depend on an open child window, the application could crash in a big way because there are no MDI child windows with which to interact at this point.

6. After you finish modifying any additional commands, save the project's RC file. At this point, you should have two menu resources: IDR_MAINFRAME and IDR_PROJNATYPE.

Step 3: Replacing the Main Frame Window

There is a fundamental difference between the main frame window of an SDI application and the main frame window of an MDI application. In order to support the additional functionality of child windows, the main frame window's class should be derived from *CMDIFrameWnd* instead of *CFrameWnd*. The following procedure changes the parent of the main frame window class to *CMDIFrameWnd*.

■ In the MAINFRM.H header file, change the following line

```
class CMainFrame : public CFrameWnd
```

to

```
class CMainFrame : public CMDIFrameWnd
```

and replace

```
protected: // create from serialization only
    CMainFrame();
    DECLARE_DYNCREATE(CMainFrame)
```

with

```
    DECLARE_DYNAMIC(CMainFrame)
public:
    CMainFrame();
```

■ In the MAINFRM.CPP file, search for *CFrameWnd* and replace it with *CMDIFrameWnd*. In the same file, replace the following line

```
IMPLEMENT_DYNCREATE(CMainFrame, CFrameWnd)
```

with

```
IMPLEMENT_DYNAMIC(CMainFrame, CMDIFrameWnd)
```

If you are the inquisitive kind, you might be wondering why the main frame window class is modified to use DECLARE_DYNAMIC instead of DECLARE_DYNCREATE. There are two reasons for this change—one rooted in the actual code generated by AppWizard, the other in the architecture of the two application types.

The Architectural Reason

In an SDI MFC application generated by AppWizard, the main frame window class is related to a specific document and view via a document template. For the application to start, a main frame window and a document-view pair must both be dynamically created simultaneously. This dynamic creation is made possible by the DECLARE_DYNCREATE macro. However, in the case of MDI applications, the main frame window is not related to any document template and can be created explicitly without its also having to create a matching document-view pair. Instead of being related to the main frame window, the document-view pairs are related to a child window. This separates the creation process and allows us to create just the main frame window initially. Therefore, the DECLARE_DYNAMIC macro is sufficient.

The Code Reason

In both SDI and MDI applications, the main frame window is created in the *InitInstance* function of the application class. However, in an SDI application, we don't actually create the main frame window. The main frame window is created because of a "request" from the document template of the application. And it just so happens that the DECLARE_DYNCREATE macro enables the creation of the frame window in this manner.

In the creation of an MDI application, the main frame window is created explicitly in the *InitInstance* function. Therefore, the class doesn't need the ability to be created dynamically. We can instead use the macro DECLARE_DYNAMIC. This macro enables the main frame window class to return run-time class information to other classes upon request.

Step 4: Adding Child Windows to the Project

For your MFC application to display child windows, you must have a class that implements an MDI child window. This class, derived from *CMDIChildWnd*, implements frame window capabilities, along with some enhancements related to MDI support. Either you can use ClassWizard to add a *CMDIChildWnd*-derived class to the target project for this step, or you can copy an existing MDI child window class. If you use ClassWizard, the template class is similar to the one created by AppWizard when the MDI option is chosen. If you use an existing class, copy both the header and implementation files (in this example, CHILDFRM.H and CHILDFRM.CPP) to the target project's main directory, and add them to the target project using the Files Into Project command from the Insert menu of Developer Studio.

After you have added the files to the project, include the header file of the new child window class in the implementation file of the project's application class. This allows the application's class access to the *CChildFrame* class when initializing the document templates of your project in the *InitInstance* function. In addition, change the following line (near the top in the new child window class) to point to the application class's header file in your project:

```
#include "projname.h"
```

Step 5: Modifying the Initialization Code of the Main Frame Window

Now that you have added a new class and resources and have changed the derivation of the frame window, the initialization code must be updated to use this new functionality. Make these modifications in the *InitInstance* function of the project's application class. The *InitInstance* function is responsible for registering and initializing all of the application's document templates. There are three parts to this process: modifying the document template initialization, creating the main frame window, and showing the window.

1. To modify the document template initialization, change the following lines in the implementation file of the project's application class

```
CSingleDocTemplate* pDocTemplate;
pDocTemplate = new CSingleDocTemplate(
    IDR_MAINFRAME,
    RUNTIME_CLASS(CMyProjDoc),
```

to

```
CMultiDocTemplate* pDocTemplate;
pDocTemplate = new CMultiDocTemplate(
    IDR_PROJNATYPE,
    RUNTIME_CLASS(CMyProjDoc),
```

The bold code lines indicate where the code has changed. This code performs the first part of document template initialization (*pDocTemplate*). It sets up a relationship between a document class (*CMyProjDoc*), a view class (*CMyProjView*), and a frame window class (*CChildFrame*). This relationship is used by the application framework when a new window needs to be created. The template tells the application framework what view class goes with the document class and the frame window class.

Now change the frame window class from your original SDI type of class (*CMainFrame*) to the new MDI class (*CChildFrame*). In the implementation file, change the following lines

```
    RUNTIME_CLASS(CMainFrame),        // Main SDI frame window
    RUNTIME_CLASS(CMyProjView));
AddDocTemplate(pDocTemplate);
```

to

```
    RUNTIME_CLASS(CChildFrame), // Custom MDI child frame
    RUNTIME_CLASS(CMyProjView));
AddDocTemplate(pDocTemplate);
```

2. Immediately after these modifications, replace these lines of code

```
// Parse command line for standard shell commands, DDE, file open
CCommandLineInfo cmdInfo;
ParseCommandLine(cmdInfo);

// Dispatch commands specified on the command line
if (!ProcessShellCommand(cmdInfo))
    return FALSE;
```

with these lines of code:

```
// Create main MDI frame window
CMainFrame* pMainFrame = new CMainFrame;
if (!pMainFrame->LoadFrame(IDR_MAINFRAME))
    return FALSE;
m_pMainWnd = pMainFrame;
```

This code creates the "container" for your MDI child windows and initializes the default menu for the application.

3. Finally, just before the end of the *InitInstance* function, add the following lines:

```
// The main window has been initialized, so show and update it
pMainFrame->ShowWindow(m_nCmdShow);
pMainFrame->UpdateWindow();
```

This code simply shows the main frame window and repaints it to update it.

Step 6: Modifying the Application's Execution

After you've made all of the recommended modifications, it's a good idea to build the project and fix any compilation and linking errors that occur. When you have a clean compilation, you can move on to the final step, modifying the application's execution, which is the most difficult step of the entire task. Because you have modified the fundamental structure of your application by converting it to an MDI application, the following assumptions that were made by the developer in the SDI version are no longer correct:

- The application's client window is always open and active. (It might not be.)

- The application's active frame window is the main window *m_pMainWnd*. (Its active frame window can be either the application frame window or a child frame window.)

- The main frame window is used to retrieve the client window. (You must call *GetActiveFrame* and then call *GetActiveView* to retrieve the client window.)

The original assumptions for an SDI application will now produce many assertions and errors, and in some cases they might cause immediate termination of the application. However, if you correct the sources of assumptions one at a time, you should be able to eliminate the majority of errors quickly.

One example of this is to check for any message handling that is sent immediately upon application initialization. Good examples of this are the message handlers for the WM_IDLE and WM_QUERYNEWPALETTE messages. If you are handling any messages of this type, check the code for assumptions regarding the application state (such as the existence of a document object or an active and visible child window). For every case, you must modify the code to check for these situations and handle them appropriately. For example, the following WM_IDLE message handler was taken from an SDI sample program; it updates a status bar pane with the current cursor location in the document.

```
BOOL CNotepadApp::OnIdle(LONG lCount)
{
    CMainFrame* pFrame = (CMainFrame*) AfxGetMainWnd();
    CStatusBar* pStatusBar = (CStatusBar*) pFrame->
    GetDescendantWindow(AFX_IDW_STATUS_BAR);

    if (pStatusBar)
    {
        CEdit &edit = ((CEditView*)pFrame->GetActiveView())->
            GetEditCtrl();
        CString s1;
        UINT i = edit.LineFromChar();
        s1.Format(_T("Ln %u"), ++i);
        pStatusBar->SetPaneText(pStatusBar->
            CommandToIndex(ID_INDICATOR_LINE), s1);
    }
    return CWinApp::OnIdle(lCount);
}
```

The following line of code from the example above indicates that the application assumes there will always be an active view:

```
CEdit &edit = ((CEditView*)pFrame->GetActiveView())->
    GetEditCtrl();
```

This is a bad assumption in an MDI application because at times there might not be any child windows open. If you were to execute this code, you would get an assertion when the *LineFromChar* function is called. To make the code work properly, format the status bar only if an active view is present. The modified code (shown in bold) might look something like this:

```
BOOL CNotepadApp::OnIdle(LONG lCount)
{
    CMainFrame* pFrame = (CMainFrame*) AfxGetMainWnd();
    CStatusBar* pStatusBar = (CStatusBar*) pFrame->
        GetDescendantWindow(AFX_IDW_STATUS_BAR);

    // If no active child frame windows are open,
    // a pointer to the main frame window is returned
    CChildFrame* pChildFrm= (CChildFrame*)pFrame->
        GetActiveFrame();
    CEditView* pView= (CEditView*)
        (pChildFrm->GetActiveView());
```

(continued)

```
if (pStatusBar && pView != NULL)
{
    CEdit &edit = pView->GetEditCtrl();
    CString s1;
    UINT i = edit.LineFromChar();
    s1.Format(_T("Ln %u"), ++i);
    pStatusBar->SetPaneText(pStatusBar->
        CommandToIndex(ID_INDICATOR_LINE), s1);
}
return CWinApp::OnIdle(lCount);
}
```

If the status bar or the view objects aren't present, you should probably call the message handler of the parent class and fall out without performing any action. Notice the call to *GetActiveFrame*; you will probably use this call when checking for the presence of child windows. It returns the active MDI frame window and, if there is no active MDI child, returns the implicit *this* pointer.

A second assumption of an SDI application is that the active frame window of the application is the main window; it fails in an MDI application because of the additional level of indirection regarding frame windows. In the case of your converted application, there are now two possible frame windows—an application frame window and a child frame window. In the SDI version of the application, the frame window was used either to access members of the frame window, such as the control bars, or to access the active view. However, in the MDI version of the application, you must determine whether you are accessing members of the main frame window or accessing views of the application. In the preceding code sample where the status bar is being updated, the first few lines work properly because the application's control bars are being accessed. However, the next few lines do not work because the code is trying to access the active view via the application's frame window. In MDI applications, you will never get an active view from the application's main frame window. You must go down one more level using *GetActiveFrame*, and then retrieve the view.

This leads nicely into a third assumption in SDI applications: that the active frame and view are retrieved using the main frame window. This cannot work in an MDI application. In most cases, the code that assumes this can be found easily by searching the source files for instances of *AfxGetMainWnd* and *m_pMainWnd*. These calls will function properly only if the control bars or the data members of the main frame window class are being accessed. If the active view or related object is being accessed, you have to address the added level of indirection by making a call to the *GetActiveFrame* function of the frame object and then using *GetActiveView* or similar calls to retrieve the active view. Once again, check for the presence of an active view before handing off the result.

To recap, check your application's code for the following:

- Message handlers that are called upon initialization

- Situations in which a view is assumed to exist

- Code that retrieves the active view using *AfxGetMainWnd* or *m_pMainWnd*

In each case, ensure that the additional level of indirection regarding frame windows in MDI applications is addressed or that return values from calls are checked for valid views.

T I P : Search the source code files for occurrences of active, frame, and view code because this is usually code that was affected in some way by the conversion from SDI to MDI.

If you have successfully completed the conversion of your application, you should now be able to build and run it. In most cases, it should run with few or no problems. However, I highly recommend that you test the functionality of your application extensively.

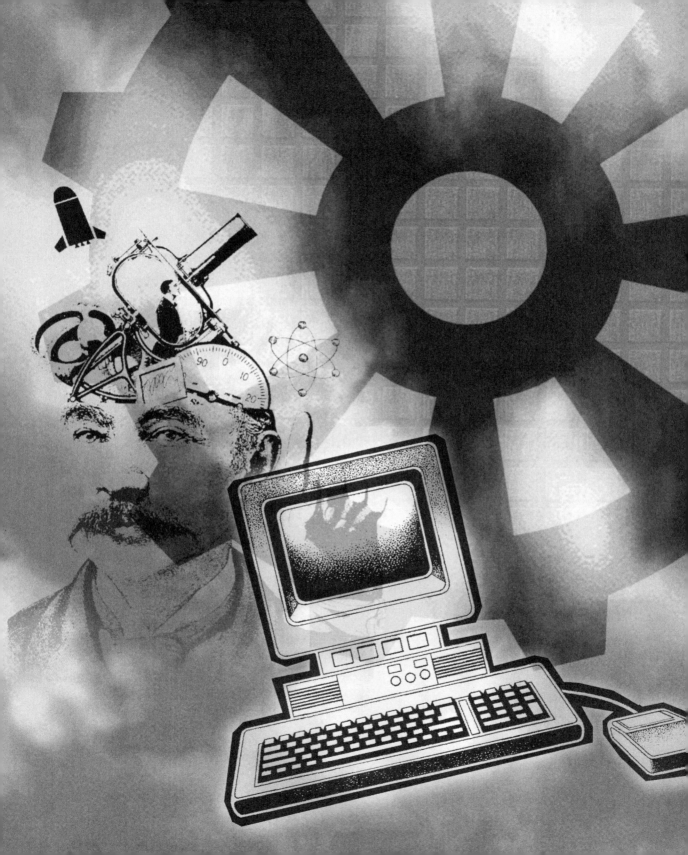

CHAPTER TWO

Application and Frame Window Architecture

The focus of this chapter is the application and frame window classes of an MFC application. As I mentioned in Chapter 1, the application object is the "core" of an MFC application. It is located in the primary layer and works closely with the document, view, and frame window objects. Although it is "invisible," it has features that are of interest to us. The frame window is a primary object that is more visible. It's more closely related to the application than either the document object or the view object and interacts with both the application and the document-view pair—it can be viewed as the "interface" between the application and the document-view pair.

The tasks included in this chapter relate in some way to either the application object or the frame window object. The following is a listing and brief description of the tasks:

- **Modifying the system menu of an MFC application** Modifies the system menu in various ways, including adding new menu commands and modifying existing menu commands.

- **Modifying the initial state of an MFC application** Demonstrates specific methods for initially minimizing or maximizing the application when it's first displayed and for altering the size and placement of the main frame window of the application.

- **Adding a progress indicator to the status bar** Demonstrates the implementation of a progress indicator in the first pane of the application's status bar.

- **Adding tooltips for modal dialog box controls** Demonstrates the implementation of tooltips for controls in a modal dialog box. Also demonstrates routing messages with respect to tooltips for controls in a modal dialog box using a nonstandard approach.

■ **Animating a bitmap in the status bar** Demonstrates the implementation of an animated 16-color bitmap in the status bar of an MFC application. This bitmap, a spinning CD, is animated in its own pane using a four-step process.

Modifying the System Menu of an MFC Application

The purpose of this task is to modify the system menu (sometimes referred to as the control menu) of an MFC application and to demonstrate some of the more popular types of system menu modifications. Modifying the system menu can provide additional information or attributes when the application (or child window) is minimized. For example, you can add a command that indicates the status of the application or a command that accesses a dialog box without having to restore the application and go through the main menu. I will discuss two types of modifications: modifications that are made to the system menu during initialization of the application and dynamic modifications that can occur whenever the system menu is accessed. Specifically, I will demonstrate how to add new commands, modify existing commands, and perform dynamic modifications. In MDI applications, the child window system menu also can be modified. Although the approach to modifying a child window system menu is similar to the approach to modifying the main system menu, there are some important differences, which are discussed in step 2 of this task.

Modifying the system menu of an MFC application consists of three steps:

1. Modifying the main system menu
2. Modifying the child window system menu
3. Handling the WM_SYSCOMMAND message

This task's project name is SYSMENU, and there are no requirements.

Step 1: Modifying the Main System Menu

The primary reason for modifying the main system menu is to expose the application attributes or the status of some task while the application is minimized so that the user can access commands without restoring the application. For example, the user might need to see the status of a lengthy process or a command that invokes a dialog box while the application remains minimized.

There are many other examples, but I leave those to the reader to discover as an exercise.

> **N O T E :** The procedure for modifying the main system menu is the same for both SDI and MDI applications.

Initial Modification

Commands that are not dynamic or that do not change have to be modified only once. For example, you would modify a command string, such as changing "Restore" to "My Restore" just once. Similarly, you would add a command that is available at all times, such as the command that invokes the About dialog box of the application, just once. Your first chance to modify the main system menu occurs after the main frame window has been created. In both SDI and MDI applications, this occurs in the *OnCreate* function.

You can retrieve a copy of the system menu with a call to the *CMenu::GetSystemMenu* function. This function takes a BOOL value as the only parameter. Because you want to modify the menu, you pass a value of FALSE. When you have a copy, make any desired modifications using member functions of the *CMenu* class.

An example of initial modification is the following: In the SYSMENU project, I modify the main system menu by changing the first command and appending a command that invokes the About box of the application. These modifications are made in a function named *ModifySysMenu*, which is called in the main frame's *OnCreate* function. The following code is taken from the body of the *ModifySysMenu* function:

```
CMenu* pSysMenu = GetSystemMenu(FALSE);
CMenu* pFrameMenu = GetMenu();
CString tmpStr;
UINT curPosID;

// Change the Restore command string
pSysMenu->GetMenuString(0, tmpStr, MF_BYPOSITION);
tmpStr = "My "+ tmpStr;
curPosID = pSysMenu->GetMenuItemID(0);
pSysMenu->ModifyMenu(0, MF_BYPOSITION | MF_STRING, curPosID,
    tmpStr);

// Append the About box command
pSysMenu->AppendMenu(MF_SEPARATOR);
pFrameMenu->GetMenuString(ID_APP_ABOUT, tmpStr, MF_BYCOMMAND);
pSysMenu->AppendMenu(MF_STRING, ID_APP_ABOUT, (LPCTSTR)tmpStr);
```

In the first section of the preceding code, I retrieve the system menu and the main frame window menu. In the second section of code, I modify the first command by adding the prefix "My" to the Restore command. The result, "My Restore," replaces the original string. The menu ID remains unchanged. In the final section, I append the About box command to the menu, which allows the user to invoke the About dialog box with one click when the application is minimized.

> **N O T E :** For new commands to execute properly, you must handle the WM_SYSCOMMAND message. This is discussed in step 3 of this task.

Dynamic Modification

Dynamic modification is useful for commands that must be checked before the system menu is displayed. These commands are available or disabled, depending on the changing conditions in the application. Examples include disabled Maximize or Minimize commands or applications that close only when certain conditions are met, such as the completion of a form or other action. Because these conditions can change at any time, they must be checked every time a user requests the system menu.

MFC provides a message (WM_INITMENU) that indicates the system menu is about to be accessed. The message is sent before the system menu is shown. To modify the system menu, add a handler for the WM_INITMENU message to your main frame class. In most cases, this class is *CMainFrame*. After you have installed the handler, you can access the system menu and make the necessary modifications. Or you can restore the default system menu by calling *GetSystemMenu* with a parameter value of TRUE. The following code sample is taken from the WM_INITMENU handler of SYSMENU's main frame class:

```
CMDIFrameWnd::OnInitMenu(pMenu);

// Retrieve copy of system menu
CMenu* pSysMenu = GetSystemMenu(FALSE);
UINT curPosID;

// Disable Maximize command
// To complete disablement, handle WM_SYSCOMMAND
curPosID = pSysMenu->GetMenuItemID(4);
pSysMenu->EnableMenuItem(curPosID, MF_GRAYED);
⋮
```

This code sample disables the Maximize command. However, to ensure that the user cannot maximize the application, you must also handle the case of

SC_MAXIMIZE in the handler for WM_SYSCOMMAND. The handler is discussed in step 3 of this task.

Step 2: Modifying the Child Window System Menu

In MDI applications, another system menu appears on every MDI child window. The same types of modifications that can be made to the main system menu also can be made to child system menus; and, with some small changes, the same procedures can be used to make these modifications.

Initial Modification

The system menu of a child window is first accessible after the child frame has processed the WM_CREATE message. To access the menu at this time, add a handler to your child frame window class for the WM_CREATE message. Any modification of the child window system menu must occur after the call to the base class's *OnCreate* function. To improve the readability of the SYS-MENU project, all modifications are made with a call to *ModifySysMenu*. The following example, taken from the child frame class, demonstrates this:

```
int CChildFrame::OnCreate(LPCREATESTRUCT lpCreateStruct)
{
    if (CMDIChildWnd::OnCreate(lpCreateStruct) == -1)
        return -1;

    ModifySysMenu();
    return 0;
}
```

An example of an initial modification is the following: the code shown below is taken from the child frame's *ModifySysMenu*, and it demonstrates some of the ways to initially modify the child frame system menu:

```
CMenu* pSysMenu = GetSystemMenu(FALSE);
CString tmpStr;

// Add Next window command
pSysMenu->AppendMenu(MF_SEPARATOR);
tmpStr = "Nex&t\tCtrl+F6";
pSysMenu->AppendMenu(MF_STRING, SC_NEXTWINDOW, tmpStr);
pSysMenu->AppendMenu(MF_SEPARATOR);

// Add tiling and cascading commands
tmpStr = "Casca&de All";
pSysMenu->AppendMenu(MF_BYPOSITION | MF_STRING,
```

(continued)

49

```
        ID_WINDOW_CASCADE, tmpStr);
tmpStr = "Ti&le All";
pSysMenu->AppendMenu(MF_BYPOSITION | MF_STRING,
        ID_WINDOW_TILE_HORZ, tmpStr);
```

In the first section of this example, I retrieve the system menu. In the second section, I add the Next command to my copy of the system menu, which allows the user to activate the next child window. This is necessary because retrieving a copy of the system menu with FALSE as the argument to *GetSystemMenu* erases this command. In the third section, I add two commands from the main menu: Cascade and Tile. I modify the menu strings slightly by adding "All" to the end of each string. The new strings are appended to the system menu, along with a separator that makes the menu more legible. Note that the command IDs for these two items are exact copies of the IDs for the Cascade and Tile commands.

Dynamic Modification

The reasons for making dynamic modifications to the main system menu apply also to child frame system menus. The following code sample is taken from the WM_INITMENU handler of SYSMENU's main frame class:

```
CMDIChildWnd::OnInitMenu(pMenu);

CMenu* pSysMenu = GetSystemMenu(FALSE);
UINT curPosID;
if (IsIconic()) // Disable tiling and cascading when
                // minimized
{
    curPosID = pSysMenu->GetMenuItemID(10);
    pSysMenu->EnableMenuItem(curPosID, MF_GRAYED);
    curPosID = pSysMenu->GetMenuItemID(11);
    pSysMenu->EnableMenuItem(curPosID, MF_GRAYED);
}
else // Enable if window is normal or maximized
{
    curPosID = pSysMenu->GetMenuItemID(10);
    pSysMenu->EnableMenuItem(curPosID, MF_ENABLED);
    curPosID = pSysMenu->GetMenuItemID(11);
    pSysMenu->EnableMenuItem(curPosID, MF_ENABLED);
}
```

The main item of interest here is the if-else block, which disables the Cascade All and Tile All commands only when the child window of the system menu being accessed is minimized. If the child window is normal or maximized, the Cascade All and Tile All commands are enabled.

N O T E : For new commands to execute properly, you must handle the WM_SYSCOMMAND message. This is discussed in step 3.

Step 3: Handling the WM_SYSCOMMAND Message

Unlike what occurs with standard menu commands, a WM_SYSCOMMAND message is sent every time the user chooses an item from the system menu. And every time a user chooses the maximize or minimize button, a WM_SYS-COMMAND message is posted. One of the message parameters is the command ID of the command chosen. To intercept events from the system menu, you must handle the WM_SYSCOMMAND message and take appropriate action for both custom commands and items that you have modified, such as a disabled Maximize command. If you do not handle these customizations, the command will be handled by the framework, which knows nothing about your modifications.

Now add the handler if you have made any changes beyond modifying command strings. For main system commands, the handler must be implemented in the main frame class; for child window system commands, the handler must be implemented in the child frame class. In the SYSMENU project, the code handles WM_SYSCOMMAND for both frame window objects.

After you have added the handler, check for your modified or new commands. To do this, compare the ID passed in against your set of modified or new command IDs. For example, in the SYSMENU project, I added an About SysMenu command; therefore, I had to check for the command ID (ID_APP-_ABOUT) and then make a call to *CSysMenuApp::OnAppAbout* to make the About SysMenu dialog box appear. The following code, taken from the body of *CMainFrame::OnSysCommand*, demonstrates the basic process:

```
CSysMenu2App* pApp = (CSysMenu2App*)AfxGetApp();

switch(nID)
{
    case SC_MAXIMIZE:
        break;
    case ID_APP_ABOUT:
    {
        pApp->OnAppAbout();
        break;
    }
    default:
    CMDIFrameWnd::OnSysCommand(nID, lParam);
}
```

In the preceding example, I checked for the Maximize (SC_MAXIMIZE) command and the About SysMenu (ID_APP_ABOUT) command. In the case of SC_MAXIMIZE, I ignore the command and return nothing because I disabled the Maximize command for the application. This prevents the user from maximizing the application with either the system menu or the Maximize button. In the case of ID_APP_ABOUT, I get a pointer to the application and call the appropriate function. In all other cases, I relay the message to the parent window.

I use the same procedure for the system menu of the child window. The following code checks for the Cascade All and Tile All commands and calls the appropriate functions. The code is taken from the body of the *CChildWnd::OnSysCommand* function:

```
// Handle the tiling and cascading commands
switch(nID)
{
    case ID_WINDOW_TILE_HORZ:
    {
        GetMDIFrame()->MDITile(MDITILE_HORIZONTAL);
        break;
    }
    case ID_WINDOW_CASCADE:
    {
        GetMDIFrame()->MDICascade();
        break;
    }
    default:
        CMDIChildWnd::OnSysCommand(nID, lParam);
}
```

In this example, I check for the Cascade All (ID_WINDOW_CASCADE) command and the Tile All (ID_WINDOW_TILE_HORZ) command. In both cases, I retrieve a pointer to the main frame window and call the appropriate function.

Additional Information

An additional modification to the *CMainFrame::ModifySysMenu* function can be made that inserts a pop-up menu into your application's system menu. Add the following code to the end of your *ModifySysMenu* function:

```
// Set up a Window State pop-up menu item
CMenu popMenu;
popMenu.CreatePopupMenu();

pSysMenu->GetMenuString(SC_MAXIMIZE, tmpStr, MF_BYCOMMAND);
```

```
popMenu.InsertMenu(0, MF_BYPOSITION, SC_MAXIMIZE, tmpStr);
pSysMenu->GetMenuString(SC_MINIMIZE, tmpStr, MF_BYCOMMAND);
popMenu.InsertMenu(0, MF_BYPOSITION, SC_MINIMIZE, tmpStr);

pSysMenu->InsertMenu(3, MF_BYPOSITION | MF_POPUP,
    (UINT)popMenu.GetSafeHmenu(), "Window States");
pSysMenu->RemoveMenu(4, MF_BYPOSITION);
pSysMenu->RemoveMenu(4, MF_BYPOSITION);
```

In the first section of this code, I create a blank pop-up menu. In the next section, I copy the existing menu strings for the Minimize and Maximize menu commands into the new pop-up menu. Finally, I insert the new menu, named Window States, into the system menu and then remove the original Minimize and Maximize items to prevent duplication.

Modifying the Initial State of an MFC Application

The purpose of this task is to modify the initial appearance of an application and its related windows. Attributes that can be modified include the automatic minimizing or maximizing of an application and the size and placement of application windows. In addition to demonstrating how to modify the main frame window, I will also demonstrate how to make these same modifications on MDI child windows. To fully demonstrate possible customizations, I will use an MDI application. The name of the project is CUSTOM, and there are no requirements.

Modifications to SDI Applications

For SDI applications, you can modify the attributes of the main frame (or application) window. Common customizations include modifying the initial state of the main frame window (whether the window is minimized or maximized) and changing the size and the position of the window on the desktop.

Minimized or Maximized?

The initial state of the main frame window (maximized or minimized) can be customized by modifying the *InitInstance* function of the main frame class. The main purpose of this function is to display the main frame window. The window style of the window object determines how the main frame window appears when it is displayed, with the default being WS_SHOWNORMAL. This style is stored in the public variable *m_nCmdShow* and can be modified easily to display the main frame window in many ways. Make the modification immediately after the call to *ParseCommandLine* of the main frame's *InitInstance* function. The following code adds the SW_SHOWMAXIMIZED style to the main frame window's styles:

```
// Maximizes main window automatically
m_nCmdShow = SW_SHOWMAXIMIZED;
```

The code shown below adds the SW_SHOWMINIMIZED style to the main frame window's styles:

```
// Minimizes main window automatically
m_nCmdShow = SW_SHOWMINIMIZED;
```

After you've changed the style, the application takes care of the rest. More styles can be found in the online documentation for Microsoft Visual C++ version 5.

Modifying the Initial Size and Position of the Main Frame Window

In addition to modifying the initial state of the main frame window, you can customize the size and the position of the window before the application first appears. The size and the position, along with other window characteristics, are stored in a CREATESTRUCT structure, which is used to create the new window object. In applications created by AppWizard, the *PreCreateWindow* member function of the main frame and view windows is automatically overridden by AppWizard. This provides access to the CREATESTRUCT structure before the window is created.

The following code sample sets the window size to half the screen size using *::GetSystemMetrics*, and then it centers the window:

```
// Size the window to 1/2 screen size, and center it
cs.cy = ::GetSystemMetrics(SM_CYSCREEN) / 2;
cs.cx = ::GetSystemMetrics(SM_CXSCREEN) / 2;
cs.y = cy / 2;
cs.x = cs.cx / 2;
```

This type of code is usually found before the call to the base member function.

Modifications to MDI Applications

In addition to the main frame and view objects, MDI applications also have child window objects. Therefore, in addition to modifying attributes of the main frame window, you also can modify attributes of the child window. However, MDI applications have a client area, generally referred to as the MDI-CLIENT area, where the child windows appear. The addition of the client area and the child window objects in an MDI application requires changing the procedures used to modify SDI applications so they will work for an MDI application. A self-centering MDI application is shown in Figure 2-1.

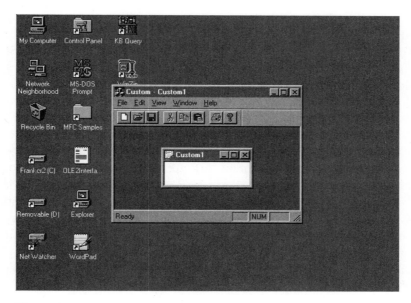

Figure 2-1.
A centered MDI application using screen size calculations.

Minimized or Maximized?

The procedure for automatically minimizing or maximizing the main frame window of an MDI application is identical to the procedure used for an SDI application except that the code is placed in a different location. Instead of placing the minimize/maximize code after the call to the *ParseCommandLine* function of the application's *InitInstance* function, place it just before the call to *ShowWindow* that shows the main frame window.

However, if you want the same effect for child windows, a little more work is required. The easiest way to customize the initial state of a child window is to override the *ActivateFrame* function of the child window class, which is usually named *CChildFrame*. This function is called by the framework before the frame window is visible. In your override of the *ActivateFrame* function, add the following code right before the call to the base class version:

```
nCmdShow = SW_SHOWMINIMIZED;
```

This causes all child windows to appear minimized initially. To display maximized child windows, use SW_SHOWMAXIMIZED.

Initial Size and Position of the Main Frame and Child Windows

Because of the similarities between the architectures, you can use the same procedures you used for SDI applications to customize the MDI main frame

55

window and the MDI child windows. Because applications created with App-Wizard automatically override the main frame and child window *PreCreateWindow* functions, all that's left to do is to add code exactly like the SDI size and position code that sets the size and the position of the main frame or child windows. However, be careful when calculating the client area of the main frame window. Once again, the MDI architecture is the reason behind this warning. As with SDI applications, there is a client area bounded by the main frame window. In a typical SDI application, the client area is completely covered by the view window object, hence, the name single document interface.

However, the client area of an MDI application can be partially or completely visible at certain times, depending on the state of the child windows and any control bars. This means that a call to the *GetClientRect* function of the frame window returns a rectangle that does *not* account for the presence of tool or status bars. Therefore, if you try to center a child window using the normal calculations (in the child's *PreCreateWindow* function), the child will not be centered because the client area is calculated only after the application becomes visible:

```
CRect client;
CMDIFrameWnd* pFrame = (CMDIFrameWnd*) AfxGetMainWnd();

// Size the window to 1/2 screen size, and center it
pFrm->GetClientRect(&client);
cs.cy = client.Height() / 2;
cs.cx = client.Width() / 2;
cs.y = ((cs.cy * 2) - cs.cy) / 2;
cs.x = ((cs.cx * 2) - cs.cx) / 2;
```

To get a centered child window, you must calculate the *actual* client area: the client area minus the area of any visible control bars. Fortunately, the *CMDIFrameWnd* class has a public member, *m_hWndMDIClient*, that helps do just that. Therefore, you can modify the calculation code slightly, as shown below. The sample will then calculate the actual client area, taking into account the presence of control bars.

```
CRect client;
CMDIFrameWnd* pFrame = (CMDIFrameWnd*) AfxGetMainWnd();

// Size the window to 1/2 screen size, and center it
::GetClientRect(pFrame->m_hWndMDIClient, &client);
cs.cy = client.Height() / 2;
cs.cx = client.Width() / 2;
cs.y = ((cs.cy * 2) - cs.cy) / 2;
cs.x = ((cs.cx * 2) - cs.cx) / 2;
```

Unfortunately, there is still a slight problem with the code sample. The *m_hWndMDIClient* data member is undocumented. This means that the behavior of this code could change in the future, so use it at your own risk. For a related method of calculating the available client area, subclass the client area and access the dimensions through the subclassed window. The Knowledge Base article "How to SubClass the MDIClient by Using MFC": Q129471 describes this procedure clearly and completely.

Adding a Progress Indicator to the Status Bar

The purpose of this task is to add a progress indicator to the status bar of an application. A progress indicator can be used to indicate the time (or bytes) remaining for the current process or as a visual indicator that the application has not frozen or silently crashed. The progress indicator is implemented with a *CProgressCtrl* class object and, when activated, covers the application status bar's first pane, which is reserved for status messages.

> **N O T E :** To clearly demonstrate the implementation of the progress indicator, this task (and the sample project) uses a simple *for* loop to demonstrate the implementation of a progress control in the status bar. I refer to this *for* loop as the "Lengthy Process." The loop, and the related interface, are used here purely for demonstration purposes only and are not intended as an example of a "real world" situation.

In the sample project, you can view the progress indicator by choosing the Lengthy Process command. When this occurs, the handler for the Lengthy Process command retrieves the dimensions of the first pane and creates the common progress control within this area, as shown in Figure 2-2 on the following page. When the *for* loop completes, the progress indicator is destroyed and control of the first pane returns to the application.

The task consists of two steps:

1. Implementing the user interface

2. Creating and displaying the progress indicator

The Lengthy Process menu command, which invokes the progress indicator control, is designed to demonstrate the progress indicator and is not a required step in this task. In a standard application, the progress indicator is invoked when a certain event, determined by the developer, begins. For this reason, you can skip step 1, which sets up the interface used in the sample

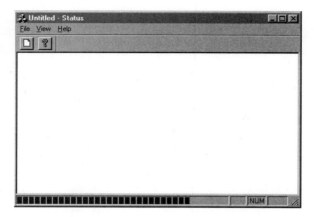

Figure 2-2.
A progress indicator, located in the first pane of the status bar.

project, and begin with step 2, which describes the code needed to implement the progress indicator. The name of the sample project is STATUS, and there are no requirements.

Step 1: Implementing the User Interface

Just for demonstration purposes, the sample project invokes the progress indicator when the user chooses the Lengthy Process menu command. To add the Lengthy Process command to the main menu, follow these steps:

1. Using the Resource Editor, add a menu command with the ID of ID_LENGTHY_PROCESS to the View menu of your application's main menu. This menu item, when chosen by the user, starts the fake process.

Properties of the Lengthy Process Menu Item

ID	Caption	Prompt
ID_LENGTHY_PROCESS	&Lengthy Process	Invokes the progress indicator in the status bar\nLengthy process.

2. Add a separator right after the new command.

3. Add a command handler for the new command to your application's *CMainFrame* class. The *CMainFrame::OnLengthyProc* function is the handler used by the sample project.

4. Save the resource file.

Step 2: Creating and Displaying the Progress Indicator

The creation and display of the progress indicator in the application's status bar is fairly simple. First you retrieve the status bar of the application, and then you calculate the size of the status bar's first pane and create the progress control and position it so that it covers the entire first pane. After the process is finished, you destroy the control.

The code for displaying a progress indicator, found in the *OnLengthyProc* function of the sample project, assumes that the status bar object of the main frame window is accessible. In applications generated by AppWizard, the status bar object (a protected data member of *CMainFrame*) is accessible only from the *CMainFrame* class or a friend of the *CMainFrame* class. For this reason, the code shown below must be added to the new command handler, *CMainFrame::OnLengthyProc.*

```
// Create CProgressCtrl as a child of the status bar
// positioned over the first pane
RECT rc;
m_wndStatusBar.GetItemRect(0, &rc);
CProgressCtrl wndProgress;
VERIFY (wndProgress.Create(WS_CHILD | WS_VISIBLE, rc,
    &m_wndStatusBar, 1));
wndProgress.SetRange(0, 50);
wndProgress.SetStep(1);

// Perform some lengthy process, simulated here with a for loop
// and the Sleep function
for (int i=0; i<50; i++)
{
    Sleep(50);
    wndProgress.StepIt();
}
```

In the first section of this code, I retrieve the dimensions of the status bar's first pane. I then create the progress indicator control, using the area of the first pane and setting the parent of the progress control equal to the frame window. I set the range and the step sizes based on the *for* loop, which has 50 parts. In the next code section, I use a *for* loop of 50 cycles to imitate a lengthy process and step the progress indicator once for each *for* loop cycle.

After you add the code on the preceding page, rebuild your project. You should now be able to display a progress indicator in the first pane of your application's status bar.

Adding Tooltips for Modal Dialog Box Controls

The purpose of this task is to add tooltips to the controls of a modal dialog box. Tooltips for the OK button, a static control, and the dialog box itself will be implemented using the *CToolTipCtrl* class. By default, MFC provides tooltips for descendants of any frame window class derived from *CFrameWnd*. If you want tooltips for other types of tools, such as other windows or rectangular regions, you'll have to roll your own.

The method used to provide tooltip support in an MFC application uses the common control class *CToolTipCtrl*. This class wraps the tooltip common control and provides an adequate amount of default support (even though the documentation is somewhat spare) to implement the common tooltips. We will add a *CToolTipCtrl* class that is responsible for three "tools"—a toolbar button, an embedded child window, or a rectangular region—to the application class. To provide a more complete demonstration, we will add tooltips for a button control, a static region, and the About dialog box. After the task has been completed, the user will see the tooltips for the dialog box or any controls inside automatically when the mouse cursor pauses over one of them, as shown in Figure 2-3.

Figure 2-3.
Tooltip for a static control.

The task consists of three steps:

1. Modifying the modal dialog box
2. Modifying the *OnInitDialog* and *PostNcDestroy* functions
3. Modifying the application class

The project is named DLGTIPS, and the requirement is a modal dialog box class used by the application. The sample project uses the About dialog box generated by AppWizard.

Background

To implement a functioning tooltip in an MFC application, you must do all of the following:

- Define the tools that will be monitored by the tooltip control.

- Activate the tooltip control(s).

- Determine when to display the tooltip.

- Provide text to display in the tooltip window when text is requested by the system.

The default support for tooltips is available only for controls (or tools) embedded in a *CFrameWnd*-derived class or for a descendant of a *CFrameWnd*-derived class. The reason for this is that *CFrameWnd* is the only class that provides a handler function for the TTN_NEEDTEXT notification. This notification is sent by the framework when the mouse has remained on the same point for about a half second and when there is a registered tool (usually a toolbar button or a menu item) that includes the current mouse position. When this situation exists, a TOOLINFO structure is initialized and passed on to the default notification handler, which in this case is *CWnd::OnToolTip-Text*. The handler retrieves the ID of the tool and any tooltip text associated with it. After the text has been retrieved, the tooltip window will be displayed. If the tool has no tooltip text, the window opens, but it is invisible.

To implement tooltips for tools inside windows that are not derived from *CFrameWnd*, you must do two things: determine when the tooltip should be displayed and provide text for the tooltip. If you implement tooltips using the *CToolTipCtrl* class, all you have to do is register the tools and provide the text for them.

Another feature of MFC that makes adding tooltips a little bit easier is the ability to manage tooltips for multiple controls using just one *CToolTipCtrl*-derived object. I demonstrate this feature in this task by adding three tools to the *CToolTipCtrl* object.

Step 1: Modifying the Modal Dialog Box

To implement tooltips for dialog box controls, you have to modify the dialog box class by doing three things:

- Adding member variables for the dialog box tools and the common tooltip control

- Adding a destructor if one does not already exist

- Overriding the *OnInitDialog* and *PostNcDestroy* functions

Adding Member Variables for Each Tool in the Dialog Box

To add tools to the tooltip common control, you must add one member variable to the dialog box class for each dialog box control. You then use the member variables when initializing the common tooltip control. A quick way to add member variables to your dialog box is to use the Resource editor and ClassWizard.

Repeat the following procedure for each dialog box control that will have a tooltip.

1. Open the dialog box resource in the Resource editor.

2. Double-click any control to which you want to add a tooltip while holding down the Ctrl key. This invokes ClassWizard and automatically opens the Member Variables page for your dialog box class.

3. Enter a name for the member variable, and select Control from the Category drop-down list box.

4. Click OK to close the dialog box.

5. Click OK to close ClassWizard, which saves your changes.

N O T E : If you want to provide tooltips for a static control (or controls), you must set the Notify style for the static control. This style allows the control to send notification messages to its parent (the dialog box), alerting the dialog box to display the tooltip for the static control.

In your dialog box class, declare a member variable pointer of type *CToolTipCtrl*, named *m_pToolTip*. In your dialog box constructor, add the following line:

```
m_pToolTip = NULL;
```

This initializes the pointer of the common tooltip control to NULL. You will use this value in the destructor to determine whether the pointer needs to be freed.

Adding a Destructor

Because memory for the *m_pToolTip* pointer was allocated in the constructor of the dialog box class, you will need a destructor to free that memory. Create one now, and add the following code, which frees up the memory you allocated for the common tooltip control:

```
if (m_pToolTip != NULL)
    delete m_pToolTip;
```

Overriding the *OnInitDialog* and *PostNcDestroy* Functions

The last modification to the dialog box class is to override the *OnInitDialog* and *PostNcDestroy* functions. You can use the Message Maps tab of ClassWizard to add these overrides.

Step 2: Modifying the *OnInitDialog* and *PostNcDestroy* Functions

Now that you have overrides of *OnInitDialog* and *PostNCDestroy*, you will have to add code to create and initialize the tooltip control. In the *OnInitDialog* function, create and initialize the common tooltip control. After all of the dialog box tools have been added, activate the common tooltip control and exit the function. Add the following code to your dialog box's *OnInitDialog* function after the call to the base class and before the return statement:

```
if (!m_pToolTip)
{
    int rt;
    m_pToolTip = new CToolTipCtrl;
    rt = m_pToolTip->Create(this);
    ASSERT(rt != 0);
    ((CDlgTipsApp*)AfxGetApp())->m_gpToolTip = m_pToolTip;

    CRect rc(11,17,29,37);
    MapDialogRect(rc);
    rt = m_pToolTip->AddTool(this, "Default MFC icon", rc,
        IDC_MFCICON);
    ASSERT(rt != 0);

    rt = m_pToolTip->AddTool(this, "About Box");
    ASSERT(rt != 0);
```

(continued)

```
rt = m_pToolTip->AddTool(&m_btnOK, "OK Button");
ASSERT(rt != 0);

m_pToolTip->Activate(TRUE);
}
((CDlgTipsApp*)AfxGetApp())->m_hwndDialog = m_hWnd;
```

In the first section of code, I create the common tooltip control and assign the result to the *m_gpToolTip* pointer, a data member of the application class. In the next section, I initialize a *CRect* object with the client coordinates of the static control. I then use this *CRect* object to add the dialog box icon to the common tooltip control, *m_pToolTipCtrl*. In the next section, I add the dialog box and the OK button to the list of tools. Finally, I activate the common tooltip control and assign the HWND of the dialog box to a data member (*m_hwndDialog*) of the application class.

In the *PostNcDestroy* function (called after the dialog box object has been destroyed), set the *m_hwndDialog* and *m_gpToolTip* data members of the application class to NULL. Add the following code to your dialog's *PostNcDestroy* function after the call to the base class:

```
((CDlgTipsApp*)AfxGetApp())->m_hwndDialog = NULL;
((CDlgTipsApp*)AfxGetApp())->m_gpToolTip = NULL;
```

The NULL value indicates to the application object that the modal dialog box has been dismissed.

Step 3: Modifying the Application Class

Because you are using a modal dialog box, you have to check for mouse messages in the application class. To do this, declare two data members in your application class: a pointer to the common tooltip control (*m_gpToolTip*) and the handle to the dialog box object (*m_hwndDialog*). The code below is taken from the sample project's application class. These data members give you access to the dialog box and to the common tooltip control of the dialog box. Be sure you set both of these data members to NULL in the constructor of the application class.

```
⋮
HWND m_hwndDialog;
CToolTipCtrl* m_gpToolTip;
```

In addition to declaring the data members, you have to override the *ProcessMessageFilter* function in the application class, which relays all messages sent to the dialog box to the common tooltip control. Override this function now. After you have done this, add the following code to the function body:

```
if (m_hwndDialog != NULL)
    if (lpMsg->hwnd == m_hwndDialog ||
    ::IsChild(m_hwndDialog, lpMsg->hwnd))
{
    if (m_gpToolTip != NULL)
        m_gpToolTip->RelayEvent(lpMsg);
}

return CWinApp::ProcessMessageFilter(code, lpMsg);
```

In the first section of the code, I check to see whether the dialog box has been created. If the check returns TRUE, I compare the handle of the message to the handle of the dialog; if there is a match, I pass on the message with a call to *RelayEvent* to the common tooltip control. If this check fails, I check whether the handle of the message matches the handle of any children of the dialog box (that is, dialog box controls). If there is a match, I pass on the message with a call to *RelayEvent* to the common tooltip control. If there is no match, I return the result of a call to the *ProcessMessageFilter* of the base class.

After you have completed these modifications, rebuild the project. You should now have tooltips for all tools, including the dialog box itself, in your dialog box.

Additional Information

For more information on providing tooltips for dialog box controls, see "Providing Tooltips for Dialog Controls" in Chapter 5. You might also want to read the related Knowledge Base article "How to Add Tooltips to OLE Controls": Q141871.

Animating a Bitmap in the Status Bar

The purpose of this task is to animate a 16-color bitmap in the status bar of an MFC application. This bitmap will be displayed in a new pane immediately preceding the three default panes (the Caps Lock, Num Lock, and Scroll Lock panes) of the MFC application. Animation is accomplished by loading a slightly different bitmap (from a series of four bitmaps) in the same status bar pane every quarter second using a system timer. The task consists of six steps:

1. Adding a *CStatusBar*-derived class to your project

2. Modifying the status bar class

3. Implementing the *DrawItem* member function of the status bar class

4. Modifying the *CMainFrame* class

5. Creating a new pane for the bitmap

6. Implementing a WM_TIMER message handler

To complete this task, you will need the following:

■ An SDI or MDI MFC application with a status bar

■ Several 16-color bitmaps to display in a status bar pane

Because this task animates the bitmaps by displaying them in a fixed sequence, the animation effect is best achieved by slightly modifying each bitmap in the sequence. The sample project, ANIMBAR, uses a sequence of four bitmaps that represents a spinning CD-ROM.

NOTE: This discussion assumes you are using a version of MFC later than 4.0. If you are using an earlier version of MFC, see the sidebar information "MFC Versions 4.*x* and Later."

Step 1: Adding a *CStatusBar*-Derived Class to Your Project

In a default MFC application created by AppWizard, a status bar is provided with basic features:

■ An area for text messages

■ State indicators for the Caps Lock, Num Lock, and Scroll Lock keys

■ The ability to toggle the visibility of the toolbar

In most applications, this functionality is sufficient, but there are always cases in which it is just not good enough. Animating a bitmap in a status bar pane happens to be one of these cases. Because we are using a class library, we can implement the functionality needed by deriving our own class from *CStatusBar*. In this step, you will add a new status bar class and implement the bitmap feature in the later steps.

Add a class derived from *CStatusBar* to your project, using your favorite method. The status bar class in the sample project is named *CMyStatusBar*. While you are adding stuff to your project, add the bitmaps (16-color only) you will be animating. Because the width and the height of the status bar pane are fixed values, the dimensions of the bitmap must be 26 pixels wide by 13 pixels high. The ANIMBAR project uses a four-element array of *CBitmap* objects (IDB_BMAP0–IDB_BMAP3) that represents a spinning CD-ROM.

Step 2: Modifying the Status Bar Class

Now that you have a *CStatusBar*-derived class, you can begin to implement the bitmap feature. In this step, you will add two data members and modify the constructor. To modify the status bar class, follow these steps:

1. Add the lines of code shown below to the definition of your new status bar class:

```
// Attributes
private:
    CBitmap m_bmpArray[4];
    int m_curBmap;
```

2. Add the following lines of code to the constructor of your new status bar class:

```
VERIFY(m_bmpArray[0].LoadBitmap(IDB_BMAP0));
VERIFY(m_bmpArray[1].LoadBitmap(IDB_BMAP1));
VERIFY(m_bmpArray[2].LoadBitmap(IDB_BMAP2));
VERIFY(m_bmpArray[3].LoadBitmap(IDB_BMAP3));

m_curBmap = 0;
```

In this step, the bitmap array *m_bmpArray* was set up to store the bitmaps used in the animation sequence. In step 3, you will modify the constructor of the status bar to load the four bitmaps that will be displayed.

Step 3: Implementing the *DrawItem* Member Function of the Status Bar Class

In this step, you will complete the modifications to the status bar class and add the code used to render the bitmap in the status bar pane. Once again, you can override a member function and place the rendering code there. This member function, *CStatusBar::DrawItem*, is called by the framework whenever the status bar items need to be redrawn. You'll have to customize the behavior of this function to properly animate your bitmap in the second status bar pane. However, because you have to control only the painting of the bitmap pane, you pass off the rest of the panes to the default function.

ClassWizard does not allow you to override the default function, so you add the function by hand. First add the following line to the public section of your status bar class declaration, which is located in the header file:

```
virtual void DrawItem(LPDRAWITEMSTRUCT lpDrawItemStruct);
```

Now add the function body shown on the following page to the implementation file of your status bar class.

```
void CMyStatusBar::DrawItem(LPDRAWITEMSTRUCT lpDrawItemStruct)
{
    switch(lpDrawItemStruct->itemID)
    {
    case 1:
        // Attach to a CDC object
        CDC dc;
        dc.Attach(lpDrawItemStruct->hDC);

        // Get the pane rectangle, and calculate
        // text coordinates
        CRect rect(&lpDrawItemStruct->rcItem);
        // Select current bitmap into a compatible CDC
        CDC srcDC;
        srcDC.CreateCompatibleDC(NULL);

        CBitmap* pOldBitmap;

        switch(m_curBmap)
        {
        case 0:
            pOldBitmap = srcDC.SelectObject(&m_bmpArray[0]);
            break;
        case 1:
            pOldBitmap = srcDC.SelectObject(&m_bmpArray[1]);
            break;
        case 2:
            pOldBitmap = srcDC.SelectObject(&m_bmpArray[2]);
            break;
        case 3:
            pOldBitmap = srcDC.SelectObject(&m_bmpArray[3]);
            break;
        }

        dc.BitBlt(rect.left, rect.top, rect.Width(), rect.Height(),
        &srcDC, 0, 0, SRCCOPY); // BitBlt to pane rect
        srcDC.SelectObject(pOldBitmap);

        // Detach from the CDC object; otherwise, the hDC will be
        // destroyed when the CDC object goes out of scope
        dc.Detach();

        return;
    }
}
```

If you have done any bitmap painting in the past, most of the preceding code will be pretty familiar to you. Basically, the logic of the function first determines the ID of the pane being notified (of the need to render itself). Because the bitmap pane is the second in a zero-based array, I check for an ID of *1*. If the ID is a match, I grab the device context for the status bar and calculate the coordinates of the bitmap pane. I then create a compatible device context and, depending on where we are in the animation sequence (*m_curBmap*), load the proper bitmap. The bitmap is then copied to the compatible device context. Finally I detach from the status bar device context and return from the *DrawItem* function. However, if the ID is not a match, I simply fall through the switch statement and pass the notification on to the default *DrawItem* function.

At this point, you have completed the implementation of the customized status bar. In the remaining steps, you will modify the frame window class so that it will use your custom status bar and create a new pane for the bitmap.

Step 4: Modifying the *CMainFrame* Class

To see the new status bar, you have to add the include file for the new status bar class and then make two modifications that affect the behavior of the main frame window object. First add the following line to the top of your *CMainFrame* header file so that you can use the *CMyStatusBar* class.

```
#include "MyStatusBar.h"
```

Now move on to the modifications for the *CMainFrame* class. The first modification involves the type of status bar class used by the main frame window. Currently the main frame window uses a default status bar class of type *CStatusBar*. This default status bar class has to be changed so that the new, customized status bar class is used instead. This is easily done by changing the following line

```
CStatusBar  m_wndStatusBar;
```

in the header file of the main frame window class to

```
CMyStatusBar  m_wndStatusBar;
```

The second modification involves the *OnCreate* function of *CMainFrame*. After the status bar has been created, it's necessary to modify the attributes of the pane containing the bitmap so that painting notifications are automatically sent to the bitmap pane when this pane needs to be repainted. In addition, you have to set the system timer for a 250-millisecond interval. This will drive the animation sequence by displaying the next bitmap in the sequence

MFC Versions 4.x and Later

In MFC versions 4 and later, the *CStatusBar* class uses the status window common control. In earlier versions, *CStatusBar* was implemented in MFC, so the procedure for displaying the bitmap differs.

In step 3, implement *CMyStatusBar::DoPaint* instead of *CMyStatus-Bar::DrawItem*. Use the following declaration for *CMyStatusBar::DoPaint*:

```
virtual void DoPaint(CDC* pDC);
```

Use the following code for the function body of *CMyStatusBar::DoPaint*:

```cpp
void CMyStatusBar::DoPaint(CDC* pDC)
{
    CRect rect;
    GetItemRect(1, &rect);  // Get pane rect

    // Exclude pane rect from paint
    pDC->ExcludeClipRect(&rect);
    CStatusBar::DoPaint(pDC);  // Paint remainder of status bar

    CRgn paneRgn;
    paneRgn.CreateRectRgnIndirect(rect);

    // Set clip region to pane rect
    pDC->SelectClipRgn(&paneRgn);

    CBitmap* pBitmap = m_pCurrentBitmap; /* pointer to current
                                            CBitmap */;

    CDC srcDC; // Select current bitmap into a compatible CDC
    srcDC.CreateCompatibleDC(NULL);
    CBitmap* pOldBitmap = srcDC.SelectObject(pBitmap);

    // BitBlt to pane rect
    pDC->BitBlt(rect.left, rect.top, rect.Width(),
        rect.Height(), &srcDC, 0, 0, SRCCOPY);
        srcDC.SelectObject(pOldBitmap);
}
```

In step 4, do not add the code below to *CMainFrame::OnCreate*:

```cpp
UINT nID, nStyle;
int cxWidth;

m_wndStatusBar.GetPaneInfo(1, nID, nStyle, cxWidth);
m_wndStatusBar.SetPaneInfo(1, nID, nStyle | SBT_OWNERDRAW,
    cxWidth);
```

in the new bitmap pane. (The actual handler for the WM_TIMER messages will be added in step 6.) Add the following code right after the call to the *Create* function of the status bar:

```
UINT nID, nStyle;
int cxWidth;
m_wndStatusBar.GetPaneInfo(1, nID, nStyle, cxWidth);
m_wndStatusBar.SetPaneInfo(1, nID, nStyle | SBT_OWNERDRAW, 23);

if (!SetTimer(100, 250, NULL))
    AfxMessageBox("No timer available");
```

In the first section of code, I retrieve the attributes of the bitmap pane, set the owner-draw attribute of the bitmap pane, and set the pane width to 26 pixels. I then attempt to start a system timer. However, because system timers are a limited resource, it's possible that no timers will be available. Therefore, if the attempt fails, I display a message box stating the failure.

Step 5: Creating a New Pane for the Bitmap

In step 5, you create a new pane for the bitmap animation. If one is not created, the animation will be rendered in the Caps Lock indicator pane. To create a new pane, follow these steps:

1. Add a new resource string named ID_INDICATOR_BMAP to the string table of your project with the caption BMAP.

2. In the implementation file of the *CMainFrame* class, modify the indicators array declaration to match the following:

```
static UINT indicators[] =
{
    ID_SEPARATOR,        // Status line indicator

    ID_INDICATOR_BMAP, // Add this line
    ID_INDICATOR_CAPS,
    ID_INDICATOR_NUM,
    ID_INDICATOR_SCRL,
};
```

By adding an entry (ID_INDICATOR_BMAP) to the array of "indicator" panes, you have created a new pane that is located immediately after the separator of the first pane.

Step 6: Implementing a WM_TIMER Message Handler

The last step in this task involves implementing a WM_TIMER message handler. In this handler, the current bitmap counter *m_curBmap* will be advanced and the bitmap pane invalidated, which causes a new bitmap to be drawn that is slightly different from the previous one. Because a WM_TIMER message is received every quarter second, four bitmaps will be drawn, resulting in a spinning CD.

First add a handler for WM_TIMER messages to your *CMainFrame* class using your favorite method. Now replace the *CMainFrame::OnTimer* function body with the following code:

```
CRect rect;

if (m_wndStatusBar.m_curBmap == 3)
    m_wndStatusBar.m_curBmap = 0;
else
    m_wndStatusBar.m_curBmap++;

m_wndStatusBar.GetItemRect(1, &rect);  // Get pane rect
m_wndStatusBar.InvalidateRect(rect, FALSE);

CFrameWnd::OnTimer(nIDEvent);
```

In the first section of code, I check the value of *m_wndStatusBar.m_curBmap* and, depending on the value, reset it to 0 or increment it by 1. I then retrieve the region occupied by the bitmap pane and pass it on to the *CStatusBar::InvalidateRect* function, which causes a repaint of my bitmap pane. Finally I pass on the timer event to the parent class and exit the function.

N O T E : The call to *CFrameWnd::OnTimer* assumes that you are working with an SDI application. If the application is an MDI application, you should make a call instead to *CMDIFrameWnd::OnTimer.*

You have now completed all of the steps required for displaying an animated bitmap in the status bar. Rebuild your project, and you will see a new pane with an animated bitmap in your application.

Additional Information

The procedure above can be modified to display only a 16-color bitmap in the status bar of an MFC application. The necessary modifications are as follows:

■ In step 2, use a *CBitmap* member function instead of a *CBitmap* array, and load only the single bitmap in the status bar's constructor. In addition, the *m_curBmap* member variable is not required.

■ The *DrawItem* function in step 3 does not need a switch statement to determine the proper bitmap to load. Just load the single bitmap stored in the *CBitmap* member variable of your status bar.

■ The *Create* function in step 4 should not create a timer.

■ Step 6 should be dropped because the timer resource was removed in step 4.

CHAPTER THREE

Document Templates

The document-view model is one of the more essential and at the same time most misunderstood features of the MFC library. After providing MFC telephone support for an extended period of time, I came to realize that, in most cases, people who do not like the document-view model do not understand two key points:

- The document-view model is *only* a model and cannot be applied to all programming questions. Therefore, in some cases, this model will not support the purpose of the developer's application.

- The document template is used to create the three necessary elements of a document type: the frame window, the document, and the view. All of these elements are created automatically by the document template and can be customized to some degree to fit your own needs. If you don't fully understand the mechanics of the document template, you will be forced to use the default template style.

In this chapter, I explain the basics of document templates—what they are, how they are used in an MFC application framework, and so forth. In addition, I explain each stage of the document creation process and describe what areas can be customized and why you might want to customize them. This chapter is not a detailed overview of document templates but an intermediate-level discussion of document template mechanics. I assume that you understand the general process of document creation. (For a complete, detailed overview of the document creation process, see "Document Templates" under "Using the Classes to Write Applications for Windows" in "Programming with MFC" in the online documentation.)

In the context of this discussion, *access point* is defined as any member function that can be overridden from a local class or as any function defined by a local class that is called automatically (by the framework) during normal program execution—specifically, a function that either is overridable or is called during the creation of a document and view with a framing window. For the purpose of this discussion, I use the member functions of a class as access points to *customize* or to *poll* the current process, such as document creation.

The chapter is broken into three general areas of discussion and three specific tasks related to document templates. The areas of general discussion are the following:

- **Overview of document templates** Highlights of the process for using a document template to create or open a document.

- **The default mechanics of document templates** A detailed description of the default mechanics of document templates in SDI and MDI applications. In addition, I discuss certain functions generated by AppWizard that allow safe customization of the document creation process.

- **Customizing the document template** An analysis of MFC functions that can be used to safely customize the default mechanics of the document template process.

Overview of Document Templates

Every MFC SDI application created by AppWizard has at least one document template. This template (referred to as the document type) creates and defines the relationships between the document, frame window, and view elements. When a new document is created or an existing document is opened, this template is used to create the elements in this order: document, frame window, and view.

For MFC MDI applications, an extra step is required to create the top-level frame window of the application before a document can be created. After this step is completed, the process used for an SDI application is used to create the requested document.

The document template, as its name suggests, maps the document, frame window, and view elements to the actual MFC classes in an application. When a user requests an application to supply a document (either existing or new), this request is passed to the appropriate document template. The document template, in turn, "requests" that each element defined by the template create itself in a specific sequence. These requests are the main purpose of the document template. All other details, such as frame window titles and the size of the view, are determined by the respective elements of the document type. Once these elements have been created, the frame window displays a view with the document's data.

The Default Mechanics of Document Templates

By default, an application created by AppWizard contains at least one document template. Because this template is responsible for creating the classes of a specific document type, the constructor requires three class names and a resource ID, as shown in the following example:

```
CSingleDocTemplate* pDocTemplate;
pDocTemplate = new CSingleDocTemplate(
    IDR_MAINFRAME,
    RUNTIME_CLASS(CSdiDoc),
    RUNTIME_CLASS(CMainFrame),        // Main SDI frame window
    RUNTIME_CLASS(CSdiView));
AddDocTemplate(pDocTemplate);
```

In this example, *CSdiDoc* is the document class, *CMainFrame* is the main frame window of the application (because the application type is SDI), and *CSdiView* is the view element. The shared resource for this document type is IDR-_MAINFRAME. This shared resource usually contains a menu and icons, which are used by all three document elements. When a template is created, it is registered with the application by a call to *AddDocTemplate*; this is the only way the application knows what document types it supports.

In addition to supplying a registered document template, the SDI application framework provides several access points (in the form of member functions) in the document-view creation process. The default support can be examined with respect to the creation of three main document type elements: the document element, the frame window element, and the view element. Because member functions for frame window and view classes are similar, I will discuss them at the same time.

One final note—in addition to the default access points of an SDI application, MDI applications have access to the creation process of the main frame window. The access points in this step (which occurs before the document element is created) are similar to the access points in the frame window and view creation steps.

Creating the Document Element

When a document is created or opened, the first task of its template is to create the document element. This is accomplished at the first access point, the document element's constructor. In an SDI application, the constructor is called only once because the framework "recycles" the document element whenever a new file is created or an existing document is opened. In an MDI application, the constructor is called every time a document is created or opened because the MDI architecture creates a separate child window for each document that is open in the application.

The second access point, *CDocument::OnNewDocument*, notifies the application each time a new document is created. You can use this function to initialize data that is common to all documents or to perform other actions, such as cleanup, before the document is created. For more information, see *CDocument::OnNewDocument* in the next task, "Customizing the Document Template" on page 80.

Figure 3-1 is the first part of a timeline that shows the functions that are called and the other events that occur when a document is created. The functions shown in bold are referred to as access points and are added automatically to the applications created by AppWizard.

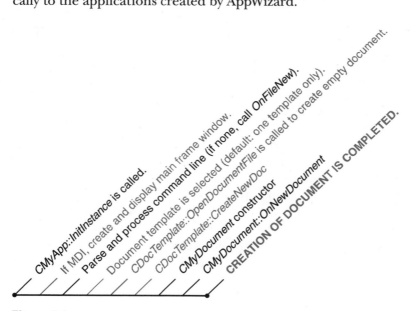

Figure 3-1.
The basic process of creating a document in an MFC application.

Creating the Frame Window and View Elements

After the document is created, the frame window, which contains the view element, is created. As in creation of the document element, the constructor is the first access point called by the framework. In most cases, this constructor does nothing beyond initializing its member variables. Figure 3-2 illustrates the second stage of the document creation timeline, showing the functions called and the other events that occur while the frame window and view are being created. The events in bold (the default access points) are created by AppWizard.

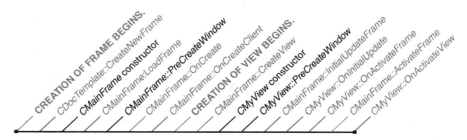

Figure 3-2.
The basic process for creating a frame window and view in an MFC application.

The next access point, the *PreCreateWindow* function, is more useful because you can modify the characteristics of the window using the CREATE-STRUCT structure that is attached to the frame window or view of the function. The CREATESTRUCT structure determines the characteristics of this object and also, among other things, the class name, styles, initial size, and menu used by the window. MFC automatically calls the *PreCreateWindow* function prior to creating the window (hence, the name of the function). As a result, this function is a good place to modify the characteristics of your window object because you do not call the *Create* function directly if you are using a document template.

The usual modification of window characteristics calls the base class implementation, properly initializing the contents. You then modify the structure values to achieve a desired effect, such as controlling the size of the frame window or registering a custom window class. The modified structure is used by the framework to create a frame window (or view) with the desired characteristics.

Customizing the Document Template

As I mentioned earlier, AppWizard creates several access points for the creation process of document, frame window, and view elements. In most cases, these are adequate for the typical document. In those cases in which a more flexible document type is needed, MFC fortunately provides additional access points where you can "plug in" your own code.

In this discussion, customizations are grouped according to the class to which they belong and the order in which they are used in the creation process. The following sections cover how to customize these elements using class library functions. A handful of functions can be used in several areas and are discussed under "Additional Functions" on page 87.

Application-Related Functions

Application-related functions include the following:

- *CWinApp::OnFileNew*
- *CWinApp::OpenDocumentFile*

CWinApp::OnFileNew

The first access point you can customize for new documents is the ID_FILE_NEW command handler. The default handler calls *CWinApp::On-FileNew*, which in turn calls *CWinApp::OpenDocumentFile*. If there is only one registered template, *CWinApp::OnFileNew* tells the document template to create a new document type. If there is more than one template, the application displays a dialog box that lists the known templates. The user must choose the proper document type, which then is created by the respective document template.

If you want to customize this process (perhaps hiding the selection process from the user, for example), add a command handler for ID_FILE_NEW using ClassWizard. This causes the ID_FILE_NEW command to be sent initially to your application's *OnFileNew* handler. In the *OnFileNew* handler, you might add some code that finds the proper template (determined by you) and creates a document-view pair. You also can create handler functions in your application's class that handle requests individually for a certain document type. (For more information on this topic, see "Choosing a Document Template Without the New Document Dialog Box" later in this chapter.) Another method for customizing the creation of new documents is described in the Microsoft Knowledge Base article "How to Create New Documents Without CWinApp::OnFileNew": Q113257.

> **N O T E :** In addition to overriding *OnFileNew,* you also can override *OnFileOpen* to customize the opening of existing documents.

CWinApp::OpenDocumentFile

If you know the filename for the document you are opening, call *CWinApp::-OpenDocumentFile* (passing the filename) to create a document-view pair. This function is commonly used in the *InitInstance* function to open a file or to bypass the New Document Type dialog box automatically. The first parameter of the command line, if the command line is not empty, can be passed via a call to *OpenDocumentFile*. If the application has only one template, a document-view pair is created using that template. If multiple document templates exist, the function tries to match the filename's extension to a template in the application's template list. If the function finds a match, a document, a frame window, and a view object are created.

Document Template–Related Functions

The primary purpose of document templates is to provide a plan for creating a specific document type. This is a one-to-one relationship: one document template produces one type of document. However, in order for an application to access document templates, it must be registered with a call to *AddDoc-Template,* usually from the application's *InitInstance* function. Any templates that are not registered with the application must be managed by the developer.

If you want to customize any part of the document creation process, you might quickly end up handling document templates and perhaps various parts of the creation process yourself. In these cases, you have access to the template list from any part of your application just by grabbing the application object and making a few calls to the *GetFirstDocTemplatePosition* function and the *GetNextDocTemplate* function. The following sample code demonstrates a common way to gain access to the list:

```
CWinApp* pApp = AfxGetApp();

POSITION curTemplatePos = GetFirstDocTemplatePosition();

while (curTemplatePos != NULL)
{
```

(continued)

```
CDocTemplate* curTemplate =
    pApp->GetNextDocTemplate(curTemplatePos);
CString str;
curTemplate->GetDocString(str, CDocTemplate::docName);
if (str == "Bounce")
{
    curTemplate->OpenDocumentFile(NULL);
    return;
}
}
```

The following functions can be used to manage or to customize various parts of the document-view creation:

- *CDocTemplate::OpenDocumentFile*

  Use this function when you need to create a document-view pair from a specific template. This function is also called by *CWinApp::-OpenDocumentFile.*

- *CDocTemplate::CreateNewFrame*

  Use this function to create a new frame window that contains a view based on the document class managed by the document template. In addition to creating a new frame window, you can base the new window on an existing document or frame window by passing an existing frame window object via this function. The result of this call is similar to the result of choosing New from the Window menu of the application. (For more information on working with *CreateNewFrame,* see the Knowledge Base article "Create Additional Views with Create-NewFrame( ) Function": Q100993.)

- *CDocTemplate::CreateNewDocument*

  Use this function to create a new document. The frame window and the view must be created in a separate step.

- *CDocTemplate::InitialUpdateFrame*

  After you have created a new frame using *CreateNewFrame,* you should call *InitialUpdateFrame* to send WM_INITIALUPDATE messages to all children within the newly created frame. This allows all children to perform any one-time initialization or actions needed before becoming visible. If there are no active views, the primary view of the frame window becomes the active view. This member function is defined in both the *CDocTemplate* and *CFrameWnd* classes. The Knowledge Base article "Create Additional Views with CreateNewFrame( ) Function": Q100993 describes how to create additional views using *CreateNewFrame* and *InitialUpdateFrame.*

Document-Related Functions

Document-related functions include the following:

- *CDocument::OnNewDocument*

- *CDocument::DeleteContents*

- *CDocument::SetModifiedFlag, CDocument::IsModified,* and *CDocument::SaveModified*

CDocument::OnNewDocument

As mentioned under "The Default Mechanics of Document Templates," *CDocument::OnNewDocument* is called when a new document is created. This function is commonly used to initialize the document's data members.

> N O T E : If the user chooses the File New command in an SDI application, the framework uses the *CDocument::OnNewDocument* function to re-initialize the existing document element rather than create a new one. Therefore, to ensure data member initialization, place your initialization code in this function instead of in the document constructor.

CDocument::DeleteContents

This little-known function provides a useful way to receive notifications that the current document is about to be destroyed. Because the default implementation of *DeleteContents* does nothing, override it in your document's class to free up any memory allocated by the document, to save any modifications to the document, or to execute other tasks that need to run before the document closes. This function is very useful in SDI applications, in which the document element is reused when a new document is opened or created.

CDocument::SetModifiedFlag, CDocument::IsModified, and CDocument::SaveModified

Because the document is responsible for its own data, it should check for any modifications and query whether the user wants to save the document when it has been modified; the *CDocument* class provides three functions and a member variable for this purpose. The member variable, named *m_bModified*, contains the modified flag; the member functions *SetModifiedFlag* and *IsModified* set and check the value of the member variable.

SaveModified calls *IsModified*, which then checks to see whether the document has been modified. If it has been modified, *IsModified* displays an MB-_YESNOCANCEL message box and handles each possible return value. If the user clicks Cancel, *SaveModified* returns FALSE, letting the calling function know to cancel the current operation.

For the user to be prompted to save the document in all possible situations, you must set the *m_bModified* flag (by calling *SetModifiedFlag*(TRUE)) when the user modifies the document. If this is done correctly, *SaveModified* is called no matter how your application is closed. This allows you to cancel the current operation. The list below shows the various ways in which *SaveModified* can be called.

Action	Called By
Exit is chosen from the top-level File menu.	*CWinApp::OnAppExit*
Close is chosen from the MDI child's File menu.	*CDocument::OnFileClose*
Close is chosen from the MDI system menu.	*CFrameWnd::OnFileClose*
Close is chosen from the system menu.	*CFrameWnd::OnFileClose*

Frame Window–Related Functions

Frame window–related functions include the following:

- *CFrameWnd::LoadFrame*

- *CFrameWnd::PreCreateWindow*

- *CFrameWnd::ActivateFrame*

CFrameWnd::LoadFrame

This function, which calls *CFrameWnd::Create,* can be used either to create and display a frame window that is based on a document template or to create a frame with a document and view without using a document template. By default, the document/frame/view object is created by the document template by filling a *CCreateContext* object and calling *CFrameWnd::LoadFrame*. To associate the frame window that is to be created with a document-view pair, pass a CCreateContext structure (with the desired document and view types) as the last argument. For example, the code sample on the next page initializes a CCreateContext structure with the current active document, *pDoc*, and the proper view, *pView*. Note that *m_pNewViewClass* is a pointer of type *CRuntimeClass* and that it allows you to specify the type of view class you want to use.

```
CCreateContext newContext;
newContext.m_pNewViewClass = pView;
newContext.m_pNewDocTemplate = NULL;
newContext.m_pLastView = NULL;
newContext.m_pCurrentFrame = NULL;
newContext.m_pCurrentDoc = pDoc;
```

"How to Create MFC Applications That Do Not Have a Menu Bar," Knowledge Base article Q131368, describes an advanced task using *CFrameWnd::Load-Frame*. The task demonstrates the steps for creating an MDI application without a menu bar. Although this method is not recommended in most cases, it is sometimes beneficial when the developer does not need menu bars for child windows.

CFrameWnd::PreCreateWindow

This member function, found in both *CFrameWnd* and *CView*, is useful when you are customizing the appearance of your frame and view windows. Overriding this function allows you to tap into the creation process of the document template window. Without this function, there would be no way to customize the creation of the window by altering the values for the CREATESTRUCT structure, which is passed in as a parameter to *PreCreateWindow*. The CREATESTRUCT structure is used by MFC as a template for building the actual window. In this structure, you have access to, among other attributes, the menu resource, the initial display size, and the name of the class on which the Microsoft Windows object is based. For a complete description of CREATESTRUCT, see the Microsoft Visual C++ version 5 online documentation.

Overriding *CFrameWnd::PreCreateWindow* is usually done to customize attributes that are separate from the client area, such as the system menu, window title, and menu resources. Some of the more common modifications that can be made to these attributes are listed below:

- Removing the application's system menu either temporarily or permanently. For details, see the Knowledge Base article "How to Remove the System Menu from an Iconized Application": Q129224.

- Changing window attributes, such as size and window styles.

- Creating an application without a menu bar. For details, see the Knowledge Base article "How to Create MFC Applications That Do Not Have a Menu Bar": Q131368.

- Changing the frame window title of an MDI child window. For details, see the Knowledge Base article "How to Change an MFC-Based MDI Child Window's Frame Text": Q99182.

■ Modifying frame windows that have a *CFormView*-derived view. For details, see the Knowledge Base article "Using CFormView in SDI and MDI Applications": Q98598.

CFrameWnd::ActivateFrame

Override this function to create an initially minimized or maximized document in an MDI application. In your override, call the parent's *ActivateFrame* function, passing SW_SHOWMINIMIZED or SW_SHOWMAXIMIZED as the parameter.

View-Related Functions

View-related functions include the following:

■ *CView::PreCreateWindow*

■ *CView::SetActiveView*

■ *CView::OnActiveFrame*

CView::PreCreateWindow

Override *CView::PreCreateWindow* to customize the client area of the frame window. An example of customizing the client area is specifying a custom window class that is used to create the actual window object. This function dynamically creates a class name, with the attributes specified by you. These attributes include the window styles used, the cursor resource used by the window, and the background brush color. For more information on custom classes, see the online documentation, the Knowledge Base article "How to Change the Mouse Pointer for a Window in MFC": Q131991, and the task "Choosing a Document Template Without the New Document Dialog Box" later in this chapter.

CView::SetActiveView

The *CView::SetActiveView* function is commonly used when dynamically switching views from the current active view to a hidden or newly created view. For an example of switching views dynamically, check out the task "Implementing Switchable Views for a Single Document" later in this chapter. There is also a Knowledge Base article, "Switching Views in a Single Document Interface Program": Q99562, that demonstrates dynamically switching a view in an SDI application and in an MDI application, respectively.

CView::OnActivateFrame

The *CView::OnActivateFrame* function, which is called whenever *CFrameWnd::-OnActivate* is called, can be used as an indicator for the gain or loss of view activation. In an MDI application, the *OnActivateFrame* function is called after the view receives a WM_INITIALUPDATE message.

Additional Functions

An additional relevant function and structure include the following:

- *CWnd::SendMessageToDescendants*
- CCreateContext structure

CWnd::SendMessageToDescendants

This function is often used to send notification messages to descendants of the frame window. One useful application is sending WM_INITIALUPDATE or WM_IDLEUPDATECMDUI to control bars or to other windows (such as individual dialog box controls) created outside the normal document-view creation process.

NOTE: Because the messages WM_INITIALUPDATE and WM-_IDLEUPDATECMDUI are private MFC messages, only windows handled by an MFC class will be able to react to them. Standard controls are not affected.

Sending WM_INITIALUPDATE or WM_IDLEUPDATECMDUI messages gives the descendants a chance to do one-time initialization. This notification simulates the traditional process of document-view creation.

CCreateContext structure

The main purpose of this structure is to provide a "context" whenever a frame window, a document, or a view element is created dynamically. The context structure is used here, just as it is for a document template, to determine what document, view, or frame window class should be created with the new element. The context structure is used most often when you dynamically create an additional view or frame element or switch views on a single document. The following example (creating a new view in an MDI application) demonstrates this use, with *pNewView* as the pointer to the view class that is being created and *pDoc* as the current active document:

```
context.m_pNewViewClass = pNewView;
context.m_pCurrentDoc = pDoc;
context.m_pNewDocTemplate = NULL;
context.m_pLastView = NULL;
context.m_pCurrentFrame = pFrame;
```

In most cases, only one or two members of the context need initialization, depending on which element is being created. Because the example is creating a new view to display the current document and to be a child of the frame window (accessed using *pFrame*), the document, view, and frame are initialized. However, the other members can be used at any time for your own needs. For examples of using *CCreateContext*, see the following Knowledge Base articles:

- Switching Views in a Single Document Interface Program: Q99562

- Replacing a View in a CMDIChildWnd Window: Q102829. (Article in its updated form was not available for inclusion in Part II of this book at press time; see the online version.)

- How to Create MFC Applications That Do Not Have a Menu Bar: Q131368

Conclusion

My purpose in this discussion of document templates has been to shed some light on the process of creating and opening documents in your MFC application. By understanding how and when the default document template is used, you can make better decisions with respect to when the default behavior is enough for the job and when it is more appropriate to customize it. In addition, you now know about a large group of functions that can enable you to customize a document template to fit your needs.

I hope you see that the document template is just another type of framework (similar to the MFC library itself) that has a large amount of default support and is easy to customize. Use the ideas in this discussion (and the functions contained in it) to dismantle the mystery of the document creation process. Make the template work for you, not against you.

To demonstrate some of the ways you can customize the document-view architecture, I have included three tasks in this chapter:

- Choosing a document template without the new document dialog box

- Adding a second view to a document

- Implementing switchable views for a single document

Choosing a Document Template Without the New Document Dialog Box

The purpose of this task is to provide a different interface for choosing new documents either automatically from a template list or graphically with a group of toolbar buttons. By default, in applications with more than one document template, a dialog box (referred to as the New Document dialog box) is displayed whenever the user opens a new document. This dialog box lists all of the available document templates for the application. After the user chooses the template type, a new document is created. However, you might prefer a more graphical interface to this list of templates, perhaps a descriptive toolbar button for each template. Or maybe you need more control over the process. For example, your application might have a document type that, when created, requires an additional document type to be created. Instead of the user having to create the second document type, your application can automatically create the additional document when the user chooses the proper document type.

In this task, I implement a command handling mechanism that searches the list of available templates and then creates a new document from the proper template. The task has five steps:

1. Adding a new type of document template

2. Modifying the application's resources

3. Modifying the application's *InitInstance* function

4. Installing the new command handlers

5. Implementing the new command handlers

W A R N I N G : If you are modifying an SDI-type application, you must create a new, empty document before the application displays itself. For more information, see "Additional Information" at the end of this task.

The project is an MDI application, and its name is NEWTMPL. The requirements for this task are:

■ A new document type consisting of a document, a frame window, a view class, and associated resources (such as an icon and a menu)

■ One or more command handlers for creating a new document

Step 1: Adding a New Type of Document Template

The default AppWizard project (either SDI or MDI) includes a fully functioning document template. This document template, which consists of frame window, document, and view elements, is automatically created and added to the application's document template list. The template list exists in the application object, and it contains all document types known by the application.

New document templates are added with a call to *AddDocTemplate*; this usually occurs in the *InitInstance* function of the application class.

In this step, you will add three new classes to provide a second document template that creates a document of type NewType. In this task, I use the following class names:

Document Template (NewType) Classes

Class Name	Description
CNewFrame	The new template's frame window element— derived from *CMDIChildWnd*
CNewDocument	The new template's document element— derived from *CDocument*
CNewView	The new template's view element—derived from *CView*

N O T E :   It's not necessary to derive the second child frame window class from *CMDIChildWnd*; you can use the base class directly by substituting *CMDIChildWnd* for *CNewFrame* in the document template definition.

Create three new classes of the types specified above using the New Class command of ClassWizard. If you already have three classes of these types, copy the header and implementation files to the directory of the project to be modified and add them to the project using the Files Into Project command on the Insert menu. These classes make up the majority of the NewType document template. In addition to these classes, you will need several resources, such as a menu, icons, and a string table entry.

Step 2: Modifying the Application's Resources

In addition to classes, each document template usually contains a set of resources that share a common resource ID. For instance, in the MDI application framework created by AppWizard, the resource ID is the name of the project with the suffix TYPE. In most cases, the resources consist of a menu, an icon for the child object, and a string that describes the various elements of the document template.

For this task, you can use a set of predefined resources, with the ID IDR_DEFAULTYPE. These predefined resources can be copied from the DEFAULT.RC file, located in the \PROJECTS\DEFAULT directory on the companion disc. The resources are made up of an icon, a menu that is based on the default menu generated by AppWizard, and the following string resource (using IDR_DEFAULTYPE as the resource ID):

```
Defaul\n\nDefaul\n\n\nDefaul.Document\Defaul Document
```

If you want to create your own resources, you will need an icon, a menu that has at a minimum all commands from the main menu resource, and a string table entry similar to the default above. For more information on strings of this type, see the Knowledge Base article "Format of the Document Template String": Q129095.

> N O T E :   Another option for new document template resources is to copy existing resources in your application's project and then modify them. For example, if your project is an MDI application, you should have resources for the original document template. Copy the icon, menu, and string entry resources into similar types using a new resource ID.

After you have the menu resource for the new template, add menu items to create each document template. For example, if the project has a Hello document and a Bounce document, add two menu items—New Hello and New Bounce—to the File menu on all of the menu resources of the project. Be sure you assign separate and distinct IDs for each item, such as ID_FILE_NEWHELLO and ID_FILE_NEWBOUNCE; you will write command handlers for these later in the task. As you edit the menu resource, there should be a New menu item or items with the ID ID_FILE_NEW that you must remove. This is the default ID used by the framework to generate new document types. Because you are bypassing this functionality, you don't need it anymore.

Step 3: Modifying the Application's *InitInstance* Function

If your application was created by AppWizard, the *InitInstance* function performs two chores that are important to this task: initializing the document template list and creating a new, empty, document type. In applications created by AppWizard, the document template list is initialized with the default document template in the first part of the application class's *InitInstance* function. The following code, taken from a default MDI application, adds the only document template that is used by the application:

```
CMultiDocTemplate* pDocTemplate;
pDocTemplate = new CMultiDocTemplate(
    IDR_MYPROJTYPE,
```

(continued)

91

```
    RUNTIME_CLASS(CProjDoc),
    RUNTIME_CLASS(CNewFrame), // Custom MDI child frame
    RUNTIME_CLASS(CProjView));
AddDocTemplate(pDocTemplate);
```

You can add your new document template right after the code above. First add the include files for the three new classes to the top of the application's implementation file. For example, if you are using *CNewFrame*, *CNewDoc*, and *CNewView*, the new code (in bold) will look like this:

```
#include "MainFrm.h"
#include "ChildFrm.h"
#include "NewTmplDoc.h"
#include "NewTmplView.h"

#include "NewFrame.h"
#include "NewDoc.h"
#include "NewView.h"
```

Add the following code right after the existing call to *AddDocTemplate*:

```
CMultiDocTemplate* pNewTemplate;
pNewTemplate = new CMultiDocTemplate(
    IDR_NEWTYPE,
    RUNTIME_CLASS(CNewDoc),
    RUNTIME_CLASS(CNewFrame), // Custom MDI child frame
    RUNTIME_CLASS(CNewView));
AddDocTemplate(pNewTemplate);
```

Notice that a new *CMultiDocTemplate* pointer (named *pNewTemplate*) is initialized with the new resource ID and the three new classes you added earlier. After the pointer is initialized, it is added to your application's template list with the call to *AddDocTemplate*.

N O T E : If your application is an SDI-type application, use *CSingleDocTemplate* instead of *CMultiDocTemplate*.

The *InitInstance* function is also where the new empty document is created. In the default application framework, the command line is parsed for any commands. These commands are then executed by the framework. If no commands are found, the ID_FILE_NEW command is handled, which usually causes a new document to be displayed in the application window. First, a *cmdInfo* object is initialized with any commands found:

```
// Parse command line for standard shell commands, DDE, file open
CCommandLineInfo cmdInfo;
ParseCommandLine(cmdInfo);
```

Then, in a call to *ProcessShellCommand*, the *cmdInfo* object is read. If no commands are found, a call to *OnFileNew* is made:

```
// Dispatch commands specified on the command line
if (!ProcessShellCommand(cmdInfo))
    return FALSE;
```

In MDI applications, you can remove this code to prevent the creation of an empty document. The application then comes up with an empty application frame, and the user must then create a new document of his or her choice using the new command handlers added in the next step. However, in SDI applications, you must create a new window before exiting the *InitInstance* function. Therefore, you should leave in this code or implement another method for creating a new window before exiting *InitInstance*.

Step 4: Installing the New Command Handlers

It's time to add some new handlers for creating new document types using a cool trick provided by the Resource editor. The following procedure for adding new command handlers will install unique handlers for each document type.

1. Open any menu resource that contains the File New commands for your document type.

2. Expand the File menu (or other top-level menu that contains your new document menu items).

3. While holding down the Ctrl key, double-click one of the new document menu items. ClassWizard should then come up with the Message Maps tab on top.

4. Add a command handler for the menu ID associated with the menu item you chose in the main frame class—in this case, *CMainFrame*. Repeat this step to add handlers for all menu items that you added in step 2. When all of the handlers have been added, save the project.

   N O T E : The class associated with this menu will be chosen by ClassWizard to handle the commands. If you want a different class (perhaps the application class), choose it from the Class Name list box and then add the handler. If the application class is chosen, the template traversal code is slightly easier to read because you have eliminated the need for an application pointer.

Because you created a unique command handler for each document type, you already know which document template should be used to create the new document. All that is left to do is to search the document template list for the proper template.

There is also an alternative method for using only one command handler for all New menu items; it parses the current message for the document type. Details about this method can be found under "Additional Information" at the end of this task.

Step 5: Implementing the New Command Handlers

You now have a command handler for each new document type, but you still have to find the right document template to create a functioning document-view pair. Fortunately, the application class contains a complete list of templates. All you have to do is traverse this list, grab the right one, and call its *OpenDocument* function.

Because the new document handlers are members of the main frame window class, you will need to get a pointer to the application object and use that pointer to access the document template list unless you chose a different class. The following code uses a call to *AfxGetApp* to accomplish this:

```
CNewTemplApp* pApp;
pApp = (CNewTemplApp *)AfxGetApp();
POSITION curTemplatePos = pApp->GetFirstDocTemplatePosition();
```

Now use *curTemplatePos* to run through the available templates and grab the proper one. The following code uses a call to *GetDocString* to match the target string with the current template's document name. If the match succeeds, you have the right one and can call *OpenDocument*. If there is no match, continue traversing the list:

```
while(curTemplatePos != NULL)
{
    CDocTemplate* curTemplate =
        pApp->GetNextDocTemplate(curTemplatePos);
    CString str;
    curTemplate->GetDocString(str, CDocTemplate::fileNewName);
    if (str == "NewType")
    {
        curTemplate->OpenDocumentFile(NULL);
        return;
    }
}
```

NOTE: In addition to *CDocTemplate::docName*, *GetDocString* can return any one of the seven elements of the document type's string resource. However, in some cases, certain values will work only in MDI-type applications. Check out *GetDocString* in the online documentation for details.

The target string (in this case, *NewType*) is determined by the proper document template resource string—in this case, the NewType document. Each of the template strings should have a different set of string elements, which allows you to distinguish between template types. I used *CDocTemplate::-docName* because it works for both SDI- and MDI-type applications.

Now that you have completed one of the handlers, use similar code for the others by changing the comparison to the new document type for which you are searching. After you have built the project, the user will be able to choose the document type he or she wants to create by executing the proper menu command.

Additional Information

Here is some additional information to help you.

Alternative Methods for Handling New Document Commands

As I mentioned earlier, there are alternative methods for installing command handlers for each document type. In one method, you have only one command handler, which contains all of the code for creating a new document. In the future, if changes to the new document logic are needed, you need modify only one function. Instead of installing a unique handler for each document type, you map every New Document menu item to the same handler (perhaps named *OnMyNewDocument*); then, before traversing the template list, determine the command ID with the following line of code:

```
idVal= LOWORD(GetCurrentMessage()->wParam);
```

You can then set up a case statement that sets the target value to the proper string value. The modified traverse function would look something like this:

```
CNewTemplApp* pApp;
pApp = (CNewTemplApp *)AfxGetApp();
POSITION curTemplatePos = pApp->GetFirstDocTemplatePosition();
// Grab the ID of the menu choice
CString targetVal;
idVal = LOWORD(GetCurrentMessage()->wParam);
switch(idVal)
{
case ID_FILE_NEWTYPE:
    targetVal = 'NewType';
case ID_FILE_OLDTYPE:
    targetVal = 'OldType';
}
```

(continued)

```
// Traverse the list to find the proper template
while (curTemplatePos != NULL)
{
    CDocTemplate* curTemplate =
        pApp->GetNextDocTemplate(curTemplatePos);
    CString str;
    curTemplate->GetDocString(str, CDocTemplate::docName);
    if (str == targetVal)
    {
        curTemplate->OpenDocumentFile(NULL);
        return;
    }
}
```

In the two methods discussed thus far, the document template variable is created on the stack. Therefore, it exists only within the scope of the *InitInstance* function. Because of this and because the order of the document templates in the document template list cannot be assumed, you must search for the proper template every time a new document is created. As it turns out, this search is unnecessary if you keep a pointer to all document templates used in the application. When placed in the application's class, these pointers allow permanent access from anywhere in the application at any time. Instead of searching, you can simply call the *OpenDocumentFile* function of the appropriate template using the stored pointer.

Modifying SDI-Type Applications

Before an SDI-type application is visible, the *m_pMainWnd* data member must point to the main frame window of the application. This means that a new, empty document must be created in order to create a valid frame window object. Unfortunately, one result of this task is that the application appears with no new document. In order for an SDI application to become visible, you must create a new, empty document during startup. After the empty document is created, the user can create new documents of his or her choice.

Additional Reading

Technical Note 22 in the Visual C++ online documentation provides an excellent description of handling standard MFC commands. There is also mention of other customizations for handling new document requests. The Knowledge Base article "How to Create New Documents Without CWinApp::-OnFileNew": Q113257 discusses yet another method of bypassing the default handling of *OnFileNew.*

The Source Code Is Your Friend!

I found the procedure used in this task (document template traversal) by stepping through the source code of *ProcessShellCommand*. In addition, the reason why *OnFileNew* is called is obvious if you continue to step through with a little patience.

Adding a Second View to a Document

The purpose of this task is to implement two different view types for a single document. The two views are shown simultaneously in a static splitter window (Figure 3-3)—each pane displaying a different view of the document data. The first view is a graphical representation derived from *CView*; the second is a control view derived from *CFormView*. Each view is able to notify the document when data is changed by the user, which "prompts" the document to update all views automatically.

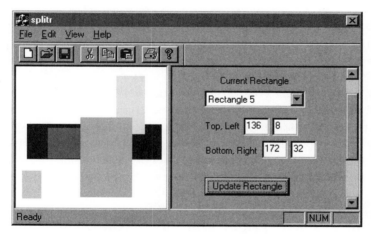

Figure 3-3.
Application with both panes visible.

This type of application is commonly referred to as a multiple view interface (MVI) application. All MVI applications must use splitter windows that come as one of two types—dynamic splitter windows, which must use the same view class for each pane, or static splitter windows, which can use different view classes for each pane. This task demonstrates the implementation of a static splitter window, which is the more complex of the two types of windows.

The task consists of two steps:

1. Adding a second view class

2. Modifying the main frame window class

The project name is SPLITR, and the requirement is a *CView*-derived class, which is used as the second view.

NOTE: Just to keep you from getting confused: in the sample project I have provided for this task, one of the data types for the document is a custom class named *CMyRect*, which has its own header and implementation files, MYRECT.H and MYRECT.CPP, respectively. In addition, the second type of view class (*CDlgView*) is derived from *CFormView* and has its own header and implementation files, DLGVIEW.H and DLGVIEW.CPP, respectively. All references to these classes are for the sample project only.

Step 1: Adding a Second View Class

Because the sample implementation uses a static splitter window, derive a second view class from *CView* (the sample derives the second view class from *CFormView*) and add it to your project. If you have an existing view class, you can simply add the files to the project by choosing the Add To Project/Files command from the Project menu. If you create the class with ClassWizard, the files are added automatically, plus you get a basic class frame with which to work. As I mentioned above, the second view class, *CDlgView*, is derived from *CFormView*. The form view contains a set of controls that allows the user to select one of five *MyRect* objects displayed in the left pane and to manipulate its values.

Step 2: Modifying the Main Frame Window Class

Now that you have two view classes, you have to modify the main frame window class, usually *CMainFrame*, to create a splitter window with two panes that display the different views. These are the modifications you will have to make:

- Adding a *CSplitterWnd* data member to the *CMainFrame* class. The data member is used later to point to the new splitter window.

- Adding the header files for the document and new view classes to the *CMainFrame* implementation file. This allows us to use the document and new view class types in the implementation code for the splitter window.

■ Overriding the *OnCreateClient* function in the *CMainFrame* class (if it is not already overidden), and adding code for creating the splitter window and its panes. This function provides a handy place to create the splitter window and its two panes.

To modify the main frame window, follow this procedure:

1. Add the splitter window data member by adding the following line to the *CMainFrame* header file:

```
    ⋮
// Attributes
protected:
    CSplitterWnd m_wndSplitter;
    ⋮
```

Declaring the data member "protected" is not required, but it does strengthen the modularity of the class.

2. In the implementation file of *CMainFrame*, add the header files for your application's document class and the view classes.

   N O T E : Including the header file of the document class (in this case, SPLITRDOC.H) is optional. In most cases, however, your second view interacts with the document, which requires the document's header file to resolve document references.

   The example below shows the lines you would add to the implementation file of the main frame class to include the SPLITR project header files for the document and two view classes:

```
    ⋮
#include "splitrDoc.h"
#include "splitrView.h"
#include "DlgView.h"
    ⋮
```

3. To properly create the splitter window and panes, override the *OnCreateClient* function using ClassWizard in the *CMainFrame* class. The result is shown below. The lines in bold were added by ClassWizard.

```
//{{AFX_VIRTUAL(CMainFrame)
public:
virtual BOOL OnCreateClient(LPCREATESTRUCT lpcs,
    CCreateContext* pContext);
```

(continued)

99

```
virtual BOOL PreCreateWindow(CREATESTRUCT& cs);
⋮
```

In the implementation file of MAINFRM.CPP, the body of the *OnCreateClient* function looks like this:

```
BOOL CMainFrame::OnCreateClient(LPCREATESTRUCT /*lpcs*/,
    CCreateContext* pContext)
{
⋮
    return CMainFrame::OnCreateClient(lpcs, pContext);
}
```

4. Add code to the *OnCreateClient* function to create and initialize the splitter panes. Because I am creating a static splitter window, I use *CSplitterWnd::CreateStatic* and *CSplitterWnd::CreateView*. The following code added to the *OnCreateClient* function creates a splitter window with one row and two columns. The left pane is created using *CSplitrView* (the initial project's class) as the view class. The second pane is created using *CDlgView* as the view class.

```
// Create a splitter with 1 row, 2 columns
if (!m_wndSplitter.CreateStatic(this, 1, 2))
{
    TRACE0("Failed to create static splitters\n");
    return FALSE;
}
// Add the first splitter pane--the default view in column 0
if (!m_wndSplitter.CreateView(0, 0,
    RUNTIME_CLASS(CSplitrView), CSize(590, 50), pContext))
{
    TRACE0("Failed to create first pane\n");
    return FALSE;
}
// Add the second splitter pane--an input view in column 1
if (!m_wndSplitter.CreateView(0, 1,
    RUNTIME_CLASS(CDlgView), CSize(0, 0), pContext))
{
    TRACE0("Failed to create second pane\n");
    return FALSE;
}
// Activate the input view
SetActiveView((CView*)m_wndSplitter.GetPane(0,1));

return TRUE;
```

After you add the new view class and implement *CMainFrame::OnCreate-Client,* your application should have a splitter window with two panes. The content of each pane depends on the *OnDraw* code in your view classes. If you have nothing in the *OnDraw* functions, these panes will be blank.

Additional Information

The SPLITR project contains additional code that synchronizes the view and document classes, specifically, code for the following functions:

- *CSplitrView::OnInitialUpdate()*
- *CDlgView::GetDocument()*
- *CDlgView::DoDataExchange(CDataExchange* pDX)*
- *CDlgView::OnInitialUpdate()*
- *CDlgView::OnUpdate*
- *CDlgView::OnUpdateRect()*

Another method for implementing multiple views on a single document (described in detail in the next task) allows a user to switch views at any time.

Implementing Switchable Views for a Single Document

The purpose of this task is to implement switchable views for the same document in an existing SDI application. In the sample application, the default view (shown in Figure 3-4 on the following page) is derived from *CView* and the second view (shown in Figure 3-5 on the following page) is derived from *CFormView.* The second view contains controls that allow the user to modify the attributes of the document's data. The document's data consists of a group of rectangles randomly generated and colored, which are drawn in the initial view and can be modified in the second view. In the procedure presented here, I use the *AddView* and *RemoveView* member functions of *CDocument.*

Initially, the document has one view—the existing view provided by the application. The user can switch the views using either the toolbar or the View menu options. The main frame window, *CMainFrame,* handles the request to switch views by creating a second view if necessary and then swapping the view IDs, hiding the current view, and showing the second view. The frame window keeps track of both views, including which of the views is the

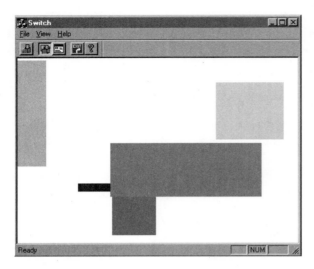

Figure 3-4.
Application with graphical view.

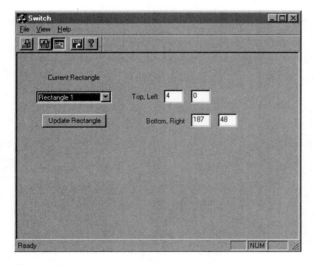

Figure 3-5.
Application with common controls view.

current one. It also handles the destruction of the second view and restoration of the initial view when the application ends or when a new document is created. The task has five steps:

1. Adding the new view class

2. Modifying the frame window class

3. Implementing the *OnViewSwitch* function

4. Re-initializing the document

5. Adding resources for switching views

The name of the project is SWITCH, and these are the requirements:

- A *CView*-derived class, which will be used as the second view

- A function, for this task named *OnViewSwitch*, that switches the current view with a hidden view

- A function, for this task named *CleanUpViews*, that resets the state of the document when a new document is requested

- Graphical resources, such as buttons or a toolbar, to switch between the views

Step 1: Adding the New View Class

The first step is to add the view to which and from which you will be switching. You can create a new view class or use an existing view class. If you are going to use an existing *CView*-derived class, you should copy the header and implementation files to the project directory and add them to the project. There are probably references (for example, *#include* directives, obsolete classes, and so on) that should be modified or removed; a quick way to track these down is to rebuild the project and fix all of the errors that pop up.

If you created the new view class with ClassWizard, modify the view's header file by changing the access specifier for the constructor, the destructor, and the *OnInitialUpdate* function from "protected" to "public." This allows the class to be created directly by other classes. You can rebuild the project, but it isn't required yet. Because the new view class will be interacting with the existing document class, it's a good idea to implement some type of *GetDocument* function in your new view class. If you access the document from the view class by name, add the document's header file to either the header or the implementation file of the view class.

TIP: If your project was created by AppWizard, you already have a working function, *GetDocument*. Make this a member function of your new view class by copying over the Debug and Release versions of the function. Make sure you grab the inline function, which is found in the header file of the view class, and the release version, which is found near the diagnostic functions.

For the second view to display the document data correctly, some type of synchronization with the document data is needed. Because the sample project uses a form view as the second view, I override *CFormView::OnInitialUpdate* and *CFormView::OnUpdate* for one-time initialization and synchronization with the document data. Use this method if your second view is derived from *CFormView*.

If your view is derived from *CView*, override the *OnInitialUpdate* and *OnActivateView* functions of your view's class. In addition to activating the view, *OnActivateView* is called when the view is being deactivated; therefore, check for this possibility and update the data only when the view is activated.

Step 2: Modifying the Frame Window Class

In a typical SDI application, switching between views is done easily in only two classes—the application class and the main frame window class. Either class is able to switch views, but if you choose the main frame window class, you save yourself a bit of typing. The sample project switches the views from the *CMainFrame* class, so I am assuming that you also are choosing *CMainFrame*. After you have chosen the class, make these modifications:

- Add the header file of the new view class to the implementation file of the chosen class.

- Add data members that will store the existing views and track the current view.

Because the switching function uses the *new* operator to create a second view, include the header file for the second view class in the implementation file of *CMainFrame*.

NOTE: Because I've used a form view in the sample project, AFXPRIV.H was included by class *CMainFrame*. This allows the class to send WM_INITIALUPDATE messages.

CMainFrame also needs a way to access both views easily. This is accomplished by adding two pointers (of type *CView*) to *CMainFrame*. These data members should be "public." To make it easier to see which view is current, add another variable named *m_currentView* of type *int*:

```
    ⋮
public:
// Attributes
    CView* m_pView1;
    CView* m_pView2;
    CView m_currentView;
    ⋮
```

In the *CMainFrame* constructor, initialize both view pointers to NULL and *m_currentView* to 1. This indicates that the current view is the original project view; the numeral *2* indicates that the current view is the new view.

```
CMainFrame::CMainFrame()
{
    m_pView1 = NULL;
    m_pView2 = NULL;
    m_currentView = 1;
}
```

Now you can implement the handler function for switching views, *On-ViewSwitch.*

Step 3: Implementing the *OnViewSwitch* Function

This is the key activity of the task. To switch views successfully, the *OnViewSwitch* function must do the following:

- Create a second view if one is needed.
- Switch the IDs of both views.
- Display the alternate view and hide the current view.
- Modify the document's list of views.

Because of the size of the *OnViewSwitch* function, I split the function into four parts for the purpose of this discussion. I will list the parts in the order in which they appear in the *OnViewSwitch* function and then discuss what they do. You can either add the body of the entire function now or add each part as it's discussed.

1. Add the code on the following page to the beginning of the *OnView-Switch* function.

```
CView* pViewAdd;
CView* pViewRemove;
CDocument* pDoc = GetActiveDocument();
BOOL bCreated = FALSE;
UINT nCmdID;

nCmdID = LOWORD(GetCurrentMessage()->wParam);

if ((nCmdID == ID_VIEW_VIEW1) && (m_currentView == 1))
    return;
if ((nCmdID == ID_VIEW_VIEW2) && (m_currentView == 2))
    return;
```

In the first section of code, I retrieve a pointer to the document and the command ID of the current message. I then use the command ID to determine whether the current view is the one chosen by the user. If so, the function returns, doing nothing. If the request is valid, the switch is initiated.

2. Add the code below immediately after the code in section 1 above:

```
if (nCmdID == ID_VIEW_VIEW2)
{
    if (m_pView2 == NULL)
    {
        m_pView1 = GetActiveView();
        m_pView2 = new CMyView2;

        m_pView2->Create(NULL, NULL, AFX_WS_DEFAULT_VIEW,
            rectDefault, this, AFX_IDW_PANE_FIRST + 1, NULL);
        bCreated = TRUE;
    }
    pViewAdd = m_pView2;
    pViewRemove = m_pView1;
    m_currentView = 2;
}
else
{
    pViewAdd = m_pView1;
    pViewRemove = m_pView2;
    m_currentView = 1;
}
```

In this section of code, if the view to which you are switching is the second view and the pointer (*m_pView2*) is NULL, the view is created and *bCreated* is set to TRUE. When both views exist, the pointers are set to their proper values.

3. Add the code below immediately after the code in section 2:

```
int nSwitchChildID = pViewAdd->GetDlgCtrlID();
pViewAdd->SetDlgCtrlID(AFX_IDW_PANE_FIRST);
pViewRemove->SetDlgCtrlID(nSwitchChildID);

// Show the newly active view, and hide the inactive view

pViewAdd->ShowWindow(SW_SHOW);
pViewRemove->ShowWindow(SW_HIDE);
```

In this section of code, I set the view ID of the newly active view to AFX_IDW_PANE_FIRST so that *CFrameWnd::RecalcLayout* will allocate to this "first pane" the portion of the frame window's client area not allocated to control bars. After the IDs have been switched, I show the newly active view and hide the other view.

4. Add the code below immediately after the code in section 3 above:

```
pDoc->AddView(pViewAdd);
pDoc->RemoveView(pViewRemove);

SetActiveView(pViewAdd);
RecalcLayout();
```

5. Finally, I replace the old view in the active document's list of views with the new view. Then I notify the new view and readjust the layout.

N O T E :   If you step through the Debug version of the *OnView-Switch* function, you will see the following warning: "Creating a pane with no *CDocument*." This warning is generated when the call to *CMyView2::Create* occurs before the call to initialize a document. The view has no document until the call to *CDocument::AddView* is made later in the function. This warning does not indicate a memory leak, illegal accessing, or any other dangerous behavior.

Step 4: Re-Initializing the Document

The application framework behaves a little differently when a new document is created in an MDI application than when it is created in an SDI application. In an SDI application, only one document, view, and frame window can be open at any one time. However, in the case of the application used in this task (which uses splitter windows), the splitter window occupies the client area of the main frame window. Each pane of the splitter has a different *CWnd*-derived object. This allows an SDI application to have more than one

CView-derived object. When a new document is requested in an SDI application, the framework reuses the existing components. This means that the existing document, view, and frame objects are wiped clean and then used to set up the new document-view pair.

Because the framework reuses the existing components in an SDI application, you must be very careful to return the document, view, and frame window objects to their original state. If you were to build your modified project right now (assuming you have a user interface for switching), you could demonstrate this need for extra care quite easily. Just start the application, switch to the second view (forcing a creation of the view), and then request a new document. You then will get a large, nasty assertion error because the detached view tried to access its document and came up with nothing. Therefore, you need to check for a couple of things before letting the application create a new document. If the second view was not created, everything is fine. If the second view was created and is the current view, you should switch views and then destroy the second view. If the second view was created and is currently detached, simply destroy the second view.

With SDI application architecture, there is really only one place to put this code, and that is in the document's override of *OnNewDocument*. It is the only place that gets called every time a new document is created. To keep the code neat and readable, the SWITCH project makes a call to *CleanUpViews* in *OnNewDocument* that determines and executes the proper action. The *CleanUpViews* function is as follows:

```
void CSwitchDoc::CleanUpViews()
{
    CMainFrame* pFrm;
    pFrm = (CMainFrame*)AfxGetMainWnd();

    if (pFrm->m_pView2 != NULL)  // Was second view created?
    {

        if (pFrm->m_currentView == 2)  // Do we need to swap in
                                       // the default view?
            pFrm->SendMessage(WM_COMMAND, ID_VIEW_VIEW1);
        pFrm->m_pView2->DestroyWindow();
        pFrm->m_pView2 = NULL;  // Restore defaults
        m_bViewCreated = FALSE;
    }
}
```

The first thing I do is determine whether the second view was created. If so, I switch views by switching to the default view (in this case, View 1) and clean up the second view. After this is done, I can destroy the window and restore the document state by setting the pointer to the second view to NULL and the view creation flag to FALSE. The architecture takes over and reuses the document-view pair with no assertions or memory leaks.

Step 5: Adding Resources for Switching Views

The remaining item in this task is providing access to view switching for the application user. I will present two possibilities but leave the implementation details up to you.

The first alternative is a graphical interface that allows the user to choose the current view at any time. The SWITCH program provides the following interface—two menu commands (View 1 and View 2) and a pair of toolbar buttons that represent these two possible views. The current view is indicated by a check mark next to the appropriate menu command and a depressed button that represents the current view. You can get an idea of how the interface works by looking at the resources for the SWITCH project and the following functions:

■ *CMainFrame::OnUpdateView1*
  This function updates the View 1 menu item.

■ *CMainFrame::OnUpdateView1*
  This function updates the View 2 menu item.

■ *CMainFrame::OnViewSwitch*
  This function is the handler for the View 1 and View 2 menu items.

Instead of allowing the user to switch views, the second alternative determines when the views need to be switched according to the occurrence or nonoccurrence of a specific event. For instance, let's say a user is changing rectangle values using the form view. When the Update Rectangle button is clicked, the application updates the document's data automatically and switches to the graphical view. If the user chooses a hypothetical Modify Values menu command to modify the current values, the view is switched to the form. When the user clicks the Update Rectangle button, the view switching function in the BN_CLICKED command handler of the form view is called. When the user chooses the Modify Values menu command, the view switching function in the Modify Values command handler is called.

After implementing the user interface of your choice, rebuild your project. You now have two views that can be switched and that display the data of a document.

Additional Information

In addition to the AddView/RemoveView method that has been described here, there is also a method that switches the views by manipulating the window IDs of the alternate views. This second method is discussed in detail in the Knowledge Base article "SAMPLE: VSWAP32 Demos Multiple-View Switching in SDI": Q141334.

Dialog Boxes

The focus of this chapter is on MFC dialog boxes. I have organized the four tasks in the chapter according to the amount of modification to the dialog box that is required. The first two tasks are examples of general modifications of the dialog box; the last two are examples of specific modifications to the various dialog box attributes. These are the tasks included in this discussion:

- **Implementing a custom DDX function** Demonstrates how to implement a custom dialog data exchange (DDX) function that displays float and double type values in an edit control without using scientific notation.

- **Customizing common dialog boxes** Demonstrates how to customize both modal and modeless MFC common dialog boxes. The task modifies the File Open dialog box (both Microsoft Windows 3.*x* style and Windows Explorer style) and the Find Text dialog box.

- **Using bitmaps as the background in a dialog box** Demonstrates how to modify the background of a dialog box using bitmaps (or a patterned brush) to customize the appearance. In addition, I handle the WM_CTLCOLOR message to blend the dialog box controls into the dialog box background.

- **Modifying the attributes of dialog box controls** Demonstrates how to modify the attributes of various common dialog box controls such as the text color used by a radio button group, the font used by a static control, and the visibility of a control.

Implementing a Custom DDX Function

The purpose of this task is to discuss and demonstrate the requirements for implementing a custom DDX function. Standard DDX functions implemented by the MFC library provide a safe way to exchange data between a control in a dialog box and a data member of the class that represents the dialog box. But despite the wide range of data types supported by these functions, you might still need to design your own customized DDX functions. Common reasons for extending the standard DDX functions include the need to exchange different data types, to add new exchange and validation procedures, and to provide custom handling for standard data types (demonstrated by this task). When implementing custom DDX functions, the hardest part is developing the code (usually divided into helper functions) that does the calculating and formatting of the data, if that is required.

The task has two steps:

- Declaring the custom DDX function
- Implementing the custom DDX function

In addition, I describe a custom DDX function that displays float values and double values without exponential notation in an edit control. The float version of the *DDX_Text* function found in the MFC library occasionally displays scientific notation.

The name of the project is CUSTDDX, and the requirement is a dialog box class with an edit control.

NOTE: This task uses multiple functions to demonstrate clearly the inner workings of *DDX_MyFloatText* and *DDX_MyDoubleText*. However, there is no rule that says your custom DDX function must have helper functions.

Step 1: Declaring the Custom DDX Function

The standard form of a custom DDX declaration is as follows:

```
DDX_function_name(pDX, nIDC, value);
```

There are three parameters to this function:

- **pDX** A pointer to a CDataExchange object. The framework supplies this object to establish the context of the data exchange, including its direction.

- **nIDC** The ID of the control in the dialog box, form view, or control view object that is exchanging data.

- **value** A reference to a data member in the dialog box, form view, or control view object.

Declare your custom DDX function, following the standard format; this makes the customized DDX function easier to identify and use. In the interest of modularity, it's a good idea to contain the declaration and implementation code in two files—a header file and an implementation file. The sample project demonstrates this modularity by declaring the custom functions in MYDDX.H and their implementation in MYDDX.CPP. In the following code sample, the custom DDX functions used in CUSTDDX are declared:

```
// Custom DDX functions
void AFXAPI DDX_MyFloatText(CDataExchange* pDX, int nIDC,
    float& value);
void AFXAPI DDX_MyDoubleText(CDataExchange* pDX, int nIDC,
    double& value);
```

Now that you have declared the custom DDX functions, move on to the real work—the actual implementation of the custom DDX functions.

Step 2: Implementing the Custom DDX Function

Another reason to keep the declaration and implementation of the custom DDX function (and any helpers) in two files is to "hide" those functions that are used internally. For example, the CUSTDDX project declares three additional functions that are used internally by the custom DDX functions; these functions are declared as follows:

```
static BOOL AFXAPI SimpleFloatParse(LPCTSTR lpszText, double& d);
static void AFXAPI MyTextFloatFormat(CDataExchange* pDX,
    int nIDC, void* pData, double value, int nSizeGcvt, int
    nSizeType);
static void StripZeros(LPTSTR szNumber);
```

The use of these functions is explained (on page 114).

The function body of a custom DDX function is broken into two parts: code that moves data from the dialog box class to the actual dialog box control, and code that moves data from the actual dialog box control to the dialog box class. Your custom function can determine the direction of transfer by checking the value of a data member (in this case, *m_bSaveAndValidate*) of the *CDataExchange* class. The following example shows the framework of a typical DDX function:

```
static void AFXAPI MyDDXFunction(CDataExchange* pDX,
    int nIDC, void* pData, double value, int nSizeGcvt, int
    nSizeType)
{
```

(continued)

113

```
// Initialization code
if (pDX->m_bSaveAndValidate)
{
    // Transfer data from the control to the class
}
else
{
    // Transfer data from the class to the control
}
}
```

At this point, I leave the actual implementation of your custom DDX function to you and continue with a discussion of the *DDX_MyFloatText* custom DDX function in the CUSTDDX project.

Discussion of the *DDX_MyFloatText* Custom DDX Function

As I mentioned before, the custom DDX functions of the CUSTDDX project are modularized. The entire body of the custom DDX functions consists of a call to *MyTextFloatFormat*, which is where the real work is done. The following is the declaration of *MyTextFloatFormat*:

```
static void AFXAPI MyTextFloatFormat(CDataExchange* pDX,
    int nIDC, void* pData, double value, int nSizeGcvt, int
    nSizeType);
```

The code sections from the *MyTextFloatFormat* function are discussed here in the order in which they appear in the function. In the code section below, some initialization and checking is done. First I check to see whether there is any data to be transferred (the assertion on *pData*); then I allocate a buffer to store the data string from the edit control of the dialog box.

```
ASSERT(pData != NULL);

HWND hWndCtrl = pDX->PrepareEditCtrl(nIDC);

// Make sure your buffer is big enough. Strings returned by
// _stprintf() using the "f" specifier tend to be longer
// than those returned using the "g" specifier.
TCHAR szBuffer[64];
```

The next code sample handles the transfer of data from the dialog box control to the class. It is executed only if *m_bSaveAndValidate* is TRUE, indicating that the transfer is from the control to the class. First the text is retrieved with a call to *::GetWindowText*. Then I call an internal helper function, *SimpleFloatParse*, to parse the text string. If the parsing fails (a valid float is not found), a message box is displayed and an exception is thrown. (For more details on the *SimpleFloatParse* function, see the MYDDX.CPP file in the CUSTDDX project.) If the parsing succeeds (a valid float is found), the value is cast to the proper data type (based on *nSizeType*) of the dialog box class. The transfer is then complete.

```
::GetWindowText(hWndCtrl, szBuffer, _countof(szBuffer));
double d;
if (!SimpleFloatParse(szBuffer, d))
{
    AfxMessageBox(AFX_IDP_PARSE_REAL);
    pDX->Fail();              // Throws exception
}
if (nSizeType == FLT_DIG)
    *((float*)pData) = (float)d;
else
    *((double*)pData) = d;
```

The following code sample handles the other half of the transfer: the transfer of data from the dialog box class to the dialog box control. First the *szBuffer* is loaded with the current data value according to the format control string. The string is then cleaned up by calling another internal helper function, *StripZeros*. (For the implementation of this function, see the MYDDX.CPP file in the CUSTDDX project.) This function removes any trailing zeros from the value. (A single zero is left after the decimal if the number has no fractional value.) The value is then transferred to the edit control of the dialog box with a call to *SetWindowText*. The transfer is then complete.

```
_stprintf(szBuffer, _T("%.*f"), nSizeGcvt, value);
StripZeros(szBuffer);
SetWindowText(hWndCtrl, szBuffer);
```

Additional Information

Some of the more common DDX functions in MFC are *DDX_Text*, *DDX_Radio*, and *DDX_Control*. For a complete listing of DDX functions, search for the string "DDX_" in the Microsoft Visual C++ version 5 online documentation. For more information on the mechanics of DDX, see Technical Note 26 in the Visual C++ online documentation.

There is another aspect of exchanging data between a dialog box control and a data member—dialog box data validation (DDV). DDV is responsible for validating the data entered into dialog box controls. Depending on the data type, the developer provides a proper range for the value or for a certain type of format. For instance, numbers of type *float* can have only one decimal point. (For more information on DDV, see Technical Note 26 in the Visual C++ online documentation.)

Customizing Common Dialog Boxes

The purpose of this task is to customize Microsoft Windows common dialog boxes using MFC classes. Windows common dialog boxes can be divided into two types:

- **Modal dialog boxes** Dialog boxes that require the user to respond before continuing the program. They include the File Open, File Save As, Print, Color, and Font common dialog boxes.

- **Modeless dialog boxes** Dialog boxes that do not require the user to respond before the program continues. The Find and Replace Text common dialog boxes are the only modeless types of dialog boxes available.

Common dialog boxes, whether they are modal or modeless, can be customized in two ways. The first type of customization changes the functionality of the dialog box without changing the appearance. The second type of modification adds or removes controls from the dialog box.

The latter type of modification alters the dialog box template and displays the modified version. For example, when you open a file using the File Open common dialog box, you can request more information from the user regarding the properties of the file. Modifications of this type can be made by deriving the class of the dialog box that is used in the File Open procedure from an MFC common dialog box class and adding code that requests additional information from the user. In this task, I demonstrate how to make the second type of modification to both modal and modeless dialog boxes by adding controls to the File Open and Find Text dialog boxes and by removing existing controls from them. This task also demonstrates how to customize both the Windows Explorer style and the earlier Windows 3.*x* style of the File Open dialog box. One example demonstrated by this task uses the class *CFileDialog* to customize the File Open dialog box. The name of the project is CMNDLGS, and the requirement is two dialog box classes derived from MFC common dialog classes, such as *CFileDialog* and *CFindReplaceDialog*.

Customizing Modal Common Dialog Boxes

Modal dialog boxes interrupt the flow of execution in a program because the user must dismiss the dialog box by clicking OK or Cancel before the program can continue. For this reason, the life cycle of the dialog box is contained within the scope of the function that invokes it. An example that is familiar to anyone who has developed an MFC application is the MFC application About dialog box created by AppWizard.

MFC supports many types of modal common dialog boxes. This task adds either a Windows 3.*x* style or a Windows Explorer style File Open dialog box. The basic procedure for implementing a customized modal common dialog box includes these steps:

1. Copying the common dialog box template

2. Customizing the common dialog box template

3. Initializing and invoking the customized dialog box

4. Handling requests from the customized dialog box

5. Providing Help for the customized dialog box

N O T E : In the interest of brevity and focus, the results of the procedures in this task differ from what is implemented in the project. If you follow the procedures in this task, your project will implement either the Windows 3.*x* style or Windows Explorer style of the File Open dialog box and a Find Text dialog box. However, the project example implements both styles of File Open dialog boxes. The Windows 3.*x* style File Open dialog box is highly modified to allow the user to select a directory instead of a file. The Windows Explorer style File Open dialog box is only slightly modified by adding a bitmap and a text string.

Step 1: Copying the Common Dialog Box Template

Each common dialog box is based on a dialog box template. Unless you are planning extensive modifications to the dialog box's appearance, customizing the original common dialog box template saves time and provides some similarity between the original version of the dialog box and your modified version.

Copy the dialog box template to your project. All common dialog box templates are stored in the Visual C++ INCLUDE directory. The Windows 3.*x* style File Open dialog box template named FILEOPENORD can be found in the FILEOPEN.DLG file. To insert a copy of the FILEOPENORD dialog box template into your project, follow this procedure:

1. Open your project's resource file (in the case of the sample project, CMNDLGS.RC) as a text file in Microsoft Developer Studio.

2. Open FILEOPEN.DLG as a text file in Developer Studio.

3. In FILEOPEN.DLG, go to the following line of text (line 7):

```
FILEOPENORD DIALOG DISCARDABLE 109, 35, 165, 134
```

4. Copy lines 7 through 84. The last line you copy should be this one:

```
END
```

5. Insert the copied text into the Dialogs section of your project's RC file.

6. Because the FILEOPENORD template contains several resource IDs, you must include the DLGS.H file in your project's RC file. The following lines of code, which are located near the top of the resource file, demonstrate the finished result:

```
#include "afxres.h"
#include "dlgs.h"
```

7. After pasting the File Open dialog box template into your project's RC file, save the changes. You should now see a new dialog box resource named FILEOPENORD.

Customizing a Windows Explorer style modal dialog box requires a procedure slightly different from the one used for customizing a Windows 3.*x* style dialog box. The Windows Explorer style dialog box does not use a standard dialog box template. Instead, you must create a new dialog box resource and allocate an area in the dialog box that will contain the controls of the dialog box. Follow the procedure below to create a new dialog resource for the Windows Explorer style dialog box.

1. To your project's resource file, add a new dialog box resource with the following styles: DS_3DLOOK, WS_CHILD, WS_CLIPSIBLINGS, DS_CONTROL, and a Border Style of none. The sample project uses the name IDD_W95_FILEOPEN for the dialog box resource.

2. Remove the OK and Cancel buttons from the new dialog box resource.

3. Add a static control of reasonable size, with an ID of *stc32* and no caption, to the dialog box template. (A rectangle of 115 by 200 pixels is sufficient.) The area of this static control should be fairly large so that the controls of the Microsoft Windows 95 File Open dialog box can be placed inside. This static control is needed only if you must have the common dialog controls placed in a certain area.

4. After you have finished customizing the dialog box resource, save the resource file.

Step 2: Customizing the Common Dialog Box Template

Now that you have a copy of the File Open dialog box in your project, you can customize it to suit your needs. Common customizations include adding, hiding, or rearranging the dialog box controls and changing other attributes of the dialog box. At this point, make any necessary modifications to the new dialog box resource.

> N O T E : If you are adding a Windows Explorer style File Open dialog box, you can hide existing controls in the dialog box template by sending the CDM_HIDECONTROL message to the *Send Message* function of the control or controls to be hidden in the *OnInitDialog* of your customized dialog box class. CDM_HIDECONTROL is discussed in the Microsoft Win32 SDK online documentation.

The Windows 3.*x* style File Open dialog box used in the project example was customized (Figure 4-1) to allow the user to select a directory instead of a file. The modifications included removing the File Name edit and list boxes, the Read-Only check box, and the List Files Of Type list box.

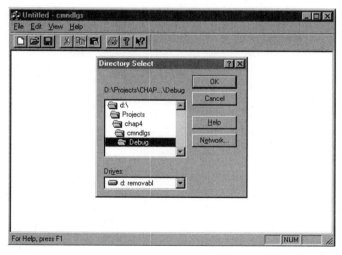

Figure 4-1.
The modified Windows 3.x style File Open common dialog box.

119

The Windows Explorer style File Open dialog box that is used in the project example was customized slightly by adding a bitmap and some text as shown in Figure 4-2.

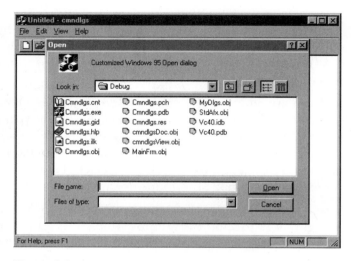

Figure 4-2.
The modified Windows Explorer style File Open common dialog box.

Step 3: Initializing and Invoking the Customized Dialog Box

After you have modified the dialog box template, you have to set up some type of interface that invokes the File Open dialog box. When you are using common dialog boxes, it is best to follow interface conventions—a File Open menu command that invokes the File Open (Windows 3.x) dialog box and an accelerator for the menu command. The menu command should be on the File menu of the application. In this task the following value is used for the menu command, which is located in the File menu:

ID	Caption	Prompt
ID_CMNDLG_FILE_OPEN	&Open...\+Ctrl+O	Open an existing document\nOpen

The following value is used for the File Open accelerator:

ID	Modifier	Key
ID_CMNDLG_FILEOPEN	Select the Ctrl checkbox.	O

N O T E : If you have a toolbar button that invokes the common File Open dialog box, change the ID to match the ID you use for the menu command. If you do not change the ID, a noncustomized File Open dialog box will appear.

You now use ClassWizard to create the class for the dialog box and to add a handler named *OnCmndlgFile* for the new menu command. *OnCmndlgFile* initializes and displays the customized dialog box. The following code, found in the header file of *CMainFrame*, declares the handler function (*OnCmndlgFile*) as a member of the *CMainFrame* class:

```
// Generated message map functions
protected:
    ⋮
    afx_msg void OnCmndlgFile();
    ⋮
```

The following code, located in the implementation file of *CMainFrame*, defines the handler function:

```
void CMainFrame::OnCmndlgFile()
{
    CMyFileOpenDlg  cfdlg(TRUE, NULL, NULL, OFN_SHOWHELP |
        OFN_HIDEREADONLY | OFN_OVERWRITEPROMPT |
        OFN_ENABLETEMPLATE, NULL, this);
    cfdlg.m_ofn.hInstance       = AfxGetInstanceHandle();
    cfdlg.m_ofn.lpTemplateName = MAKEINTRESOURCE(FILEOPENORD);
    cfdlg.m_ofn.Flags           &= ~OFN_EXPLORER;

    if (IDOK == cfdlg.DoModal())
    {
        WORD wFileOffset;
        char szBuffer[128];

        wFileOffset = cfdlg.m_ofn.nFileOffset;
```

(continued)

121

```
       cfdlg.m_ofn.lpstrFile[wFileOffset-1] = 0;

       wsprintf(szBuffer, "Selected directory was %s",
           (LPSTR)cfdlg.m_ofn.lpstrFile);

       AfxMessageBox((LPSTR)szBuffer, MB_OK);
    }
}
```

In the first section of code in the *OnCmndlgFile* function, I create an instance of the *CMyFileOpenDlg*-derived class with the necessary flags. In the second section of code, I assign the File Open (Windows 3.*x*) dialog box template to the FILEOPEN structure, FILEOPENORD, and properly initialize the instance handle. This is done to ensure that the application that created the dialog box receives all messages from the dialog box. I then remove the OFN-_EXPLORER flag because I am using the Windows 3.*x* style for the File Open dialog box. In the last section of code, I check the return of the call to *DoModal.* If the user has clicked OK, I display a message box that shows the name of the directory selected by the user.

One final note regarding the creation of dialog boxes: it is common practice to override the *OnInitDialog* member function of the dialog box class. This allows you to handle any initialization issues before the dialog box appears to the user.

In this task, I used the *OnInitDialog* function to add a particular window style, WS_EX_CONTEXTHELP, to the dialog box. This adds a question mark to the title bar of the dialog box, which allows the user to invoke the context help for the dialog box. I also hid all unused windows so that the tab order of the dialog box would not be disrupted. The following code demonstrates this:

```
CFileDialog::OnInitDialog();

CenterWindow();

ModifyStyleEx(0, WS_EX_CONTEXTHELP);

GetDlgItem(stc2)->ShowWindow(SW_HIDE);
GetDlgItem(stc3)->ShowWindow(SW_HIDE);
GetDlgItem(edt1)->ShowWindow(SW_HIDE);
GetDlgItem(lst1)->ShowWindow(SW_HIDE);
GetDlgItem(cmb1)->ShowWindow(SW_HIDE);
GetDlgItem(chx1)->ShowWindow(SW_HIDE);

SetDlgItemText(edt1, "Junk");
```

To initialize and invoke the File Open (Windows Explorer style) common dialog box, use code similar to the code in the *CMainFrame::OnCmndlgFile95* function:

```
void CMainFrame::OnCmndlgFile95()
{
    CMyFileOpen95Dlg cfdlg(TRUE, NULL, NULL, OFN_HIDEREADONLY |
        OFN_EXPLORER | OFN_OVERWRITEPROMPT |
        OFN_ENABLETEMPLATE, NULL, this);
    cfdlg.m_ofn.hInstance = AfxGetInstanceHandle();
    cfdlg.m_ofn.lpTemplateName =
        MAKEINTRESOURCE(IDD_W95_FILEOPEN);

    if (IDOK == cfdlg.DoModal())
    {
        WORD wFileOffset;
        char szBuffer[128];

        wFileOffset = cfdlg.m_ofn.nFileOffset;  // For convenience
        wsprintf(szBuffer, "Selected file was %s",
            (LPSTR)cfdlg.m_ofn.lpstrFile);

        AfxMessageBox((LPSTR)szBuffer, MB_OK);
    }
}
```

The only difference between the code for initializing and invoking the File Open (Windows Explorer style) dialog box and the code for initializing and invoking the File Open (Windows 3.*x* style) dialog box is found in the first section of code. The OFN_EXPLORER flag is now included because we are creating a Windows Explorer style of File Open dialog box, and the template name has changed to use the new dialog box template created in step 1.

Step 4: Handling Requests from the Customized Dialog Box

When the modal dialog box appears, you will have to handle all of the events from the dialog box controls that you've added to the template. In addition, you will have to retrieve information from the dialog box if the user has closed the dialog box by clicking OK. For an example, see the control event handler *CMyFRDlg::OnFindAll* in the file MYDLGS.CPP, located in the CMNDLGS project.

To add a control event handler using ClassWizard, follow this procedure:

1. Load your project into Developer Studio, and open ClassWizard.

2. Click the Message Maps tab, and select your dialog box class from the list of available classes.

3. Select the object ID of the control whose event you want to handle.

4. From the list on the right, select the message for the event you want to handle. For example, you could add a handler for the BN_CLICK message of a common button control.

5. Click Add Function.

6. Click OK.

7. Repeat this procedure for all of the other controls that were added to the dialog box template.

Check the return value from the call to the dialog box's *DoModal* function to determine what action the user chose. For example, if the return value is equal to IDOK, the user has clicked OK. In this case, collect any needed information from the dialog box and perform the appropriate tasks. The following code is taken from the last part of the *CMainFrame::OnCmndlgFile* function and demonstrates code that executes when OK is clicked:

```
if (IDOK==cfdlg.DoModal())
{
    WORD wFileOffset;
    char szBuffer[128];

    wFileOffset = cfdlg.m_ofn.nFileOffset;
    cfdlg.m_ofn.lpstrFile[wFileOffset-1]=0;
    wsprintf(szBuffer, "Selected directory is %s",
        (LPSTR)cfdlg.m_ofn.lpstrFile);

    AfxMessageBox((LPSTR)szBuffer, MB_OK);
}
```

Step 5: Providing Help for the Customized Dialog Box

The last step in adding a customized common dialog box to your application is to provide help for the dialog box. For Windows 3.*x* style modal dialog boxes, you will have to add two kinds of help—help for the entire dialog box and context help for individual controls. For modal dialog boxes in the Windows Explorer style, you will have to add only one kind of help—context help for individual controls.

N O T E : Under Windows 95, common dialog boxes provide only context-sensitive help.

Both context-sensitive help and help for the entire dialog box require the project to have its own Help file. The default Help file support (including a basic Help file) installed by AppWizard is sufficient for this task. For the remainder of this discussion, it is assumed that you have default help support for the application. (For information about adding context-sensitive help to an existing project, see "Adding Context-Sensitive Help" in the Scribble tutorial, which can be found in the online documentation for Developer Studio.)

Adding Help for the entire dialog box   Help for the entire dialog box is required only if you are adding common dialog boxes of the Windows 3.*x* style. In this case, you have to add a Help button and an associated Help topic to your dialog box. If the application's default Help support was created by AppWizard, topics already exist in the Help file for each of the common dialog boxes. In addition, this Help file opens automatically to the proper topic when the user clicks Help in your customized common dialog box. For instance, if the user chooses Help in your customized File Open dialog box, the application Help file opens to the Open File dialog box topic. The only thing you have to do is update the appropriate Help topic in the RTF file (the source text used to build the Help file) of the application by adding the information on the new controls and removing the information on the controls that you deleted from the common dialog box template. When you are done, your Help topic will provide full support for your customized common dialog box.

> N O T E :   If your application's Help file was not created by AppWizard, you must manually add a Help topic for your dialog box.

Adding context-sensitive Help for dialog box controls   The method for adding context-sensitive Help is a four-step process:

1. Adding the context-sensitive style to the common dialog box

2. Generating help IDs for new controls in the common dialog box

3. Handling the WM_HELPINFO message

4. Displaying the appropriate topic in your application's Help file

Adding the context-sensitive style can be performed in two ways. The first opportunity occurs when you add the dialog box resource to your project's RC file. After you have added the dialog box resource, you can open the properties for the dialog box resource and select the Context Help style check box found on the Extended Styles tab. The second opportunity occurs when you initialize the dialog box itself. In the *OnInitDialog* function of your dialog box class, place the following code after the call to the base class:

```
ModifyStyleEx(0, WS_EX_CONTEXTHELP);
```

Help IDs for controls are used to map the Help request to an existing Help topic in the application's Help file. You can create a Help ID for a control by bringing up the properties for the control in your dialog box and selecting the Help ID check box on the General page. Save the file; a new Help ID for the control is generated automatically by the Resource editor and added to the project's RESOURCES.HM file. This file contains the Help IDs generated by the Resource editor. After you have added Help IDs for all new controls in the dialog box, save the RC file.

You must include the RESOURCES.HM file in the HPJ file of the application so that the Help IDs can be used by the Help file. Assuming that RESOURCES.HM is located in the application's root directory, add the following line in the [MAP] section of the application's HPJ file:

```
#include <..\resource.hm>
```

This line adds the IDs generated by the Resource editor to the existing IDs of the Help file, which are then used by the Help compiler when building the application's Help file. For the mapping to work, there has to be a related Help topic for each control. Therefore, add a topic for each new control, using its associated Help ID for the context string, to the source file AFXCORE.RTF. If the application was created with AppWizard, the file should be located in the HLP subdirectory of your project.

Now use ClassWizard to add the WM_HELPINFO message handler to your common dialog box class. Add code to the WM_HELPINFO message handler that opens the correct topic in your application's Help file. Generally, your code should check each Help ID for a match with the Help IDs of your new controls. If a match is found, call WinHelp with the Help ID. If no match is found, pass the message to the parent class. The following code sample, which is taken from the CMNDLGS sample program, demonstrates this:

```
BOOL CMyFile95Dlg::OnHelpInfo(HELPINFO* pHelpInfo)
{
    UINT helpContext = pHelpInfo->dwContextId;

    if ((helpContext == 0x808203e9))
    {
        WinHelp(helpContext);
```

```
        return TRUE;
    }
    else
        return CFileDialog::OnHelpInfo(pHelpInfo);
}
```

The first line sets *helpContext* equal to the Help ID of the topic being requested. This makes the function more readable. Next, I use an *if* statement to check the Help ID against the Help ID of a new control. If the IDs match, I make a call to WinHelp, passing along the proper ID. If the Help ID does not match the new control, it is passed along to the parent class for proper handling.

Customizing Modeless Common Dialog Boxes

As I mentioned earlier, the primary difference between modal and modeless dialog boxes is that modeless dialog boxes, although they are visible, allow the program to continue execution. Because of this flexibility, the modeless dialog box object is constructed using the new operator, which allocates memory from the application's heap for the object. Therefore, the scope of the object is extended beyond the function in which it was created. Extending the scope is necessary because we don't know when the dialog box will be dismissed by the user.

The basic procedure for implementing a customized common dialog box of the modeless type is similar to the procedure used for a modal dialog box except for some variation in step 3 (initializing and invoking the customized dialog box) and step 4 (handling requests from the customized dialog box). Because of this similarity, steps 1, 2, and 5 below will mostly just reference the corresponding step in the customization procedure for the modal dialog box. The Find Text common dialog box will be used as an example of customizing a modeless common dialog box.

Step 1: Copying the Common Dialog Box Template

The only difference in this step between customizing a modeless dialog box and customizing a modal dialog box is what dialog box template you use. The Find Text template we are using for a modeless dialog box can be found in the FINDTEXT.DLG file. To insert a copy of this resource into your project, follow this procedure:

1. Open your project's resource file (in the case of the sample project, CMNDLGS.RC) as a text file in Developer Studio.

2. Open FINDTEXT.DLG as a text file in Developer Studio.

3. In FINDTEXT.DLG, locate line 8:

```
FINDDLGORD DIALOG LOADONCALL MOVEABLE DISCARDABLE
```

4. Copy lines 8 through 53. The last line copied should be the following:

```
END
```

5. Insert the copied text into the dialogs section of your project's RC file, and save the changes. You should now see a new dialog box resource named FINDDLGORD.

Step 2: Customizing the Common Dialog Box Template

You can now customize the dialog box resource as you like. (See "Step 2: Customizing the Common Dialog Box Template" under the task "Customizing Common Dialog Boxes" on page 119 for details.) The sample project makes the following additions to the Find Text dialog box: a new button and two static strings that display the number of occurrences for a particular string in the current file. A common push button control (named Find All) with an ID of IDC_FINDALL was added. Two Static Text controls also were added: the first, IDC_FOUND, displays the number of occurrences of a string of text; the other, IDC_STATIC, is used as a label. The result is shown in Figure 4-3.

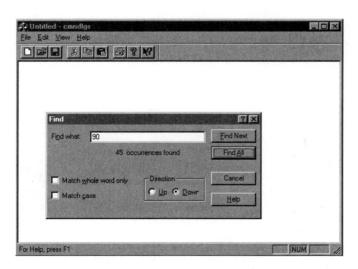

Figure 4-3.
The modified Find Text common dialog box.

N O T E : If you run the CMNDLGS sample program, you will notice that the number of occurrences always is shown as 45. Obviously, this is not true; in the interest of time, I simply handled the event and updated the strings. This illustrates sufficiently the point of the customization.

Step 3: Initializing and Invoking the Customized Dialog Box

After the dialog box template has been modified, you will have to set up some type of interface that invokes the Find Text dialog box. When you are using common dialog boxes, it is best to follow existing interface conventions—a Find menu command with the Ctrl-F accelerator that invokes the Find Text dialog box. The menu command should be on the Edit menu of the application. The task uses the following value for the Find menu command, which is located in the Edit menu:

ID	Caption	Prompt
ID_CMNDLG_EDIT_FIND	&Find...\tCtrl+F	Finds the specified text\Find

The following value is used for the Find Text accelerator:

ID	Modifier	Key
ID_CMNDLG_EDIT_FIND	Select the Ctrl checkbox.	F

Now add a handler named *OnCmndlgFind* to the *CMainFrame* class using ClassWizard. This handler initializes and displays the Find Text dialog box. The following code, found in the header file of *CMainFrame*, declares the handler function (*OnCmndlgFind*) as a member of the *CMainFrame* class.

```
// Generated message map functions
protected:
    ⋮
    afx_msg void OnCmndlgFind();
    ⋮
```

And the following code, found in the implementation file for *CMainFrame*, defines the handler function:

```
void CMainFrame::OnCmndlgFind()
{
    m_pFindDlg= new CMyFRDlg;
    m_pFindDlg->m_fr.hInstance = AfxGetInstanceHandle();

    m_pFindDlg->m_bFindDialog= TRUE;
    m_pFindDlg->m_fr.lpTemplateName =
    MAKEINTRESOURCE(FINDDLGORD);
    m_pFindDlg->Create(TRUE, NULL, NULL, FR_DOWN |
        FR_ENABLETEMPLATE | FR_SHOWHELP, this);
}
```

In the first section of code, I create an instance of the *CFindReplaceDialog*-derived class from the application's memory heap. Then I assign the Find Text dialog box template to the FINDREPLACE structure, FINDDLGORD, and create the dialog box with a call to the *Create* member function.

One final note regarding the creation of dialog boxes: it is common practice to override the *OnInitDialog* member function of your dialog box class. This allows you to handle any initialization issues before the dialog box appears to the user. In this task, I used the *OnInitDialog* function to add a certain window style (WS_EX_CONTEXTHELP) to the dialog box. This adds a question mark button on the right side of the title bar in the dialog box, which allows the user to invoke the context help for the dialog box. In addition, I disabled the Find All button. The disabled state of the Find All button mimics the behavior of the Find button by being enabled only when text is present in the Find What edit box. The following code sample, taken from the *CMyFRDlg::OnInitDialog* function, demonstrates adding the WS_EX_CONTEXTHELP style and disabling the Find All button:

```
CFindReplaceDialog::OnInitDialog();

ModifyStyleEx(0, WS_EX_CONTEXTHELP);

GetDlgItem(IDC_FINDALL)->EnableWindow(FALSE);

return TRUE;
```

Step 4: Handling Requests from the Customized Dialog Box

After the modeless dialog box is up, you have to handle all of the events from the dialog box controls that were added to the template. (See step 4 of the modal dialog box procedure for details.) The following code sample, taken from the *CMyFRDlg::OnFindall* handler, demonstrates one method of handling control notifications by modifying a static text control when the Find All button is clicked.

```
CEdit* pFindEdit= (CEdit*)GetDlgItem(edt1);
CString findStr;

pFindEdit->GetWindowText(findStr);
// Search the current document or other processing
// For test purposes, output a fake number

GetDlgItem(IDC_FOUND)->SetWindowText("45");
```

However, because the modeless dialog box is invoked with a call to *Create* (not *DoModal*), there is no return value from a call to *DoModal* that you can check. Instead, you must implement a way to be notified of find/replace requests—referred to as a callback function. Notification can be implemented by handling a registered message named WM_FINDREPLACE; you can then call any member function of the *CFindReplaceDialog* class from this callback function and take the appropriate action. To implement this callback function, follow this procedure:

1. Add the boldface line below to the header file of your mainframe class, preferably in the protected message section:

```
// Generated message map functions
protected:
afx_msg LRESULT OnFindReplace(WPARAM wParam, LPARAM lParam);
```

2. Add the following lines to the implementation file of your mainframe class, somewhere after the #include lines:

```
static UINT NEAR WM_FINDREPLACE =
    ::RegisterWindowMessage(FINDMSGSTRING);
```

3. Add the following line to the main frame window's message map, which is located in the implementation file of the mainframe class:

```
ON_REGISTERED_MESSAGE(WM_FINDREPLACE, OnFindReplace)
```

4. Add the function body shown on the following page to the implementation file of your mainframe class.

```
LRESULT CMainFrame::OnFindReplace(WPARAM wParam, LPARAM
    lParam)
{
    CFindReplaceDialog* dlg
        = CFindReplaceDialog::GetNotifier(lParam);

    // Add any code for handling Find and/or Replace requests
    // here
    return (LRESULT)0;
}
```

The first section of the code retrieves a pointer to the Find Text dialog box object. Use this pointer to gather information about a search request or about the condition of the dialog box object by accessing member functions of the *CFindReplaceDialog* class. Some examples of information you can obtain include the following:

- Whether the dialog box is exiting

- When a search request is made

- What type of replacement to make when the search text is found

Because there is no MFC support for searching and replacing text, you must support these requests yourself. For more information, see the *CFindReplaceDialog* overview in the Visual C++ online documentation.

Step 5: Providing Help for the Customized Dialog Box

You should now provide both general dialog box help and context-sensitive help for each new control added. See step 5 of the modal dialog box procedure for details. The main difference for a modeless dialog box is the context IDs of the controls added to the dialog box resource. In the task project, I generate a Help ID for the Find All button. I then check for this ID in the *OnHelpInfo* function of the *CMyFRDlg* class. The code for doing this is essentially the same as the code found in step 5 of the modal dialog box procedure.

Additional Information

For additional reading on common dialog boxes, search for the string "Common Dialog Box Library" in the Microsoft Win32 SDK online documentation. In addition, Technical Note 50, also found in the online documentation, discusses common OLE and MFC dialog box resources. The Microsoft Knowledge Base article "How to Customize the Common Print Dialog": Q132909 also provides additional information on common dialogs.

Using Bitmaps as the Background in a Dialog Box

The purpose of this task is to demonstrate how to use a bitmap for the background of a dialog box. I demonstrate three methods of using bitmaps for doing this:

- The *StretchBlt* method, which simply places the bitmap in the dialog box without regard to centering. The bitmap will fill the entire background.

- The *BitBlt* method, which centers the bitmap in the dialog box. This approach is a variation of the *StretchBlt* method, and it uses a smaller bitmap.

- The bitmap brush method, which uses the bitmap as a brush object to paint the background. It produces a patterned background.

In addition to bitmap manipulation, I also demonstrate a method for rendering common dialog box controls "transparent." I use 16-color bitmaps as examples because you can create this type of bitmap with the Resource editor or with Paintbrush, the Windows application. The name of the sample project is BKBMPS. To perform the following procedures, you will need these things:

- Three 16-color bitmaps of any size

- Handler functions for the WM_ERASEBKGND, WM_INITDIALOG, and WM_CTLCOLOR messages

Because the bitmaps used in this task do not change at any time, I can save time (and unnecessary work) by loading them only once (during creation of the main frame window).

```
VERIFY(m_bkBmap.LoadBitmap(IDB_BKBMAP));
VERIFY(m_bmapBrush.LoadBitmap(IDB_BMAPBRUSH));
VERIFY(m_bmapCentered.LoadBitmap(IDB_BMAPCENTER));
```

After the three bitmaps (IDB_BKBMAP, IDB_BMAPBRUSH, and IDB-_BMAPCENTER) have been loaded, they are stored in three data members of the *CMainFrame* class, defined as follows:

```
// Attributes
public:
    CBitmap m_bkBmap;
    CBitmap m_bmapBrush;
    CBitmap m_bmapCentered;
```

The *StretchBlt* Method

The *StretchBlt* method has three main steps:

1. Adding supporting code for the bitmap

2. Initializing the attributes of the bitmap object

3. Handling the WM_ERASEBKGND message and making a call to the *StretchBlt* function

Handling the WM_ERASEBKGND message, which is called when the dialog box background needs repainting, allows you to customize the painting of the dialog box background. The handler function for the message *CWnd::OnEraseBkgnd* provides a device context representing the object you are painting, which, in this case, is the background of the dialog box. Inside the handler for the WM_ERASEBKGND message, you will make the call to *StretchBlt.* Figure 4-4 shows the finished result.

Figure 4-4.
A dialog box that shows the StretchBlt *method.*

Step 1: Adding Supporting Code for the Bitmap

Let's begin by first setting up the support for the bitmap that will be used as the background. The bitmap should be monochrome, 8-color or 16-color. Bitmaps of 256 colors or more need additional palette support, which is discussed under "Additional Information" on page 142. For the purpose of this discussion, I assume that you will be using this bitmap in an existing dialog box class, although the method can be used in other ways, such as display in a *CView*-derived class. The task uses a dialog box class, *CBmapDlg*, for the display of the bitmap.

In the header file for the target dialog box class (the one displaying the bitmap), add the following data members:

```
// Attributes
protected:
    CDC m_dcMem;          // Compatible memory DC for dialog
    CBrush m_brush;       // Handle of null brush

    BITMAP m_bmInfo;      // Bitmap information structure
    CPoint m_pt;          // Position for upper left corner of
                          // bitmap in dialog
    CSize m_size;         // Size (width and height) of bitmap
                          // in dialog
```

The access level of the bitmap attributes (data members) can be either public or protected. In this task, they are declared protected because the dialog box is the only class accessing them. As the comments describe, these data members represent the different aspects of the bitmap that are needed by the *StretchBlt* function.

Step 2: Initializing the Attributes of the Bitmap Object

The data attributes of the bitmap object must be initialized before the dialog box appears. A good place to do this is in the handler function for the WM_INITDIALOG message. Add this handler function (named *OnInitDialog*) to your dialog box class, either by using ClassWizard or by manually adding the code. After the handler function has been added, add the following code to the body of the function:

```
CMainFrame* pFrm = (CMainFrame*)AfxGetMainWnd();
CBitmap* dlgBmap;

dlgBmap = &(pFrm->m_bkBmap);
RECT rectClient;
// Load null brush;
m_brush.CreateStockObject(NULL_BRUSH);
```

First I access the main frame window to retrieve a pointer to the bitmap that is to be used. I keep the bitmap in the *CMainFrame* object so that I only have to load once—during the creation of the main frame window. (Loading the bitmap is a somewhat expensive action in terms of execution time.) I could just as easily load the bitmap during the creation of the dialog box, but this would result in a slower display of the dialog box, plus wasted work because the bit-map never changes content. The brush being created is used to blend the common controls of the dialog box into the background bitmap.

The following code, found in the *CBmapDlg::OnInitDialog* function, initializes the various attributes of the bitmap object:

```
// Get bitmap information
dlgBmap->GetObject(sizeof(BITMAP), &m_bmInfo);

GetClientRect(&rectClient);

m_size.cx = rectClient.right;      // Zero based
m_size.cy = rectClient.bottom;     // Zero based
m_pt.x = rectClient.left;
m_pt.y = rectClient.top;

// Get temporary DC for dialog--will be released in DC
// destructor
CClientDC dc(this);

// Create compatible memory DC using the dialog's DC
VERIFY(m_dcMem.CreateCompatibleDC(&dc));

m_dcMem.SelectObject(dlgBmap);
```

First, I store the bitmap information and retrieve the dimensions of the client area of the dialog box. Then I store the bitmap size (which is used in the call to *StretchBlt*) in the *m_size* data member and the coordinates of the upper left corner of the client area in the *m_pt* data member. Finally, I create a device context for the bitmap that is compatible with the device context of the dialog box and select the bitmap into the compatible device context. This allows the call to *StretchBlt* to make use of the background bitmap.

Step 3: Handling the WM_ERASEBKGND
Message and Making a Call to the *StretchBlt* Function
The final step provides a handler for the WM_ERASEBKGND message. As you would for the WM_INITDIALOG handler, add this message handler to the class representing the bitmap background dialog box. In the body of the message handler *OnEraseBkgnd*, add the following call to *StretchBlt*:

```
pDC->StretchBlt( m_pt.x, m_pt.y, m_size.cx, m_size.cy,
    &m_dcMem, 0, 0, m_bmInfo.bmWidth-1,
    m_bmInfo.bmHeight-1, SRCCOPY );
return TRUE;
```

This call uses the information from the data members *m_size, m_dcMem, m_pt,* and *m_bmInfo* to properly stretch the bitmap to the edges of the dialog box client area. If you are curious about the purpose of the hollow brush, check out the information on transparent controls in "Additional Information" on page 142.

After you have added the code to the *OnEraseBkgnd* handler, rebuild the project; you now should have a dialog box with a bitmap background.

> N O T E : Instead of *CDC::StretchBlt*, we could have used a call to *CDC::BitBlt* in the WM_ERASEBKGND handler. However, because the bitmap is not stretched or shrunk to cover the entire client area when you use *CDC::BitBlt*, there might be areas that never would be updated. This results in a very confusing dialog box background. The *BitBlt* method discussed in the next section provides one solution to this problem.

The *BitBlt* (or Centered Bitmap) Method

The *BitBlt* method is similar to the *StretchBlt* method. But the *BitBlt* method adds some code that centers the bitmap and paints the area of the client area not covered by the bitmap. As for all of the methods in this task, the *BitBlt* method is independent of other methods. Like the *StretchBlt* method, the *BitBlt* method has three main steps:

1. Adding supporting code for the bitmap
2. Initializing the attributes of the bitmap object
3. Handling the WM_ERASEBKGND message and making a call to the *BitBlt* function

The task uses the dialog box class *CBmapCenterDlg* to demonstrate this method. Figure 4-5 on the following page shows the finished result.

Step 1: Adding Supporting Code for the Bitmap

In addition to the data members that are added in the *StretchBlt* method, another data member (*m_bkBrush*) must be added to store the background brush. The following is the resultant block of necessary data members:

```
// Attributes
protected:
    CDC m_dcMem;          // Compatible memory DC for dialog
    CBrush m_brush;       // Handle of hollow brush
    CBrush m_bkBrush;     // Handle of background brush
```

(continued)

```
BITMAP m_bmInfo;      // Bitmap information structure
CPoint m_pt;          // Position for upper left corner of
                      // bitmap
CSize m_size;         // Size (width and height) of bitmap
```

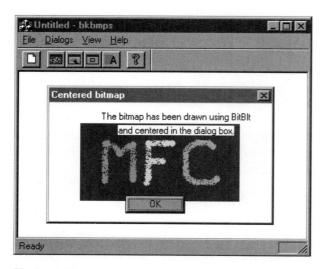

Figure 4-5.
A dialog box that shows the BitBlt *method.*

Step 2: Initializing the Attributes of the Bitmap Object

The data members are initialized in the handler for the WM_INITDIALOG message, as they are in the *StretchBlt* method. Add this handler now.

Because some of the same techniques are used in both the *StretchBlt* and *BitBlt* methods, the code for initializing the attributes is similar for both methods. However, instead of modifying the bitmap size to fit the entire client area, you must figure out the values for the size and for the coordinates of the upper left corner of the dialog box client area. In addition, the background brush, *m_bkBrush*, must be initialized. The code below should be added to the body of your newly added *OnInitDialog* function. The modified code is shown in boldface type.

```
CMainFrame* pFrm = (CMainFrame*)AfxGetMainWnd();
CBitmap* dlgBmap;

dlgBmap = &(pFrm->m_bmapCentered);

RECT rectClient;
```

```
// Load a hollow brush and create another
// brush with the default background color
m_brush.CreateStockObject(NULL_BRUSH);
m_bkBrush.CreateSolidBrush(::GetSysColor(COLOR_WINDOW));

// Get bitmap information
dlgBmap->GetObject(sizeof(BITMAP), &m_bmInfo);

GetClientRect(&rectClient);
//Check to see whether bitmap is larger than target area
if (m_bmInfo.bmWidth > rectClient.right)
    m_size.cx = rectClient.right;
else
    m_size.cx = m_bmInfo.bmWidth;      // Zero based

if (m_bmInfo.bmHeight > rectClient.bottom)
    m_size.cy = rectClient.bottom;
else
    m_size.cy = m_bmInfo.bmHeight;     // Zero based

m_pt.x = (rectClient.right - m_size.cx) / 2;
m_pt.y = (rectClient.bottom - m_size.cy) / 2;

// Get temporary DC for dialog, will be released in DC
// destructor
CClientDC dc(this);

// Create compatible memory DC using the dialog's DC
VERIFY(m_dcMem.CreateCompatibleDC(&dc));

m_dcMem.SelectObject(dlgBmap);

return TRUE;
// Return TRUE unless you set the focus to a
// control. EXCEPTION: OCX Property Pages should
// return FALSE.
```

The first modification simply creates a brush with the color defined by the system for a dialog box background. The *::GetSysColor* function is used to retrieve the exact color needed. The second modification is to the size and location of the bitmap. I use values from the call to *GetClientRect* to center the bitmap. In addition, if the bitmap is larger than the client area of the dialog box, the width and height of the bitmap are set to the width and height of the client area and the upper left corner of the bitmap is set to (0, 0).

Step 3: Handling the WM_ERASEBKGND
Message and Making a Call to the *BitBlt* Function

The final component is the handler for the WM_ERASEBKGND message. Add this message handler to the class representing the bitmap background of the dialog box. In most cases, the bitmap will be smaller than the client area of the dialog box. This means that the area surrounding the bitmap must also be painted in the WM_ERASEBKGND handler. This is where the *m_bkBrush* member comes in handy. The background is painted in a two-step process. First the client area is painted using the current system color for window client areas; then the bitmap is displayed in the center. The result is a centered bitmap with a background of the current window client color. The following code should be added to the *OnEraseBkgnd* handler after the call to the base class function:

```
RECT rectClient;
CBrush bkBrush;

GetClientRect(&rectClient);
pDC->FillRect(&rectClient, &m_bkBrush);

pDC->BitBlt(m_pt.x, m_pt.y, m_size.cx, m_size.cy,
    &m_dcMem, 0, 0, SRCCOPY);
```

After you have added the code to the *OnEraseBkgnd* handler, rebuild the project. You should have a centered bitmap in the background of the dialog box.

The Bitmap Brush Method

The bitmap brush method is very useful if you want a patterned background. Instead of using a single bitmap to partially or completely cover the background area, I will use a patterned brush that has been created using an 8x8, 16-color bitmap. Bitmaps of other sizes can be used, but the patterned brush will initialize using only the upper left grid of 8x8 pixels of the bitmap. This method is also the easiest of the three, requiring only a *CBrush* data member, an 8x8 pixel bitmap, and two handler functions. The bitmap brush method consists of three steps:

1. Adding supporting code for the bitmap

2. Initializing the attributes of the bitmap object

3. Handling the WM_CTLCOLOR message

The task uses the *CBmapBrushDlg* dialog box class to demonstrate this method. Figure 4-6 shows the finished result.

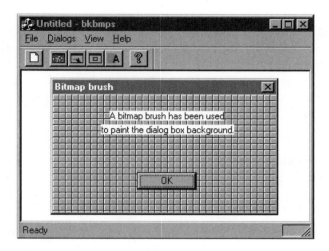

Figure 4-6.
A dialog box that shows the bitmap brush method.

Step 1: Adding Supporting Code for the Bitmap
Add the *CBrush* data member to the dialog box class that will be using the background brush. The *m_brush* data member stores the pattern brush once it is created.

```
// Attributes
CBrush m_brush;          // Background brush
```

Step 2: Initializing the Attributes of the Bitmap Object
Add a handler for the WM_INITDIALOG message to the dialog box class of your application. In the body of the *OnInitDialog* function, add the following code:

```
CMainFrame* pFrm = (CMainFrame*)AfxGetMainWnd();
CBitmap* pDlgBmap;

pDlgBmap = &(pFrm->m_bmapBrush);

// Create bitmap brush;
m_brush.CreatePatternBrush(pDlgBmap);
```

141

In the code on the preceding page, I first retrieve the loaded bitmap from the main frame window class. Then I use the bitmap to create a patterned brush with a call to *CreatePatternBrush.*

Step 3: Handling the WM_CTLCOLOR Message

Add a handler to the same dialog box class for the WM_CTLCOLOR message. I use this message instead of WM_ERASEBKGND because it expects a brush for the background painting. In the body of the handler function *OnCtlColor,* I simply return the handle of my newly created brush and let MFC do the rest of the work:

```
return (HBRUSH)m_brush;
```

After you have added this last piece of code, rebuild the project. You should now have a dialog box with a patterned background.

Additional Information

Every control in a dialog box can be thought of as being rendered in two surfaces: a foreground surface and a background surface. If you can control the rendering of these surfaces, you can create some interesting effects. The BK-BMPS project demonstrates one such effect for static controls—a "transparent" control. Basically, this means that the background of the control is the same as the background of the dialog box. This effect is achieved in three steps:

- Creating the null brush

- Handling the WM_CTLCOLOR message

- Making a call to *CDC::SetBkMode*

In some of the code samples for the three methods that have been discussed here, you might have noticed the presence of a brush object. Created by a call to *CreateStockObject,* the brush object is a "null" brush, which means that any surface painted by the brush will not change its current color or pattern. You can think of it as a paint brush that uses transparent paint. The process is as follows.

1. Create a null brush. The BKBMPS project declares an object of type *CBrush* as a data member of the dialog box class:

```
// Attributes
protected:
    CBrush m_brush;     // Null brush for control blending
    CBrush m_bkBrush;   // Background brush
```

2. Initialize the brush object with a call to *CreateStockObject*. This can be done in the *OnInitDialog* function of your dialog box class. The BK-BMPS project initializes the brush with the following code, which is located in *OnInitDialog*:

```
⋮
m_brush.CreateStockObject(NULL_BRUSH);
⋮
```

3. Add a handler for the WM_CTLCOLOR message to the dialog box class, and modify the handler function to match the code below:

```
HBRUSH CMyDlg::OnCtlColor(CDC* pDC, CWnd* pWnd, UINT nCtlColor)
{
    pDC->SetBkMode(TRANSPARENT);
    return (HBRUSH)m_brush;
}
```

Now you should be able to build the project and have any static text controls in your dialog box use the background of the dialog box as the background of the control, whatever that background is. You also can change the appearance of other control types using this method. For information on changing the appearance of other controls, see these Knowledge Base articles:

- How to Handle OCM_CTLCOLOREDIT Reflected Messages: Q148242

- Changing the Background Color of an MFC Edit Control: Q117778

Modifying the Attributes of Dialog Box Controls

The purpose of this task is to demonstrate three types of modifications to dialog box controls.

- Coloring individual controls
- Modifying the font used by a control or controls
- Hiding static text and common controls

In most cases, these modifications can be applied to either child controls embedded in a view or to controls in a form view. In addition, I will demonstrate the instant updating of control states. All of the modifications can be used either separately or together; however, each type is completely independent of the others.

The name of the task project is DLGCTRL, and the requirement is a dialog box class containing several common controls.

Coloring Individual Controls

In this procedure, the text color of a group of radio buttons is modified according to the choice of the user and the color change occurs immediately after the user chooses the color. The procedure also can be used to change the text color of other common controls that contain text. The following four steps provide a basic framework for coloring individual dialog box controls:

1. Implementing user interface
2. Notifying the dialog box of a color change by the user
3. Processing and storing the color choice
4. Dynamically updating the control group

Step 1: Implementing the User Interface

The first step is to create an obvious interface that allows the user to modify an attribute of the control. In this case, the attribute I use is the text color for a group of radio buttons. Each radio button has a different caption—black, red, green, or blue. The user chooses the color he or she wants, and then the entire set is updated to display its text in the chosen color.

Step 2: Notifying the Dialog Box of a Color Change by the User

After you have an interface in place, you can set up some type of notification for the dialog box of a color change. This allows you to update the controls immediately after the user chooses a different color. The easiest way to set up notification is to create a notification handler using ClassWizard for each control in which you are interested. Your notification handler then should retrieve the choice and implement the color change immediately or implement it the next time the dialog box is visible. This handler (or handlers) is usually found in the class representing the dialog box.

TIP: If you do not want the color change to be updated immediately, you can skip this step and proceed to the next step, "Processing and Storing the Color Choice."

The DLGCTRL project has a BN_CLICKED notification handler for each radio button, which I added using ClassWizard. For clarity, I routed all notifications to the same handler. The following code fragment is taken from the message map of the dialog box class:

```
BEGIN_MESSAGE_MAP(CMyDlg, CDialog)
    //{{AFX_MSG_MAP(CMyDlg)
    ⋮

    ON_BN_CLICKED(IDC_BLACK, OnColorChange)
    ON_BN_CLICKED(IDC_BLUE, OnColorChange)
    ON_BN_CLICKED(IDC_GREEN, OnColorChange)
    ON_BN_CLICKED(IDC_RED, OnColorChange)
    ⋮

    //}}AFX_MSG_MAP
END_MESSAGE_MAP()
```

Step 3: Processing and Storing the Color Choice

When you receive a BN_CLICKED message, which indicates that the user has chosen a color, you have to determine what color was chosen and then do one of two things: change the color immediately or store the new color and use it the next time the dialog box is visible. Depending on the type of interface you have implemented for your dialog box, add code that retrieves the color and then either immediately changes it or stores it for later use.

In this task I use a group of radio buttons. Whenever I receive a *BN_CLICKED* message, I change the color of the radio button text immediately and store the current color for later use. To implement the storage of the color, I declared a data member of type *int* in the *CMainFrame* class:

```
⋮
// Attributes
public:
    int m_BtnTextColor;
⋮
```

In addition, I declare two data members in the *CMyDlg* class of the task project that will store the color value in the dialog box class and initialize the radio button group when the dialog box is displayed:

```
⋮
    COLORREF m_curColor;

// Dialog Data
    //{{AFX_DATA(CMyDlg)
    enum { IDD = IDD_DIALOG1 };
    int    m_color;
    //}}AFX_DATA
⋮
```

After the user chooses a color (in this case, clicks a button), the *OnColorChange* function is called. This function retrieves the color and computes the respective COLORREF value by calling *UpdateData*, stores the new value

145

for future use, and then updates the radio button group with the new color. The function is as follows:

```
void CMyDlg::OnColorChange()
{
    UpdateData(TRUE);
    SetRadioBtnColor();
    PaintRadioBtns();
}
```

For full details of the helper functions *SetRadioBtnColor* and *PaintRadioBtns*, see MYDLGS.CPP in the CTRLDLG project.

Step 4: Dynamically Updating the Control Group

At this point, I have implemented an interface that allows the user to choose the color of a radio button group. In addition, with the help of *PaintRadioBtns*, I am updating the color of the controls immediately after the user chooses a color. However, I still have no way of painting individual controls with the proper color. To do this, I have to be able to modify the default behavior of painting for that control (or controls). Fortunately, there is a message perfectly suited to this need—WM_CTLCOLOR, which is sent by a child control that is about to be drawn. The message handler *OnCtlColor* provides the ID of the control making the request, the device context of the control, and the type of control (such as a button control or an edit control). Therefore, to modify the radio buttons dynamically, I have to handle the WM_CTLCOLOR message in the dialog box class. This is done easily with ClassWizard. The resultant handler function, *OnCtlColor*, is as follows:

```
HBRUSH CMyDlg::OnCtlColor(CDC* pDC, CWnd* pWnd, UINT nCtlColor)
{
    HBRUSH hbr = CDialog::OnCtlColor(pDC, pWnd, nCtlColor);

    // TODO: Change any attributes of the DC here

    // TODO: Return a different brush if the default is not desired
    return hbr;
}
```

Because I want to modify the appearance of specific controls, I will modify the function to set the text color of only the controls with the proper ID. The result is as follows:

```
HBRUSH CMyDlg::OnCtlColor(CDC* pDC, CWnd* pWnd, UINT nCtlColor)
{
    HBRUSH hbr = CDialog::OnCtlColor(pDC, pWnd, nCtlColor);
```

```
if (IsRadioButton(pWnd->GetDlgCtrlID()))
{
    pDC->SetTextColor(m_curColor);
}
return hbr;
}
```

IsRadioButton is another function of *CMyDlg*, which returns TRUE if the given ID matches the ID of a radio button. All other IDs are ignored, and the remaining controls are painted using the default method of the application framework.

At this point, you can rebuild the project, and you'll be able to modify the color of the text in your dialog box controls.

Modifying the Font Used by a Control or Controls

The following steps provide a basic framework for changing the font of individual controls:

1. Loading a different font

2. Modifying the *OnInitDialog* function

3. Changing the font for the window

Step 1: Loading a Different Font

There are many different ways to load a font, depending on the type of information that is available to you. The simplest way to load a font for MFC applications is to create a CFont object and then initialize the object with a call to the *CreateFontIndirect* function. The *CMyDlg::LoadFont* function is used by the CTRLDLG project to load the font specified by *m_fontName*, a data member of the dialog box class *CMyDlg*:

```
BOOL CMyDlg::LoadFont()
{
    LOGFONT logFont;

    logFont.lfHeight = -12;
    logFont.lfWidth = 0;
    logFont.lfWeight = FW_NORMAL;
    logFont.lfItalic = FALSE;
    logFont.lfUnderline = FALSE;
    logFont.lfStrikeOut = FALSE;
    logFont.lfEscapement = 0;
    logFont.lfOrientation = 0;
```

(continued)

147

```
lstrcpy(logFont.lfFaceName, m_fontName);
    return m_curFont.CreateFontIndirect(&logFont);
}
```

Step 2: Modifying the *OnInitDialog* Function

A good place to initialize the attributes of a dialog box, such as the font of a control, is in the WM_INITDIALOG message handler function (*OnInitDialog*) because, before the dialog box is visible, the dialog box object and its controls are created and available to you. You can add this function to your dialog box class using ClassWizard. After you have added this handler, make a call to *LoadFont,* and if the return is successful, the font can be used by any control in the dialog box.

Now that you have the font, you need access to the control that will use the font. This is done by making a call to the *CWnd::GetDlgItem* function and passing the ID of the control that is desired as the parameter, as shown below:

```
CWnd* pWnd = GetDlgItem(IDC_FONTTEXT);
```

> **N O T E :** The *CWnd* pointer that is returned from the call to *Get-DlgItem* is a temporary pointer. This means it should be used only within the function where *GetDlgItem* was called. The destruction of these temporary pointers is handled in the idle time processing of the application. When the application is idle, the *CWinApp::OnIdle* function is called, which destroys all temporary pointers.

Step 3: Changing the Font for the Window

Now that you have a pointer to the window of the control, you can call *SetFont* for that window, passing in the newly created font object.

The following code, which demonstrates all three steps of changing a font used by a control, is taken from the body of *CMyDlg::OnInitDialog*:

```
CDialog::OnInitDialog();

if (LoadFont())
{
    CWnd* pWnd = GetDlgItem(IDC_FONTTEXT);
    pWnd->SetFont(&m_curFont, FALSE);
}
else
    AfxMessageBox("Font creation failed!");

// Additional initialization
:
return TRUE;
```

After you have completed these modifications, you can rebuild the project and change the font of any dialog box control.

Hiding Static Text and Common Controls

The method for changing a font for a specific control demonstrated in step 2 of the previous procedure also can be used to hide the common controls of a dialog box. For example, in the *OnInitDialog* function of the dialog box class, check to see whether controls should be visible or hidden. If you want the controls to be visible, retrieve the window of each control and call *ShowWindow* with the value SW_SHOW. If you want the controls to be hidden, call *ShowWindow* with the value SW_HIDE. When the necessary controls have been hidden or revealed, the dialog box can be displayed.

In the CTRLDLG project, I make a call to *SetVisibleTextState* in the *OnInitDialog* function *CMyDlg*. This function checks the Boolean value *CMyDlg::-m_visible*; if the value is FALSE, it hides two controls (with the respective ID values IDC_STATIC1 and IDC_STATIC2). If the value is TRUE, the two controls are visible. The following code for showing and hiding the controls is taken from the body of *CMyDlg::SetVisibleTextState*:

```
CWnd* pCtrl;
CWnd* pCtrl2;

pCtrl = GetDlgItem(IDC_STATIC1);
pCtrl2 = GetDlgItem(IDC_STATIC2);

if (m_visible)
{
    pCtrl->ShowWindow(SW_SHOW);
    pCtrl2->ShowWindow(SW_SHOW);
}
else
{
    pCtrl->ShowWindow(SW_HIDE);
    pCtrl2->ShowWindow(SW_HIDE);
}
```

At this point, you can rebuild the project and show or hide the static text of a dialog box.

CHAPTER FIVE

Controls

The focus of this chapter is the customization and extension of MFC applications in relation to Microsoft Windows common controls. Each task demonstrates a way to either customize the default behavior of some control-related aspect of an MFC application (for example, sharing menu resources between child windows) or extend the default behavior in some way (for example, providing tooltips for view regions). The chapter includes the following tasks:

- **Sharing the main frame window menu between MDI children** This task modifies the default management of child menu resources by sharing a menu resource between child windows. Instead of loading a menu resource for each child window, the existing main menu is modified for the needs of the active child window.

- **Transferring strings between a list box and a *CStringArray* object** This task extends the common dialog box list box controls by adding the ability to transfer strings to and from a list box. An array of strings is used to initialize and later store strings from the list box control. This technique can also be used, with modification, for combo boxes.

- **Tabbing between child window controls in a non–dialog box view** This task demonstrates extending the default behavior of child window controls in a view by adding the ability to tab between child controls in a *CView*-derived class.

- **Adding tooltips for view regions and child windows** This task extends the tooltip capabilities of an MFC application by implementing tooltips for controls and rectangular regions embedded in a child window.

- **Enabling a nested pop-up menu** This task demonstrates a technique that enables a nested pop-up menu only if one or more menu items are enabled. The pop-up menu is otherwise disabled.

Sharing the Main Frame
Window Menu Between MDI Children

The purpose of this task is to share the main frame window menu resource between MDI child windows. Instead of loading a new menu resource for each type of MDI child window, the existing menu resource can be dynamically modified by adding and removing menu commands, based on the needs of the individual MDI child window. Sharing one menu resource is suited for child windows that are similar in functionality yet require unique menu commands. By using one main menu resource instead of a unique menu for each type of child window, you can conserve the amount of resources needed by the application. The task consists of four steps:

1. Adding a new document template class

2. Modifying the application class

3. Modifying the main frame window class

4. Modifying the child frame window class

The sample project is named MDIMENU, and there are two requirements:

- An MDI application with two or more document templates

- A menu resource that will be used as the main menu by two or more child windows

In the MDIMENU sample project, I use two document types: Rect (which draws four random rectangles) and Ellipse (which draws four random ellipses). The menu resource shared by these document templates is named IDR-_SHAREDMENU. For demonstration purposes, I modify the shared menu resource by displaying either the About Ellipse or the About Rect command on the application's Help menu (Figure 5-1), depending on which document type is active at the time.

Step 1: Adding a New Document Template Class

One of the main functions of a document template is to collect the resources for its specific document type. When a new document is created, the document's template is responsible for creating and loading the resources for that document. When the last open document of the specific document type is destroyed, the template automatically frees up all memory and resources that were associated with the document type. However, this presents a problem if another

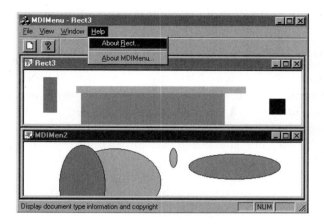

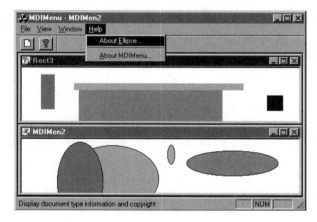

Figure 5-1.
The two versions of the Help menu for the MDIMENU application.

document type is sharing the same menu resource and is still active. Therefore, to share a menu resource successfully, you must prevent the menu resource from being deleted until all active documents are closed. The solution is to derive your own document template class from *CMultiDocTemplate* and modify the template's destructor so the menu resource is deleted only when the last active document sharing that menu is closed.

1. Add a new class derived from *CMultiDocTemplate* to your project. This new class will implement the shared resource template. (In the sample project, I call my derived class *CSharedTemplate*).

2. Now modify the destructor of the new class by adding this line:

```
m_hMenuShared = NULL;
```

This line of code sets the *m_hMenuShared* data member of the document template to NULL. If *m_hMenuShared* were not set to NULL, the base class would delete the menu resource (not knowing that it is being shared), causing the application to assert immediately. However, when the value is NULL, the base class assumes that there is no menu resource to delete. The actual deletion of the menu resource is handled in the next step.

N O T E : Don't waste time trying to find some documentation on *m_hMenuShared* because it's not documented. As is true for all of the undocumented data members and functions I've used in this book, the use of undocumented class members by MFC is subject to change without warning and should be done with caution.

Step 2: Modifying the Application Class

When an MFC application shuts down, the application object is the last object that is destroyed. For this reason, the application class is an ideal place for managing document templates. Use this class to store the pointers to all registered document templates and the handle of the shared menu resource. Then when the user exits the application, it's safe to delete the shared menu resource. The modifications to the application class include adding new data members and functions and modifying an existing function.

Adding New Data Members and a Function

In this section, we add data members to the application class and override the *CWinApp::ExitInstance* function.

To store the handle of the menu resource, add the following lines of code to the declaration of your application's class, which is found in the header file of the application class:

```
public:
    HMENU m_sharedMenu;
```

Right after this declaration, declare a pointer of type *CSharedTemplate* (or the name used when you created the new template class in step 1) for each document template you want to register in your application. Don't forget to include the header file for the new shared template class in the header file of the application class. The following code sample, from the header file of the sample project's application class, declares two pointers to the registered document templates of the application:

```
CMultiDocTemplate* m_pEllipse;
CMultiDocTemplate* m_pRect;
```

In addition to adding new data members, you also have to override the *ExitInstance* function in your application class. Do this now. Then add the following line of code to your *ExitInstance* function right before the call to *CWinApp::ExitInstance*:

```
::DestroyMenu(m_sharedMenu);
```

This line of code deletes the shared menu resource.

Modifying the *InitInstance* Function

In this section, we modify the *InitInstance* function of the application class by loading the shared menu resource and using the *CSharedTemplate* class to register the document templates used by the application.

In the *InitInstance* function of your application class, add the lines of code shown below before any document templates are registered. Be sure you use the ID of your shared menu resource instead of IDR_SHAREDMENU in the call to *::LoadMenu*.

```
// Initialize shared menu resource
m_sharedMenu = ::LoadMenu(m_hInstance,
    MAKEINTRESOURCE(IDR_SHAREDMENU));
```

After loading the menu resource, modify the method by which the document template is registered with the application using the *CSharedTemplate* class. The resulting document templates will be stored in the appropriate template pointers of your application class. To modify the registering of the document template:

1. Change the template class used to create the document template to *CSharedTemplate* (or whatever name you used in step 1).

2. Store the result of the document template creation in the appropriate template pointer, which is located in the application class.

3. Set the *m_hSharedMenu* data member of the template pointer used in step 2 equal to *m_sharedMenu*.

Use this procedure to modify the registration of any remaining document templates in your application. The code for your single document template

155

should be similar to the following example, which is taken from the *InitInstance* function of the sample project's application class:

```
m_pEllipse = new CSharedTemplate(
    IDR_MDIMENTYPE,
    RUNTIME_CLASS(CMDIMenuDoc),
    RUNTIME_CLASS(CChildFrame), // Custom MDI child frame
    RUNTIME_CLASS(CMDIMenuView));
m_pEllipse->m_hMenuShared = m_sharedMenu;
```

Step 3: Modifying the Main Frame Window Class

Because the main frame window class is the owner of the main menu, it is a good place to modify the menu and to handle commands that appear in all variations of the main frame window menu. To allow modification of the menu at any time, we have to add a group of functions that, when called, modify the main menu for each document type sharing the main menu resource.

In the header file of your main frame class, declare a public member function in a manner similar to the following declaration:

```
void FuncName();
```

For each additional document type that shares the main menu resource, declare a similar function.

For the two document templates used in the sample project, I declared the following two functions in the header file of the main frame window class:

```
void ModifyEllipseMenu();
void ModifyRectMenu();
```

Note that these functions will be called from the MDI_ACTIVATE message handlers of each child window class, which you will add in step 4.

In the body of each menu modification function that you have declared, add the code that will modify the main frame window menu. The code below is taken from the *CMainFrame::ModifyEllipseMenu* function of the sample project:

```
CMenu* pMenu = GetMenu();
CMenu* pAbtMenu = pMenu->GetSubMenu(3);

if (pAbtMenu->GetMenuItemID(0) == ID_APP_ABTRECT)
{
    pAbtMenu->DeleteMenu(0, MF_BYPOSITION);
    pAbtMenu->DeleteMenu(0, MF_BYPOSITION);
}

if (pAbtMenu->GetMenuItemID(0) != ID_APP_ABTELLIPSE)
{
```

```
pAbtMenu->InsertMenu(0, MF_BYPOSITION, MF_SEPARATOR);
pAbtMenu->InsertMenu(0, MF_BYPOSITION, ID_APP_ABTELLIPSE,
    "About &Ellipse...");
}
```

In the first section of this code, I retrieve the Help menu of the main frame window. In the second section of code, I check for the presence of the About Rect menu command. If the check succeeds, I delete the first two menu commands in preparation for adding Ellipse-specific menu commands. Finally, I check for the absence of the About Ellipse menu command. If the check fails, I add the necessary menu items and exit the function.

The last modification to the main frame window class is adding handlers for any menu commands that were added as a result of modifying the main menu. In your main frame window class, use your favorite method to implement handlers for menu commands that are dynamically added to the main menu. In the sample project, I added handlers for two new menu commands: About Rect and About Ellipse. The following code is the handler for the About Rect command and is taken from the implementation file of class *CMainFrame*:

```
CAboutRectDlg aboutDlg;
aboutDlg.DoModal();
```

This handler creates a *CAboutRectDlg* object and then displays it for the user.

Step 4: Modifying the Child Frame Window Class

Whenever a new child window is activated in standard MFC applications, the main menu is updated by swapping the main menu resource with the menu resource of the child window. Because the same menu resource is used for all child windows, the main menu must be updated at the appropriate time. You can easily determine the appropriate time by handling the WM_MDIACTIVATE message in the child windows of your application; the message is sent when a child window is about to be activated.

1. Add a handler for the WM_MDIACTIVATE message to the child frame window class. You will use this handler to modify the main menu, depending on which child window is being activated.

2. Modify the main menu by adding a call to the appropriate function from the group you added when you modified the main frame window class.

3. Repeat these two steps for the other document templates in your application.

> **N O T E :**   Because the method for modifying the main menu of a child window is the same for all child windows, I will modify one type of child window and leave modification of the remaining classes as an exercise for the reader.

The following example, taken from the sample project, demonstrates the WM_MDIACTIVATE message handler for the *CRectFrame* class:

```
CMDIChildWnd::OnMDIActivate(bActivate, pActivateWnd,
    pDeactivateWnd);

if (bActivate)
{
    CMainFrame* pFrm;

    pFrm = (CMainFrame*)GetMDIFrame();
    if (pFrm != NULL)
        pFrm->ModifyRectMenu();
}
```

In the first section of this code, I call the base class handler. I then check to see whether the child window is being activated. If the check succeeds, I retrieve a handle to the main frame window, which contains the menu modification functions. I then call the appropriate function for the Rect document type, in this case *ModifyRectMenu*.

After you have made all the necessary modifications to each child frame window class, rebuild the project. Your child windows will now share one common menu resource, which is modified dynamically for each type of child window.

Transferring Strings Between a List Box and a *CStringArray* Object

The purpose of this task is to implement a function that transfers character strings of type *CString* to and from the list box control of a modal dialog box. A *CStringArray* object, initialized in the sample project's *CDlgxmplDoc* constructor, stores the list box strings. The data transfer is accomplished with the *StringTransfer* function. To transfer strings at the proper time (before the modal dialog box is displayed and after the user chooses the OK button), we override and modify the *OnInitDialog* and *OnOK* functions in the dialog box class containing the list box control.

In this task, I use a *CStringArray* object to store the strings being transferred. I chose this data type because a *CStringArray* object provides a clean, high-level interface to basic functions on arrays containing strings. With some minor modifications of the *StringTransfer* function (which are not addressed in this task), other data types and storage methods can be used with equal success.

The task consists of three steps:

1. Adding the *StringTransfer* function to the project

2. Overriding and modifying the *OnInitDialog* function

3. Overriding and modifying the *OnOK* function

N O T E :   This task demonstrates data transfer with a list box control. However, with some slight modifications, a combo box control can be used as discussed in step 1 below.

The sample project name is DLGXMPL, and there are two requirements:

■ A modal dialog box with either a combo box or a list box control

■ A data member of type *CStringArray* (In the task, this data member, *m_lstBoxArray*, is part of the *CDlgxmplDoc* class.)

Step 1: Adding the *StringTransfer* Function

The *StringTransfer* function is the workhorse of this task; it is responsible for transferring an array of *CString* objects (in this task, a *CStringArray* object) either to or from a list box control. Inside this function, an *if* statement determines the direction of transfer and transfers *CString* objects, one string at a time. The *StringTransfer* function takes two parameters: a pointer to a list box control, and a Boolean value that indicates the direction of transfer. In the sample project, this function is declared as a member of the *CDlgxmplDoc* class.

T I P :   The *StringTransfer* function also can be modified to use a combo box instead of a list box. Because of the similarity between the *CListBox* and *CComboBox* classes, substitute a *CComboBox* pointer for every occurrence of a *CListBox* pointer in the *StringTransfer* function. After making this substitution, you can then use the function to transfer *CString* objects to and from a combo box.

1. In the header file of your document class, add the following definition:

```
void StringTransfer(CListBox* pListBox,
    BOOL bDir);
```

2. In the implementation file of your document class, add the following function declaration:

```
void DlgxmplDoc::StringTransfer(CListBox* pListBox, BOOL bDir)
{
    CString str;
    int count;

    if (bDir)  // Transfer array contents to list box
    {
        for (int i = 0; i < m_lstBoxArray.GetSize(); i++)
        {
            str = m_lstBoxArray[i];
            pListBox->AddString((LPCTSTR)str);
        }
    }
    else    // Transfer list box contents to array
    {
        int count;
        count = pListBox->GetCount();

        m_lstBoxArray.RemoveAll();
        for (int i = 0; i < count; i++)
        {
            pListBox->GetText(i, str);
            m_lstBoxArray.Add(str);
        }
    }
}
```

The first thing the *StringTransfer* function does is determine the direction of data transfer. This is accomplished by checking the value of the *bDir* parameter. If *bDir* is TRUE, strings are transferred from the string array to the list box control. In this case, I add each string array element to the list box control that is pointed to by *pListBox* with a call to the *AddString* function. However, if *bDir* is FALSE, strings are transferred from the list box control to the string array. First I determine the number of strings contained by the list box. I retrieve each string from the list box, starting with the first listed string, and set the *i*th array element (which is determined by the current *for* loop index) equal to the current string value. Then I increment the index of the string array and read the next string. After the last string of the list box control has been read and stored, the program control exits the function.

Step 2: Overriding and Modifying the *OnInitDialog* Function

Now that you have added the *StringTransfer* function to the application, you have to determine when and how it should be called. Because the list box control is located in a modal dialog box, the best method for initializing the contents is to override the *OnInitDialog* function in your dialog box class. If your dialog box class does not override this function, override it now. After you override the function, modify the function body by adding the following code (after the initial call to *OnInitDialog*):

```
CDlgxmplDoc* pDoc;
CFrameWnd* pFrm = (CFrameWnd*)AfxGetMainWnd();
pDoc = (CDlgxmplDoc*)pFrm->GetActiveDocument();

pDoc->StringTransfer(&m_listBox, TRUE);

return TRUE;
```

In the first section of code, I retrieve a pointer to the document object. This pointer is used in the next line to make a call to the *StringTransfer* function. In addition to the address of the dialog box's list box control (*m_listBox*), I pass a value of TRUE, indicating that the array will be used to initialize the list box control.

This completes one side of the data transfer. The other side of the data transfer involves transferring the list box strings to the *CStringArray*, as demonstrated in the next step.

Step 3: Overriding and Modifying the *OnOK* Function

Modal dialog boxes can be dismissed by clicking either OK or Cancel. To properly update the array of strings, you should accept changes to the array only if the user dismisses the dialog box by clicking OK. You can determine when the user clicks OK by overriding the *OnOK* function in your dialog box class. If your dialog box class does not override this function, override it now.

In the *OnOK* function of your dialog box class, add the following code before the call to the base class *OnOK* function:

```
CDlgxmplDoc* pDoc;
CFrameWnd* pFrm = (CFrameWnd*)AfxGetMainWnd();
pDoc = (CDlgxmplDoc*)pFrm->GetActiveDocument();

pFrm->StringTransfer(&m_listBox, FALSE);
```

The preceding code is similar to the code of the *OnInitDialog* function that you added in step 1. A pointer to the document is retrieved and used to call the *StringTransfer* function. Notice that the Boolean value is FALSE, which indicates that strings from the list box control will be transferred to the string array.

After you have modified the *OnOK* function, rebuild the project. Your list box control now initializes itself with strings from your array and transfers any changes (additions or deletions) when the user clicks OK.

Additional Information

The procedure presented in this task for modal dialog boxes also can be used for modeless dialog boxes.

Tabbing Between Child Window Controls in a Non–Dialog Box View

The purpose of this task is to enable tabbing between child window controls outside a dialog box or form view, where common window controls provide minimal functionality. One of the more useful features that isn't available outside these environments is the ability to tab from one control to the next, just as you can among a group of controls in a dialog box.

In this task, I use a custom notification method to implement tabbing and assume that the controls will be used in some *CView*-derived object. Each control class is derived from an MFC control class, and the WM_CHAR message is added to the control's message map. When the Tab key is pressed, the control with the focus sends a user-defined message to the parent view. The parent view determines which control has the current focus and switches the focus to the next control in line.

The task consists of four steps:

1. Adding new control classes to the project
2. Adding WM_CHAR handlers to the control classes
3. Modifying the existing view class
4. Adding a user-defined message handler to the view class

The sample application is an SDI application that uses button, edit, and slider control types. The name of the project is TABVW, and there are no requirements.

T I P :   The same functionality can be achieved by an override and a call to *IsDialogMessage*! If you want to use the quick method, skip to "Additional Information." I present the long version here to illustrate how to use custom messages and to demonstrate various techniques for embedding common controls.

Step 1: Adding New Control Classes to the Project

One standard approach for placing a functional Windows common control (or controls) in a *CView*-derived class is to implement each control as a child window of the view class. You can do this by having the view construct the control type that is needed and then by calling the control's *Create* function. This function creates the proper control and attaches it to the control object in the view. For more information on this topic, see "Using Common Controls as a Child Window" in Technical Note 60 of the Visual C++ online documentation.

However, if you need the control to act as a notifier for custom events, the standard approach is inadequate. What you need is your own control class that is able to handle WM_CHAR messages and notify its parent (the view class) when the Tab character is received. This new control class can be derived from any one of the MFC common control classes, such as *CButton* or *CSliderCtrl*.

Because I don't know your intended purpose in following this task, I am assuming the simplest case for the purpose of this discussion—that you have one or more control classes derived from *CButton* or the like and that you want to place them directly in the main view of an SDI application. If you already have control classes that have been derived from MFC common control classes, feel free to substitute them for the sample classes used here. First add the control classes that you will be using to your project. Now, using your favorite method, add the data members of various types from your new control classes to either the project's main view class or a *CView*-derived class of your choice.

N O T E :   If you use ClassWizard to create the new control classes, they will be added to the project automatically. In addition, you can choose the existing files in the project in which the class is declared and defined.

In the sample project, three different control types (button, edit, and slider) are implemented in two files, MYCTRLS.H and MYCTRLS.CPP. The code shown in bold in the following code fragment, which is taken from the declaration of the *CTabVwView* class, declares five controls as data members of *CTabVwView.*

```
// Attributes
public:
    CTabVwDoc* GetDocument();

// Embedded controls
    CMyButton* m_pCtrl1;
    CMyEdit* m_pCtrl2;
    CMyButton* m_pCtrl3;
    CMyEdit* m_pCtrl4;
    CMySlider* m_pCtrl5;
```

At this point, each control has very little functionality beyond what it inherits from its parent. In the next step, the functionality is improved by adding the WM_CHAR handler.

Step 2: Adding WM_CHAR Handlers to the Control Classes

Now that you've added the controls, you can add the ability to both check for the Tab key and somehow notify the parent when this event occurs. The parent is responsible for switching focus because it is the only class that has knowledge of all the child window controls. Notification should occur only if one of the controls has input focus and the Tab key is pressed. This imitates the behavior of controls in a dialog box or form view. Because the user can tab from any control, each control must check for the Tab event. A good way to detect Tab keypresses is with a WM_CHAR handler. Therefore, for each new control in the view, add a handler for the WM_CHAR message.

After you have added the handler to every control class, add the following code, or if you used ClassWizard, replace the existing handler code with the following:

```
CWnd* pParentWnd = GetParent();

if (nChar == 0x09) // Tab key pressed, notify parent
    pParentWnd->PostMessage(WM_SWITCHFOCUS,
        (WPARAM)((CWnd*)this), 0);
else
    CEdit::OnChar(nChar, nRepCnt, nFlags);
```

In this code, I retrieve a pointer to the control's parent class, which in this case is the view class of the application. Next I check the character received for a match against the Tab character. If there is a match, I notify the parent with a call to *PostMessage*. Because this is a custom event, there are no predefined messages to use as a parameter for the *PostMessage* function. I use the message WM_SWITCHFOCUS, which is a custom message I discuss later in step 4. For now, assume that the view object knows what to do when the user-defined message is received. If there is no match, the character is passed on to the parent's handler and no action is taken.

> **N O T E :** I use *PostMessage* because it allows me to send the message and immediately return without waiting for the handling of the message. If you want to wait for the window that received the message to handle the message and then return, call *SendMessage*.

Step 3: Modifying the Existing View Class

You can now modify the intended parent class to properly create, store, and destroy the new controls. The simplest method, used in the sample project, makes use of the public pointers we declared in step 2:

```
// Attributes
public:
    ⋮
    CMyButton* m_pCtrl1;
    CMyEdit* m_pCtrl2;
    CMyButton* m_pCtrl3;
    CMyEdit* m_pCtrl4;
    CMySlider* m_pCtrl5;
```

In the view's constructor, initialize these pointers to NULL. This allows you to quickly determine (in the destructor) which pointers need cleaning up by checking the pointer state:

```
CTabviewView::~CTabviewView()
{
    if (m_pCtrl1)
        delete m_pCtrl1;
    if (m_pCtrl2)
        delete m_pCtrl2;
// Check remaining control pointers
    ⋮
}
```

Now create each instance of the control type using the *new* operator. A good place to do this is in the view class's override of *OnInitialUpdate*. Using your favorite method, override *OnInitialUpdate* in your view class and create each control, using the *new* operator and the control's *Create* function. The following example is from the override of the *OnInitialUpdate* function in the TABVW sample project. The *rect* variable is used to align the controls in columns and rows, with each control the same size.

```
void CTabVwView::OnInitialUpdate()
{
    CView::OnInitialUpdate();

    CRect rect(50, 50, 125, 80);

    m_pCtrl1 = new CMyButton();
    m_pCtrl1->Create(_T("Button 1"), BS_PUSHBUTTON | WS_CHILD
        | WS_VISIBLE, rect, this, 1010);

    rect.left = rect.left+95;
    rect.right = rect.right+95;
    m_pCtrl2 = new CMyEdit();
    m_pCtrl2->Create(ES_AUTOHSCROLL | WS_BORDER | WS_CHILD
        | WS_VISIBLE, rect, this, 1020);
// Remaining controls created
    ⋮
```

Now that the controls have been placed in the view and can clean up after themselves, it's time to add message handlers that will be used for notifying the parent view class.

Step 4: Adding a User-Defined Message Handler to the View Class

In step 2, I mentioned that the control notifies the parent with a user-defined message, WM_SWITCHFOCUS. Even though MFC has an incredible list of message types, it would be impossible for Microsoft to foresee the needs of every application developed with MFC. Therefore, Microsoft has added support for user-defined messages to handle the rest. In this case, I wanted to notify the view to change focus via the control's message maps. There isn't a message that fits that need, so I created one.

User-defined messages are any messages that are not standard Windows WM_MESSAGE messages. There should be an ON_MESSAGE macro statement in the message map for each user-defined message that must be mapped to a message-handler function. In addition, these messages must be defined in the range WM_USER through 0x7FFF; in this task, I use a random number for the value. Even though the custom message is being used only by the view and control classes, I made the message available application-wide. The procedure on the facing page demonstrates how to define and handle a user-defined message.

1. Define the user-defined message by adding the following lines to the header file of the application object:

```
// User-defined messages
////////////////////////////////////
#define WM_SWITCHFOCUS (WM_USER + 119)
```

2. Add a handler for the custom message in the implementation file of the control's parent class (probably a view) by adding the following line to the message map of the control's parent class (which should be *CView*-derived):

```
    ON_MESSAGE(WM_SWITCHFOCUS, OnSwitchFocus)
```

3. Declare the handler function, *OnSwitchFocus*, of the custom message in the header file of the view class as follows:

```
afx_msg LRESULT OnSwitchFocus(WPARAM wParam, LPARAM lParam);
```

4. Define the body of the handler function:

```
LRESULT CTabVwView::OnSwitchFocus(WPARAM WParam, LPARAM LParam)
{
    return (LRESULT)0;
}
```

Now that the custom message (and its handler) have been defined and declared, complete the job by adding logic to the body of *OnSwitchFocus* to switch between controls. *OnSwitchFocus* has to determine which control has the focus and, on the basis of that result, switch to the next control in line. Add the following code to *OnSwitchFocus*, right before the *return* statement:

```
CWnd* pFocusWnd = (CWnd*)WParam;
CWnd* pNextWnd = pFocusWnd->GetNextWindow();
if (!pNextWnd)
    pNextWnd = GetWindow(GW_CHILD);

if (pNextWnd)
{
    pNextWnd->SetFocus();
    return 0L;
}

AfxMessageBox("Tab received but no control has focus");

    return (LRESULT)0;
```

The first section of the preceding code makes the second section a little easier to read by casting the control that fired off the notification to a *CWnd* pointer. I then set the focus to the next window in the Z-order. If necessary, the focus is automatically wrapped around to the first control.

Now that you have successfully built the project, you should have dialog box–like behavior in your view window.

Additional Information

If you don't have the time or energy for the preceding procedure, give this one a whirl.

1. In the view class that will contain the controls, add "public" pointer members of various control types, such as *CSliderCtrl* and *CButton*.

2. In your constructor and destructor, initialize and clean up the pointers. (For an example, see above under "Step 3: Modifying the Existing View Class.")

N O T E : For this method to work properly, each control must have the WS_TABSTOP style; otherwise, it will be ignored in the tabbing order.

3. Override the *PreTranslateMessage* function in the view's class.

4. In the override of *PreTranslateMessage*, replace the code in the function body with the following code:

```
if (!::IsDialogMessage(m_hWnd, pMsg))
    return CView::PreTranslateMessage(pMsg);
else
    return TRUE;
```

This code hands off the messages that are received to *IsDialogMessage*. If the message contains keyboard events, *IsDialogMessage* handles them as if the view were a dialog box, in which case the function tabs to the next control. If a message does not contain any keyboard events, the message is handed off to the parent class. As noted in the online documentation, a message processed by *IsDialogMessage* must not be passed to either the *TranslateMessage* function or the *DispatchMessage* function because *IsDialogMessage* performs all necessary translating and dispatching of messages.

Adding Tooltips for View Regions and Child Windows

The purpose of this task is to add tooltips for four child window items—two standard button controls and two rectangular regions. These items (shown in Figure 5-2) are implemented as members of an MDI child window. By default, tooltips are provided only in *CFrameWnd*-derived windows because *CFrameWnd* handles the TTN_NEEDTEXT notifications and loads the string resources according to the ID of the window or the ID of the tool in a toolbar. If you want tooltips for other types of tools, such as other windows or rectangular regions, you have to roll your own.

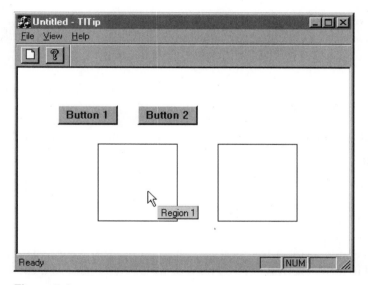

Figure 5-2.
Tooltip for a rectangular region.

There are two methods you can use to provide tooltip support in an MFC application:

- **Using the *OnToolHitTest* function and TTN_NEEDTEXT notification** Overrides *CWnd::OnToolHitTest* and tests for hits on tools in the application. If the tooltip test is successful, the text for the tooltip is then provided by handling the TTN_NEEDTEXT notification.

■ **Using the *CToolTipCtrl* class** Uses the *CToolTipCtrl* class to create and manage a list of tooltips for an application.

The first of these methods is the one used in this task. For information on the second method, see "Adding Tooltips for Modal Dialog Controls" in Chapter 2. The task consists of four steps:

1. Adding tools to the application

2. Modifying the *OnInitialUpdate* function

3. Overriding the *CWnd::OnToolHitTest* function

4. Handling the TTN_NEEDTEXT notification

The name of the project is TLTIP, and the requirement is one or more tools (regions, controls, and so forth) that will be embedded in the view class.

Background

To implement a functioning tooltip in an MFC application, you must perform some (or all) of the following steps:

■ Define the tools that will be monitored by the tooltip control.

■ Activate the tooltip control(s).

■ Determine when to display the tooltip.

■ Provide text to display in the tooltip window when text is requested by the system.

The default support for tooltips is available only for controls (or tools) embedded in a *CFrameWnd*-derived class or for a descendant of a *CFrameWnd*-derived class because *CFrameWnd* is the only class that provides a handler function for the TTN_NEEDTEXT notification. This notification is sent by the framework when the mouse has remained on the same point for about half a second and there is a registered tool (usually a toolbar button or menu item) that includes the current mouse position. When this happens, a TOOLINFO structure is initialized and passed on to the default notification handler, which in this case is *CWnd::OnToolTipText*. The handler retrieves the ID of the tool and the string resource, if any, with the same ID. After the text is retrieved, the tooltip window is displayed. If the tool has no tooltip text, the window still opens, but it's invisible.

To implement tooltips for tools inside windows that are not derived from *CFrameWnd*, you must do two things: determine when the tooltip should be displayed (by overriding *CWnd::OnToolHitTest*) and provide text for the tooltip if text is needed (handling the TTN_NEEDTEXT notification).

Step 1: Adding Tools to the Application

Tooltips can be used for a variety of tools—all types of Windows controls or regions in a view. For this task, I assume you will use tools that are embedded in a *CView*-derived class.

    The first step is to add the necessary tools to your project. For example, you might choose to add new button classes, or you might choose simply to declare one or more *CRect*-type data members to represent rectangular regions in the view class.

    After you have added your tools to the project, add a string for each new tool to the string table of your project. Remember the IDs of the new strings because they will be used to identify the tooltip text for the new tools. In this sample project, I created two strings:

- IDS_RECT, with the caption "Region 1"
- IDS_RECT2, with the caption "Region 2"

For this task, I used two common button controls and two regions. I define the tools (in TLTIPVIEW.H) as members of class *CTlTipView*:

```
// Attributes
public:
  ⋮
    // Child window controls
    CButton* m_pBtn1;
    CButton* m_pBtn2;

    // Rectangular regions
    CRect m_rect1;
    CRect m_rect2;
```

In the constructor for *CTlTipView*, I initialize both *CButton* pointers to NULL. In the destructor for *CTlTipView*, I check the value of each pointer and call the *delete* operator if the value is not equal to NULL.

Step 2: Modifying the *OnInitialUpdate* Function

A good place to initialize and to enable tooltips for the embedded tools is in the *OnInitialUpdate* function of your view class. Because AppWizard doesn't override this function, you should override it now. After overriding the function in your view class, add code that creates the two common button controls and then enables tooltips for the view. The following is an example of how this might be done:

```
CView::OnInitialUpdate();

CRect rect(50, 50, 125, 75);
m_pBtn1 = new CButton;
m_pBtn1->Create(_T("Button 1"), BS_PUSHBUTTON | WS_CHILD |
    WS_VISIBLE, rect, this, IDS_BTN1);
rect.left += 100;
rect.right += 100;
m_pBtn2 = new CButton;
m_pBtn2->Create(_T("Button 2"), BS_PUSHBUTTON | WS_CHILD|
    WS_VISIBLE, rect, this, IDS_BTN2);

// Initialize regions
m_rect1.SetRect(100, 100, 200, 200);
m_rect2.SetRect(250, 100, 350, 200);

EnableToolTips(TRUE);
```

In the first section of the code, after calling *CView::OnInitialUpdate*, I create the button controls, using the *rect* variable to make both buttons the same size. In the second section, I initialize the values for the two rectangular regions used by the class *CTlTipView*. And finally, I make a call to *EnableToolTips*. Just as the name suggests, this function enables tooltips for the view window of the application.

Step 3: Overriding the *CWnd::OnToolHitTest* Function

Now that you have four tools created and initialized by the view object, you have to override the *CWnd::OnToolHitTest* function to provide tooltips when the user pauses the mouse cursor over one of the four tools. The default behavior of *CWnd::OnToolHitTest*, which is found in the MFC source file WINCORE.CPP, checks only for the presence of a child window. If the function does not find a child window, disabled or otherwise, that contains the point being checked, it returns the value –1.

Because you also want to provide tooltips for the two rectangular regions, you must customize the behavior of this function to check for rectangular regions in addition to child windows. The following procedure overrides the *OnToolHitTest* function in the application's view class.

1. In the "protected" section of your view class's header file, add the following declaration:

```
protected:
    ⋮
int OnToolHitTest(CPoint point, TOOLINFO* pTI)
    const;
```

2. In the implementation file of your view class, add this definition:

```
int CTlTipView::OnToolHitTest(CPoint point, TOOLINFO* pTI)
    const
{
// Code will be added later
}
```

3. After you override the *OnToolHitTest* function, you can add code that checks for hits on the two tool regions. If the check comes back negative, you call the base class implementation to check for hits on the two embedded buttons. Add the following code to the body of the overridden *OnToolHitTest* function:

```
// Check for hits on the rectangles
if ((m_rect1.PtInRect(point)) || (m_rect2.PtInRect(point)))
{
    // Set up TOOLINFO structure
    ASSERT(pTI != NULL);
    pTI->hwnd = m_hWnd;
    if (m_rect1.PtInRect(point))
    {
        pTI->rect = m_rect1;
        pTI->uId = IDS_RECT1;
    }
    else
    {
        pTI->rect = m_rect2;
        pTI->uId = IDS_RECT2;
    }
    pTI->lpszText = LPSTR_TEXTCALLBACK;
    return 1;
}
return CView::OnToolHitTest(point, pTI);
```

In the first section of code, I check to see whether *point,* passed in by the framework, is contained in either region. If *point* is contained in either region, I initialize a TOOLINFO structure with information on the tool that is currently being queried. This information includes the handle of the parent window (the application's view), the area of the tool, the ID of the tool, and finally, the text for the tool. Because I am handling the TTN_NEEDTEXT notification, I pass the value LPSTR_TEXTCALLBACK, which sends a TTN_NEEDTEXT notification to the parent of the tool, in this case *m_hWnd*. If *point* is not contained by the two regions, I call the base class implementation.

Step 4: Handling the TTN_NEEDTEXT Notification

If you rebuild your project at this point in the procedure, you would get tool-tips for all four tools. However, you wouldn't be able to see the tooltip window because no tooltip text has been given to the framework to display. To fix this, you must handle the TTN_NEEDTEXT notification and provide tooltip text for the appropriate control. The following procedure overrides the *CWnd::On-ToolTipNotify* function and installs a notification handler for TTN_NEEDTEXT in the message map of your application's view class.

1. In the "protected" section of your view class (found in the header file), add the following declaration:

```
protected:
⋮
BOOL CTlTipView::OnToolTipNotify(UINT id, NMHDR *pNMH, LRESULT
    *pResult);
```

2. In the implementation file of your view class, add the line of code shown in bold to the message map of your view class:

```
BEGIN_MESSAGE_MAP(CTlTipView, CView)
    // {{AFX_MSG_MAP(CTlTipView)
    ⋮
    // }}AFX_MSG_MAP
    ON_NOTIFY (TTN_NEEDTEXT,0,OnToolTipNotify)
END_MESSAGE_MAP()
```

This code maps the TTN_NEEDTEXT notification to the handler function *CTlTipView::OnToolTipNotify*.

3. In the implementation file of your view class, add the following definition:

```
void CTlTipView::OnToolTipNotify(NMHDR *pNMH, LRESULT
    *pResult)
{
// Code will be added later
}
```

4. Now that you have a handler function for the TTN_NEEDTEXT notification, you must add code to the handler that supplies each tool with its related text. The related text is determined by examining the NMHDR structure passed to the *OnToolTipNotify* function. Add the code below to the body of the overridden *OnToolTipNotify* function:

```
TOOLTIPTEXT *pTTT = (TOOLTIPTEXT *)pNMH;
UINT nID = pNMH->idFrom;
if (pTTT->uFlags & TTF_IDISHWND)
{
    // idFrom is actually the HWND of the tool
    nID = ::GetDlgCtrlID((HWND)nID);
    ASSERT(nID != 0);
    pTTT->lpszText = MAKEINTRESOURCE(nID);
    pTTT->hinst = AfxGetResourceHandle();
}
else
{
    pTTT->lpszText = MAKEINTRESOURCE(nID);
    pTTT->hinst = AfxGetInstanceHandle();
}
```

In the first section of code, I attempt to retrieve the ID of the tool (assuming that it is a child window) from the NMHDR structure. If I am successful, I retrieve the string that matches the ID of the control, set the instance of the application, and exit the function. If there is no control ID, I check for the IDs of the regions IDS_RECT1 and IDS-_RECT2. If either region is found, I retrieve the string that matches the ID of the region, set the instance of the application, and exit the function.

N O T E : In the preceding handler code, the string resources added in step 1 were used by passing the string ID to the MAKE-INTRESOURCE macro. I could just as easily have used a string constant for the *lpszText* member.

Additional Information

For more information on providing tooltips for dialog box controls, see the section "Adding Tooltips for Modal Dialog Controls" in Chapter 2. You might also want to read one or more of the Microsoft Knowledge Base articles listed on the following page.

- DOCERR: How to Display Tool Tips After Calling EnableToolTips: Q140595 (Article in its updated form was not available for inclusion in Part II of this book at press time; see the online version.)

- How to Add Tooltips to OLE Controls: Q141871

- How to Add Tooltips for Controls on an MFC Modal Dialog Box: Q141758 (Article in its updated form was not available for inclusion in Part II of this book at press time; see the online version.)

Enabling a Nested Pop-Up Menu

In an MFC application, each item in a menu or submenu can be either enabled or disabled by calling its related command-update handler through the ON_UPDATE_UI macro. Usually, this message handler is called only once—before the menu item is displayed to the user. Inside the menu items handler, you determine whether the menu item is enabled or disabled. However, in the case of nested pop-up menus, the handler for the first menu item in the pop-up can be called in two different cases. (See the example in Figure 5-3.) This can cause the nested pop-up to be enabled, even if there are no enabled menu items on the pop-up menu itself. Therefore, you have to take steps to ensure that the pop-up menu is enabled only under the appropriate conditions.

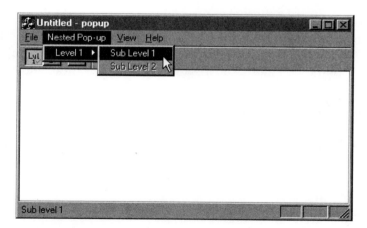

Figure 5-3.
The nested pop-up menu of the sample project POPUP.

This task (with the sample project POPUP) demonstrates a technique that enables the nested pop-up menu but only if one or more items on the pop-up menu are enabled. If no menu items are enabled, the nested pop-up menu is disabled. The task consists of two steps:

1. Modifying the *CMainFrame* window class
2. Implementing the command-update handler

To complete this task, you will need an SDI or MDI MFC application with a nested pop-up menu containing one or more menu items.

Step 1: Modifying the *CMainFrame* Window Class

In this step, we modify the main frame window class by adding Boolean data members for each pop-up menu item in the project and modifying the *CMainFrame* constructor. These data members (which are named *m_bSublevel1* and *m_bSublevel2* in this example) are used to track whether the pop-up menu item should be enabled (a value of TRUE) or disabled (a value of FALSE).

Add a data member for each menu item in your nested pop-up menu. After you have added these variables, initialize the new data members in the constructor of the *CMainFrame* class by adding the following code to your *CMainFrame* constructor:

```
m_bSublevel1 = FALSE;
m_bSublevel2 = FALSE;
```

> N O T E : For this update technique to work properly, you will have to keep the Boolean variables that represent each pop-up menu item up-to-date. For instance, if a pop-up menu item is disabled by some event, you should immediately update the Boolean variable related to the menu item. (See the POPUP sample project for an example.)

Step 2: Implementing the Command-Update Handler

Now you can implement the command-update handler for the first pop-up menu item. The logic used in this handler enables the pop-up menu, depending on the state of its menu items. However, before you get into implementing the actual code, I should explain a few things about pop-up menus and the ON_UPDATE_COMMAND_UI macro.

The ON_UPDATE_COMMAND_UI macro maps command-update command messages to an appropriate message handler. For the first item in the nested pop-up menu, this handler is called in two different cases. In the first case, the command-update handler is called for the pop-up menu itself. This is necessary because the pop-up menu does not have its own ID; therefore, the ID of the first menu item is used to refer to the entire pop-up menu. In the second case, the handler is called just before the pop-up menu items are to be drawn. In this case, the ID (passed into the handler function) refers to just the first menu item.

Now comes the important part. If you look at the *CCmdUI* object passed in as a parameter to the handler function, you will notice that the value of the *m_pSubMenu* data member differs, depending on which case you are dealing with. In the first case (updating the pop-up menu), the *m_pSubMenu* member variable of the *CCmdUI* object is non-NULL and points to the pop-up menu to be displayed. In the second case (updating the individual menu items of the pop-up menu), the *m_pSubMenu* member variable of the *CCmdUI* object is NULL. You can use this difference to properly enable or disable the nested pop-up menu by checking the value of the *m_pSubMenu* member variable. For instance, if there are no enabled items in the nested pop-up menu and *m_pSubMenu* is non-NULL, the pop-up menu should not be enabled. However, if one or more items are enabled and *m_pSubMenu* is non-NULL, the pop-up menu should be enabled.

The first thing you have to do is add a command-update handler for the first menu item of the nested pop-up menu. So add a handler and the ON-_UPDATE_COMMAND_UI macro now, using your favorite method. After you add the handler, modify the function by replacing the current body of the handler function with the following:

```
if (pCmdUI->m_pSubMenu != NULL)
{
    // Enable entire pop-up if Sub level 1 and Sub level 2
    // are enabled
    BOOL bEnable = m_bSublevel1 || m_bSublevel2;

    // Check to see whether we need to enable the pop-up menu.
    pCmdUI->m_pMenu->EnableMenuItem(pCmdUI->m_nIndex,
        MF_BYPOSITION | (bEnable ? MF_ENABLED :
        (MF_DISABLED | MF_GRAYED)));
    return;
}
// Otherwise, enable just the Sub level 1 command
pCmdUI->Enable(m_bSublevel1);
```

The main part of the logic is contained in the *if* statement. If *pCmdUI->m_pSub-Menu* is not equal to NULL, the program is displaying the menu, which contains the nested pop-up menu. In this case, you will have to determine whether any pop-up menu items are enabled. You can do this by setting a local variable, *bEnable*, to the result of ORing the menu item variables. The result is then used in a call to the *EnableMenuItem* function of the pop-up menu. After updating the pop-up menu item, exit the function. If the *if* test fails, which indicates that the pop-up menu items need to be updated, simply update the first item in the pop-up menu using the current value of the *m_bSublevel1* variable.

Additional Information

For additional information on the ON_UPDATE_COMMAND_UI macro and the routing of other default messages, see Technical Note 21 in the Microsoft Visual C++ online documentation.

CHAPTER SIX

ActiveX Controls and OLE

In this chapter, we take a quick peek at the world of Microsoft ActiveX controls. Over the last year, through Microsoft's commitment to Internet programming, a wealth of functionality has been exposed through the MFC library. One of the major components of the library is the ActiveX control support. Using MFC and also Microsoft Developer Studio, you can have an ActiveX control framework up and running in no time. To properly discuss all of the possibilities of ActiveX control development is far beyond the scope of this book. However, here I hope to provide you with a few interesting tasks that you can use when developing ActiveX controls. I am including four ActiveX tasks as well as one task (exposing MFC collections to a Microsoft Visual Basic application) that is extremely useful for developers who need to share collections of objects between Visual Basic applications and MFC applications.

- **Making an ActiveX control safe for scripting and initializing** Demonstrates the steps for implementing the *IObjectSafety* interface for an ActiveX control. The *IObjectSafety* interface is used by Microsoft Internet Explorer to determine whether a control is safe for scripting or initializing.

- **Loading an ActiveX control property asynchronously** Demonstrates the asynchronous loading of a bitmap using a custom property (Image-Path) of an ActiveX control.

- **Implementing a Custom Interface Using an MFC Out-of-Process Server** Demonstrates the required steps for implementing a custom interface.

- **Exposing the accelerator table of an ActiveX control to Visual Basic applications** Shows how Visual Basic containers differ from MFC containers when determining the mnemonics supported by an ActiveX control. It then shows how to detail the workaround that allows a control to return an accelerator table that works for both Visual Basic and MFC containers.

■ **Exposing MFC collections to a Visual Basic application** Shows how to implement an automation method for a document object that returns a collection of the current objects in the document. The collection consists of an enumerated array of VARIANT-type objects that can be used by Visual Basic applications.

Making an ActiveX Control Safe for Scripting and Initializing

The purpose of this task is to enable an ActiveX control to be safe for scripting and initializing when queried by its container. Being safe for scripting and initializing is needed when the control is used within Microsoft Internet Explorer versions 3 and later. Every control contained in an HTML page that is loaded by Internet Explorer is checked for support of the *IObjectSafety* interface. The process that Internet Explorer uses to query the control is shown in Figure 6-1. If the *IObjectSafety* interface is not supported, the user is warned by Internet Explorer that the control could be malicious and is asked whether the user still wants to download the control. By implementing this interface, an ActiveX control can state which of the interfaces it implements are safe for scripting, initializing, or both.

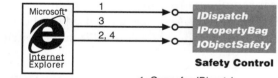

1. Query for *IDispatch*.
2. If present, ask to enable scripting safety.
3. Query for *IPropertyBag*.
4. If present, try to set initializing safety.

Figure 6-1.
Initial interaction between Internet Explorer and an ActiveX control that supports the IObjectSafety *interface.*

This task consists of four steps:

1. Adding the *IObjectSafety* interface

2. Modifying the control class

3. Implementing the *AddRef, Release,* and *QueryInterface* functions

4. Implementing the *Get/SetInterfaceSafetyOptions* functions

The name of the sample project is IMAGE, and it requires an ActiveX control project.

Step 1: Adding the *IObjectSafety* Interface

Because the *IObjectSafety* interface is already defined by the ActiveX SDK, all you have to do to use the interface in your control is include the header file that defines the interface (OBJSAFE.H), which is found in the MFC\INCLUDE directory. In addition, you have to include the header file INITGUID.H, which is used in step 2 of this task. You won't be modifying the header files; therefore, you should include them in STDAFX.H because STDAFX.H is a precompiled header file and is compiled only when its state changes. The first build that occurs after you add the header files will compile OBJSAFE.H and INITGUID.H into the precompiled header. Successive builds will then use the precompiled header instead of recompiling everything.

In the STDAFX.H header file of your project, add the following lines:

```
#include "objsafe.h"
#include "initguid.h"
```

Now that you have included the appropriate header files, you can add the *IObjectSafety* interface to the control class of the project.

Step 2: Modifying the Control Class

In this step, we declare the *IObjectSafety* interface, four protected member variables, and an enumerated type in the control class. The following list describes the purpose of each member variable and the enumerated type:

- *m_supportedScriptingOptions* Stores the safety options that are related to scripting and are supported by the control

- *m_supportedInitOptions* Stores the safety options that are related to initializing and are supported by the control

- *m_enabledScriptingOptions* Stores the safety options that are related to the scripting currently enabled by the control

- *m_enabledInitOptions* Stores the safety options that are related to the initializing currently enabled by the control

- *SafetyOptions* An enumerated type that stores the current safety options that are supported by the control

183

Follow the procedure below to modify the control class:

1. In the "public" section of your control class, add the following lines of code:

    ```
    DWORD m_supportedScriptingOptions;
    DWORD m_supportedInitOptions;
    DWORD m_enabledScriptingOptions;
    DWORD m_enabledInitOptions;
    ```

    The first two lines of code declare the variables that store the scripting and initializing options the control supports. The second two lines declare the variables that store the scripting and initializing options currently enabled for the control.

2. In the "public" section of your control class declaration, add the following lines of code:

    ```
    enum SafetyOptions
    {
        SupportedScriptingOptions =
            INTERFACESAFE_FOR_UNTRUSTED_CALLER,
        SupportedInitOptions =
            INTERFACESAFE_FOR_UNTRUSTED_DATA
    }
    ```

    This enumerated type stores the safety options for scripting and initializing that are currently supported by the control:

    ❑ INTERFACESAFE_FOR_UNTRUSTED_CALLER:
    This option, which indicates safe for scripting, declares that no matter how malicious a script is, the automation model of the control does not allow any harm to the user, either in the form of data corruption or in the form of security leaks.

    ❑ INTERFACESAFE_FOR_UNTRUSTED_DATA:
    This option, which indicates safe for initialization, declares that the control is guaranteed to do nothing bad, no matter what type of data is used to initialize the control.

3. Save your changes to this file.

4. Add the following lines of code to your control's constructor, which is found in the implementation file:

    ```
    m_supportedScriptingOptions = SupportedScriptingOptions;
    m_supportedInitOptions = 0;
    ```

```
m_enabledScriptingOptions = 0;
m_enabledInitOptions = 0;
```

The first two lines of code allow your control to be marked as safe for scripting but not safe for initializing. The second two lines of code set *m_enabledScriptingOptions* and *m_enabledInitOptions* to zero, which indicates that the control has not yet been queried for safety options.

N O T E : For the purpose of discussion, the task and sample project implement support for the INTERFACESAFE_FOR_UN-TRUSTED_CALLER safety option only. When implementing *IObjectSafety* for your control, you must decide what options to support.

5. Save your changes to this file.

After declaring the four protected member variables, declare the *IObjectSafety* interface using the following procedure:

1. Add the following lines of code to the header file of the control class in the "protected" section:

```
BEGIN_INTERFACE_PART(MySafetyObj, IObjectSafety)
INIT_INTERFACE_PART(CImageCtrl, MySafetyObj)
    STDMETHOD(GetInterfaceSafetyOptions)(REFIID, DWORD*,
        DWORD*);
    STDMETHOD(SetInterfaceSafetyOptions)(REFIID, DWORD,
        DWORD);
END_INTERFACE_PART(MySafetyObj)

DECLARE_INTERFACE_MAP()
```

N O T E : Substitute the name of your control class for *CImageCtrl* and the new name of the nested class for *MySafetyObj*.

2. Save these changes to your header file.

In this, the BEGIN_INTERFACE_PART and END_INTERFACE_PART macros define a nested class, in this case *XMySafetyObj*. The *X* in *XMySafetyObj* is used only to differentiate nested classes from global classes (which start with "C") and from interface classes (which start with "I"). A nested member of this class is now created: *m_xMySafetyObj*. Because the BEGIN_INTERFACE_PART and END_INTERFACE_PART macros automatically declare the *AddRef, Release,* and *QueryInterface* functions, you have to declare only the two functions specific to this interface: *GetInterfaceSafetyOptions* and *SetInterfaceSafetyOptions*. (For more information on the macros and other related topics, see Technical Note 38 in the Microsoft Visual C++ online documentation.)

After you declare the *IObjectSafety* interface, you have to define the globally unique identifier (GUID) of the interface and map the interface to your control. Define the GUID in the control's implementation file using the DEFINE_GUID macro. I usually add this line after the declaration of the two interfaces exposed by the control. The following code sample defines the GUID for the *IObjectSafety* interface:

```
DEFINE_GUID(IID_IObjectSafety, 0xcb5bdc81, 0x93c1, 0x11cf, 0x8f,
0x20, 0x0, 0x80, 0x5f, 0x2c, 0xd0, 0x64);
```

> **N O T E :**   Each interface and type of COM object are accessed by a universally unique identifier (UUID), also known as a GUID. A UUID is a 128-bit value used for identifying an entity uniquely within COM/OLE. Interface identifiers (IIDs) and class identifiers (CLSIDs) are two of the most important kinds of UUIDs. OLE defines an interface ID for each interface; the ID is used in manipulating the interfaces. For more information, see *IUnknown::QueryInterface* in *OLE 2 Programmer's Reference,* Volume 1 (Microsoft Press, 1995).

Remember the INITGUID.H file you included in step 1? Even though you defined the GUID for the *IObjectSafety* interface using the DEFINE_GUID macro, it still needs initializing. This is what the INITGUID.H file does for you. (Check out the Microsoft Knowledge Base article "Avoiding Error LNK2001 Unresolved External Using DEFINE_GUID": Q130869 for more information on how this is achieved.) And although you have declared the *IObjectSafety* interface as part of your control, you must still map the *IObjectSafety* interface (which you declared earlier in this step) to the nested class of your control. Do this by adding the following lines of code to your control's implementation file right after the declaration of your control's dispatch map:

```
BEGIN_INTERFACE_MAP(CImageCtrl, COleControl)
    INTERFACE_PART(CImageCtrl, IID_IObjectSafety, MySafetyObj)
END_INTERFACE_MAP()
```

Substitute the names used by your control for the control name and the nested class that implements the *IObjectSafety* interface.

Step 3: Implementing the *AddRef*, *Release*, and *QueryInterface* Functions

The three functions automatically declared when you declare the new interface (*AddRef, Release,* and *QueryInterface*) are part of an important OLE interface:

186

IUnknown. IUnknown enables clients (objects using your control) to retrieve pointers to other interfaces supported by your control and to manage the existence of the object through the *IUnknown::AddRef* and *IUnknown::Release* functions. All other COM interfaces are inherited, directly or indirectly, from *IUnknown*. Therefore, the *AddRef, Release,* and *QueryInterface* functions are the first entries in the virtual table for every interface.

Your control is derived (eventually) from *CCmdTarget*, so you can delegate the implementation of *AddRef, Release,* and *QueryInterface* to *CCmdTarget*. This is made possible by three functions in MFC: *ExternalAddRef, ExternalRelease,* and *ExternalQueryInterface*. Each function provides the standard data-driven implementation based on your object's interface map. In other words, you pass on the cost of implementation to *CCmdTarget*. The following procedure for implementing the *IUnknown* interface adds this functionality to your control class.

1. Add the following lines to the implementation file of your control class after any handler function definitions:

```
STDMETHODIMP_(ULONG) CImageCtrl::XMySafetyObj::AddRef()
{
    METHOD_MANAGE_STATE(CImageCtrl, MySafetyObj)
    ASSERT_VALID(pThis);

    return pThis->ExternalAddRef();
}
```

This defines the *AddRef* function of the *IUnknown* interface. Substitute the name of your nested class for *XMySafetyObj* and *MySafetyObj* and the name of your control class for *CImageCtrl*.

2. Add the following lines after the *AddRef* definition to the implementation file of your control class:

```
STDMETHODIMP_(ULONG) CImageCtrl::XMySafetyObj::Release()
{
    METHOD_MANAGE_STATE(CImageCtrl, MySafetyObj)
    ASSERT_VALID(pThis);

    return pThis->ExternalRelease();
}
```

This defines the *Release* function of the *IUnknown* interface. Once again, substitute the name of your nested class for *XMySafetyObj* and *MySafetyObj* and the name of your control class for *CImageCtrl*.

3. Add the following lines after the *Release* definition to the implementation file of your control class:

```
STDMETHODIMP CImageCtrl::XMySafetyObj::QueryInterface(
    REFIID iid, LPVOID FAR* ppvObj)
{
    METHOD_MANAGE_STATE(CImageCtrl, MySafetyObj)
    ASSERT_VALID(pThis);

    return pThis->ExternalQueryInterface((void *)&iid, ppvObj);
}
```

This defines the *QueryInterface* function of the *IUnknown* interface. OK, all together now: substitute the name of your nested class for *XMySafetyObj* and *MySafetyObj* and the name of your control class for *CImageCtrl*.

4. Save these changes to your implementation file.

You've now finished implementing the *IUnknown* interface. In reality, you did little more than delegate the work. But that is the point of using a class library—if your parent class can do the work, let it!

Step 4: Implementing the *Get/SetInterfaceSafetyOptions* Functions

In this step, you will implement the *GetInterfaceSafetyOptions* function, which indicates the current safety options supported by your control, and learn about the issues related to implementing the *SetInterfaceSafetyOptions* function. To correctly implement *GetInterfaceSafetyOptions*, you have to return the options that the control can support (in this case, only those safe for scripting) and the current values of *m_enabledScriptingOptions* and *m_enabledInitOptions* when the client requests the current safety options.

Returning the Current Safety Options for Your Control

The *GetInterfaceSafetyOptions* function is called when the client requests the current safety options that are supported. Add the following code to your control's *GetInterfaceSafetyOptions* function:

```
STDMETHODIMP CImageCtrl::XMySafetyObj::GetInterfaceSafetyOptions(
    REFIID riid, DWORD __RPC_FAR *pdwSupportedOptions,
    DWORD __RPC_FAR *pdwEnabledOptions)
{
    METHOD_MANAGE_STATE(CImageCtrl, MySafetyObj)
```

```
    ASSERT_VALID(pThis);

    if (!pdwSupportedOptions || !pdwEnabledOptions)
        return E_POINTER;
    if (riid == IID_IDispatch)
    {
        *pdwSupportedOptions = pThis->m_supportedScriptingOptions;
        *pdwEnabledOptions = pThis->m_enabledScriptingOptions;
        return S_OK;
    }
    else if (riid == IID_IPersistPropertyBag)
    {
        *pdwSupportedOptions = pThis->m_supportedInitOptions;
        *pdwEnabledOptions = pThis->m_enabledInitOptions;
        return S_OK;
    }
    else
    {
        *pdwSupportedOptions = *pdwEnabledOptions = 0;
        return E_FAIL;
    }
}
```

> **N O T E :** Replace *CSafeCtrl* with the name of your control class and *MySafetyObj* with the name of your nested class in the call to METHOD_MANAGE_STATE. Note that the code only checks the *IDispatch* and *IPropertyBag* interfaces, which vary depending on the type of control.

In the first section of code, the control's module-specific information is stored in the MFC global state using METHOD_MANAGE_STATE, and the *pThis* pointer is checked for validity. The interface passed in is then checked to see whether it is one that the control supports (either *IDispatch* or *IPropertyBag*). If it is, the option allowed (*m_supportedScriptingOptions* or *m_supportedInitOptions*) and the option currently enabled (*m_enabledScriptingOptions* or *m_enabledInit-Options*) are returned. If the interface passed in is not *IDispatch* or *IProperty-Bag,* E_FAIL is returned.

Setting the Current Safety Options for the Image Control

You will have to do three things when you implement the *SetInterfaceSafety-Options* function:

■ Determine what safety options the control can support: none, safe for scripting, safe for initializing, or safe for both scripting and initializing.

- Allow external clients to enable the safety options supported by the control using the *SetInterfaceSafetyOptions* function.

- Modify the actions of the control if one or more of the safety options are enabled.

Let's tackle these in order.

Determining what safety options are supported by the control   This task is difficult to discuss with authority at this time because the criteria for what makes an ActiveX control safe for scripting or for initializing are still in development. The situation is complicated by the fact that for each control there will be a unique solution for making that control safe for scripting or for initializing. However, in a discussion of this issue, John Elsbree (a Microsoft MFC developer) and I came up with a few commonsense guidelines you can use until more specific criteria are published by Microsoft's MFC group.

To be safe for scripting, a control must not do any of the following:

- Delete, modify, or add files located on the control user's system without first asking permission.

- Allocate or lock overly large amounts of system resources for its own use.

To be safe for initializing, a control must not do either of the following:

- Make use of data for initialization purposes without first verifying that the data comes from a "safe" source.

- Perform any action on the control user's system, such as deleting or adding files, without first asking permission.

Now, having said all of that, let me add one more thing: the bottom line is that you, as the control developer, are the only one who can determine whether your control can be marked as safe for scripting or initializing.

Allowing modification of safety options by external clients   After you have determined what safety options you support, if any, you must add code to the *SetInterfaceSafetyOptions* function that will enable these options when this is requested by the client. You can use the following code sample as a guideline for your implementation of *SetInterfaceSafetyOptions*. The code is taken from *CImageCtrl::SetInterfaceSafetyOptions*.

```
STDMETHODIMP CImageCtrl::XMySafetyObj::SetInterfaceSafetyOptions(
    REFIID riid, DWORD dwOptionSetMask,
    DWORD dwEnabledOptions)
{
    METHOD_MANAGE_STATE(CImageCtrl, MySafetyObj)
    ASSERT_VALID(pThis);

    if (riid == IID_IDispatch)
    {
        if ((dwOptionSetMask & pThis->m_supportedScriptingOptions)
            == dwOptionSetMask)
        {
            DWORD dwNewOptions = dwOptionSetMask & dwEnabledOptions;
            pThis->m_enabledScriptingOptions =
                (pThis->m_enabledScriptingOptions &
                ~dwOptionSetMask) | dwNewOptions;
            return S_OK;
        }
        else
            return E_FAIL;
    }
    else if (riid == IID_IPersistPropertyBag)
    {
        if ((dwOptionSetMask & pThis->m_supportedInitOptions)
            == dwOptionSetMask)
        {
            DWORD dwNewOptions = dwOptionSetMask &
                dwEnabledOptions;
            pThis->m_enabledInitOptions =
                (pThis->m_enabledInitOptions &
                ~dwOptionSetMask) | dwNewOptions;
            return S_OK;
        }
        else
            return E_FAIL;
    }
    else
        return E_FAIL;
}
```

In the first section of code, I again store the control's module-specific information in the MFC global state using METHOD_MANAGE_STATE and check the *pThis* pointer for validity. I then check the interface that has been passed in to see whether it is an interface I support (either *IDispatch* or *IPersistProperty-Bag*). If it is, I perform a little sleight-of-hand (using bitwise AND operators) to determine whether the options being changed are supported by my control (in this case, options that are safe for scripting). If the safety option is not equal to safe for scripting, I return E_FAIL, informing the client that it is unsafe for scripting. However, if the safety option is safe for scripting, I set *m_enabledScriptingOptions* to the option requested and return S_OK. If the interface passed in is not *IDispatch* or *IPersistPropertyBag*, I return E_FAIL.

Modifying control actions that could compromise safety   Now that you allow your safety options to be changed, you must ensure that any action performed by your control, such as file access, file modification, or allocation of resources, are within the guidelines of the current safety options of the control. Examine your control code, looking for any areas that are potentially unsafe. Such areas are commonly found in the handlers for your control's properties or methods and in the internal code that accesses resources outside the control's own resources, such as an external bitmap or text file. If you find a potentially unsafe area, encapsulate it with a conditional that checks the current safety options of the control. If the area in question can be executed without compromising the safety of the control, execute it. If it cannot, either disable the functionality or modify the code so that the safety of the control is maintained.

An example of this type of modification can be found in the implementation of the ImagePath property, which is a custom property of the sample project. The ImagePath property accepts a string that describes the location of the bitmap to be loaded. To be able to mark the control as safe for scripting, I accept, for example, only images found on other Web sites (that is, having an http://prefix)—well, it's a pretty weak example, but it is an example nonetheless! This is done by checking the path for the prefix "http://"; if the prefix is found, the path is valid. If the control has not been marked as safe for scripting, the check is not performed and any path is accepted. This check is done before setting the property and loading the bitmap by making a call to *CImageCtrl::ValidImagePath*.

NOTE: Because bitmaps are static images, they cannot contain viruses (yet!), and they are thus unable to do anything except be displayed. Therefore, a bitmap is safe for loading even if the control is not marked as safe for scripting or for initializing.

The following code is from the *CImageControl::ValidImagePath* function:

```
// If control is not marked as SfS, accept any path;
// else accept only paths that have the http://
// prefix
CString strPath = path;
```

```
if (!m_enabledScriptingOptions)
    return TRUE;
else
{
    int retVal = strPath.Find("http://");
    if (retVal == 0)
        return TRUE;
    else
        return FALSE;
}
```

The first section of code initializes a temporary *CString* object with the value of the path to be checked. The next section is an *if* statement that checks the status of the control's safety options. If the control has not been marked as safe for scripting, *m_enabledScriptingOptions* is equal to 0, no check is performed, and *ValidImagePath* returns TRUE. However, if the control has been marked, the string is tested for the presence of the "http://" prefix. If the prefix is found, *ValidImagePath* returns TRUE. If no prefix is found, the path is invalid and *ValidImagePath* returns FALSE.

After you have modified any unsafe areas of your control code, rebuild the project. Your control can now mark itself as safe for scripting or for initializing or both.

Loading an ActiveX Control Property Asynchronously

The purpose of this task is to asynchronously load a 16-color bitmap image (represented by the custom ImagePath property) of an ActiveX control. Asynchronous loading is designed for properties that are downloaded in a large stream, such as bitmaps and video data. Because the data can be retrieved from the source in an incremental or progressive fashion, the control works cooperatively with other controls that also might be retrieving data. The sample program, IMAGE, demonstrates this by loading a bitmap image file when the control's client sets the ImagePath property. The task consists of nine steps:

1. Adding a class derived from *CCachedDataPathProperty*

2. Adding attributes for the bitmap property

3. Implementing the *ResetData* function

4. Implementing the *OnDataAvailable* function

5. Adding data members and functions to the control class

6. Modifying the Get and Set functions for the ImagePath property

7. Modifying the *DoPropExchange* function

8. Overriding and modifying the *OnResetState* function

9. Calling *InternalSetReadyState* at the correct times

The name of the project is IMAGE. The requirement for the task is an ActiveX control project.

WARNING: If you are using variable names other than the ones I use in this task, you must modify the four functions copied in step 4.

Step 1: Adding a Class Derived from *CCachedDataPathProperty*

For an ActiveX control to implement an asynchronous property correctly, the property must be implemented with a class derived from *CCachedDataPath-Property*. This MFC class provides several functions and overrides that make implementing asynchronous properties a little easier. It even provides a *CMemFile* data member for storing the image you will download. Using your favorite method, add a class derived from *CCachedDataPathProperty* to your ActiveX control project. In the sample project, this class is named *CBitmapProperty*.

Step 2: Adding Attributes for the Bitmap Property

Because you are downloading a bitmap, you have to customize the *CBitmap-Property* class to store important information about the bitmap file. Add the following code to the "public" section of the *CBitmapProperty* class:

```
CBitmap m_Bitmap;          // Class for the bitmap
CSize m_BitmapSize;        // Size of the bitmap, in bytes
BITMAPINFO256 m_bmInfo;    // Structure derived from
                           // BITMAPINFO
enum DLState
{
    dlNone,                // Not downloading
    dlFileHeader,          // Downloading file header
    dlInfoHeader,          // Downloading BITMAPINFO
    dlColorTable,          // Downloading color table
    dlDone                 // Downloading complete
} m_dlState;               // ENUM type representing the
                           // current download state
int m_nScanLine;           // Height (in lines) of bitmap
```

In the header file *CBitmapProperty*, add the following code before the declaration of the *CBitmapProperty* class:

```
struct BITMAPINFO256 : public BITMAPINFO
{
    RGBQUAD bmiOtherColors[255];
};
```

This declares a structure, derived from BITMAPINFO, that will be used to store information about the bitmap.

Step 3: Implementing the *ResetData* Function

In some cases, the ImagePath property can be interrupted during downloading. If the property is interrupted during downloading, it should be cleared and reloaded. The *CCachedDataPathProperty* class provides a function (*ResetData*) that, when called, notifies the container that the control properties have changed and all information loaded asynchronously (in our case, the ImagePath property) is no longer useful. Override the *ResetData* function now, and replace the function body with the following code:

```
CCachedDataPathProperty::ResetData();
m_dlState = dlNone;
if (m_Bitmap.m_hObject != NULL)
    m_Bitmap.DeleteObject();

m_cache.SetLength(0);
m_cbRead = 0;
m_nScanLine = 0;
```

In this code, I call the base class's *ResetData* function, reset the download state (*m_dlState*) to 0, and delete the *m_bitmap* object if it is not equal to NULL. I then reset the cache (*m_cache*), the number of bytes read (*m_cbRead*), and the current line being read (*m_nScanLine*) back to 0. After I exit *ResetData*, the ImagePath property is ready to be reloaded.

Step 4: Implementing the *OnDataAvailable* Function

The *OnDataAvailable* function is one of the most important functions available to classes derived from *CCachedDataPathProperty*. This function is called by the framework to provide data to the client as soon as the data becomes available during asynchronous binding operations. The default implementation does nothing, so you have to override *OnDataAvailable* and then provide your own implementation. (Because *OnDataAvailable* is a large function, the following discussion about implementing it is not a comprehensive one. For more detail, see the *CBitmapProperty::OnDataAvailable* function in the sample project.) To successfully download the bitmap file, you have to do several things when you implement *OnDataAvailable*:

1. Initialize the property attributes by calling *ResetData* if this is the first time *OnDataAvailable* has been called.

2. Check to see whether any new data from the bitmap file has been downloaded. If there is no new data, exit *OnDataAvailable*. If there is new data to read, proceed.

3. Depending on the current state of the download (not started, reading file header, reading info header, reading color table), attempt to read the next section of the bitmap file.

4. If you can read the next section of the bitmap file, store the data in the cache file, initialize the appropriate attributes of the *CBitmapProperty* class with the new data, and increment the download state flag. If these operators are not successful (the current section being read was not downloaded completely), set a flag indicating the failure.

5. Check the download state flag. If the value indicates that downloading is not complete and the current section of the file has been read, return to step 3 of this list.

6. Continue until either the file read fails or the file has been downloaded completely.

7. Just before exiting *OnDataAvailable*, inform the control of the current state of the download.

NOTE: To give you an idea of why I don't just show you the actual implementation of *OnDataAvailable*, it took about 100 lines of code to implement the seven steps in this list correctly! And that's not all. The *OnDataAvailable* function makes use of three *additional* helper functions that I didn't even mention—quite a chunk of code!

Override *OnDataAvailable* now, and complete the procedure on the next page, which walks you through copying the necessary functions from the sample project into your project.

WARNING: If you have not followed the same naming conventions for member variables, classes, and functions that I've used in this task, you *must* modify the names used in the four functions that you will copy over. If you do not do this, you will be buried in a mountain of errors!

1. From your project, open the header file that contains the declaration of the *CBitmapProperty* class.

2. Add the following lines to your declaration of *CBitmapProperty*:

```
// Operations
public:
    BOOL ReadStruct(DWORD& rdwSize, void* pb, int cLen);
    int ReadArray(DWORD& rdwSize, void** pb, int cElem, int
        cMax);
```

3. Save your changes, and close the file.

4. From your project, open the implementation file of the *CBitmapProperty* class.

5. Open the BITMAPPROPERTY.CPP file from the IMAGE sample project.

6. Copy *CBitmapProperty::OnDataAvailable* from the IMAGE sample project, and paste it into the implementation file of your *CBitmapProperty* class.

7. Copy *AfxTransferFileContent* from the IMAGE sample project, and paste it into the implementation file of your *CBitmapProperty* class.

8. Copy *CBitmapProperty::ReadStruct* from the IMAGE sample project, and paste it into the implementation file of your *CBitmapProperty* class.

9. Copy *CBitmapProperty::ReadArray* from the IMAGE sample project, and paste it into the implementation file of your *CBitmapProperty* class.

10. Save your changes, and close the file.

After you complete this procedure, continue on and modify the existing ActiveX control class.

Step 5: Adding Data Members and Functions to the Control Class

Now that you have implemented the cached bitmap object, you have to modify the existing ActiveX control class to expose and manage this property. In this step, you will add a data member for *CCachedDataPathProperty*, the Get/ Set ImagePath property, and a stock event named ReadyStateChange. To add new members to the control class, follow the procedure on page 198.

1. In the header file of your control class, add a "public" data member named *m_bmProp*, of type *CBitmapProperty*.

2. Add the ReadyStateChange stock event to your control class using ClassWizard.

3. Add a custom property using the following parameters:

   ❏ External name: ImagePath

   ❏ Type: BSTR

   ❏ Implementation: Get/Set methods

   ❏ Get function: default value

   ❏ Set function: default value

   ❏ Parameter list: *lpszNewValue*, type LPCTSTR

4. Save all changes.

Step 6: Modifying the Get and Set Functions for the ImagePath Property

Currently the Get/Set functions of the ImagePath property do nothing. You have to modify the *GetImagePath* function to return the current value of Image-Path and modify the *SetImagePath* function to update the ImagePath property with the new path given by the control's client. In the *GetImagePath* function of your control, replace all code with the following:

```
return m_bmProp.GetPath().AllocSysString();
```

In the *SetImagePath* function of your control, replace all code with the following:

```
Load(lpszNewValue, m_bmProp);
Invalidate(FALSE);
SetModifiedFlag();
```

The first thing I do is call the *Load* function, which initiates the asynchronous transfer. I invalidate the control to force a repaint and then set the control's modified flag to indicate that the property value has changed.

Step 7: Modifying the *DoPropExchange* Function

Because the ImagePath property is asynchronous and is implemented with *CCachedDataPathProperty*, you have to modify the *DoPropExchange* function of the control. Add the following lines to your control's *DoPropExchange* function after the call to the base class *DoPropExchange* function:

```
if (pPX->IsLoading())
    InternalSetReadyState(READYSTATE_LOADING);
PX_DataPath(pPX, _T("ImagePath"), m_bmProp);
```

This code accomplishes two things. When the ImagePath property begins to load, the control's internal state is changed automatically with a call to *Internal-SetReadyState*. This updates the clients of the control with respect to the current state. (This is discussed in detail in step 9.) Also, the ImagePath property is correctly serialized with a call to *PX_DataPath*.

Step 8: Overriding and Modifying the *OnResetState* Function

In step 3, I discussed the reason behind overriding the *ResetData* function for the asynchronous bitmap property. Similar reasoning also applies to the internal state of your control. Overriding the *OnResetState* function allows you to be notified when the properties of the control should be set to their default values. It turns out to be a simple override because all you have to do is let the bitmap object know that it needs to reset its data and then make a call the base class function. Override this function in your control class, and replace the existing code with the following code:

```
m_bmProp.ResetData();
COleControl::OnResetState();  // Resets defaults found in
                             // DoPropExchange
```

Step 9: Calling *InternalSetReadyState* at the Correct Times

The last thing you have to do is update the state of the control with regard to the asynchronous ImagePath property. This allows the client (or clients) of the control to be notified when the state of the control changes. When a control is first loaded, it is not ready for interaction automatically—perhaps a critical property has to be loaded, or some calculations have to be performed. In any case, after the control has accomplished the minimal requirements to become interactive (as determined by the control developer), it must notify the client by making a call to *InternalSetReadyState*. Depending on what parameter is passed to this function, the client can determine to some degree the current state of the control. The parameter of the *InternalSetReadyState* function can have the following values:

■ READYSTATE_UNINITIALIZED
    This is the default initialization state.

■ READYSTATE_LOADING
    The control is loading its properties.

199

- READYSTATE_LOADED

  The control has been initialized.

- READYSTATE_INTERACTIVE

  The control has enough data to be interactive, but not all asynchronous properties have been loaded.

- READYSTATE_COMPLETE

  The control has all of its data.

At this point, examine your control and determine the points at which the control changes state (the five values above). Keep in mind that your control does not need to inform the client (or clients) of all five state changes. However, from the client's point of view, the point at which the control first becomes interactive (able to communicate and to accept limited commands from the client) is the most important state change. You must inform the client when this change occurs. Figure 6-2 shows how the ImagePath property is loaded and the points at which the sample control changes state.

After you have determined the points at which the state changes, add calls to *InternalSetReadyState* using the appropriate parameter for each call. Be sure that you make at least one call to the *InternalSetReadyState* function at some point in your project using READYSTATE_INTERACTIVE for the value.

After adding code for each state change in the control, save your changes and rebuild the project. Your control now exposes an asynchronous property named ImagePath. When the user changes the value of this property by supplying a path to the image, the file is asynchronously retrieved.

Additional Information

Because rendering the downloaded image was not related to the task at hand, I have not discussed it. For the code that does this, check out the *CImageCtrl::-OnDraw* function, which is found in the implementation file of the *CBitmap-Property* class. In this function, if the ImagePath property is uninitialized, the client area of the control is painted black. When the control receives the proper path, the bitmap is rendered in the client area of the control. The Image control also exposes a custom property named AutoSize. If this property is enabled, the size of the control is set automatically to the size of the bitmap. If the property is disabled, the control does not resize the new image when it is loaded.

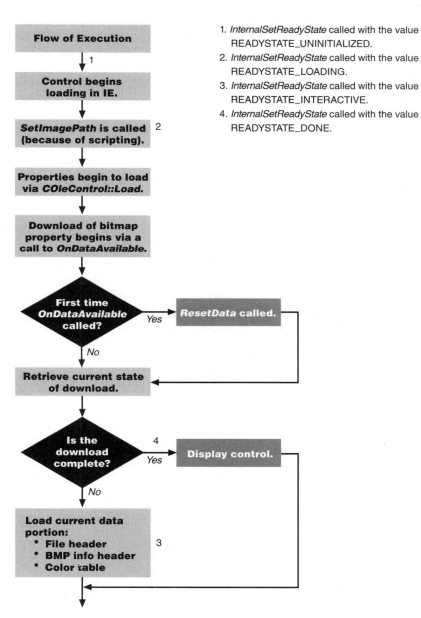

1. *InternalSetReadyState* called with the value READYSTATE_UNINITIALIZED.
2. *InternalSetReadyState* called with the value READYSTATE_LOADING.
3. *InternalSetReadyState* called with the value READYSTATE_INTERACTIVE.
4. *InternalSetReadyState* called with the value READYSTATE_DONE.

Figure 6-2.
Process for loading the ImagePath property.

Implementing a Custom Interface Using an MFC Out-of-Process Server

The purpose of this task is to implement a custom interface, derived from *IUnknown*, from a *CCmdTarget*-derived class. Unlike COM interfaces, custom interfaces are not supported by the system. The main reason for developing one is to expose other interfaces that are specific to a user-defined object or data type. Because a custom interface is implemented from an out-of-process server (which means that it is a stand-alone executable), it also makes use of a marshaling DLL. This DLL is responsible for routing information from the external client to the custom interface of the *CCmdTarget*-derived object, which is found in the out-of-process server.

The MYPT sample used in this task contains a creatable OLE Automation object (*CMyPointObj*) that wraps a *CPoint*-type class. In the first part of this task, the interface exposes three methods that allow an external client to get and set the current value of a point object and to perform a translation on that point. In the second part of this task, a marshaling DLL (MYPTDLL) is created to act as a proxy between the *CMyPointObj* object and the external client. The task consists of nine steps:

1. Declaring the custom interface
2. Generating the GUID for the custom interface
3. Adding include files to the project
4. Adding a *CCmdTarget*-derived class to the project
5. Modifying the new *CCmdTarget*-derived class
6. Implementing the *IUnknown* portion of the custom interface
7. Implementing the *IMyPoint* portion of the custom interface
8. Creating the marshaling DLL
9. Using the custom interface and the marshaling DLL

To complete this task, you will need an MFC application.

Step 1: Declaring the Custom Interface

Declaring a custom MFC interface is similar to declaring a custom C++ class. MFC provides three macros that make the declaration fairly straightforward and painless:

■ **DECLARE_INTERFACE_** Begins the declaration of a custom interface. Use this macro to declare a name for your custom interface and the base interface from which you are deriving it (for example, *IUnknown* or *IDispatch*).

■ **STDMETHOD** Declares an interface function whose return is of type HRESULT (the standard return type for OLE-related functions). Use this macro to declare interface methods that will return an HRESULT, such as NOERROR.

■ **STDMETHOD_** Declares an interface function whose return is not of type HRESULT. Use this macro to declare interface methods that return a type other than HRESULT, such as *long*.

It's good practice to declare the interface in a separate header file. This makes it easy to include the interface in the project wherever it's needed. Add the following code to a new text file, and save it in your project's directory as IMYPT.H:

```
#ifndef _IMYPT_H
#define _IMYPT_H

#undef INTERFACE
#define INTERFACE    IMyPoint

DECLARE_INTERFACE_(IMyPoint, IUnknown)
{
    //** IUnknown methods **
    STDMETHOD(QueryInterface) (THIS_ REFIID riid,
        LPVOID FAR* ppvObj) PURE;
    STDMETHOD_(ULONG, AddRef) (THIS) PURE;
    STDMETHOD_(ULONG, Release) (THIS) PURE;

    //** IMyPoint methods **
    STDMETHOD(GetValues) (long * xVal, long * yVal) PURE;
    STDMETHOD(SetValues) (long xVal, long yVal) PURE;
    STDMETHOD(TranslatePoint) (long translationVal) PURE;

};
typedef IMyPoint FAR *LPMyPoint;

#endif
```

The first section of this code redefines INTERFACE as equal to *IMyPoint*. This redefinition ensures that the declaration of the interface structure is proper for both C and C++. In C source files, this redefinition allows forward references (as a substitute for the implicit *this* pointer) of the class name (in this case, *IMyPoint*). However, in C++ source files this redefinition is not needed because the implicit *this* pointer already exists in the C++ language. Therefore, the whole redefinition becomes a null operation. If you really want to dig into this stuff, check out OBJBASE.H, which is located in the \DEVSTUDIO\VC\INCLUDE directory.

In the next section of code, the DECLARE_INTERFACE_ macro is used to begin a new interface named *IMyPoint*, which is derived from the *IUnknown* interface. After the DECLARE_INTERFACE_ macro, I declare the *IUnknown* portion of the custom interface. The *IUnknown* interface functions are required for every OLE interface.

In the final section of code, I declare the three *IMyPoint* functions: *GetValues*, *SetValues*, and *TranslatePoint* (Figure 6-3). Finally, I close the declaration of the custom interface and define a pointer of type *far* for the interface. This defines a convenient method of access for the application. In step 5 of this task, you will use IMYPT.H to implement the *IMyPoint* interface for your new automation class, which is added in step 4.

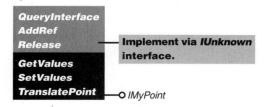

Figure 6-3.
The IMyPoint *custom interface.*

Step 2: Generating the GUID for the Custom Interface

In addition to the interface declaration performed in step 1, one more item is required to complete the interface declaration—the interface's GUID. This ID is used by external clients to request a specific interface. You can think of it as a kind of kind of baggage claim ticket. You don't get your bag unless you have the ticket. Because there are many custom interfaces floating around, we need a method of generating GUIDs that avoids an ID conflict. It just so happens that Microsoft's Win32 SDK has a cool little application, GUIDGEN.EXE, that does exactly this. The program guarantees a unique identifier in the format that is needed. In your case, you need a GUID for use in a call to DEFINE_GUID.

Using GUIDGEN, create a unique identifier for the *IMyPoint* interface now. Copy the DEFINE_GUID option of the new GUID, and paste it to the end of the IMYPT.H file before #endif. The result should look like this:

```
// {8F8FEFB0-23A7-11d0-B694-00AA00574A50}
DEFINE_GUID(IID_IMyPoint,
0x8f8fefb0, 0x23a7, 0x11d0, 0xb6, 0x94, 0x0, 0xaa, 0x0, 0x57, 0x4a,
    0x50);

typedef IMyPoint FAR *LPMyPoint;

#endif
```

Unless GUIDGEN is broken, your GUID should differ from the GUID above (hence its name, globally unique identifier).

Step 3: Adding Include Files to the Project

In this step, you'll be adding two include files to the project. These files (AFX-OLE.H and INITGUID.H) add OLE support to the project and initialize the GUID used by the custom interface. You won't be modifying these files at all, so include them in the STDAFX.H file, which is the source for the precompiled header file.

Add the following two lines to the end of your project's STDAFX.H file:

```
#include <afxole.h>
#include <initguid.h>
```

The declaration of the custom interface is now complete.

N O T E : If the INITGUID.H file is not included, you will get a LNK2001 error, which can cause quite a bit of frustration. (I speak from experience!) The text for the LNK2001 error is not very helpful until you figure out that the DEFINE_GUID macro is generating an external reference to the GUID of the *IMyPoint* interface. This is a result of not including the INITGUID.H include file, which actually initializes the GUID. For a more detailed explanation of this behavior, check out the Knowledge Base article "Avoiding Error LNK2001 Unresolved External Using DEFINE_GUID": Q130869.

Step 4: Adding a *CCmdTarget*-Derived Class to the Project

Now that you have declared the custom interface, you need something from which to hang the interface. A *CCmdTarget*-derived class will do nicely. There is not a lot to say about this step; just add a new class with the following properties to your project using ClassWizard:

- Name: *CMyPointObj*

- Base class: *CCmdTarget*

- OLE Automation: creatable by type ID

Step 5: Modifying the New *CCmdTarget*-Derived Class

Before you modify the *CMyPointObj* class, let me briefly hit the high points of how MFC implements additional interfaces on a *CCmdTarget*-derived object. Through the magic of several macros, which you will be using later, a nested class can be defined for any class derived from *CCmdTarget*. This nested class, which is a friend of the outer class, represents the custom interface and handles all requests from external clients. You can access the nested class from the outer class through a member variable (*m_xMyPointObj*), which also is automatically declared by the interface macros. Figure 6-4 illustrates this class.

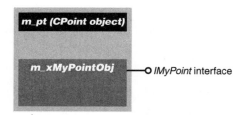

Figure 6-4.
The MyPointObj *class structure.*

In this step, you will include the IMYPT.H file, a data member, and a nested class that implements the *IMyPoint* interface within the class *CMyPointObj*. Follow the procedure below to add the *IMyPoint* interface.

1. Add the following line to the top of the header file for the *CMyPointObj* class:

```
#include "IMyPt.h"
```

This allows you to use the interface in the *CMyPointObj* class.

2. Add a "public" data member to the declaration of the *CMyPointObj* class:

```
CPoint m_pt;
```

This variable stores the current *x* and *y* values of the point object.

3. Modify the constructor for the *CMyPointObj* class by initializing *m_pt* to (0, 0):

```
CMyPointObj::CMyPointObj()
    :m_pt(0, 0)
```

4. Add the custom *IMyPoint* interface to the *CMyPointObj* class:

```
// IMyPoint interface
BEGIN_INTERFACE_PART(MyPointObj, IMyPoint)
    STDMETHOD(GetValues) (long*, long*);
    STDMETHOD(SetValues) (long, long);
    STDMETHOD(TranslatePoint) (long);
END_INTERFACE_PART(MyPointObj)
```

This code defines an embedded class that implements the custom *IMyPoint* interface for your automation object. (For details on what this chunk of code does, see "Making an ActiveX Control Safe for Scripting and Initializing" on page 182 of this chapter.)

5. Save your changes to this file.

At this point, you have completed the declaration of the custom interface. Now you have to implement the *IUnknown* (step 6) and *IMyPoint* (step 7) functions of the custom interface.

Step 6: Implementing the *IUnknown* Portion of the Custom Interface

One of the more involved steps in this type of task is the implementation of the custom interface functions. One of the main benefits of using predefined COM interfaces is that you are customizing only those functions whose default behavior is not adequate for your needs. Unfortunately, you will also be responsible for developing the default behavior of each of these customized functions. One of the benefits of being the author is that I can make the examples as hard or as easy as I deem necessary; so for this task, the interface code is going to be pretty simple because the point is to implement a custom interface—not design the ultimate custom interface.

In this step, you have to declare an additional interface map for the *CMyPointObj* class and implement the *IUnknown* functions of the *IMyPoint* interface. (The actual *IMyPoint* functions—*GetValues*, *SetValues*, and *Translate-Point*—are implemented in step 7.) But before you tear off to implement the *IUnknown* interface functions, define the interface for the *CMyPointObj* class. Add the following lines to the implementation file of *CMyPointObj* inside the definition of the interface map for the new *CMyPointObj*:

```
INTERFACE_PART(CMyPointObj, IID_IMyPoint, MyPointObj)
```

This code hooks the interface you declared in step 5 to the actual *CMyPointObj* class, which means that all calls to this interface will be handled by the nested *XMyPointObj* object.

> **N O T E :** If you don't hook the interface to the automation class, the result can be quite amusing, albeit frustrating at first. While I was coding the sample for a similar task, I declared and implemented the interface but forgot to hook it to the object. The result: a successful build and several minutes of head-scratching, trying to figure out why the heck my interface functions weren't getting called.

When you are implementing the *IUnknown* interface, you can reap one of the many benefits of MFC. Because the *CMyPointObj* class is derived (eventually) from *CCmdTarget*, you can delegate the implementation of the *AddRef*, *Release*, and *QueryInterface* functions to *CCmdTarget*. This is easily accomplished by using three MFC functions: *ExternalAddRef*, *ExternalRelease*, and *External-QueryInterface*. Each of these functions provides the standard data-driven implementation based on your object's interface map. In other words, you pass on the cost of implementation to *CCmdTarget*. The following procedure for implementing the *IUnknown* interface functions adds this support to the *CMyPointObj* class.

1. Add the following lines to the implementation file of the *CMyPointObj* class after any handler function definitions:

```
STDMETHODIMP_(ULONG) CMyPointObj::XMyPointObj::AddRef()
{
    METHOD_PROLOGUE(CMyPointObj, MyPointObj)
    ASSERT_VALID(pThis);

    return pThis->ExternalAddRef();
}
```

2. Add the following lines after the *AddRef* definition:

```
STDMETHODIMP_(ULONG) CMyPointObj::XMyPointObj::Release()
{
    METHOD_PROLOGUE(CMyPointObj, MyPointObj)
    ASSERT_VALID(pThis);

    return pThis->ExternalRelease();
}
```

3. Add the following lines to the implementation file of your control class after the *Release* definition:

```
STDMETHODIMP CMyPointObj::XMyPointObj::QueryInterface(REFIID
    iid, LPVOID FAR* ppvObj)
{
    METHOD_PROLOGUE(CMyPointObj, MyPointObj)
    ASSERT_VALID(pThis);

    return pThis->ExternalQueryInterface((void *)&iid, ppvObj);
}
```

4. Save your changes.

Now you have implemented the *IUnknown* interface functions, and once again, the parent class did the work. In the next step, you will implement the remaining functions, which are the custom part of the *IMyPoint* interface.

Step 7: Implementing the *IMyPoint* Portion of the Custom Interface

In step 6, you handed off the majority of work to predefined functions of the *CCmdTarget* class. Unfortunately, implementing the custom functions of the *IMyPoint* interface requires a little more effort. The following procedure for implementing the *IMyPoint* interface functions adds the definitions and function bodies for all three of its functions.

1. Add the following code to the implementation file of the *CMyPointObj* class:

```
STDMETHODIMP CMyPointObj::XMyPointObj::GetValues(long* pXVal,
    long* pYVal)
{
    METHOD_PROLOGUE(CMyPointObj, MyPointObj)
    ASSERT_VALID(pThis);
```

(continued)

```
    *pXVal = pThis->m_pt.x;
    *pYVal = pThis->m_pt.y;

    return NOERROR;
}
```

I retrieve a valid *this* pointer to the outer class so that I can access the *m_pt* member. Then I initialize the pointers passed in with their respective values from *m_pt*. Finally, I exit the function and return NO-ERROR.

2. Add the following code to the implementation file of the *CMyPoint-Obj* class after the *GetValues* function:

```
STDMETHODIMP CMyPointObj::XMyPointObj::SetValues(long xVal,
    long yVal)
{
    METHOD_PROLOGUE(CMyPointObj, MyPointObj)
    ASSERT_VALID(pThis);

    pThis->m_pt.x = xVal;
    pThis->m_pt.y = yVal;

    return NOERROR;
}
```

This code is just the reverse of the *GetValues* function. I accept two values from the client and set the *m_pt* member to these values.

3. Add the following code to the implementation file of the *CMyPoint-Obj* class after the *SetValues* function:

```
STDMETHODIMP CMyPointObj::XMyPointObj::TranslatePoint(long
    value)
{
    METHOD_PROLOGUE(CMyPointObj, MyPointObj)
    ASSERT_VALID(pThis);

    pThis->m_pt.x += value;
    pThis->m_pt.y += value;

    return NOERROR;
}
```

This code performs a mathematical translation of the *m_pt* member by adding the value passed in to both the *x* and *y* values of *m_pt*.

4. Save your changes.

You now have completed the implementation of the custom interface. The remaining portion of the task involves the implementation of the marshaling DLL.

Step 8: Creating the Marshaling DLL

In the introduction to this task, I briefly mentioned a marshaling DLL. It is pertinent at this point to explain why you should care about marshaling DLLs. So let's assume that you have two applications: an out-of-process server (the server for *CMyPointObj*) and an external client that wants an instance of *CMyPointObj*. Because the server is an out-of-process server, its process space is different than the process space of the external client. This is a problem if the client and the server want to interact because the addresses of the data members and functions in each application are different. It's impossible for either the server or the client to access the data members or functions of the other. The situation has be fixed so that the code for the interaction between them uses the proper offsets with respect to data member and function addresses. (Boy, talk about an obvious lead-in!)

Thankfully, there is a technique called *marshaling* that does exactly the type of address fixup you require. Unfortunately, the marshaling DLL responsible for the interaction between the server and the client is not strictly an MFC thing, and the process for building a marshaling DLL is pretty involved. Let's take a look at what it takes to create one. The process can be divided into four parts:

1. Creating the IDL file

2. Compiling the IDL file

3. Building the marshaling DLL project

4. Creating the REG file and registering the marshaling DLL

Because this book is about MFC tasks, not marshaling DLLs, I'll discuss only parts 1, 2, and 4 because they are closely related to the MFC side of things. I'll leave the discussion of part 3 for Kraig Brockschmidt's *Inside OLE 2,* Second Edition (Microsoft Press, 1995).

> N O T E : Because you will be building a DLL project that is separate from the automation object's project, it's a good idea to make a directory for the DLL source code. The source code for the sample's marshaling DLL is in the MYPTDLL directory.

Creating the IDL File

We begin the process of creating a marshaling DLL by creating an Interface Description Language (IDL) file for the custom interface, in this case *IMy-Point*. The IDL file describes the interface by defining the interface's GUID and the number of methods the interface exposes. If you have worked with Object Description Language (ODL) files and type libraries, you will recognize much of the syntax used in the IDL file. The two languages are very similar. The IDL file needs a section for each custom interface that is exposed by the server. It also needs a section that describes the incoming and outgoing parameters for each function of each custom interface. For example, if the server implements two custom interfaces, *IMyInterfaceOne* and *IMyInterfaceTwo*, there will be four sections in the IDL: two sections for the interface IDs and two for the custom interface functions. For this task, you will create a simple IDL file that contains information for the *IMyPoint* interface. The procedure is described below.

1. In the directory of your marshaling DLL, create a new text file.

2. Describe the ID of the custom interface:

```
[
    object,
    uuid(8F8FEFB0-23A7-11d0-B694-00AA00574A50),
    pointer_default(unique)
]
```

Note that the UUID you just added matches the ID of the *IMyPoint* custom interface.

3. After the object section, describe the attributes of the *IMyPoint* interface:

```
interface IMyPoint: IUnknown
{
    import "unknwn.idl";

    HRESULT GetValues([out, ref] long* xVal,
        [out, ref] long* yVal);
    HRESULT SetValues([in] long xVal, [in] long yVal);

    HRESULT TranslatePoint([in] long translationVal);
}
```

4. Save the new text file as MYPOINT.IDL.

Compiling the IDL File

Just as you would for ODL files, you have to compile a new IDL file to generate the source code used by the marshaling DLL. Visual C++ provides a program that uses IDL files to create some of the source files for the marshaling project—MIDL.EXE. You provide the remaining files for the DLL project.

To compile the IDL file, execute the following command (in the directory of the IDL file) from a command prompt:

```
midl MyPoint.idl
```

During the compilation, four files are generated:

- **DLLDATA.C** Source file that contains additional information on the marshaling DLL

- **MYPOINT.H** Header file that defines the custom interface for both C and Visual C++ compilers

- **MYPOINT_I.C** Source file that contains additional interface information

- **MYPOINT_P.C** Source file that contains code for the interface proxy and stubs

In addition to the newly generated files, you will need two files, RCSUPPORT.H and RCSUPPORT.CPP, for building the DLL. They can be found in the \CHAP6\TASKDIR2\MYPTDLL directory on the companion CD-ROM. These two files automatically cause the remote procedure call (RPC) libraries to be linked with your DLL. If they aren't included in the project, you will get several errors relating to unresolved externals. These files, and others referenced in Brockschmidt's book, will be used to create the marshaling DLL.

Building the Marshaling DLL Project

To build the DLL, you will have to do a little extracurricular reading. The two best sources I have found are these:

- *Inside OLE 2,* by Kraig Brockschmidt (Chapter 6), which is the best reference for building the actual marshaling DLL—very good stuff.

- *Object Linking and Embedding (OLE) Programmer's Reference* (Microsoft Press, 1992), "OLE Custom Interfaces Appendix," which is a good reference for the Win32 API side of things when marshaling. Be fore-warned: the discussion is quite dense and not MFC-related in any way.

There are also some technical notes in the Visual C++ online documentation and a reference section in the Windows NT 3.5 SDK that might be helpful:

- MFC Technical Note 11: "Using MFC as Part of a DLL"

- MFC Technical Note 33: "DLL Version of MFC"

- MFC Technical Note 38: "MFC/OLE IUnknown Implementation"

- MFC Technical Note 39: "MFC/OLE Automation Implementation"

- Windows NT 3.5 SDK, RPC Reference

After you have successfully built the DLL, proceed on to the next step to create the REG file and register the marshaling DLL.

Creating the REG File for the Marshaling DLL

Now it's time to create the REG file for the marshaling DLL. The purpose of the REG file is to register the marshaling DLL with the system registry. This ensures that the system will be able to find and invoke the DLL whenever an external client attempts to create an instance of the *CMyPointObj* object. The REG file describes the *IMyPoint* custom interface (the ID of the interface, the class ID of the proxy stub, and the number of functions—including the *IUnknown* functions—implemented by the interface) and the marshaling DLL (the interface it implements and the location of the DLL). To create the REG file, follow this procedure:

1. In your marshaling DLL directory, create a new text file.

2. Provide registry key values for different attributes of the interface using the GUID generated for your custom *IMyPoint* interface:

```
REGEDIT
HKEY_CLASSES_ROOT\Interface\{8F8FEFB0-23A7-11d0-B694-
    00AA00574A50} = IMyPoint
HKEY_CLASSES_ROOT\Interface\{8F8FEFB0-23A7-11d0-B694-
    00AA00574A50}\ProxyStubClsid32 = {8F8FEFB0-23A7-11d0-
    B694-00AA00574A50}
HKEY_CLASSES_ROOT\Interface\{8F8FEFB0-23A7-11d0-B694-
    00AA00574A50}\NumMethods = 6
```

3. Immediately after the interface attributes section, provide registry key values for the marshaling DLL using the GUID generated for your custom *IMyPoint* interface:

```
HKEY_CLASSES_ROOT\CLSID\{8F8FEFB0-23A7-11d0-B694-00AA00574A50} =
    IMyPoint Proxy/Stub Factory
HKEY_CLASSES_ROOT\CLSID\{8F8FEFB0-23A7-11d0-B694-
    00AA00574A50}\InprocServer32  = d:\projects\MarshTst\Debug\
    MarshTst.dll
```

Please note that your DLL path and GUID will differ from the above examples.

4. Save the file as MYPTDLL.REG.

After you have successfully built the DLL, register it by executing the MYPTDLL.REG file.

Step 9: Using the Custom Interface and the Marshaling DLL

You have now created a stand-alone server for the *CMyPointObj* object that implements a custom interface *IMyPoint*. This server (MYPT.EXE) and the custom interface are dependent on the marshaling DLL (MYPTDLL) that you have built. (See Figure 6-5.) When you distribute the custom interface, you have to provide three items: the stand-alone server, the marshaling DLL, and the REG file for the marshaling DLL. Your customer will register the marshaling DLL by double-clicking the REG file and then will use an external client (which he or she probably developed) to create and manipulate an instance of the *CMyPointObj* object, or whatever object you end up developing.

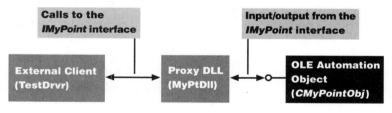

Figure 6-5.
Client/Proxy/Custom Interface interaction.

For the purposes of this demonstration, I have created an external client—a dialog box–based application named TESTDRVR.EXE (Figure 6-6 on the following page)—that you can use to test the *IMyPoint* interface.

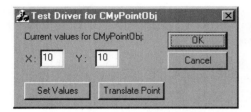

Figure 6-6.
The TestDrvr application.

The current values of the *CMyPointObj* object are displayed in the edit fields and can be changed by entering new values and clicking Set Values. In addition, you can invoke the *TranslatePoint* function using a predefined value by clicking Translate Point. The *x* and *y* edit fields are updated automatically with the new function value.

Additional Information

For more information on implementing a COM interface, check out "Making an ActiveX Control Safe for Scripting and Initializing" on page 2 of this chapter, which describes how to implement a COM interface (that is, an interface supported by the operating system).

Exposing the Accelerator Table of an ActiveX Control to Visual Basic Applications

Visual Basic and MFC have different requirements for the entries in their accelerator tables. The purpose of this task is to demonstrate how you can create an accelerator table that allows both MFC control containers and Visual Basic control containers to understand the accelerator table format. Accommodating the different requirements of MFC and Visual Basic accelerator table entries means a departure from the standard method of handling mnemonic keys. In this task, I demonstrate a method for accommodating these requirements through customizing the *OnGetControlInfo, PreTranslateMessage,* and *OnMnemonic* functions of the ActiveX control class and for handling the "m" mnemonic key in both MFC and Visual Basic control containers. The task consists of three steps:

1. Overriding *OnGetControlInfo, PreTranslateMessage,* and *OnMnemonic* for the control

2. Modifying the *OnGetControlInfo* function

3. Modifying the PreTranslateMessage and OnMnemonic functions

The name of the sample project is ACCEL, and you will need these items:

- An MFC application that implements an ActiveX control

- One or more mnemonics supported by the control

Background

An ActiveX control overrides the virtual *COleControl::OnGetControlInfo* function to allow the control's container to get a description of the mnemonic key commands for the control. When it is called, the *OnGetControlInfo* function returns, among other things, an initialized structure of type CONTROL-INFO. This structure contains a handle to an accelerator table that is used by the container to check for mnemonic keys handled by the control. The accelerator table consists of accelerator keys, each of which is defined by the AC-CEL structure. The ACCEL structure contains the following members: *fVirt, key,* and *cmd.* One of the differences between Visual Basic containers and MFC containers is the contents of these ACCEL data members as shown in the following table.

Requirements for MFC Containers	Requirements for Visual Basic Containers
The *fVirt* member must be FALT or 0.	The *fVirt* member must be a combination of (FVIRTKEY l FALT) or (FVIRTKEY l FALT l FSHIFT).
The *key* member must be lowercase.	The *key* member must be uppercase.
The *cmd* member is ignored.	The *cmd* member must not be equal to 0.

N O T E : For more information on the ACCEL structure, see the Visual C++ online documentation.

MFC and Visual Basic ActiveX control containers also differ in the way they handle mnemonic processing when a control is UI active. When handling

217

keyboard input, MFC containers check first to see whether an ActiveX control has the focus. If it has the focus, the framework calls the control's *PreTranslateMessage* function. For an ActiveX control's mnemonics to function correctly when it is UI active, it must override the *PreTranslateMessage* function and check for special key combinations that the control supports.

Step 1: Overriding the *OnGetControlInfo, PreTranslateMessage,* and *OnMnemonic* Functions for the Control

The first step in providing an accelerator table for Visual Basic and MFC containers is to override the *PreTranslateMessage, OnMnemonic,* and *OnControlInfo* functions in your ActiveX control. Override these functions now using Class-Wizard or by opening the control's implementation file and using the Wizard bar at the top of the edit window. After you override these functions, you will add code to each function that correctly sets up the accelerator table and handles mnemonic key events.

Step 2: Modifying the *OnGetControlInfo* Function

As I've already mentioned, the control's *OnGetControlInfo* function is called by the container to retrieve a description of the control's mnemonic keys. This is where you must initialize the accelerator table entries requested by the container. The following procedure for implementing *OnGetControlInfo* adds the necessary code to the body of the *OnGetControlInfo* function.

Add the following code to the control's implementation file right after the opening brace of the *OnGetControlInfo* function:

```
HACCEL hAccel = NULL;
TCHAR ch = 'm';
ACCEL accKey[4];

accKey[0].fVirt = FVIRTKEY | FALT;
accKey[1].fVirt = FVIRTKEY | FALT | FSHIFT;
accKey[0].key = accKey[1].key = LOBYTE(VkKeyScan(ch));
accKey[0].cmd = accKey[1].cmd = 1;

accKey[2].fVirt = FALT;
accKey[3].fVirt = 0;
accKey[2].key = accKey[3].key = ch;
accKey[2].cmd = accKey[3].cmd = 1;

hAccel = CreateAcceleratorTable(accKey, 4);
if (hAccel != NULL)
{
```

```
    // Fill in the CONTROLINFO structure passed in
    pControlInfo-> hAccel = hAccel;
    pControlInfo-> cAccel = 4;
    pControlInfo-> dwFlags = 0;
}
else
    COleControl::OnGetControlInfo(pControlInfo);
```

The first three lines of code declare an accelerator table handle, a TCHAR (for the mnemonic key value), and an array of four ACCEL structures. For the purpose of this demonstration, I have hardcoded an "m" as the mnemonic key of the control. Lines 4–7 of the code initialize the first two entries in the accelerator table for use by Visual Basic control containers. Lines 8–11 of the code initialize the last two entries in the accelerator table for use by MFC control containers. The remaining code creates the accelerator table and, if the creation of the table is successful, fills in the CONTROLINFO structure that was passed in. If the accelerator table is not created, the base class implementation is called instead.

Step 3: Modifying the *PreTranslateMessage* and *OnMnemonic* Functions

The final step in this task ensures that the mnemonics of an ActiveX control function properly when the control is UI active. Use the following procedure to modify these functions:

1. Modify the *PreTranslateMessage* function by replacing the body of the function with the following code:

```
if (pMsg->message == WM_SYSKEYDOWN)
{
    if ((pMsg->wParam == 'm') || (pMsg->wParam == 'M'))
    {
        // Do mnemonic key processing here
        return TRUE;
    }
}
return COleControl::PreTranslateMessage(pMsg);
```

The code first checks for the Alt-M (or Alt-m) key combination, which indicates that a mnemonic is being accessed. If the test is successful, any processing of the mnemonic is done. This is where you, the developer, take over. The function then returns TRUE, indicating that the key was handled. If the test was not successful, pass the call on to the base class.

2. Now modify the *OnMnemonic* function by replacing the body of the function with the following code:

```
if (pMsg->message == WM_SYSKEYDOWN ||
    (pMsg->message == WM_SYSKEYDOWN))
{
    if ((pMsg->wParam == 'm') || (pMsg->wParam == 'M'))
    {
        // Do mnemonic key processing here
        return;
    }
}
COleControl::OnMnemonic(pMsg);
```

This code is nearly the same as the *PreTranslateMessage* code that you added except that if the test fails, the *OnMnemonic* function of the base class is called (because, obviously, you are in the override of the *OnMnemonic* function).

After you have saved your changes and recompiled, your control will handle the "m" mnemonic key correctly in both Visual Basic and MFC control containers.

Exposing MFC Collections to a Visual Basic Application

The purpose of this task is to enable Visual Basic applications to retrieve a collection (an array of data objects, such as numeric data or strings) from an MFC document object that supports OLE Automation. When you are sharing data between Visual Basic and MFC applications, the major problem is finding a data type that is understood by both types of applications.

In this task, I will demonstrate how to add an OLE Automation method to a document object, which will allow external clients (other applications) to retrieve a collection from the MFC document object. The collection, which is implemented by *CMyCollection*, then creates an enumerated array of *CString* objects. The *IDispatch* interface of the collection is passed back to the client, which allows access to the document's collection, as shown in Figure 6-7. The collection that you will add to your project contains an enumerated array (implemented by class *CEnumVARIANT*) of VARIANT objects. The array is enumerated to allow the client to step through the collection or make copies

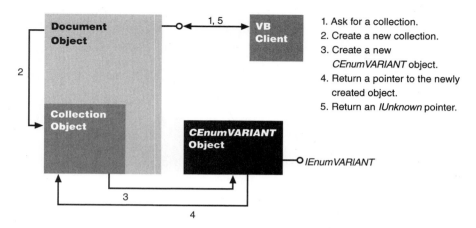

Figure 6-7.
The creation and handoff of a collection object.

of the collection. (For more information on the VARIANT data type, see the Visual C++ online documentation.)

> N O T E :   Actually, the array is composed of *COleVariant* objects, but they can emulate a VARIANT data type when necessary.

The sample project (VBCOLL) exposes a collection with the following elements:

■ A collection object implemented by class *CMyCollection* and derived from *CCmdTarget*.

■ An enumerated array object of *CString*-type values implemented by *CEnumVARIANT*. Each value is packed into a VARIANT data type using the *COleVariant* class.

■ A document object implemented by class *CVBCollDoc*, which exposes the collection via an OLE Automation property (collection).

The task consists of six steps:

1. Adding the enumerated array class

2. Adding the collection class

3. Modifying the collection class

4. Adding the _NewEnum property

5. Adding other properties and methods to the collection class

6. Modifying the document class

The name of the sample project is VBCOLL, and you will need the following items:

■ An MFC application with a document object that supports OLE Automation

■ An array of data that is suitable for exposure as a collection

Step 1: Adding the Enumerated Array Class

The implementation of the enumerated array (which in this task is *CEnum-VARIANT*) is made simple by deriving it from an undocumented class, in this case *CEnumArray*. The *CEnumArray* class, declared in DEVSTUDIO\MFC\SRC-\OLEIMPL2.H, is also used as a base class for other enumerated array classes in MFC. As it happens, these other enumerated classes are undocumented as well! In any event, the *CEnumArray* class provides an enumerated array of void* pointers and a COM interface (*IEnumVoid*) with several useful methods for array use. You will derive an enumerated array of *COleVariant* objects from the *CEnumArray* class and also add a modified destructor and *OnNext* function to the class. I use *COleVariant* objects because they provide a convenient C++ interface between MFC objects and VARIANT structures. As usual, when using undocumented classes, the implementation of *CEnumArray* can be modified at any time.

To implement this functionality, you must include the header file that declares the *CEnumArray* class and tell Developer Studio where to look for the file. The following procedure shows the steps involved in defining the *CEnum-Array* class in a project.

N O T E : To include the OLEIMPL2.H header file in your project, you must install the MFC source code on your hard drive.

1. Append the following lines to your project's STDAFX.H header file:

```
#include "afxole.h"
#include "oleimpl2.h"
```

2. Save your changes.

3. Choose Settings from the Project menu.

4. Click the C/C++ tab.

5. Choose Preprocessor from the Category drop-down list box.

6. In the Additional Include Directories edit box, enter the full path of the directory in which the MFC source code was installed.

7. Click OK.

Now that you have defined the base class you are using, you can add the *CEnumVARIANT* class. Because it is a small class, I will show you just the class declaration (and implementation); you then can save them in separate text files in your project. The declaration of *CEnumVARIANT* is as follows:

```
class CEnumVARIANT: public CEnumArray
{
public:

    CEnumVARIANT(const COleVariant* pVAR, UINT nSize) :
        CEnumArray(sizeof(COleVariant), pVAR, nSize, FALSE) {}
    ~CEnumVARIANT();

protected:
    virtual BOOL OnNext(void* pv);

public:
    DECLARE_INTERFACE_MAP()
};
```

This code declares a constructor that passes its parameters to the *CEnumArray* constructor. A destructor and a virtual function, *OnNext*, are also declared. Finally, I declare an interface map (which will be defined later). Save this code in a text file in the project directory as ENUMVAR.H.

The implementation of *CEnumVARIANT* is as follows:

```
#include "stdafx.h"
#include "EnumVar.h"

BEGIN_INTERFACE_MAP(CEnumVARIANT, CEnumArray)
    INTERFACE_PART(CEnumVARIANT, IID_IEnumVARIANT, EnumVOID)
END_INTERFACE_MAP()

CEnumVARIANT::~CEnumVARIANT()
{
    if (m_pClonedFrom == NULL)
        delete [] (COleVariant*)m_pvEnum;
}
```

(continued)

```
BOOL CEnumVARIANT::OnNext(void* pv)
{
    VARIANT var;
    if (!CEnumArray::OnNext(&var))
        return FALSE;

    VariantCopy((VARIANT*)pv, &var);
    return TRUE;
}
```

In the first section of code, I define an interface (*IEnumVoid*) that will be used by the enumerated array. In the next section of code, the destructor is defined. In this destructor, I first check whether the object has been used for making copies. If it hasn't (which means it's safe to destroy it), I delete the array using the *delete* operator. Finally, I define the *OnNext* function, which copies the next array element, if there is one, into the parameter (*pv*) passed in. Save this code in a text file in the project directory as ENUMVAR.CPP. When you have saved both files, add them to your project.

Step 2: Adding the Collection Class

Now that you have a valid enumerated array object, you need a collection object that contains the enumerated array. The main purpose of the collection object is to control access to the array through the collection object's interface. Because the collection class is also a fairly simple class, use ClassWizard to add it to your project. Call the class *CMyCollection*, derive it from *CCmdTarget*, and then enable OLE Automation. In step 3, you will make the class more useful by adding some functionality.

Step 3: Modifying the Collection Class

In this step, you will modify the constructor of the *CMyCollection* class slightly. To modify the *CMyCollection* class, follow this procedure:

1. In the header file (H) of the *CMyCollection* class, change the line

   ```
   CMyCollection();
   ```

   to the following:

   ```
   CMyCollection(CVBCollDoc* pDoc);
   ```

2. Add a document pointer of the appropriate type, named *m_pDoc*, to the collection class.

3. Save your changes to this file.

4. In the implementation file (CPP) of the *CMyCollection* class, replace the constructor declaration with the following code:

```
CMyCollection::CMyCollection(CVBCollDoc* pDoc)
{
    m_pDoc = pDoc;

    EnableAutomation();
}
```

This code accepts a document pointer and uses its value to initialize the member variable that you added above. Note that you should change the type of the document pointer to the type you use in your project.

5. Include the header file of your document object in the implementation file of the collection class; make sure it precedes the header file of the collection class. The following code is taken from the sample project:

```
#include "VBCollDoc.h"
#include "MyColl.h"
```

6. Save your changes to this file.

Step 4: Adding the _NewEnum Property

In this step, you add the _NewEnum property, which is an important part of the collection class object. It allows Visual Basic applications to step through each item of the exposed collection using a *for* loop. (For more information on this special property, see "Implementing the _NewEnum Property" in the SDK online documentation of Visual C++.) You can't add the property using ClassWizard because the property now has two requirements that make this impossible:

- It must be named _NewEnum and must not be localized.

- It must have DISPID = DISPID_NEWENUM (−4).

The procedure on the following page shows how to add the _NewEnum property to your project.

1. In the header file of the *CMyCollection* class, modify the dispatch map declaration to match the code below. (The new code is shown in bold.)

```
DECLARE_MESSAGE_MAP()
// Generated OLE dispatch map functions
//{{AFX_DISPATCH(CMyCollection)
afx_msg short GetCount();
//}}AFX_DISPATCH
afx_msg LPUNKNOWN GetNewEnum();
```

2. In the implementation file of the *CMyCollection* class, modify the dispatch map definition to match the code below. (The new code is shown in bold.)

```
BEGIN_DISPATCH_MAP(CMyCollection, CCmdTarget)
    //{{AFX_DISPATCH_MAP(CMyCollection)
    DISP_PROPERTY_EX(CMyCollection, "Count", GetCount,
        SetNotSupported, VT_I2)
    //}}AFX_DISPATCH_MAP
    DISP_PROPERTY_EX_ID(CMyCollection, "NewEnum",
        DISPID_NEWENUM, GetNewEnum, SetNotSupported,
        VT_UNKNOWN)
END_DISPATCH_MAP()
```

3. In the same file, add the following definition of the *GetNewEnum* function:

```
LPUNKNOWN CMyCollection::GetNewEnum()
{
    // Create and fill array of COleVariant objects here
    COleVariant* pVar = new COleVariant[m_pDoc->m_nElts];
    for (int i = 0; i < m_pDoc->m_nElts; i++)
        pVar[i] = m_pDoc->m_Elts[i];

    CEnumVARIANT* pEnum = new CEnumVARIANT(pVar,
        m_pDoc->m_nElts);
    return &pEnum->m_xEnumVOID;
}
```

This function creates an array of *COleVariant*-type objects and initializes each element with a *CString* value from the document object. It then creates an enumerated array using the *COleVariant* array and passes back a pointer to the *IUnknown* interface of the enumerated array.

NOTE: In case you're wondering how the *CString* objects are destroyed (and if you aren't, you should be), the destructor for the *COleVariant* class makes a call to *VariantClear*. Because *CString* objects are stored in a VARIANT as a BSTR, *VariantClear* will free the string automatically. (It's features like this that make using a class library pretty nice!)

4. In the ODL file of the project, add the following line after the initial comments:

```
#define DISPID_NEWENUM (-4)
```

This defines the ID of the _NewEnum property.

5. In the same file, locate the dispatch interface declaration of the collection object. It should look similar to the code shown here:

```
dispinterface IMyCollection
{
    properties:
        // NOTE - ClassWizard will maintain property
        // information here.
        // Use extreme caution when editing this section.
        //{{AFX_ODL_PROP(CMyCollection)
        [id(1)] short Count;
        //}}AFX_ODL_PROP
```

6. Immediately after the //}}AFX_ODL_PROP comment, add the following line:

```
[id(DISPID_NEWENUM)] IUnknown* _NewEnum;
```

This defines the _NewEnum property.

7. Save all changes to your project.

At this point, the _NewEnum property is implemented.

Step 5: Adding Other Properties and Methods to the Collection Class

It's now time to add two properties (Count and Item) and a method (*Add*) to the collection class.

The Count Property

The Count property (of type Get/Set) returns the number of objects in the collection. Because the document object is the only one that should change the object count, the *Set* function is not supported. Use ClassWizard to add this custom property to your collection class specifying the values below.

- External name: *Count*
- Type: short
- Implementation: Get/Set methods
- Get function: default value
- Set function: no value
- Parameter list: none

Replace the existing function body for the *GetCount* function (found in the implementation file of the *CMyCollection* class) with the following line:

```
return m_pDoc->m_Elts.GetSize();
```

The Item Property

The Item property (of type Get/Set) returns the item at the specified location in the collection. Use ClassWizard to add this custom property to your collection class specifying the values below.

- External name: *Item*
- Type: BSTR
- Implementation: Get/Set methods
- Get function: default value
- Set function: no value
- Parameter list: *nIndex*, type *long*

Replace the existing function body for the *GetItem* function (found in the implementation file of the *CMyCollection* class) with the following code:

```
CheckIndex(nIndex);
return m_pDoc->m_Elts.ElementAt((int)
    nIndex).AllocSysString();
```

For the Item property to function properly, you must check the index passed in to the method with a call to *CheckIndex*. This helper function determines whether the index value is greater than 0 and less than or equal to the index of the last item in the collection. The following procedure adds the *CheckIndex* function to your *CMyCollection* class.

1. In the header file of the *CMyCollection* class, add the following code to the "public" section of *CMyCollection*:

```
void CheckIndex(long nIndex);
```

2. In the implementation file of the *CMyCollection* class, add the following code to define the *CheckIndex* function:

```
void CMyCollection::CheckIndex(long nIndex)
{
    if (nIndex <= 0 || nIndex >= m_pDoc->m_Elts.GetSize())
        AfxThrowOleDispatchException(10000,
            T("Index value out of range"));
}
```

The *Add* Method

The *Add* method allows the external client to add items to the collection. Use ClassWizard to add this custom property to your collection class and specify the values below.

- External name: *Add*
- Internal name: *Add*
- Return type: *long*
- Parameter list: *newVal*, LPCTSTR

Replace the existing function body for the *Add* method (found in the implementation file of the *CMyCollection* class) with the following code:

```
m_pDoc->m_Elts.Add(newVal);
return m_pDoc->m_Elts.GetSize();
```

Step 6: Modifying the Document Class

In this task, the document's role is to store the data objects (in this case, of type *CString*) and, when requested, return a collection of these objects for use by external clients. To expose this collection to external clients, the document object must support OLE Automation and must expose a Get/Set custom property that returns a collection on demand. To add this functionality, the document class is modified by defining two new member variables and a custom Get/Set property, named Collection.

Add the following lines of code to the "protected" section of your document class located in the header file:

```
friend class CMyCollection;
CStringArray m_Elts;
```

The first line of code declares the *CMyCollection* class as a friend of your document class. This allows *CMyCollection* to access the document's "protected" and "private" members—which is useful when creating a collection. The remaining line declares an array of *CString* objects, *m_Elts*.

The last item of business is to implement the custom Collection property, which is used by external clients for requesting a collection of the current objects in the document object. This custom property will not allow the client to "set" a collection, only to retrieve one. First add the custom Collection property to your document class with the following properties using ClassWizard:

- External name: *Collection*
- Type: LPDISPATCH
- Implementation: Get/Set methods
- Get function: default value
- Set function: no value
- Parameter list: none

Now modify the *GetCollection* function by replacing the existing body of code with the following code:

```
CMyCollection* pCollection = new CMyCollection(this);
return GetIDispatch(FALSE);
```

Basically, the function creates a collection, passing in a pointer to itself, and then returns the *IDispatch* of the new collection. The parameter of the *GetIDispatch* call is FALSE because you don't want the reference count of the *IDispatch* interface to be incremented. You are returning only the interface of the collection object and not creating an instance of the object, so you should not increment the reference count.

After you have made these changes, rebuild the project; your document will expose a collection method that can be used by external clients for retrieving a collection of current document objects.

Additional Information

I have included two Visual Basic files (VBTEST.FRM and VBTEST.VBP) on the companion CD-ROM that you can use for adding new items to the collection and viewing the contents of an item at a given index in the collection. To use the test form (VBTEST.FRM), load the VBTEST.FRM or VBTEST.VBP file into Visual Basic version 4. The form will load, and you can then retrieve and interact with the enumerated collection.

CHAPTER SEVEN

Bits and Pieces

This chapter is a grab bag of tasks. There are a couple tasks relating to OLE, one about resource-only DLLs, and one about saving the state of an application, as you will see in the list below. Enjoy!

- **Building an MFC resource-only DLL** Demonstrates a technique for building an MFC-extension DLL that contains only resources and a process for using resources from a DLL in an MFC application.

- **Implementing drag and drop capability between child windows** Demonstrates implementation of OLE drag and drop capabilities in the child windows of a typical MDI application. Each child window allows you to drag and drop selected text strings either in other areas of the same client window or in a separate child window of the application. This technique can be adapted to work with Microsoft Windows common controls that use text as input/output data.

- **Using a custom class factory in an MFC application** Demonstrates how to customize versions of the DECLARE_OLECREATE and IMPLEMENT_OLECREATE macros. The macros have been customized by changing the class factory class from *COleObjectFactory* to a *COleObjectFactory*-derived class.

- **Saving the state of an MDI application upon exiting** Demonstrates how to create or update a Registry key so that it will store various aspects of an MFC application upon exiting. Examples of application information to be stored in the Registry include the size and the position of the main window and the state (maximized or normal) of any active child windows.

Building an MFC Resource-Only DLL

The purpose of this task is to create an MFC-extension DLL that contains only resources. Such an approach provides several advantages:

- It reduces the size of the MFC executable by moving large, expensive (in terms of size) resources into a separate DLL.

- It makes it possible for you to create localized copies of the resources in separate DLLs—for example, converting all of the English strings of an MFC application to French and then storing the converted strings in a French resource DLL.

- It provides an efficient way of updating the resources in an application. Instead of revising an entire application and its resources, you can revise just the resources, which are in the DLL, and then just hand out new copies of the DLL.

I use the sample projects MAIN (the calling application) and MYRES (the DLL) to demonstrate how resources are retrieved from the DLL and used by the application. This is done by moving all of the resources except the version number from the MAIN project into the MYRES DLL project. I then redirect the location of the resources for the MAIN project to an instance of the MYRES DLL. The task consists of four steps:

1. Creating the DLL project

2. Adding resources to the DLL project

3. Modifying the *InitInstance* function of the calling application

4. Implementing the *ExitInstance* function of the calling application

To complete this task, you will need an SDI, MDI, or dialog box–based MFC application.

NOTE: If you don't want to mess around with the Visual C++ IDE, copy the MYRES project (Chap7\TaskDir1\MyRes) from the companion CD-ROM and use it as your framework.

Step 1: Creating the DLL Project

Creating the framework of the DLL project is simple if you don't mind using the Microsoft Visual C++ Integrated Development Environment. Basically, you create an MFC extension DLL using the following procedure:

1. Choose New from the File menu in the Microsoft Developer Studio IDE.

2. Click the Projects tab in the New dialog box.

3. Double-click MFC AppWizard (DLL).

4. Enter a name for your project. In the sample, I use MYRES. Click OK.

5. Click Finish in the MFC AppWizard dialog box to create the project framework.

The project is, indeed, a framework. It contains no classes, just a few source files and some resources. In step 2, you will flesh out the project by adding resources taken from the application MAIN.

Step 2: Adding Resources to the DLL Project

Now that you have created the DLL project, you can add other resources. Here are the most common methods for doing this:

- Adding other RC files to your DLL project (If you add other resource files to the project, don't forget to add the include files used by these new resources.)

- Creating new resources for the DLL project

- Copying resources from a project's RC file to your DLL's RC file

For the MYRES sample project, I copied the RC file (and the \RES directory) from the MAIN project to the MYRES project. I then added the RC file to the DLL project and deleted all resources except the version number from the MAIN project. I did this to show that the resources used by the MAIN application come from the DLL and not from the application. I also changed the name of the output file for the Debug build from MYRES.DLL to MYRESD.DLL. This was done to distinguish between the Debug and Release versions of the DLL. You can make this change by clicking the Link tab of the Project Settings dialog box inside the Developer Studio IDE and then modifying the Output File value.

N O T E : If you are using the Developer Studio IDE, you must have an RC file for the project or all access to ClassWizard will be disabled.

You should now be able to build the DLL with no problems. The resultant DLL can be found in either the \DEBUG or the \RELEASE subdirectory of your DLL project directory, depending on the version you have built. Copy the DLL to the \SYSTEM subdirectory of Microsoft Windows 95 or the \SYSTEM32 directory of Microsoft Windows NT version 4 so that your calling application can use this DLL. In the next step, you will redirect the source of the resources used by your application to the resource-only DLL.

Step 3: Modifying the *InitInstance* Function of the Calling Application

Under normal circumstances, an MFC application contains all of its own resources. However, in this case, you have moved the resources into a separate DLL (MYRES). Now you need some way to tell your application to look in the DLL for whatever resource it needs. Doing this requires some modification of the *InitInstance* function of the calling application—specifically, by adding a data member to the class (*m_hInstRes*) and by making calls to *AfxSetResourceHandle* (sets the default resource location of an application) and *LoadLibrary* (loads the specified DLL into memory). This redirects all resource requests from the application to the DLL.

> N O T E : In this task, I assume that all resources for the application are located in a single DLL. It is also possible to switch between locations for specific resources when needed by resetting the resource handle with another call to *AfxSetResourceHandle*.

To modify the *InitInstance* function, follow this procedure:

1. Define the *m_hInstRes* data member by adding the following line to the header file of the application class:

```
HINSTANCE m_hInstRes;
```

2. Add the following lines to the beginning of your application's *InitInstance* function:

```
#ifdef _DEBUG
// Load the Debug version of the localized resources
    m_hInstRes = LoadLibrary("MyResd.dll");
#else
// Load the Release version of the localized resources
    m_hInstRes = LoadLibrary("MyRes.dll");
#endif
ASSERT(m_hInstRes != NULL);
AfxSetResourceHandle(m_hInstRes);
```

In this code, I check to see whether the application is a Debug version or a Release version. I then make a call to the *LoadLibrary* function, passing the name of the appropriate DLL. (For a Debug build, this is MYRESD.DLL; for a Release build, this is MYRES.DLL.) I then reset the resource handle of the application to the DLL by making a call to the *AfxSetResourceHandle* function, passing the handle of the DLL. From now on, the application will always look in the DLL for the required resources.

> N O T E : The preceding code assumes that the DLL is named MYRESD/MYRES.DLL and that different builds (Debug and Release) of the DLL exist. If this is not true for your application, modify the code accordingly.

Step 4: Implementing the *ExitInstance* Function of the Calling Application

The final step in this task is to override the *ExitInstance* function of your application class and add some code that frees the DLL before the application exits.

Override the *ExitInstance* function of your application class now. Replace the function body with the following code:

```
// In case you load multiple DLLs, be sure you free them,
// and avoid calling FreeLibrary with a NULL pointer
FreeLibrary(m_hInstRes);

return CWinApp::ExitInstance();
```

After you have made these changes, rebuild the project. If you have copied the resource DLL to the appropriate system directory, your application will now retrieve all needed resources from the loaded DLL.

Additional Information

For details of how to localize resources in separate DLLs, check out Technical Note 57: "Localization of MFC Components" in the Developer Studio online documentation. For details of how to export MFC classes from a DLL, see Technical Note 11: "Using MFC as Part of a DLL" in the Developer Studio online documentation.

The Microsoft Knowledge Base also contains articles that are related to this topic:

- How to Localize Application Resources with Foundation Classes: Q147149 (Article in its updated form was not available at press time; see the online version.)

- PRB: MFC Loads Wrong Resource in Extension DLL: Q150121

Implementing Drag and Drop Capability Between Child Windows

The purpose of this task is to implement the ability to drag and drop text strings between two child windows of an existing MDI application. This procedure uses the OLE drag and drop functionality provided by the *COleDropTarget* class as well as several virtual functions related to OLE drag and drop: *OnDragEnter, OnDragOver, OnDrop,* and *OnDragLeave.* Note that this procedure can also be used with some modification to allow dragging and dropping between any two window objects, such as two common controls. For more information about this option, see "Additional Information" at the end of this task.

A drag and drop operation has two parts: handling the source of the drag and drop operation and handling the drop target. For a drag and drop operation to be successful, there are several small tasks that must be completed for each part. To handle the source of a drag and drop operation, the following tasks must be completed by the data source (the object where the drag and drop operation starts):

- Determining the start of a valid drag and drop operation

- Packing the data to be dragged into a *COleDataSource* object and calling its *DoDragDrop* member function

To handle the drop target, the following tasks must be completed:

- Adding a *COleDropTarget* data member to the view class and registering it as a drop target with the operating system.

- Overriding the *OnDragEnter, OnDragOver,* and *OnDragLeave* functions of the drop target class and returning a value other than the default value DROPEFFECT_NONE, which indicates no drop allowed. You can use either the DROPEFFECT_MOVE return value or the DROP-EFFECT_COPY return value to indicate the proper action to be taken by the data source.

- Overriding the *OnDrop* function of the drop target class to unpack and insert the data upon completion of a drag and drop operation.

Because MFC's implementation of OLE drag and drop is very flexible, there are many possible types of drag and drop operations, each with different attributes. For example, both copying or moving entire classes and just copying or moving a single numeric value can be implemented by the code that packs and unpacks the data source object. For this task, the drag and drop operation has the following attributes:

■ Some text must be selected in the source window.

■ The user must press and hold the left mouse button over the selected text and drag the selection outside of a 5x5 pixel region to initiate a drag and drop operation. This region is centered on the location of the cursor when the left mouse button is pressed.

■ The contents (the selected text) are inserted at the nearest text index of the drop target when the item is dropped (Figure 7-1).

■ The operation can be canceled at any time during the drag operation either by pressing the Esc key or by clicking the right mouse button.

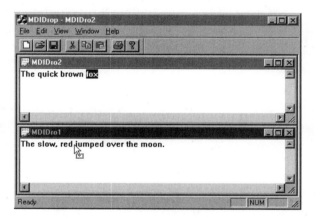

Figure 7-1.
Dropped text inserted between the words "red" and "jumped."

The task consists of nine steps:

1. Initializing the OLE system libraries

2. Adding data members to the project's view class

3. Implementing the *OnLButtonDown* function

4. Adding the *InSelRegion* helper function

5. Implementing the *OnMouseMove* function

6. Implementing the *OnLButtonUp* function

7. Registering the application's drop target

8. Implementing the *OnDragEnter* and *OnDragOver* functions

9. Implementing the *OnDrop* function

The name of the sample project is MDIDROP; to complete this task you will need the following things:

- An MDI MFC application

- The application's view class derived from *CEditView*

Step 1: Initializing the OLE System Libraries

For OLE drag and drop operations to function within your application, you must include AFXOLE.H and initialize the OLE system libraries. To include the AFXOLE.H file in your project, add the following line to the project's STADAFX.H file:

```
#include <afxole.h>
```

Initialize the OLE system libraries by making a call to the global function *AfxOleInit*. A good place for this call is in your application's *InitInstance* function, so add the following lines to the beginning of that function:

```
// Initialize the OLE libraries
if (!AfxOleInit())
{
    AfxMessageBox("Ole Initialization Failed");
    return FALSE;
}
```

This code attempts to initialize the OLE libraries. If it fails, a message box is displayed, indicating the failure.

Step 2: Adding Data Members to the Project's View Class

Begin implementing the data source by adding eight data members to the project's view class. The data members store several values that will indicate the status of the drag and drop operation. (More detail about these data members will be provided in the appropriate steps of the task.) Add the following code to the header file of your view class:

```
COleDataSource m_dataSrc;     // Source of data for operation
COleDropTarget m_dropTarget;  // The drop target for the
                              // operation
```

```
CRect m_dragRect;            // must be outside this area
                             // before a drop is accepted
CString m_dragString;        // The string being dragged

BOOL m_bLBDown;              // Was the WM_LBUTTONDOWN message
                             // handled?
BOOL m_bIsTextSelected;      // Is there any selected text?
BOOL m_bValidDragStart;      // A valid drag and drop operation
                             // has been started
BOOL m_bCheckForDrop;        // Have we checked for a valid
                             // drop?
```

Typically, you initialize these data members in the constructor of the view class. Add the code shown below to your view class's constructor. The values of these data members represent the state of the data source before a drag and drop operation has been initiated. The Boolean values are all FALSE, which indicates that no operation has been initiated and that the area and its contents are cleared:

```
m_bLBDown = FALSE;
m_bIsTextSelected = FALSE;
m_bValidDragStart = FALSE;
m_bCheckForDrop = FALSE;
m_dragRect.SetRect(0, 0, 0, 0);
m_dragString = "";
```

The next four steps are where the real work of implementing the data source occurs.

Step 3: Implementing the *OnLButtonDown* Function

Because every drag and drop operation is initiated by the user pressing the left mouse button, a good place to start setting up the drag and drop operation is in the WM_LBUTTONDOWN event handler (*OnLButtonDown*).

Before jumping into the code that you will need to add, let's review the logic you will have to implement in this handler. For a drag and drop operation to be valid, two things must be true:

■ Some or all of the text in a child window has been selected.

■ The user has pressed the left mouse button somewhere within the selected text area.

If these two conditions are true, the user possibly has started a new drag and drop operation. I say "possibly" because the user must drag the selection outside the *m_dragRect* region before the drag is actually accepted as a drag and

drop action. However, after the initial requirements of a drag and drop operation have been met, set some flags (indicating that a possible drag and drop
operation has started) and capture the mouse input until the operation is
complete or has been canceled. Now that you're clear on the logic, add the
code. Add a handler to your view's class to handle the **WM_LBUTTONDOWN**
message, and then add the following lines of code to your new *OnLButtonDown*
function:

```
BOOL    ptInRegion = FALSE; // Is the cursor over the selected
                            // text?
CEdit&  tmpEdit = GetEditCtrl();
HLOCAL  hBuff = tmpEdit.GetHandle();
CHAR*   szBuff = (CHAR*)LocalLock(hBuff);
CHAR*   szDragString;
DWORD   PtPos;
int     ptIndex, nStartChar, nEndChar, nLen;

tmpEdit.GetSel(nStartChar, nEndChar);
nLen = nEndChar - nStartChar;
szDragString = m_dragString.GetBufferSetLength(nLen);
memcpy(szDragString, szBuff + nStartChar, nLen);
LocalUnlock(hBuff);
m_dragString.ReleaseBuffer();
m_bLBDown = TRUE;

if (nLen > 0) // Possible drag operation
{
    // Check to see whether LBDown is in seltext region
    PtPos = tmpEdit.CharFromPos(point);
    ptIndex = LOWORD(PtPos);
    m_bValidDragStart = InSelRegion(point, ptIndex);

    if (!m_bValidDragStart) // Clicked outside selected region
        CEditView::OnLButtonDown(nFlags, point);
    else
    {
        SetCapture();
        m_dragRect.SetRect(point.x - 5, point.y - 5,
            point.x + 5, point.y + 5);
        m_bCheckForDrop = TRUE;
    }
}
else
    CEditView::OnLButtonDown(nFlags, point);
```

In the first section of code, I initialize the *ptInRegion* flag to FALSE and retrieve a handle to the edit control that is embedded in the view object. I then

lock a local buffer (*hBuff*), which causes the entire contents of the edit control to be loaded into *szBuff*. In the next section of code, I retrieve the start and end positions of the selected text. The pointer to a local string buffer (*szDragString*) is then set to the *m_dragString* member variable and the selected contents of the edit control are copied into *szDragString*, which automatically copies the same text into *m_dragString*. Finally, the *m_dragString* buffer is unlocked, and *m_LBDown* is set to TRUE. I then check to see whether the string containing the selected text is empty (indicating that no text is selected). If no text is selected, I can safely ignore this event and pass it on to the default handler. If text is selected, I proceed to the second part of validation: has the user clicked within the selected text region?

Because I am working with edit controls that are embedded in each child window, I am able to calculate the dimensions of the rectangle containing the selected text and determine whether the mouse click occurred within the text string. This is accomplished in the next section of code (an *if* statement) by determining the text index of the string and making a call to a helper function (*InSelRegion*), which will be added in step 4. If *InSelRegion* returns FALSE, the user has not clicked within the selected text rectangle. This means that a drag operation has not started; therefore, I can safely ignore the WM_LBUTTONDOWN event and pass the event on to the default handler. However, if *InSelRegion* returns TRUE, a valid drag operation has been started; then I proceed to the *else* body of the *if* statement.

In the *else* body of code, I capture all further input from the mouse and set the *m_dragRect* data member to a 5x5 pixel region, centered on the point in the region where the left mouse button was pressed. I use this region in the WM_MOUSEMOVE handler to determine whether the drag and drop operation should be completed. (This is discussed further in step 6.) Finally, I set another flag that tells me to allow drop attempts to be made.

Step 4: Adding the *InSelRegion* Helper Function

In the previous step, you made a call to the *InSelRegion* helper function. The purpose of this function is to check the location of the cursor when the left mouse button is pressed against the selected text region. If there is an intersection, TRUE is returned. If there is no intersection, FALSE is returned. Add this function now by adding the following line in the header file of your view class:

```
BOOL InSelRegion(CPoint pt, int ptIndex);
```

In the implementation file of your view class, add the following code:

```
BOOL CMDIDropView::InSelRegion(CPoint pt, int ptIndex)
{
    CEdit& tmpEdit = GetEditCtrl();
    DWORD txtPos;
    int startIndex, endIndex;

    txtPos = tmpEdit.GetSel();
    startIndex = LOWORD(txtPos);
    endIndex = HIWORD(txtPos) - 1;

    if ((ptIndex >= startIndex) && (ptIndex <= endIndex))
        return TRUE;
    else
        return FALSE;
}
```

In the first section of this code, I retrieve the embedded edit control and declare some local variables. In the next section of code, I retrieve the current selection and calculate the start and end indexes of the selected text. Finally, I compare this range against *ptIndex*, the index of the mouse click. If *ptIndex* is within the range, I return TRUE. If it is outside the range, I return FALSE.

Step 5: Implementing the *OnMouseMove* Function

In the previous step, you determined at what point a valid drag and drop operation was initiated by the user. Now you have to implement the "dropping" of the item being dragged. To make the code easier to read, I use the WM-_MOUSEMOVE handler (*OnMouseMove*) to implement dropping the dragged item. I have seen other methods that place the "drop code" in the WM-_LBUTTONDOWN handler, but the placement of this code seems to be a matter of choice. In any event, at this point you have to implement the following logic: if you are checking for a drop event (*m_CheckForDrop* is TRUE) and the current location of the cursor is outside the valid drop region (*m_dragRect*), copy or move the selected text to the valid drop target by calling *DoDragDrop*. However, if you aren't checking for a drop event (*m_CheckForDrop* is FALSE) or if the current cursor location is inside the valid drop region, ignore this event and call the default handler.

Add a handler to your view's class to handle the WM_MOUSEMOVE message, and add the following lines of code to the beginning of your new *OnMouseMove* function:

```
DWORD numBytes;
HGLOBAL hgData;
LPTSTR lpData;
DROPEFFECT dropEffect;

if (m_bCheckForDrop && !(m_dragRect.PtInRect(point)))
{ // Valid drag, do drop
    ReleaseCapture();
    m_bCheckForDrop = FALSE;

    numBytes = (DWORD)m_dragString.GetLength();
    // Create global memory for sharing drag and drop text
    hgData = GlobalAlloc(GPTR,numBytes + 1);
    ASSERT(hgData != NULL);

    // Lock global data (get pointer)
    lpData = (LPTSTR)GlobalLock(hgData);
    ASSERT(lpData != NULL);

    strcpy(lpData, m_dragString);
    GlobalUnlock(hgData);

    m_dataSrc.CacheGlobalData(CF_TEXT, hgData);
    dropEffect = m_dataSrc.DoDragDrop(
        DROPEFFECT_COPY | DROPEFFECT_MOVE, NULL);
    if ((dropEffect&DROPEFFECT_MOVE) == DROPEFFECT_MOVE)
        GetEditCtrl().Clear();
    m_dataSrc.Empty();
}
else
    CEditView::OnMouseMove(nFlags, point);
```

In the first section of code, I declare some local variables. In the *if* statement that follows the declarations, if *m_bCheckForDrop* is TRUE and the current drop location is outside the valid drop region, I have a valid drop. Next I allocate enough global memory to store the selected string and retrieve a pointer to it. In the next section, I copy the selected string into the global memory pointer. I then cache the data in the data source object (*m_dataSrc*) and call the *DoDragDrop* function of *m_dataSrc*. Finally, I use an *if* statement check to see whether the drag and drop operation was a copy or a move. If it was a move, I clear the selected text from the source with a call to the view object's *Clear* function.

Step 6: Implementing the *OnLButtonUp* Function

Because the end of a valid drag and drop operation is indicated by the user re-leasing the left mouse button, the WM_LBUTTONUP handler (*OnLButtonUp*) is a great place to re-initialize the drag and drop data members you added in step 2. This allows your child windows to look for the next possible drag and drop operation. Implement this cleanup now. Add a handler to your view's class to handle the WM_LBUTTONUP message, and add the following lines of code to your new *OnLButtonUp* function:

```
m_bLBDown = FALSE;
if (m_bCheckForDrop)
{
    CEdit& tmpEdit = GetEditCtrl();
    DWORD ptChar;
    int ptIndex;

    ReleaseCapture();
    m_bCheckForDrop = FALSE;
    ptChar = tmpEdit.CharFromPos(point);
    ptIndex = LOWORD(ptChar);
    tmpEdit.SetSel(ptIndex, ptIndex);
};
CEditView::OnLButtonUp(nFlags, point);
```

In the first section of this code, I set *m_lbDown* to FALSE; then, if *m_bCheckForDrop* is TRUE, I release the mouse capture, set *m_bCheckForDrop* to FALSE, and clear any current text selection. If I am not checking for a drop event, the default handler is called.

This concludes the implementation of the drop source. In the remaining three steps, you will implement the drop target side of things.

Step 7: Registering the Application's Drop Target

For a Windows object to be a valid drop target, it must contain a *COleDropTarget* data member or a data member derived from *COleDropTarget*; the object must be registered. This means that for this task each child window object must have a data member of this type (completed in step 2) and the drop target must be registered with Windows. You register your child windows by making a call to the *Register* function of the drop target data member that you added in step 2.

Register the child window now by adding the following code line to the *OnCreate* function of your view class after the call to the base class's *OnCreate* function:

```
m_dropTarget.Register(this);
```

N O T E : There is a function, *COleDropTarget::Revoke*, that removes the window from the list of valid drop targets. However, because both drop targets are valid child window objects, *Revoke* is automatically called by the *OnClose* function of each child window when the window is destroyed.

Step 8: Implementing the *OnDragEnter* and *OnDragOver* Functions

In step 5, you made a call to the drop source's *DoDragDrop* function. You might remember that you also checked the return value to see whether the original data should be moved (DROPEFFECT_MOVE) or should be copied (DROPEFFECT_COPY). This return value is determined by three functions of the view class—*OnDragEnter, OnDragOver,* and *OnDragLeave.*

The default behavior for *OnDragEnter* and *OnDragOver* returns the value DROPEFFECT_NONE, which indicates that the current target is not valid for dropping. However, if these two functions are overridden in the application's view class, drop operations will be allowed in any child window of the application. The overrides of these functions are the same, so you can tackle both at once.

N O T E : For this task, there is no need to override the *OnDrag-Leave* function.

To implement *OnDragEnter* and *OnDragOver,* follow this procedure:

1. In your application's view class, override the *OnDragEnter* and *On-DragOver* functions using your favorite method.

2. Replace the body of each overridden function with the following code:

```
// Check whether the control key was pressed
if ((dwKeyState & MK_CONTROL) == MK_CONTROL)
    return DROPEFFECT_COPY; // Copy the source text
else
    return DROPEFFECT_MOVE; // Move the source text
```

3. Save your changes.

The code you just added checks the *dwKeyState* variable for the value of MK_CONTROL, which indicates that the user pressed the Ctrl key before starting the drag and drop operation. According to the Windows style guide, this indicates a copy operation, not a move. Therefore, you should return DROPEFFECT_COPY. Going back to the code you added in step 5, you can see that the return value is compared to DROPEFFECT_MOVE and, if true, the original text is deleted:

```
m_dataSrc.CacheGlobalData(CF_TEXT, hgData);
dropEffect = m_dataSrc.DoDragDrop(
    DROPEFFECT_COPY | DROPEFFECT_MOVE, NULL);
if ((dropEffect&DROPEFFECT_MOVE) == DROPEFFECT_MOVE)
    GetEditCtrl().Clear();
m_dataSrc.Empty();
```

Step 9: Implementing the *OnDrop* Function

You have now implemented all of the drag and drop capability except for one part—the code that handles the drop event. Once again, MFC saves the day by providing a handy little virtual function (*CView::OnDrop*) that you can override to handle drop events for a window. By default, *OnDrop* does nothing and returns FALSE. You are going to need better results than that if you want drag and drop capability! First override *OnDrop* in your application's view class. Then replace the body of that override with the following code:

```
HGLOBAL  hGlobal;
LPCSTR   pData;
int charPos, charIndex;
CEdit&   tmpEdit = GetEditCtrl();
DWORD oldSel;

// Get text data from COleDataObject
hGlobal = pDataObject->GetGlobalData(CF_TEXT);

// Get pointer to data
pData = (LPCSTR)GlobalLock(hGlobal);
ASSERT(pData != NULL);

// Set text in dropped window
charPos = tmpEdit.CharFromPos(point);
charIndex = LOWORD(charPos);

oldSel = tmpEdit.GetSel();
tmpEdit.SetSel(charIndex, charIndex);
tmpEdit.ReplaceSel(pData);
tmpEdit.SetSel(oldSel);

// Unlock memory
GlobalUnlock(hGlobal);

return TRUE;
```

Let's quickly run through the code and see what it does. In the first section, I declare some local variables and retrieve a reference to the embedded edit control. Next I retrieve the text with a call to *GetGlobalData*. Then I get a pointer to the text and drop the text into the current window. I determine the location of the text by choosing the closest text index to the current position of the pointer. Finally, I unlock the global memory and exit the function.

After this code has been added and the project rebuilt, you can drag and drop selected text from one child window to another.

Additional Information

In a sense, this task has already demonstrated dragging text between two common controls. The data source and drop target are *CView*-derived windows, each of which contains an embedded edit control. This means that the procedure for implementing drag and drop between child windows can be used, with some modification, for implementing drag and drop between other types of common controls. To find out how to implement this functionality for common controls on non–Windows 95 platforms, see the Knowledge Base article "SAMPLE: Using MFC OLE Drag & Drop to Drag Text Between Windows": Q135299. The article also contains a sample that demonstrates the procedure discussed.

With the introduction of Windows 95, the underlying implementation for common controls changed significantly. An article in the Knowledge Base has a sample that addresses these changes: "DRAGD95.EXE:SAMPLE:OLE Drag/Drop in Windows 95 Common Controls": Q152092.

Using a Custom Class Factory in an MFC Application

The purpose of this task is to customize the creation process of a creatable OLE Automation object that can be created at run time in an MFC application. The task deals specifically with OLE Automation objects that are creatable by type ID—a method of creation that makes use of the macros DECLARE_OLECREATE and IMPLEMENT_OLECREATE.

> N O T E : The declaration and definition of these macros can be found in the header file AFXDISP.H, which is located in the \MFC\INCLUDE directory.

In this task, I will demonstrate how to customize the DECLARE-_OLECREATE and IMPLEMENT_OLECREATE macros using a class derived from *COleObjectFactory*. These macros automatically use an instance of the *COleObjectFactory* class to create an instance of your Automation object for external clients. You can then customize various default aspects of the class factory (the object that is implemented by the *COleObjectFactory*-derived class) by overriding virtual functions of the *COleObjectFactory* base class. The task consists of four steps:

1. Defining custom macros in the project

2. Using the custom macros in the Automation object

3. Adding a new class factory class to the project

4. Modifying the class factory class

An OLE Automation object (*CMyAutoObj*) is contained in the sample project MYFACT; external clients can create this object using a set of customized macros. These macros, MYDECLARE_OLECREATE and MYIMPLEMENT-_OLECREATE, use a class factory class derived from *COleObjectFactory* (*CMyFactory*) instead of the *COleObjectFactory* class. To complete the task, you will need the following things:

- An MFC application project that provides OLE support.

- A creatable OLE Automation object that will use the custom class factory. Objects of this type can be created by external clients and can make use of the DECLARE_OLECREATE and IMPLEMENT_OLE-CREATE macros.

Step 1: Defining Custom Macros in the Project

As I mentioned above, the DECLARE_OLECREATE and IMPLEMENT-_OLECREATE macros allow an instance of your OLE Automation object to be dynamically created. To customize this dynamic creation process, you must implement an exact copy of each macro, with the following exception: instead of using the *COleObjectFactory* class, use your own class derived from *COleObjectFactory*. First define the custom versions of the DECLARE_OLE-CREATE and IMPLEMENT_OLECREATE macros in the header file of the Automation object. Then add the following lines to the top of the header file:

```
#define MYDECLARE_OLECREATE(class_name) \
public: \
    static AFX_DATA CMyFactory factory; \
    static AFX_DATA const GUID guid; \

#define MYIMPLEMENT_OLECREATE(class_name, external_name, \
    l, w1, w2, b1, b2, b3, b4, b5, b6, b7, b8) \
    AFX_DATADEF CMyFactory class_name::factory(class_name::guid, \
        RUNTIME_CLASS(class_name), FALSE, _T(external_name)); \
    const AFX_DATADEF GUID class_name::guid = \
        { l, w1, w2, { b1, b2, b3, b4, b5, b6, b7, b8 } }; \
```

This code is an exact copy of the code found in AFXDISP.H except for the class factory name and custom macro names. The class that is referenced in the macros, *CMyFactory*, will be derived from *COleObjectFactory* in step 3 below.

Now that the macros have been defined, you can modify the Automation object class to make use of them.

Step 2: Using the Custom Macros in the Automation Object

This step is fairly easy because all you need to do is change two lines of code. In the header file of the Automation object class, locate the macro DECLARE_OLECREATE and change its name to MYDECLARE_OLECREATE. In the implementation file of the Automation object class, locate the macro IMPLEMENT_OLECREATE and change its name to MYIMPLEMENT_OLE-CREATE. After you have made these changes, you can add the class factory that is used by the MYDECLARE_OLECREATE and MYIMPLEMENT_OLE-CREATE macros.

Step 3: Adding a New Class Factory Class to the Project

The final piece of this task adds and implements the class factory class used by your Automation object. I divide this step into two parts, deriving the class factory class from *CCmdTarget* and modifying the new class, because ClassWizard does not support adding classes derived directly from *COleObjectFactory*. I suggest using ClassWizard to add the class because you can get a usable framework by deriving from *CCmdTarget*, which saves some typing.

So add a new class derived from *CCmdTarget* using ClassWizard. (Class and source filenames can be of your choosing.) Now that you have an actual class factory class, you will have to fix a little problem that was skipped over in

step 2. If you recall, the MYDECLARE_OLECREATE and MYIMPLEMENT-
_OLECREATE macros make references to the *CMyFactory* class. At the time,
you didn't have a header file that defined the *CMyFactory* class. Now that you
do, include the *CMyFactory* header file right after the custom macro declarations in the implementation file of your OLE Automation object. This prevents any compilation errors that might result from a lack of definition for
CMyFactory.

> **N O T E :** The name of the class used in the sample is *CMyFactory*.
> The header file is named MYFACTORY.H, and the implementation
> file is named MYFACTORY.CPP.

Step 4: Modifying the Class Factory Class

Because you had to derive the class factory class from *CCmdTarget*, you must
now modify the derivation of that class to *COleObjectFactory*. Use the following
procedure to modify the class factory class. All changes are confined to the
header and implementation files of the new class.

1. Change all occurrences of *CCmdTarget* to *COleObjectFactory*.

2. Delete the DECLARE_DYNCREATE macro from the header file.

3. Change the declaration of the constructor, located in the header file,
   to the following:

```
public:
    CMyFactory(REFCLSID clsid,
        CRuntimeClass* pRuntimeClass, BOOL bMultiInstance,
        LPCTSTR lpszProgID);
```

4. Change the access specifier of the destructor, located in the header
   file, from "protected" to "public."

5. Delete the IMPLEMENT_DYNCREATE macro from the implementation file.

6. Change the definition of the constructor, located in the implementation file, to the following:

```
CMyOleObjectFactory::CMyOleObjectFactory(REFCLSID clsid,
    CRuntimeClass* pRuntimeClass, BOOL bMultiInstance,
    LPCTSTR lpszProgID):
    COleObjectFactory(clsid, pRuntimeClass,
    bMultiInstance, lpszProgID)
{
}
```

7. Save your changes to the source files.

After you have completed these changes, rebuild your project. When creating an instance of itself, the Automation object will now use a class factory derived from *COleObjectFactory*, and you will now be able to modify the class factory as you see fit.

Saving the State of an MDI Application upon Exiting

The purpose of this task is to enable an MFC MDI application to save the state of its various attributes (such as the size and the position of the main frame window) to the system Registry before the application exits. When the application is reopened, the saved information is used to restore application attributes to their previous state.

> **N O T E :** For information about implementing this same functionality for SDI and dialog box–based applications, see "Additional Information" at the end of this task.

Attributes that are commonly saved range from application-wide information (such as what control bars were docked or visible) to specific items (such as the value for a specific control in a dialog box). For the purpose of this demonstration, the following attributes are stored by the sample project (INIFILE) in the system Registry under the key RedRoad Inc.:

- The size and position of the main frame window.
- The state of the child window (maximized or normal).
- The state (docked or undocked, visible or hidden) of the status bar and the toolbar. If the toolbar is undocked, the current position is also saved.

This task consists of nine steps:

1. Modifying the *InitInstance* function of the application class
2. Overriding the *ExitInstance* function of the application class
3. Implementing the *InitialShowWindow* function
4. Adding helper functions for the *InitialShowWindow* function
5. Implementing the *OnClose* function of the main frame window

6. Adding data members to a child window

7. Adding the *Initialize* and *Terminate* functions to a child frame window

8. Implementing the *ActivateFrame* function of a child frame window

9. Implementing the *OnSize* function of a child frame window

To complete this task, you will need an MFC MDI application.

Step 1: Modifying the *InitInstance* Function of the Application Class

You will be storing attributes related to both the main frame and child frame windows, so the application object is a good place to notify both the main frame window and the child frame windows of their creation. This notification allows the windows to retrieve any attribute values that can affect the appearance of the windows. Use the following procedure to modify the *InitInstance* function.

1. Add the following lines of code to the implementation file of your application class right after the message map declaration:

```
static TCHAR szCompanyName[] = _T("RedRoad Inc.");
```

This code defines the name of a key in the system Registry that your application uses to store attributes. This key is located in the HKEY_CURRENT_USER\Software directory of the system Registry. Storing attributes in the system Registry is essential for applications that are Windows 95 compliant. If you are modifying a non–Windows 95 application, however, and want to use an INI file instead of the system Registry, see "Additional Information" at the end of this task. Naturally, you should replace the *szCompanyName* string with the name of your company.

2. Add the following lines of code to the beginning of the application's *InitInstance* function:

```
SetRegistryKey(szCompanyName);
CChildFrame::Initialize();
```

This code sets the Registry key to *szCompanyName* and notifies the child frame window object of its creation. At this point, the *Initialize* function has not yet been added to the child frame class. It will be added in step 7.

3. In the *InitInstance* function, find the line of code that makes a call to the *ShowWindow* function. Replace it with the following code:

```
pMainFrame->InitialShowWindow(m_nCmdShow);
```

This code causes the main frame window to retrieve its size and state attributes from the Registry key and to use these values to display itself. At this point, the *InitialShowWindow* function has not yet been added to the main frame class. It will be added in step 3.

4. Save your changes.

Now that you have set up a framework for notifying the window objects before their creation, add code that notifies the child frame window of its termination. (The mechanism for notifying the main frame window to save its attributes is discussed in step 5.)

Step 2: Overriding the *ExitInstance* Function of the Application Class

The purpose of this step is to provide a mechanism for notifying the child window of its termination so that it can save its current attributes to the system Registry before termination. The simplest method involves overriding and modifying the *ExitInstance* function. Using your favorite method, override the function now, and then replace the existing function code with the following code:

```
CChildFrame::Terminate();
return CWinApp::ExitInstance();
```

This code simply calls the *Terminate* function of the child window object (which is added in step 7) and then returns the value of the call to *CWinApp::ExitInstance*.

This completes the modifications to the application class.

Step 3: Implementing the *InitialShowWindow* Function

It's now time to implement the *InitialShowWindow* function. This function, called from the newly modified *InitInstance* function of the application class, reads main frame window attributes and toolbar states from the Registry key and then displays the main frame window and its control bars using the values from the Registry key. Use the procedure on the following page to add the *InitialShowWindow* function to your project.

1. Add this code to the header file of the main frame window class:

```
public:
    void InitialShowWindow(UINT nCmdShow);
```

2. Save your changes.

3. Add the following lines to the implementation file of your main frame window class (position is not important):

```
////////////////////////////////////////////
// Helpers for saving/restoring window state
static TCHAR szSection[] = _T("Settings");
static TCHAR szWindowPos[] = _T("WindowPos");
static TCHAR szCBarSection[] = _T("Control Bars");
static TCHAR szFormat[] = _T("%u,%u,%d,%d,%d,%d,%d,%d,%d,%d");
```

The first three lines define three strings, each representing a section in the Registry key. The fourth string defines a format that will contain the size and position of the main frame window.

4. Add the following code to the implementation file of your main frame window class:

```
void CMainFrame::InitialShowWindow(UINT nCmdShow)
{
    // Retrieve position of the window before displaying
    WINDOWPLACEMENT wp;
    wp.length = sizeof (WINDOWPLACEMENT);
    if (!ReadWindowPlacement(&wp))
    {
        ShowWindow(nCmdShow);
        return;
    }
    if (nCmdShow != SW_SHOWNORMAL)
        wp.showCmd = nCmdShow;
    WriteWindowPlacement(&wp);
    LoadBarState(szCBarSection);
    SetWindowPlacement(&wp);

    ShowWindow(wp.showCmd);
}
```

This code first reads the attributes from the Registry key and initializes a WINDOWPLACEMENT structure, *wp*. The state of the control bars is then read, the size of the main frame window is restored, and finally, a call is made to *ShowWindow*, which displays the main frame window using the *wp* variable.

5. Save your changes.

Step 4: Adding Helper Functions
for the *InitialShowWindow* Function

Did you notice the calls the *InitialShowWindow* function made to the *ReadWindowPlacement* and *WriteWindowPlacement* functions? In case you were wondering about them, you haven't added them yet. The *InitialShowWindow* function uses these two helper functions to read and write entries to and from the Registry key. For *InitialShowWindow* to work properly, you must add the *ReadWindowPlacement* and *WriteWindowPlacement* helper functions to the main frame window class. To add them, follow this procedure:

1. Add the following lines of code to the implementation file of the main frame window class:

```
static BOOL ReadWindowPlacement(LPWINDOWPLACEMENT pwp)
{
    CString strBuffer = AfxGetApp()->
        GetProfileString(szSection, szWindowPos);
    if (strBuffer.IsEmpty())
        return FALSE;

    WINDOWPLACEMENT wp;
    int nRead = _stscanf(strBuffer, szFormat,
        &wp.flags, &wp.showCmd,
        &wp.ptMinPosition.x, &wp.ptMinPosition.y,
        &wp.ptMaxPosition.x, &wp.ptMaxPosition.y,
        &wp.rcNormalPosition.left, &wp.rcNormalPosition.top,
        &wp.rcNormalPosition.right,
        &wp.rcNormalPosition.bottom);

    if (nRead != 10)
        return FALSE;

    wp.length = sizeof wp;
    *pwp = wp;
    return TRUE;
}
```

The first section of this code retrieves the size and the position of the main frame window from the Registry key using the strings *szSection* and *szWindowPos*. If the buffer is empty (indicating that no information was found), the *ReadWindowPlacement* function returns FALSE, indicating failure. The second section of the code uses the size and position values from the *szFormat* string to initialize a temporary WINDOWPLACEMENT variable. If the initialization is successful, *pwp* is set equal to *wp* and the function returns TRUE, indicating success.

2. Add the following lines of code to the implementation file of the main frame window class:

```
static void WriteWindowPlacement(LPWINDOWPLACEMENT pwp)
{
    TCHAR szBuffer[sizeof("-32767") * 8 +
        sizeof("65535") * 2 + 1];

    wsprintf(szBuffer, szFormat,
        pwp->flags, pwp->showCmd,
        pwp->ptMinPosition.x, pwp->ptMinPosition.y,
        pwp->ptMaxPosition.x, pwp->ptMaxPosition.y,
        pwp->rcNormalPosition.left, pwp->rcNormalPosition.top,
        pwp->rcNormalPosition.right,
        pwp->rcNormalPosition.bottom);
    AfxGetApp()->WriteProfileString(szSection,
        szWindowPos, szBuffer);
}
```

The first section of this code allocates a temporary character buffer to store the string retrieved from the Registry key. The buffer is then initialized with values from the WINDOWPLACEMENT pointer that was passed in. Once initialized, the buffer is written to the Registry key in the *szSection* section under the *szWindowPos* heading.

3. Save your changes.

Now that you have added the ability to read values from the application's Registry key, you have to add the ability to store the attributes of the main frame window (and the control bars) in the application's Registry key at the proper time.

Step 5: Implementing the *OnClose* Function of the Main Frame Window

To save the current state of the main frame window, you need a way to store its attributes before its termination. You can do this by overriding the *OnClose* function of the main frame window object and then adding code that writes the values to the system Registry. Using your favorite method, override the *OnClose* function of the main window class.

After you override the *OnClose* function, replace any existing function code with the following code:

```
void CMainFrame::OnClose()
{

    // Before it is destroyed, save the position of the
    // window
    WINDOWPLACEMENT wp;
    wp.length = sizeof (WINDOWPLACEMENT);
    if (GetWindowPlacement(&wp))
    {
        wp.flags = 0;
        if (IsZoomed())
            wp.flags |= WPF_RESTORETOMAXIMIZED;
        // And write it to the Registry
        WriteWindowPlacement(&wp);
    }
    SaveBarState(szCBarSection);

    CMDIFrameWnd::OnClose();
};
```

The first section of this code initializes a temporary WINDOWPLACEMENT structure with a call to the *GetWindowPlacement* function. If this call is successful, the code checks to see whether the main window is maximized and adds the WPF_RESTORETOMAXIMIZED flag if it is needed. A call is then made with these new values to the *WriteWindowPlacement* helper function that was added in step 4. Finally, the state of the control bars is saved, and the *OnClose* function of the base class is called.

This completes the modifications to the main frame window class.

Step 6: Adding Data Members to the Child Window

For child windows, there are several attributes that can be saved from session to session:

- The state of the child window (maximized, minimized, or normal)

- The type of child window that is open

- The last file viewed

Unfortunately, I have room here to demonstrate the tracking of only one attribute—the state of the child window. This tracking is accomplished using two data members (*m_nDefCmdShow* and *m_nDefCmdShowOld*) and four functions (*Initialize, Terminate, OnActivate,* and *OnSize*). The data members store the current state and the previously saved state of the child window. One group of functions, which consists of the *Initialize* and *Terminate* functions, reads and writes the child window state from the application's Registry key. The second group of functions, which consists of the *OnActivateFrame* and *OnSize* functions, tracks changes in the child window state and ensures that new child windows always use the current value, *m_defShowCmd*.

To implement this functionality, add several data members to the child frame window class, as described below:

1. Add the following lines of code to the "protected" section of the child window class, which is found in the header file of the child frame window class:

```
static int m_nDefCmdShow;
static int m_nDefCmdShowOld;
```

These two members store the current and previous values of the child window state.

2. Save your changes.

3. In the implementation file of your child window class, add the following lines of code after the message map declaration:

```
int CChildFrame::m_nDefCmdShow = SW_SHOWMAXIMIZED;
int CChildFrame::m_nDefCmdShowOld = SW_SHOWMAXIMIZED;

static TCHAR szSec[] = _T("Settings");
static TCHAR szShowCmd[] = _T("ShowCmd");
```

The first section of this code initializes the two static data members (*CChildFrame::m_nDefCmdShow* and *CChildFrame::m_nDefCmdShow-Old*) to SW_SHOWMAXIMIZED. This forces all child windows to be displayed initially as maximized. In the second section of code, the *szSec* and *szShowCmd* strings are defined. These strings contain the name of the Registry key section and the attribute name, respectively.

4. Save your changes.

Step 7: Adding the *Initialize* and *Terminate* Functions to the Child Frame Window

You might recall that at one point you modified the *InitInstance* function in the application class to make a call to a function of the child window class, named *Initialize*. In addition, you modified the *ExitInstance* function to make a call to a function of the main frame window class, named *Terminate*. Well, you are now ready to implement these functions.

The purpose of the *Initialize* function is to retrieve the default state of child windows from the application's Registry key and to initialize the static data members that were declared in step 6. The purpose of the *Terminate* function is to check the current child window state against the value in the application's Registry key and, if the values differ, to store the new value in the Registry key. Because both of these functions are custom functions, you add them to the child window class manually. To implement the *Initialize* and *Terminate* functions, follow this procedure:

1. Add the following code to the header file of the child window class:

   ```
   // Operations
   public:
       static void Initialize();
       static void Terminate();
   ```

2. Save your changes.

3. In the implementation file of the child window class, add the following code:

   ```
   void CChildFrame::Initialize()
   {
       m_nDefCmdShow = AfxGetApp()->GetProfileInt(szSec,
           szShowCmd, m_nDefCmdShow);
       m_nDefCmdShowOld = m_nDefCmdShow;
   }
   ```

   This code retrieves the default state of the child window from the application's Registry key and initializes *m_nDefCmdShowOld* with this value.

4. Immediately after the *Initialize* function body, add the code below:

   ```
   void CChildFrame::Terminate()
   {
       if (m_nDefCmdShow != m_nDefCmdShowOld)
       {
           AfxGetApp()->WriteProfileInt(szSec, szShowCmd,
               m_nDefCmdShow);
           m_nDefCmdShowOld = m_nDefCmdShow;
       }
   }
   ```

This code first checks the current default state of the child window object (*m_nDefCmdShow*) against the previously saved state (*m_nDef-CmdShowOld*). If there is a difference, the new value is written to the application's Registry key and *m_nDefCmdShowOld* is updated with the current value.

5. Save your changes.

You can now initialize *m_nDefCmdShow* and *m_nDefCmdShowOld* with the value that is found in the application's Registry key. When the application exits, check the current value (which has possibly been changed by the user) and, if it differs from the Registry key value, update the Registry key value.

Step 8: Implementing the *ActivateFrame* Function of the Child Frame Window

Because you are tracking the child window state, it would be a good idea to use it when creating new child windows. A good way to do this is to override the *ActivateFrame* function. You can use the override to ensure that any new child window initially appears in the proper state—that is, either maximized or normal. Override the function now, and replace the existing body of code with the following code:

```
void CChildFrame::ActivateFrame(int nCmdShow)
{
    if (nCmdShow == -1)
        nCmdShow = m_nDefCmdShow;   // Use our default
    CMDIChildWnd::ActivateFrame(nCmdShow);
}
```

This code checks the current value of *nCmdShow* and, when the values don't match, uses the stored value (*m_nDefCmdShow*). The child window is then displayed with a call to the *ActivateFrame* function of the base class.

Step 9: Implementing the *OnSize* Function of the Child Frame Window

At this point, you have code that saves the current value of the child frame window upon exit and then uses this value when creating new child frame windows. However, it would be nice if it were possible to update the value of the child window state whenever the user restores a maximized child window or maximizes a child window. This can be done by overriding another function (*OnSize*) in the child window class. The *OnSize* function is called every time the state of the child window is changed. Override the *OnSize* function now, and replace the existing body of code with the following code:

```
void CChildFrame::OnSize(UINT nType, int cx, int cy)
{
    CMDIChildWnd::OnSize(nType, cx, cy);
    if (!IsWindowVisible())
        return;

    switch (nType)
    {
        case SIZE_MAXIMIZED:
            m_nDefCmdShow = SW_SHOWMAXIMIZED;
            break;
        case SIZE_RESTORED:
            m_nDefCmdShow = SW_SHOWNORMAL;
            break;
    }
}
```

This code first calls the default handler and then checks to see whether the window is visible. When the window isn't visible, there isn't any need to track the state of the child window, so the function exits immediately. However, when the window is visible, a *switch* statement is used to determine the current state of the child window (maximized or normal). The *switch* statement then stores the current value in *m_defCmdShow* and exits the function.

Rebuild the project. Your application will now save the size and the position of the main frame window, the state of the child window (maximized or normal), and the state (docked or undocked, visible or hidden) of the status bar and the toolbar in a key of the system Registry.

Additional Information

For an MDI application, you must use the system Registry to achieve this functionality if the application is to be Windows 95 compliant. However, if your MDI application doesn't have to be Windows 95 compliant, you can use the INI file approach. The only change you have to make is to remove the call to the *SetRegistryKey* function in the *InitInstance* function of the application. This causes an INI file to be created automatically for the application (if one does not already exist) and all attributes to be automatically written to and read from this file.

For an SDI application, you will have to modify the procedure that has been described in this task to achieve this functionality. The code that saves the size, position, and state of the control bars—the bulk of which is found in step 3 and step 5—remains the same. If you want to save the state of the main frame window, modify the procedure and code found in steps 6 through 9. Of course you should make all changes to the main frame window class instead of the child frame window class. I leave the details as an exercise for the reader.

Because the structure of a dialog box–based application is different from the structure of an SDI or MDI application, the only useful information that can be taken from this chapter is how to set up the Registry key (using a call to the *SetRegistryKey* function) and the use of the *WriteProfileInt* and *GetProfileInt* function calls.

MFC Database Classes

When the Data Access Objects (DAO) database classes were first introduced in MFC version 4, users began to ask a logical question: which set of classes is used in what circumstances? The answer to that question depends entirely on what is to be implemented, so it is impossible to answer the question without going into a lot of detail for each individual case. Nevertheless, I can comment briefly on the subject here.

The set of choices you have for creating database applications is vast. It is actually a continuum of choices, with desktop database applications at one end and strict client/server database applications at the other end. Probably the only two choices that might seem obvious are using the MFC DAO database classes with Microsoft Access 97 MDB data and using the MFC ODBC database classes with Microsoft SQL Server version 6.x. The members of each of these two pairings were for the most part designed to work together, and both pairings are very efficient. But you probably already knew about these choices—what about everything else? Briefly, here is a process for making your decision:

- Decide what data source you have to use. How robust does your database have to be? How many people will need access to the data at one time? The data source you select often determines what database classes you'll use.

- Decide what tool you'll use to create the interface. The more flexibility your users need in the interface, the more careful you have to be in designing it. Designing an interface in which the user clicks buttons to print predetermined reports is completely different from one in which the user creates his or her own queries and prints the results. For example, if you have to use list boxes filled with data that doesn't change much and you've selected a server-based data source, it would make more sense to store the data locally rather than on the server.

■ Decide what network you're going to use, if any. There are a number of types of networks in use today, and each one has an effect on how data moves across the network. I don't have room to discuss networks in this chapter, but understanding how to optimize your database application is necessary if you are to avoid pitfalls in your network schema.

■ Create prototype applications before starting down an implementation path. There is so much to plan in advance of any implementation that developing a prototype becomes an essential part of the process, not merely an option. It will require a significant amount of time to construct your prototype application in such a way that the elements that work can be transferred easily to start the actual application—you might do well in the prototyping stage, but the job isn't finished until your solution works in the actual implementation.

Comparing the MFC Database Classes

Let's focus first on the common database functionality in the two sets of classes:

■ Both sets of classes support scrolling through recordsets.

■ ODBC classes rely on the underlying driver.

■ DAO classes have better support for MDB, which is good for installable ISAMs, and which is the same support as the ODBC database classes for server-based data.

■ Both sets of classes support transactions:

❑ ODBC classes support transactions at the database level.

❑ DAO classes support transactions at the workspace level.

■ The recordset update functions of the two classes are almost identical.

■ Both sets of classes support locking records during updates.

■ Both sets of classes support detection of field data changes.

■ Both sets of classes have Move operations.

■ Both *CDatabase* and *CDaoDatabase* can detect whether a data source accepts transactions. Transaction requirements have been considerably relaxed in the ODBC database classes as of MFC version 4.2.

■ Database objects in both classes allow you to set a predetermined query timeout period.

■ Both classes can execute direct SQL statements.

In addition, the ODBC database classes have functionality that is not included in the DAO database classes:

- The ODBC database classes are multithreaded as of MFC version 4.2. To take advantage of this capability, you must use a multithreaded ODBC driver. DAO 3.5 is apartment-model threaded.

- The bulk row fetching functionality is new in MFC version 4.2. Additional navigation capabilities have been added.

- In response to many requests, the Visual C++ team has added better support for console database applications. These are the new options in *CDatabase::OpenEx*:

  - *CDatabase::noOdbcDialog*: Does not display the ODBC connection dialog box, regardless of whether enough connection information is supplied.

  - *CDatabase::forceOdbcDialog*: Always displays the ODBC connection dialog box.

In turn, the DAO database classes have functionality that is not included in the ODBC database classes:

- The Workspace, TableDef, and QueryDef objects are unique to the DAO database classes. There are no direct equivalents for them in the ODBC database classes.

- *CDaoTableDef* and *CDaoQueryDef* functionality can generally be reproduced with direct ODBC calls, such as those found in the CATALOG2 sample.

- *CDaoDatabase* supports the creation of TableDefs, QueryDefs, and Relations.

- *CDaoRecordset* has slightly better navigation functionality, including these operations:

  - Find

  - Percent position

  - Seek

- The ability to create fields and indexes at run time using a *CDaoTableDef* object is a wonderful advantage, as is the data validation that supports it.

■ *CDaoQueryDef* objects can be created using fields and indexes and then stored for repeated use.

■ *CDaoQueryDef* objects can also control ODBC timeouts.

Understanding the DAO SDK Classes

The DAO SDK includes some C++ database classes that are separate and distinct from the MFC DAO database classes and encapsulate the individual objects in the DAO hierarchy. Although you can mix DAO SDK C++ classes with MFC DAO database classes, the DAO SDK C++ classes do not follow the MFC guidelines for operator overloading. Please exercise caution when using the classes together. (For more information on this topic, see the article "The DAO of Databases: Using Data Access Objects and the Jet Engine in C++" in *Microsoft Systems Journal,* January, 1996.) The following table compares features of the DAO SDK and MFC DAO database classes.

DAO SDK Database Classes	MFC DAO Database Classes
Simple migration from Visual Basic	Simple migration from MFC ODBC database classes
Direct mappings to DAO's OLE Automation objects	Conforms to MFC standard two-phase construction
More Jet/DAO functionality	AppWizard and ClassWizard support
Doesn't conform to MFC standard two-phase construction	Hides more difficult DAO functionality

Using DAO SDK classes is easier for developers accustomed to writing applications with Microsoft Visual Basic. Developers who already use MFC ODBC database classes will find the architecture and use of MFC DAO classes more familiar.

Using the MFC Database Classes

When you write applications using the MFC ODBC classes, you can connect to any data source for which you have an ODBC driver. The operation of ODBC Driver Manager and ODBC drivers is transparent in applications you write with these classes, but the individual driver capabilities affect the functionality of an application. Generally, MFC dynasets require an ODBC driver with level 2 API conformance. You can use updatable and read-only snapshots and forward-only recordsets if your data source driver conforms to the level 1 API set, but you can't use dynasets. However, if a level 1 driver supports extended fetching and keyset-driven cursors, it will also support dynasets.

When you write applications using the MFC DAO classes, your best performance will be with the Microsoft Access databases because they are native to Microsoft Jet. Microsoft Access 97 for Microsoft Windows 95 has a database format that is native to DAO version 3.5. You'll get the fastest performance when you use a Microsoft Access 97 database. A separate DLL does provide access to Microsoft Jet version 1.*x* and version 2 databases. But in Microsoft Jet version 3, the storage engine and format were completely revised. Given the large number of structural changes, Jet version 3 treats version 2 databases as external indexed sequential access method databases (ISAMs). This has an impact on performance, so if you have not already considered upgrading your Access database, this is a good reason to think about doing so.

You also can access installable ISAM databases and ODBC data sources. ISAM databases such as Microsoft Visual FoxPro and Borland dBASE can be opened directly or attached to Access databases for the best performance. Remember that Access version 1.*x* and version 2 databases fall into this category. You can reach ODBC data sources such as Microsoft SQL Server and Oracle Server through ODBC, so you have the option of using DAO for those data sources also. An ODBC data source is any database management system (DBMS) for which you have the appropriate ODBC driver. For Microsoft Visual C++ versions 2 and later, you need 32-bit ODBC drivers—except on Win32s, where you need 16-bit ODBC drivers.

If you like, you can use the new DAO 3.5 ODBCDirect objects through direct calls to these OLE objects, but MFC does not have wrapper classes for them.

Here are some general principles to follow as you decide which set of database classes to use:

- ODBC database classes work best with server-based data such as SQL Server and Oracle Server.

- ODBC database classes work best with an application that has to be written in a generic enough form that it can be used with a wide range of data sources; this is one of ODBC's strengths.

- DAO database classes are best used with desktop databases, and then only sparingly if you are using server-based data. Queries for server-based data must be carefully optimized.

269

■ Attaching external tables to Access provides faster performance than opening data sources directly when you are using the DAO database classes. Tests show slightly faster performance with desktop data and dramatically increased performance with server-based data.

■ With desktop data, DAO database classes can be faster than ODBC database classes with some operations but slower with others. There is usually no clear winner, so creating prototypes with both sets of classes for your specific data sources might be the only way to determine which type of database class works best for your project.

The time you spend creating prototypes is time well spent. You are more likely to find and correct problems early in the product cycle when you take the time to plan and create a prototype for your application.

Stretching the MFC Database Classes

MFC database classes were designed with specific uses in mind. The ODBC database classes let you get data from any data source type for which you have an ODBC driver. The DAO database classes are generally more suited for use with desktop data sources, although they have greater built-in functionality. However, there might be many occasions when you want to stretch the original intent of each set of database classes. For example, you might want to open a SQL Server database directly instead of attaching it to an Access database as the documentation recommends. I've included some of these types of tasks in this chapter, but be aware that you must evaluate carefully whether using them will give you optimal results for your individual situation.

Some of the tasks are documented in the Visual C++ online help, but step-by-step instructions might not be supplied for them in the documentation, or the instructions might not be easily inferred. Some of the tasks will be easier to accomplish if you have Visual C++ Enterprise Edition, but this edition is not required to complete the task.

I decided to rely heavily on AppWizard for the tasks presented in this chapter because it saves so much time when you set up the field data members for your database. In nearly all of the sample applications, I use the record view and demonstrate its flexibility for a variety of situations. For two of the tasks, I use a *CDialog*. Rather than trying to supply a single database for all of these tasks, I decided to take advantage of the sample databases included with the data source types used in this chapter. All of these sample databases are included on the companion CD-ROM, with the exception of the SQL Server and Oracle Server sample databases.

This chapter includes the following tasks:

- Opening a FoxPro database directly with DAO database classes

    The Jet database engine includes an internal driver for reading FoxPro data sources. I've included sample applications for the three most recent releases of Microsoft Visual FoxPro that contrast the use of the different releases.

- Opening SQL Server directly with DAO database classes

    This is a task that is frequently requested by developers, but I emphasize again that performance might not be optimal with this method of getting data from the database. Nevertheless, it is useful in some situations to be able to open the SQL Server data source directly, such as when you are creating temporary tables.

- Opening Oracle directly with DAO database classes

    With the release of Microsoft ODBC Driver for Oracle, you might want to try this task just to get the default ODBC connect string that you can use in this task and the other applications for Oracle Server.

- Attaching FoxPro to an Access database using DAO database classes

    This handy task creates a utility for creating blank Access MDB files and attaching FoxPro and Visual FoxPro DBF tables to the MDB file programmatically. Gallery components make up the bulk of the code, and they are sure to save you a lot of time in creating the utility. The dialog box for this application has edit controls for each element of the connect string that is required for attaching a FoxPro table.

- Attaching SQL Server to an Access database using DAO database classes

    This handy task creates a utility for creating blank Access MDB files and attaching SQL Server tables to the MDB file programmatically. Gallery components also make up the bulk of the code for this task. The dialog box for this application has edit controls for each element of the connect string that is required for attaching a SQL Server table.

- Attaching Oracle to an Access database in DAO database applications

    This task briefly discusses how to attach an Oracle database to an Access MDB file.

- Mixing static and dynamic binding in DAO database classes

    This task shows how to create a standard AppWizard-generated application that uses *CRecordset::DoFieldExchange* with calls to *CRecordset::GetFieldValue* for populating a Microsoft ActiveX control with employees' photos. The method is similar to the one demonstrated in the first task of the chapter, "Opening a FoxPro Database Directly with DAO Database Classes."

■ Opening a recordset on a stored procedure using ODBC database classes

Stored procedures can be wonderfully useful for returning recordsets of all sizes. In this example, I use a standard AppWizard-generated database application and supplement it with a second dialog box whose edit controls are populated by records returned from the stored procedure.

■ Using output parameters with the ODBC API and ODBC database classes

This task builds on the project code of the preceding task and adds another button to the record view. This new button runs a stored procedure that does not return records; rather, it calculates a figure and displays the results to the user in a message box.

Opening a FoxPro Database Directly with DAO Database Classes

The purpose of this task is to demonstrate how to open a FoxPro database directly without first attaching it to an Access table. DAO can read FoxPro DBF files rather easily; but reading Visual FoxPro database container (DBC) files requires a little more work.

The task consists of twelve steps:

1. Preparing the FoxPro database
2. Attaching the table to Access
3. Building the ACCSPICT control from the MFC DAOCTL sample
4. Running AppWizard on the MDB file
5. Removing the Photo field from *DoFieldExchange* using ClassWizard
6. Designing the record view
7. Inserting the ACCSPICT control
8. Changing *GetDefaultDBName* for the recordset
9. Adding a function to the document header
10. Adding code to *OnInitialUpdate* to open the recordset

11. Adding code to display the Employee Photo field

12. Compiling and running the application

Step 1: Preparing the FoxPro Database

If you are using FoxPro version 2.6, use the Customer database in the CATA-LOG sample for this step. You will need all of the sample files in the subdirectory in which you intend your application to be used. For this data source, you can now skip to step 2.

If you are using Visual FoxPro version 3, use the Customer table in the TASTRADE sample database and export it to a Visual FoxPro version 3 DBF format as described below. If you are using Visual FoxPro version 5, use the Employee table in the TASTRADE database and export it to a Visual FoxPro version 3 DBF format as described below. In both versions of Visual FoxPro, the table is bound to the DBC file.

1. Start Visual FoxPro version 3 or version 5, and open the TASTRADE sample project.

2. Export the Customer database for Visual FoxPro version 3 or the Employee database for Visual FoxPro version 5 as a Visual FoxPro version 3 DBF file to a temporary directory.

3. Copy the accompanying FPT (memo) and CDX (index) files to that temporary directory, but do not include any INF files. Ultimately, you'll also need the DBC file and any other tables in that file because your DAO database application will open the DBC file directly.

Step 2: Attaching the Table to an Access Database

Use Access to attach the DBF table to the MDB file.

1. Start Access, and create a blank database.

2. Choose Get External Data/Link Tables from the File menu. Select Microsoft FoxPro Database (DBF) from the Files Of Type drop-down list box, and navigate to your data source.

3. Select the DBF file, and click Link. Then select the index file from the next dialog box.

   ❏ For FoxPro version 2.5, select CNO as the unique identifier for the index.

❑ For Visual FoxPro version 3, select the CUSTOMER_ID as the unique identifier for the index.

❑ For Visual FoxPro version 5, select LAST_NAME as the unique identifier for the index.

Click OK when Access has successfully linked the table.

4. Open the linked table in design mode. Access warns you that this table is a linked table and you will not be able to modify its properties. That's OK, because you're just going to look at the structure of the table. You also will not be able to open the table in datasheet mode, but that's not necessary anyway because you're going to use the record view form to display your data.

5. Notice that Access has truncated some of the field names to ten characters. Leave them that way—if you lengthen the names, your DAO database application won't find the fields in your table. If you attach the table to Access first, this will help you determine what DAO will expect.

Step 3: Building the ACCSPICT OLE Control from the MFC DAOCTL Sample

You can skip this step if you have already built and registered this control. If not, continue as described below.

1. Load the Visual C++ version 5 Professional or Enterprise distribution CD, and copy all of the files for the DAOCTL sample.

2. Open the ACCSPICT ActiveX control project, and build a Release version of the control. Building this control registers the OCX with your system and adds it to the Component And Controls Gallery. Close the project workspace.

If you copy the OCX to your Windows 95 or Microsoft Windows NT directory and register the OCX there using REGSRV32, you can remove the sample files and still have the OCX available. But I encourage you to build the other control and sample container and study the code. It's an excellent sample.

Step 4: Running AppWizard on the MDB File

In this task, you can create any one of three applications, depending on the sample database you're using: FoxPro version 2.6, Visual FoxPro version 3, or Visual FoxPro version 5. Just follow the directions for your version.

1. Start Microsoft Visual Studio, and create a new MFC AppWizard (EXE) project. Name it *DirFox2*, *DirFox3*, or *DirFox5*, as appropriate.

2. In AppWizard Step 1, choose Single Document interface.

3. In AppWizard Step 2, choose A Database View Without File Support. For the data source, select DAO, and click the browse button (...). Select the MDB file you have just created, and then select Table as the recordset type.

   ❏ For FoxPro version 2.6 and Visual FoxPro version 3, select the Customer table from the next dialog box.

   ❏ For Visual FoxPro version 5, select the Employee table from the next dialog box.

4. For Visual FoxPro version 5 only, select ActiveX controls in AppWizard Step 3 to provide container support.

5. Accept the defaults on the remaining AppWizard steps (or, if you like, make changes), and then click OK to create the files.

Step 5: Removing the Photo Field
from *DoFieldExchange* Using ClassWizard

For FoxPro version 2.6 or Visual FoxPro version 3, skip to step 6; the Customer table in the sample database that comes with these software packages doesn't have a photo field.

For Visual FoxPro version 5, first look at the *CDirFox5Set* class; notice that the data members have the same names (preceded by $m\_$) and field name truncation that they have in Access. You can change the names of the data members if you like, but you must then also change them elsewhere in the code, and it's probably not worth the effort to do so.

To display the Photo field from this database, you have to use the AccessPict control from the Components And Controls Gallery. You won't be using the *DoFieldExchange* mechanism to retrieve the value from each field, so you have to remove it from the *DoFieldExchange* code using ClassWizard.

1. Start ClassWizard; then click the Member Variables tab. In the Class Name drop-down list box, select the *CDirFox5Set* class.

2. Scroll down until you see the [PHOTO] field. Select it, and then click Delete Variable. Click OK to close ClassWizard.

You'll add code that retrieves the Photo field a little later on. In the constructor for the recordset, notice that the data member *m_nFields* has been decremented from 19 to 18. You'll see also that data members for the two Memo fields are not initialized because it's not necessary to do so.

Step 6: Designing the Record View

Use the Resource editor to design the record view. For ideas on how to lay out the information, see the layout for this sample on the companion CD-ROM.

1. Lay out static controls in the dialog box for the field titles and edit controls for the fields from the Employee table in whatever format you like. In Visual FoxPro version 5, leave room for the control that will display the employee's photo.

2. When you're satisfied with the layout, hold down Ctrl and double-click each edit control. Then select the member variable that corresponds to the field name from the Member Variable Name drop-down list box in ClassWizard. In the Visual FoxPro version 5 Notes fields, under the Styles tab in the Edit Properties box, add the Multiline, Vertical Scroll, and AutoVScroll properties.

Step 7: Inserting the ACCSPICT Control

If you're using FoxPro version 2.6 or Visual FoxPro version 3, skip this step. If not, continue with the procedure below.

1. Choose Add To Project/Components And Controls from the Project menu. Choose Registered ActiveX Controls. Select AccessPict control, and then click Insert. Then click OK. The list of classes to be added to the project is displayed. Click OK to add the control to your Resource editor toolbox and the code to your project. Close the Components And Controls Gallery dialog box.

2. Click and drag the OCX toolbox button to your form, and give the control proportions normally associated with an ID photo. Hold down Alt and double-click the control to open the Properties dialog box (if you don't already have it open), and click the Control tab. Click the Stretch To Fit and Preserve Ratio options, and remove the text from the Caption property.

3. Hold down Ctrl and double-click the control to bring up the Class-Wizard Add Member Variable dialog box. Name the control *m_ctl-Picture*. Notice that Control is already selected in the Category drop-down list box and that the Variable type is *CAccessPict*. Click OK to add the variable.

Step 8: Changing *GetDefaultDBName* for the Recordset

You're now going to change the data source from the MDB file you used with
AppWizard to one of the following: the FoxPro version 2.6 DBF file, the Visual
FoxPro version 3 DBC file, or the Visual FoxPro version 5 DBC file.

1. In the ClassView pane, double-click the *GetDefaultDBName* member
   function from the recordset class.

2. Remove the reference to the physical file location, and leave only the
   following line:

   ```
   return _T("");
   ```

   You'll open the recordset directly in the view's *OnInitalUpdate* member function.

Step 9: Adding a Function to the Document Header

To open a table directly, you have to be able to get a pointer to the database
from the document header file. In the //Attributes section under "public:", add
the following code:

```
CDaoDatabase m_database;
CDaoDatabase* GetDatabase()
{
    return &m_database;
}
```

Having a *CDaoDatabase* data member in the view makes it easy to specifically open a database; the *GetDatabase* function returns the needed reference
to the data member.

Step 10: Adding Code to *OnInitialUpdate* to Open the Recordset

Using the appropriate class names and file locations for your project, replace
the default implementation of the *OnInitialUpdate* member function with the
appropriate code, as shown below.

For FoxPro version 2.6, use the following code:

```
CDirFox26Doc* pDoc = (CDirFox26Doc*)GetDocument();
CDaoDatabase* pDatabase = pDoc->GetDatabase();

m_pSet = &GetDocument()->m_dirFox26Set;
m_pSet->m_pDatabase = pDatabase;
m_pSet->m_pDatabase->Open(
```

(continued)

277

```
    _T("C:\\MFC Workshop\\Chap8\\DirFox26\\Catalog26"),
    FALSE, FALSE, _T("FoxPro 2.6"));
CDaoRecordView::OnInitialUpdate();
```

For Visual FoxPro versions 3 and 5, use the code below. (If you are using version 3, substitute "Fox3" for "Fox 5" in the code.)

```
CDirFox5Doc* pDoc = (CDirFox5Doc*)GetDocument();
CDaoDatabase* pDatabase = pDoc->GetDatabase();

m_pSet = &GetDocument()->m_dirFox5Set;
m_pSet->m_pDatabase = pDatabase;
m_pSet->m_pDatabase->Open(
    _T("C:\\MFC Workshop\\Chap8\\DirFox5\\tastrade5\\tastrade.dbc"),
    FALSE, FALSE, _T("FoxPro DBC"));
CDaoRecordView::OnInitialUpdate();
```

The first two lines of code for each example create a pointer to the document object and obtain a pointer to the database object. The third line of code is the standard implementation for a record view. The fourth line of code sets the data members to the correct pointers, and the fifth line opens the DBF or DBC file. Notice that for FoxPro version 2.6, you're pointing to the directory in which the table's files are located; for Visual FoxPro version 3 and version 5, you're supplying the path to the DBC file. DAO uses the DBC file to find the correct table to open.

By explicitly opening a database and then a recordset, you can specify the necessary connection information to open the table directly. The default implementation of *CDaoRecordView::OnInitialUpdate* checks to see whether a database or a recordset is already open. If you do not create and open the database object yourself, the framework implicitly creates and opens the database object for you.

If you like, you can compile the application at this point and see the data in the form you've created. For Visual FoxPro version 5, you can see all of the data with the exception of the photo. (You'll add the code for the photo in the next step.) If you're using FoxPro version 2.6 or Visual FoxPro version 3, you're now finished with the application.

Step 11: Adding Code to Display the Employee Photo Field

As you scroll through the recordset, the *DoFieldExchange* member function retrieves the values for each field. Because you eliminated the [PHOTO] field from that list, the value is not being retrieved as you scroll. It's possible to retrieve the value by calling *CDaoRecordset::GetFieldValue* and using the picture control's member functions to put the photo in the control. This retrieval has to occur twice:

■ When the record view first initializes (so that the photo for the first record is displayed)

■ After each move to the next record

Add a data member to the view to store the value for each photo.

1. In the view's header file just below the //}}AFX_DATA section, add the following line of code:

```
COleVariant m_varPhoto;
```

2. In the implementation for the record view's *OnInitialUpdate*, add the following code after the call to *CDaoRecordView::OnInitialUpdate*:

```
try
{
    m_varPhoto = m_pSet->GetFieldValue("[photo]");
    m_ctlPicture.SetData(&m_varPhoto);
}
catch (COleException* e)
{
    e->Delete();
}
```

3. Start ClassWizard, and then click the Message Maps tab. Select the view class name from the Object IDs list. Scroll down until you find the *On-Move* member function, and double-click it to add it to the list of member functions. Then click Edit Code.

4. Replace the call to *CDaoRecordView::OnMove* between the braces with the following code:

```
CDaoRecordView::OnMove(nIDMoveCommand);

m_varPhoto = m_pSet->GetFieldValue("[photo]");
try
{
    m_varPhoto = m_pSet->GetFieldValue("[photo]");
    m_ctlPicture.SetData(&m_varPhoto);
    return TRUE;
}
catch (COleException* e)
{
    e->Delete();
    return FALSE;
}
```

Step 12: Compiling and Running the Application

Now compile and run the application. You will see the photo for each record appear when you scroll through the data. The default implementation of *CDaoRecordView* takes care of populating the record view with fields from the database; the separate call to *GetFieldValue* and *SetData* displays the photo as you scroll through the database.

Additional Information

It's essential that the memo field files for any database reside in the same sub-directory as the table files. MFC throws an exception if it cannot locate the memo files.

Opening SQL Server Directly with DAO Database Classes

The purpose of this task is to demonstrate how to open a SQL Server database table directly without first attaching it to an Access table. I don't recommend as a rule that you open a SQL Server database directly because the performance is not optimal. However, it is possible to do this, and there are occasions when it makes sense to do it. Therefore, I've included the steps for the procedure here. You could easily substitute another server-based data source in these steps, provided you have the correct ODBC connect string. To open an Oracle Server database directly, see the next task, "Opening Oracle Directly with DAO Database Classes." Also, be sure you read the "Additional Information" section at the end of this task.

The task consists of seven steps:

1. Attaching the table to Access
2. Running AppWizard on the MDB file
3. Designing the record view
4. Changing *GetDefaultDBName* for the recordset
5. Adding a function to the document header
6. Adding code to *OnInitialUpdate* to open the recordset
7. Compiling and running the application

Step 1: Attaching the Table to an Access Database

This procedure assumes that you have already created a data source name (DSN) for your SQL Server data source with ODBC Administrator. (See the Visual C++ online help for instructions on how to create a DSN.) Use Access to attach the DBF table to the MDB.

1. Start Access, and create a blank database.

2. Choose Get External Data/Link Tables from the File menu. Select ODBC Databases( ) from the Files Of Type drop-down list box. A list of ODBC data sources will appear.

3. Select your ODBC data source, and supply a user ID and a password (if one is required). Select dbo.Authors from the list of tables that appears. Click OK when Access has successfully linked the table.

4. Open the linked table in design mode. Access warns you that the table is a linked table and that you will not be able to modify its properties. That's OK because you're just going to look at the structure of the table.

5. Access might truncate some of the field names to ten characters. Leave them that way—if you lengthen the names, your DAO database application might not be able to find the fields in your table. If you attach the table to Access first, this will help you determine what DAO will expect.

Step 2: Running AppWizard on the MDB File

Now you'll run AppWizard and use the Access database you created; afterward you can delete the database.

1. Start Developer Studio, and create a new MFC AppWizard (EXE) project (and workspace). Name it *SSDir.*

2. In AppWizard Step 1, choose Single Document interface.

3. In AppWizard Step 2, choose A Database View Without File Support. Select DAO for the data source, and click the browse button (...). Select the MDB file you have just created, and then select Dynaset as the recordset type.

4. Select the dbo.Authors table from the next dialog box.

5. Accept the defaults on the remaining AppWizard steps (or, if you like, make changes), and click OK to create the files.

Step 3: Designing the Record View

Use the Resource editor to design the record view. For ideas on how to lay out the information, see the layout for this sample on the companion CD-ROM.

1. Lay out static controls for the field titles and edit controls for the fields from the EMPLOYEES table in whatever order you prefer.

2. When you're satisfied with the layout, hold down Ctrl and double-click each edit control. Then select the member function that corresponds to the field name from the Member Variable Name drop-down list box in ClassWizard.

Step 4: Changing *GetDefaultDBName* for the Recordset

You're now going to change the data source from the MDB file you used with AppWizard to the SQL Server table.

1. In the ClassView pane, double-click the *GetDefaultDBName* member function from the recordset class.

2. Remove the reference to the physical file location, and leave only the following line:

```
return _T("");
```

You'll open the recordset directly in the view's *OnInitalUpdate* member function.

Step 5: Adding a Function to the Document Header

To open a table directly, you have to be able to get a pointer to the database from the document header file. In the //Attributes section under "public:", add the following code:

```
CDaoDatabase m_database;
CDaoDatabase* GetDatabase()
{
    return &m_database;
}
```

Having a *CDaoDatabase* data member in the view makes it easy to specifically open a database; the *GetDatabase* function returns the needed reference to the data member.

Step 6: Adding Code to *OnInitialUpdate* to Open the Recordset

Using the appropriate class names and file locations for your project, replace the default implementation of the *OnInitialUpdate* member function with the following code (between the existing braces):

```
CSSDirDoc* pDoc = (CSSDirDoc*)GetDocument();
CDaoDatabase* pDatabase = pDoc->GetDatabase();

m_pSet = &GetDocument()->m_sSDirSet;
m_pSet->m_pDatabase = pDatabase;
m_pSet->m_pDatabase->Open(NULL, FALSE, FALSE,
    _T("ODBC;DATABASE=PUBS;UID=sa;PWD=;DSN=SQLServerPubs;"));
CDaoRecordView::OnInitialUpdate();
```

The first two lines of code create a pointer to the document object and obtain a pointer to the database object. The third line of code is the standard implementation for a record view. The fourth line of code sets the data members to the correct pointers, and the fifth line opens the table. The last line of code is the standard implementation for *OnInitialUpdate.*

By explicitly opening a database and then a recordset, you can specify the necessary connection information to open the table directly. The default implementation of *CDaoRecordView::OnInitialUpdate* checks to see whether a database or a recordset is already open. If you do not create and open the database object yourself, the framework implicitly creates and opens the database object for you.

Step 7: Compiling and Running the Application

Compile the application using the Win32 Debug configuration, and put a breakpoint on the *OnInitialUpdate* member function. Step through the code to see how the new implementation supplies the database pointer and opens the database in advance of *CRecordView*'s calls to open the database.

Additional Information

Opening a table directly is an attractive option for desktop data sources. By opening a table using a *CDaoTableDef,* you can take advantage of several member functions available only to TableDef objects. You can only open dynasets and snapshots on an ODBC data source directly, however, so these advantages could be lost. In addition, performance might not be optimal if your queries cause DAO to do local processing before sending the query to the server. For more information on the impact of local processing on queries, consult the *Microsoft Jet Database Engine Programmer's Guide* (Microsoft Press, 1995).

Be wary also of creating joins between different types of database. Although it is possible to do this with DAO, it is one of the slowest types of queries to run. Optimize your joined tables as much as possible, and limit the number of fields in each half of the join.

Opening Oracle Directly with DAO Database Classes

The purpose of this task is to demonstrate how to open an Oracle Server database table directly without first attaching it to an Access table. Typically, you'll find that performance is better if you use ODBC database classes with Oracle server, but there might be occasions when you need to use the DAO database classes instead.

The most difficult step in opening any server-based data source is setting up the correct ODBC connect string. Even if the connect string is documented in your ODBC driver's Help file, you might have to experiment with the string until you find the right combination of elements. Be persistent—you'll figure it out.

The new ODBC Driver for Oracle ships with Visual C++ version 5, and I've used that driver in this example. Be sure to study the driver help file for additional information on connecting to an Oracle data source.

The sample database used here is the DEMO database, which can be accessed using the default user schema SCOTT and the password TIGER. The connect string you'll add to the application uses SCOTT and TIGER to get to the EMPLOYEE table.

The task consists of seven steps:

1. Attaching the table to Access
2. Running AppWizard in the MDB file
3. Designing the record view
4. Changing *GetDefaultDBName* for the recordset
5. Adding a function to the document header
6. Adding code to *OnInitialUpdate* to open the recordset
7. Compiling and running the application

Step 1: Attaching the Table to an Access Database

Use Access to attach the DBF table to the MDB file.

1. Start Access, and create a blank database.

2. Choose Get External Data/Link Tables from the File menu. Select ODBC Databases() from the Files Of Type drop-down list box. A list of ODBC data sources will appear.

3. Select your ODBC data source, and supply a user ID and a password (if one is required). From the list of tables that appears, select the EMPLOYEE table. (The prefix on the table name might vary.) Click OK when Access has successfully linked the table.

4. Open the linked table in design mode. Access warns you that the table is a linked table and that you will not be able to modify its properties. That's OK, because you're just going to look at the structure of the table.

5. Access might truncate some of the field names to ten characters. Leave them that way—if you lengthen the names, your DAO database might not be able to find the fields in your table. If you attach the table to Access first, this will help you determine what DAO will expect.

Step 2: Running AppWizard on the MDB File

Now you'll run AppWizard and use the Access database you created; afterward you can delete the database.

1. Start Visual Studio, and create a new MFC AppWizard (EXE) project. Name it *OrclDir*.

2. In AppWizard Step 1, choose Single Document interface.

3. In AppWizard Step 2, choose A Database View Without File Support. For the data source, select DAO; then click the browse button (…). Select the MDB file you have just created, and then select Dynaset as the recordset type.

4. Select the DEMO.EMPLOYEE table from the next dialog box. (The prefix on the table might vary.)

5. Accept the defaults on the remaining AppWizard steps (or, if you like, make changes), and then click OK to create the files.

Step 3: Designing the Record View

Use the Resource editor to design the record view. For ideas on how to lay out the information, see the layout for this sample on the companion CD-ROM.

1. Lay out static controls for the field titles and edit controls for the fields from the DEMO.EMPLOYEE table in whatever format you like.

2. When you're satisfied with the layout, hold down Ctrl and double-click each edit control. Then select the member variable that corresponds to the field name from the Member Variable Name drop-down list box in ClassWizard.

Step 4: Changing *GetDefaultDBName* for the Recordset

You're now going to change the data source from the MDB file you used with AppWizard to the SQL Server table.

1. In the ClassView pane, double-click the *GetDefaultDBName* member function from the recordset class.

2. Remove the reference to the physical file location, and leave only the following line:

```
return _T("");
```

You'll open the recordset directly in the view's *OnInitalUpdate* member function.

Step 5: Adding a Function to the Document Header

To open a table directly, you have to be able to get a pointer to the database from the document header file. In the //Attributes section under "public:", add the following code:

```
CDaoDatabase m_database;
CDaoDatabase* GetDatabase()
{
    return &m_database;
}
```

Having a *CDaoDatabase* data member in the view makes it easy to specifically open a database; the *GetDatabase* function returns the needed reference to the data member.

Step 6: Adding Code to *OnInitialUpdate* to Open the Recordset

Using the appropriate class names and file locations for your project, replace the default implementation of the *OnInitialUpdate* member function with the following code (between the existing braces):

```
COrclDirDoc* pDoc = (COrclDirDoc*)GetDocument();
CDaoDatabase* pDatabase = pDoc->GetDatabase();

m_pSet = &GetDocument()->m_orclDirSet;
```

```
m_pSet->m_pDatabase = pDatabase;
m_pSet->m_pDatabase->Open(NULL, FALSE, FALSE,
    _T("DSN=OracleServer;CONNECTSTRING=server;PWD=tiger;UID=scott;"));
m_pSet->Open(dbOpenDynaset, _T("Select * from Employee"));
CDaoRecordView::OnInitialUpdate();
```

The first two lines of code create a pointer to the document object and obtain a pointer to the database object. The third line of code is the standard implementation for a record view. The fourth line of code sets the data members to the correct pointers, and the fifth line opens the table. The sixth line of code opens the recordset as a dynaset with a specific SELECT statement. The last line of code is the standard implementation for *OnInitialUpdate.*

By explicitly opening a database and then a recordset, you can specify the necessary connection information to open the table directly. The default implementation of *CDaoRecordView::OnInitialUpdate* checks to see whether a database or a recordset is already open. If you do not create and open the database object yourself, the framework implicitly creates and opens the database object for you.

Step 7: Compiling and Running the Application

Compile the application using the Win32 Debug configuration, and put a breakpoint on the *OnInitialUpdate* member function. Step through the code to see how the new implementation supplies the database pointer and opens the database in advance of the *CRecordView* calls to open the database.

Additional Information

MFC database classes were designed primarily with Microsoft data sources in mind, but they are flexible in their implementation. The MFC database classes work well with Oracle, and AppWizard handles the mapping of field data types well. You probably won't have to make adjustments to data types after you use AppWizard with the Oracle table attached to Access. For a list of the Oracle and ODBC data type mappings, see "Mapping Data Types" in the Microsoft ODBC Driver For Oracle Help file (MSORCL10.HLP).

Attaching FoxPro to an Access Database Using DAO Database Classes

The purpose of this task is to create a utility that attaches external data sources to a blank MDB programmatically. This dialog box–based application can be constructed quickly using the Gallery components supplied on the companion

CD-ROM. The overall process of attaching a table involves two, or sometimes three, operations:

1. Creating the blank database.

2. Attaching the external table to the database.

3. [Optional.] Displaying the newly created database and its attached tables in the MFC sample DAOVIEW. The DAOVIEW application can be launched directly from your application.

The MFC sample DAOTABLE already had the necessary code to create a blank database, so I used several files from that project and designed a dialog box that is based on the data source type. Rather than reinvent an application to display the results of the utility, I used DAOVIEW. I created Gallery components and exported them to OGX files, which are located on the companion CD-ROM. Setting up these dialog boxes took a bit of time, so use the components to construct the utility. Then study the code at your leisure. The task consists of nine steps:

1. Creating the DAOVIEW application

2. Creating the dialog box–based application

3. Inserting the dialog component

4. Inserting the AddDBDlg component

5. Inserting the support files

6. Inserting the ExecButton component

7. Adding the database header files and #defines

8. Adjusting the initialization for the ExecButton command

9. Compiling and running the application

Step 1: Creating the DAOVIEW Application

You can skip this step if you have already built this sample. Otherwise, follow the procedure below.

1. Load the Visual C++ version 5 Professional or Enterprise Edition distribution CD-ROM, and copy all of the files for the DAOVIEW sample.

2. Open the DAOVIEW project, and build a Release version of the sample. Close the project workspace. For ease of use, I suggest that you place a copy of the EXE file in your Microsoft Windows directory.

Step 2: Creating the Dialog Box–Based Application

You'll create a utility that makes an empty Access MDB file and attaches a Fox-Pro table to the MDB file.

1. Create a new MFC AppWizard (EXE) project (with a workspace), and name it *AccFox*. Then, in AppWizard Step 1, select Dialog Box–based application.

2. In AppWizard Step 2, select a title for your dialog box.

3. Accept the defaults for the remainder of the AppWizard steps. Then click OK to create the application.

Step 3: Inserting the Dialog Box Component

The dialog box you add in this step replaces the dialog box that was supplied by AppWizard when you created the application. It contains all of the controls that are necessary for gathering information from the user in preparation for attaching a FoxPro or Visual FoxPro table. To save yourself time setting up this utility, use the ACCFOXDLG.OGX Developer Studio component included in the source code found on the distribution CD-ROM.

1. Choose Add To Project/Components And Controls from the Project menu.

2. Navigate to the location of the OGX file, select the file, and then click Import. Because the OGX components that are added to the project have the same name as your project, Developer Studio appends a numeral *1* to your filenames.

3. Open the Resource editor, and delete the default dialog box supplied by AppWizard. Rename the new dialog box by removing the numeral *1* from the end of the resource ID. Do a global search for the IDD_ACC-FOX_DIALOG1 resource ID, and remove the numeral *1* from any other references. The compiler will then automatically pick up the correct resource IDs and other elements of the dialog box.

The top third of the dialog box provides a place to enter a database path for the MDB file. If the MDB does not yet exist, the utility programmatically creates it (see step 4 below). If the database exists, the utility opens the MDB. When the MDB is open, the controls in the middle third of the dialog box are enabled. Here the user enters the database path and table name and clicks Attach Table To MDB. A *CDaoTableDef* object is created, the table is appended, and the tabledef is closed. The code for the dialog box is found in class *CAcc-FoxDlg*, which is also inserted into the project.

The Visual FoxPro version 3 and version 5 tables that are contained in a DBC file are considered "bound" tables and must be exported from the DBC file before they can be attached to an MDB file. You must use Visual FoxPro (either version 3 or version 5) to export the table as a "Visual FoxPro 3.0 (DBF)." FoxPro 2.*x* (DBF) tables are not bound tables and can be attached to an MDB without any preparation.

Step 4: Inserting the AddDBDlg Component

Now add a second dialog box and its corresponding class. This component is borrowed from the DAOTABLE sample.

1. Choose Add To Project/Components And Controls from the Project menu.

2. Navigate to the location of the ADDDBDLG.OGX file, select the file, and then click Import. The header file, the implementation file, and the dialog box resource are added to your project.

This dialog box collects the information required to programmatically create an empty MDB file and supplies the information as parameters to *CDaoDatabase::Create*. DAO version 3 (on which the MFC DAO database classes are based) is selected by default. This dialog box appears only if the user elects to create an empty database rather than open an existing MDB.

Step 5: Inserting the Support Files

There are two support files for this application that are also borrowed from the DAOTABLE sample—DATABASE.H and DATABASE.CPP.

1. Choose Add To Project/Files from the Project menu.

2. Navigate to the location of the DATABASE.H and DATABASE.CPP files on the companion CD-ROM.

3. Select these files, and then click OK.

The DATABASE.H and DATABASE.CPP files contain global helper functions that can create, open, and close a DAO database specified by the user in the first edit control. Error handling checks for the existence of an MDB file and then offers the user a chance to create the database if it doesn't exist. No resources are associated with these files.

Step 6: Inserting the ExecButton Component

The *CExecButton* class contained in this Gallery component uses the *WinExec* API function to launch DAOVIEW from the application you're creating.

1. Choose Add To Project/Components And Controls from the Project menu.

2. Navigate to the location of the EXECBUTTON.OGX file, select the file, and then click Import. The header file and the implementation files will be added to your project. Close the Components And Controls Gallery dialog box.

The *CExecButton* class is based on the *CButton* class. Using MFC's support for message reflection, you can launch another application by clicking a button resource associated with this class. Message reflection lets you reuse your *CWnd*-derived classes more readily; it works via *CWnd::OnChildNotify*, using ON_XXX_REFLECT message map entries. Message reflection allows the notification messages to be handled in either the child control window or the parent window, or in both windows, which eliminates the need to have the message handler code duplicated in every class that has to handle that message. (MFC Technical Note 62 describes message reflection in detail.)

It is possible to start the DAOVIEW application while the utility is active. The *CExecButton* class has a data member named *m_command* that is initialized in *CAccFoxDlg::OnInitDialog* to contain the path to DAOVIEW.EXE. When the user closes the MDB, the name of the database is appended to the *m_command* data member, and the Open MDB in DAOVIEW button is enabled. If the user clicks this button, the database is ready for browsing when DAOVIEW starts.

Step 7: Adding the Database Header Files and #defines

These #defines make it easy to follow the logic in the code for these support files.

1. Open the STDAFX.H file, and add the following line of code:

```
#include <afxdao.h>              // MFC support for DAO
```

This adds the DAO database class support for your application.

2. Open the ACCFOX.H file, and add the #defines on the following page just below the include statement for RESOURCE.H.

```
#define SUCCESS 1
#define FAILURE 0
#define FATAL -1
```

3. Choose Update All Dependencies from the Build menu for both the Debug and Release build configurations.

Step 8: Adjusting the Initialization for the ExecButton Command

I've used my Windows directory plus the DAOVIEW.EXE file to initialize the value for the *m_daoView.m_command* member variable. If you place DAOVIEW-.EXE in a different location, you will have to adjust this variable to match your configuration.

1. Open the ACCFOXDLG1.CPP file, and locate the *OnInitDialog* member function.

2. Find the following line, and adjust it if necessary. Be sure you leave in the double backslashes.

```
// Initialize CExecButton command
m_daoView.m_command = _T("C:\\win95\\daoview.exe ");
```

Step 9: Compiling and Running the Application

Now that all of the components, support files, and #defines are in place you're ready to compile.

1. Compile the application, and fix the errors if there are any.

2. Run the application in Debug mode if you like, and step through the code.

3. Follow the instructions in the dialog box for creating and attaching tables. Insert the data without quotes or other delimiters.

4. After you have either opened or created an MDB file, you can attach tables using a name for the table and the path to the subdirectory containing the table files. Internally, this application uses the table name to retrieve the correct table from the database and gives the TableDef object the same name.

5. Click Attach Table. The application locates the path you've entered and uses the DBC file or the DBF table name to open a *CDaoTableDef* and append the table to the TableDefs collection.

6. To view the database with its newly attached tables in DAOVIEW, you must first close the database by clicking Close MDB.

7. Click Open MDB In DAOVIEW. DAOVIEW appears with the MDB displayed. You can look at the contents of the table, show the data, and even create new queries.

8. Click Exit to close the ACCFOX application.

Additional Information

The dialog box for this application reminds you that DAO requires FoxPro version 2.6 free tables (DBF) format or Visual FoxPro version 3 DBC files to open the database. If you use a DBC file, be sure the tables for the entire database are in the same subdirectory, but do not include any INF files. DAO will accept the default values and expect to find the index (CDX) files, memo (FPT) files, and related files in the same subdirectory as the DBF or DBC files.

Attaching SQL Server to an Access Database Using DAO Database Classes

The purpose of this task is to create a utility that attaches external data sources to a blank MDB programmatically. This dialog box–based application is customized to the requirements for attaching Microsoft SQL Server 6.*x* to the MDB file. The overall process of attaching a table involves two or three operations:

1. Creating the blank database

2. Attaching the external table to the database

3. [Optional.] Displaying the newly created database and its attached tables in the MFC sample DAOVIEW (The DAOVIEW application can be launched directly from your application.)

After you've been working a long time on a particular piece of an application, it's useful to be able to save that component and to be able to reuse it. You'll most likely want to add components to the Gallery when you add a resource to your application, refine the resource (such as a dialog box), and associate a class with it.

For this task, I created Gallery components and exported them to OGX files, which are located on the companion CD-ROM. Setting up the dialog boxes took some time, so again, use the Gallery components to construct the utility. Then study the code at your leisure. I'll explain the code that is added by each component as you add components to the project.

The task consists of nine steps:

1. Creating the DAOVIEW application
2. Creating the dialog box–based application
3. Inserting the dialog box component
4. Inserting the AddDBDlg component
5. Inserting the support files
6. Inserting the ExecButton component
7. Adding the database header files and #defines
8. Adjusting the initialization for the ExecButton command
9. Compiling and running the application

Step 1: Creating the DAOVIEW Application

You can skip this step if you have already built this sample. Otherwise, follow this procedure.

1. Load the Visual C++ version 5 Professional or Enterprise Edition distribution CD-ROM, and copy all of the files for the DAOVIEW sample.
2. Open the DAOVIEW project, and then build a Release version of the sample. Close the project workspace. For ease of use, I suggest that you place a copy of the EXE file in your Windows directory.

Step 2: Creating the Dialog Box–Based Application

You'll create a utility that makes an empty Access MDB file and attaches a SQL Server table to the MDB file.

1. Create a new MFC AppWizard (EXE) project (with a workspace), and name it *AccSql.* In AppWizard Step 2, select a title for your dialog box.
2. Accept the defaults for the remainder of the AppWizard steps, and then click OK to create the application.

Step 3: Inserting the Dialog Box Component

The dialog box you add in this step replaces the dialog box that was supplied by AppWizard when you created the application. It contains all of the controls that are necessary for gathering information from the user in preparation for attaching a FoxPro or Visual FoxPro table. To save yourself time setting up this utility, use the ACCSQLDLG.OGX Developer Studio component included in the source code found on the distribution CD-ROM.

1. Choose Add To Project/Components And Controls from the Project menu.

2. Navigate to the location of the OGX file, select the file, and then click Import. Because the OGX components added to the project have the same name as your project, Developer Studio appends a numeral *1* to your filenames.

3. Open the Resource editor, and delete the empty dialog box supplied by AppWizard. Rename the new dialog by removing the numeral *1* from the end of the resource ID. Now do a global search for the IDD-_ACCSQL_DIALOG1 resource ID, and remove the numeral *1* from any other references in your project. The compiler then will automatically pick up the correct resource IDs and other elements of the dialog box.

The top third of the dialog box provides a place to enter a database path for the MDB file. If the MDB does not yet exist, the utility programmatically creates it (see step 4 below). If the database exists, the utility opens the MDB. When the MDB is open, the controls in the middle third of the dialog box are enabled. Here the user enters the database path and table name and clicks Attach Table To MDB. A *CDaoTableDef* object is created, the table is appended, and the tabledef is closed. The code for the dialog box is found in class *CAccSqlDlg*, which is also inserted into the project.

Step 4: Inserting the AddDBDlg Component

Now add a second dialog box and its corresponding class. This component is borrowed from the DAOTABLE sample.

1. Choose Add To Project/Components And Controls from the Project menu.

2. Navigate to the location of the ADDDBDLG.OGX file, select the file, and then click Import. The header file, the implementation file, and the dialog box resource are added to your project.

This component, the support files inserted in step 5 below, and the *CExecButton* component inserted in step 6 are the same ones used in the previous task ("Attaching FoxPro to an Access Database Using DAO Database Classes") except that the correct #include files are supplied for this version of the utility.

The Database Definition dialog box collects the information required to programmatically create an empty MDB file and supplies the information as parameters to *CDaoDatabase::Create*. DAO version 3 (on which the MFC DAO database classes are based) is selected by default. This dialog box appears only if the user elects to create an empty database rather than open an existing MDB.

Step 5: Inserting the Support Files

There are also two support files for this application that are borrowed from the DAOTABLE sample—DATABASE.H and DATABASE.CPP.

1. Choose Add To Project/Files from the Project menu.

2. Navigate to the location of the DATABASE.H and DATABASE.CPP files on the companion CD-ROM.

3. Select these files, and then click OK.

The DATABASE.H and DATABASE.CPP files contain global helper functions that can create, open, and close a DAO database specified by the user in the first edit control. Error handling checks for the existence of an MDB file and then offers the user a chance to create the database if it doesn't exist. No resources are associated with these files.

Step 6: Inserting the ExecButton Component

The *CExecButton* class contained in this Gallery component uses the *WinExec* API function to launch DAOVIEW from the application you're creating.

1. Choose Add To Project/Components And Controls from the Project menu.

2. Navigate to the location of the EXECBUTTON.OGX file, select the file, and then click Import. Developer Studio adds the header file and the implementation files to your project.

The *CExecButton* class is based on the *CButton* class. Using MFC's support for message reflection, you can launch another application by clicking a button resource associated with this class. Message reflection lets you reuse your *CWnd*-derived classes more readily; it works via *CWnd::OnChildNotify*, using ON_XXX-_REFLECT message map entries. Message reflection allows these notification messages to be handled in either the child control window or the parent window, or in both windows, which eliminates the need to have the message handler code duplicated in every class that has to handle that message. (MFC Technical Note 62 describes message reflection in detail.)

It is possible to start the DAOVIEW application while the utility is active. The *CExecButton* class has a data member named *m_command* that is initialized in *CAccSqlDlg::OnInitDialog* to contain the path to DAOVIEW.EXE. When the user closes the MDB, the name of the database is appended to the *m_command* data member and the Open MDB In DAOVIEW button is enabled. If the user clicks this button, the database is ready for browsing when DAOVIEW starts.

Step 7: Adding the Database Header Files and #defines

These #defines make it easy to follow the logic in the code for these support files.

1. Open the STDAFX.H file, and add the following line of code:

```
#include <afxdao.h>              // MFC support for DAO
```

This adds the DAO database class support for your application.

2. Open the ACCSQL.H file, and add the following #defines right after the include statement for RESOURCE.H:

```
#define SUCCESS 1
#define FAILURE 0
#define FATAL -1
```

3. Choose Update All Dependencies from the Build menu for both the Debug and Release build configurations.

Step 8: Adjusting the Initialization for the ExecButton Command

I've used my Windows directory plus the DAOVIEW.EXE file to initialize the value for the *m_daoView.m_command* member variable. If you place DAOVIEW.EXE in a different location, you will have to adjust this variable to match your configuration.

1. Open the ACCSQLDLG1.CPP file, and locate the *OnInitDialog* member function.

2. Navigate to the following line, and adjust it if necessary. Be sure you leave in the double backslashes.

```
// Initialize CExecButton command
m_daoView.m_command = _T("C:\\win95\\daoview.exe ");
```

Step 9: Compiling and Running the Application

Now that all of the components, support files, and #defines are in place, you're ready to compile.

1. Compile the application, and fix the errors if there are any.

2. Set up an ODBC DSN for your SQL Server database using ODBC Administrator.

3. Run the application in debug mode if you like, and step through the code.

4. Follow the instructions in the dialog box for creating and attaching tables. Insert the data without quotes or other delimiters.

5. After you have either opened or created an MDB file, you can attach tables using the information from ODBC Administrator for the DSN.

6. Click Attach Table. The application constructs the connect string and uses the table name to open a *CDaoTableDef* and append the table to the TableDefs collection.

7. To view the database with its newly attached tables in DAOVIEW, you first must close the database by clicking Close MDB.

8. Click Open MDB In DAOVIEW. DAOVIEW appears with the MDB displayed. You can look at the contents of the table, show the data, and even create new queries.

9. Click Exit to close the ACCSQL application.

Additional Information

The class *CExecButton* is a subclassed button control that uses message reflection to launch the DAOVIEW application. Because the application adds tables to an MDB file, the database is opened automatically with an administrative lock on the database. It is necessary to first close the database; then you can look at it in DAOVIEW. By enabling and disabling the buttons in the correct sequence, the application guides you through the process of creating the database and attaching the tables. The ACCSQL application stays open in case you want to go back and add more tables. Type in the name of the database, and click Connect To MDB to continue the process.

Attaching Oracle to an Access Database in DAO Database Applications

You can attach an Oracle data source to an Access database by using the Access DBMS. Access works with ODBC to request the necessary information for connecting to the data source, and then it obtains a list of all available data sources. To connect properly to an Oracle data source, you will have to know the database alias (usually the server name), the user ID, the password, and the data source name. The Microsoft ODBC Driver For Oracle Help file (MSORCL-10.HLP) has good information about connecting to this data source type through ODBC. See also "Opening Oracle Directly with DAO Database Classes" on page 284 in this chapter for an example of an ODBC connect string to the Oracle sample database Employee.

Mixing Static and Dynamic Binding in DAO Database Classes

The purpose of this task is to demonstrate the mixing of static and dynamic binding by retrieving only part of a record, instead of an entire record, to improve efficiency in an application. Because of the greater size of some fields (a binary field, for example), it isn't always a good idea to retrieve a value for the fields each time you move through a recordset. Using DAO database classes, you can bind fields dynamically (that is, on demand) in combination with the static field binding that AppWizard provides.

The data source for this procedure contains a binary field in the form of an employee photo. Even though it is possible to retrieve the value of the field using *DoFieldExchange*, it isn't very useful if you can't display it. The MFC sample DAOCTL uses an ActiveX control named AccessPict that you can build and use in an ActiveX container. You'll use functions from that control to display the data in the control.

The task consists of eleven steps:

1. Building the ACCSPICT OLE control from the MFC DAOCTL sample

2. Creating the application

3. Removing the Photo data member

4. Designing the record view

5. Inserting the ACCSPICT control

6. Adding the Photo dialog box

7. Creating the dialog box class for the Photo dialog box

8. Adding the #include references for the Photo dialog box and the recordset

9. Creating the message handler for the Photo dialog box button

10. Overriding the WM_INITDIALOG message for the *CPhotoDlg* class

11. Compiling and running the application

Step 1: Building the ACCSPICT OLE Control from the MFC DAOCTL Sample

Build the picture control before creating the sample application. You can skip this step if you have already built and registered this control.

1. Load the Visual C++ version 5 Professional or Enterprise Edition distribution CD-ROM, and copy all of the files for the DAOCTL sample.

2. Open the ACCSPICT ActiveX control project, and build a Release version of the control. Building this control registers the OCX with your system and adds it to Component Gallery. Close the project workspace.

If you copy the OCX to your Windows 95 or Windows NT directory and register the OCX there (using REGSRV32), you can remove the sample files and still have the OCX available. But I encourage you to build the other control and the sample container and to study the code. It's an excellent sample.

Step 2: Creating the Application

You'll create an application named *StatDyn* using AppWizard.

1. Start Visual Studio, and create a new MFC AppWizard (EXE) project (with a workspace). Name it *StatDyn*.

2. In AppWizard Step 1, choose Single Document interface.

3. In AppWizard Step 2, choose A Database View Without File Support. For the data source, select DAO and then click the browse button (…). Select the Microsoft Access For Windows 97 Northwind database, and select Table as the recordset type.

4. Select the Employees table from the next dialog box, and click OK.

5. In AppWizard Step 3, select ActiveX Controls to provide container support.

6. Accept the defaults on the remaining AppWizard steps (or, if you like, make changes), and click OK to create the files.

Step 3: Removing the Photo Data Member

When you selected Table-type recordset, the framework used the fields in the table to create a list of fields in the *DoFieldExchange* member function. You're going to dynamically retrieve the value of the Photo field, so you don't want the *DoFieldExchange* function to retrieve it for you. Use *GetFieldValue* to put the photo in a separate dialog box.

> **T I P :**   I like to use ClassWizard because I prefer to see everything in one dialog box. Most of the time, you can accomplish the same tasks with the WizardBar, and it's a lot more convenient. Just substitute WizardBar actions wherever I mention ClassWizard.

1. Open ClassWizard, click the Member Variables tab, and select *CStatDynSet*.

2. Delete the member variable for the [PHOTO] field (*m_Photo*), and click OK.

If you forgot to select Table when you used AppWizard, don't panic. Changing the default open type is as simple as changing *m_nDefaultType* in the recordset constructor to the following:

```
m_nDefaultType = dbOpenTable;
```

Step 4: Designing the Record View

Use the Resource editor to design the record view. For ideas on how to lay out the information, see the layout for this sample on the companion CD-ROM.

1. Lay out the static controls in the dialog box for the field titles and edit controls for the fields from the Employees table in whatever format you like. For the Notes field, under the Styles tab in the Edit Properties box, add the Multiline, Vertical Scroll, and AutoVScroll properties.

2. When you're satisfied with the layout, hold down Ctrl and double-click each edit control. Then select the member variable that corresponds to the field name from the Member Variable Name drop-down list box.

3. Add a button to the record view. Change the resource ID to IDC-_PHOTOBUTTON, and change the caption to See Photo. (You'll add the message handler for this button in step 9 on page 304.)

4. Compile the application, and look at it. Make adjustments until you're satisfied with the layout.

Step 5: Inserting the ACCSPICT Control

The interface for the Gallery has changed slightly, but it's still easy to use.

1. Open Components And Controls Gallery. Then open the Registered ActiveX Controls folder.

2. Click the AccessPict control, and then click Insert. A list of the classes that are to be added to the project is displayed.

3. Click OK to add the control to the Resource editor toolbox and the code to your project. Then click Close.

Step 6: Adding the Photo Dialog Box

Create a dialog box just big enough to display the picture.

1. In Resource pane, right-click Dialog, and then choose Insert Dialog. Give the dialog box a custom resource ID (something like IDD_PHOTO-DIALOG).

2. In the toolbox, click and drag the new ACCSPICT OCX icon to the dialog box. Increase the size of the picture control to the proportions of a normal ID photo. (You will probably want to experiment with the size.)

3. Remove the Cancel button, and rename the caption of the OK button to &Close. (I like to center the Close button below the picture control.)

4. Right-click the ACCSPICT control, and choose Properties to open the Properties dialog box (if you don't already have it open). Click the Control tab. Select the Stretch To Fit and Preserve Ratio options, and remove the text from the Caption property. When you're satisfied with the layout of the photo dialog box, go on to step 7.

Step 7: Creating the Dialog Box Class for the Photo Dialog

Now add a *CDialog*-derived class for this dialog resource.

1. Double-click the photo dialog in the Resource editor to open Class-Wizard. ClassWizard offers you the chance to create a class corresponding to this dialog box.

2. Select Create A New Class if it is not already selected, and then click OK. Name the class *CPhotoDlg*, and accept the remaining defaults. ClassWizard now displays the Member Variables tab for this new class.

3. Select the picture control, and click Add Variable. Name the variable *m_ctlPicture*. The category is Control, and class *CAccessPict* is the variable type. Click OK to accept the name.

4. Click the Class Info tab for class *CPhotoDlg*. Under Foreign Class, select *CStatDynSet*. In the Foreign Variable edit box, enter *m_pSet*. Click OK to close ClassWizard.

Step 8: Adding the #include References for the Photo Dialog and the Recordset

To complete the connection of the photo dialog to the application, you have to add #include directives for the photo dialog and a forward declaration of the recordset class.

1. In the header file for the photo dialog class (PHOTODLG.H), just above the class declaration, add the following code:

```
class CStatDynSet;
```

2. In the implementation file for the view (STATDYNVIEW.CPP), just below the #include for the recordset (STATDYNSET.CPP), add this line:

```
#include "PhotoDlg.h"
```

3. In the implementation file for the photo dialog (PHOTODLG.CPP), just above the #include for the dialog box header (PHOTODLG.H), add this line:

```
#include "StatDynSet.h"
```

Step 9: Creating the Message
Handler for the Photo Dialog Box Button

Add a message handler for the See Photo button. This function calls *DoModal*, which then calls *OnInitDialog*.

1. With the form view displayed in the Resource editor, hold down Ctrl and double-click the photo button to create the handler for the button.

2. Add the following code for the implementation of the function:

```
CPhotoDlg dlg;
dlg.m_pSet = &GetDocument()->m_statDynSet;
dlg.DoModal();
```

This code declares an instance of the dialog box class, initializes the *m_pSet* data member to the same recordset the view is using, and calls *DoModal*.

Step 10: Overriding the WM_INITDIALOG
Message for the *CPhotoDlg* class

Now add the message handler that retrieves the employee photo.

1. Open ClassWizard, and click the Message Maps tab. From the Class Name drop-down list box, select *CPhotoDlg*. Select *CPhotoDlg* also in the Object IDs list, and scroll down through the list of messages until you find WM_INITDIALOG.

2. Double-click WM_INITDIALOG to create the message handler; then click Edit Code to go to the implementation file.

3. Just below the call to *CDialog::OnInitDialog*, replace the //TO DO comment with the following code:

```
// Retrieve the photo from the current record, and display it
   try
   {
       COleVariant varPhoto =
           m_pSet->GetFieldValue("[photo]");
       m_ctlPicture.SetData(&varPhoto);
   }
   catch (COleException* e)
   {
       e->Delete();
       AfxMessageBox(T_("Photo unavailable"));
   }
```

This allows you to create and delete the *COleVariant* object that will retrieve the employee's photo. The *COleVariant* is automatically deleted when the *OnInitDialog* function returns TRUE. You retrieve the value only when you want it, which speeds up the retrieval of data.

Step 11: Compiling and Running the Application

You're ready to compile and run the application. Scroll through the data, and click the See Photo button. You'll see the picture in a separate dialog box.

Additional Information

This example is just a beginning to the possibilities for mixing static and dynamic binding. You also can create custom DFX routines that conditionally bind fields as you want to bind them. (See Technical Note 53: "Custom DFX Routines for DAO Database Classes," which provides more information on this subject.)

Opening a Recordset on a Stored Procedure Using ODBC Database Classes

The purpose of this task is to demonstrate the use of a stored procedure for obtaining frequently updated data and displaying it in a recordset. This procedure uses the project code base named *SPROC*.

The application uses two recordsets. You'll start with a standard AppWizard-generated application and then add a dialog box and also a second recordset class for handling the stored procedure. The application consists of the usual record view that displays information about an author, but it has a button that displays a second dialog box. As you scroll through the records, you can see the titles for a particular author in the second dialog box by clicking the button on the record view.

N O T E : It is not necessary to use Visual C++ Enterprise Edition for this procedure; you can accomplish all of the tasks listed using Visual C++ Professional Edition. In some steps, I have included instructions specifically for Visual C++ Enterprise Edition.

The task consists of eleven steps:

1. Creating an ODBC database application

2. Designing the record view

3. Adding a second recordset

4. Adding to the *GetDefaultConnect* string for the recordsets

5. Adding data members for the stored procedure parameters

6. Adding the Show Titles dialog box

7. Adding the handlers for the Previous and Next buttons

8. Adding the directives for the Show Titles dialog box

9. Adding the handler for the Show Titles dialog box

10. Adding the stored procedure to the SQL Server PUBS database

11. Compiling and running the application

Step 1: Creating an ODBC Database Application

This procedure assumes that you have already created a DSN for your SQL Server data source with ODBC Administrator. (See the Visual C++ online help for instructions on how to create a DSN.)

1. Create a new MFC AppWizard (EXE) project, and name it *SProc*.

2. In AppWizard Step 1, choose Single Document interface.

3. In AppWizard Step 2, choose A Database View Without File Support. For the data source, select ODBC from the Database Options dialog box. Then select the DSN you use for SQL Server's PUBS database. Supply the necessary login information to connect to the data source.

4. Select the dbo.Authors table from the Select Database Tables dialog box.

5. Accept the defaults on the remaining AppWizard steps (or, if you like, make changes), and then click OK to create the files.

Step 2: Designing the Record View

Use the Resource editor to design the record view. For ideas on how to lay out the information, see the layout for this sample on the companion CD-ROM.

1. Lay out the static controls for the field titles and edit controls for the fields from the Authors table in whatever order you prefer. Leave space for a button that you'll add in step 9 to display the second dialog box.

2. When you're satisfied with the layout, hold down Ctrl and double-click each edit control. Then select the member variable that corresponds

to the field name from the Member Variable Name drop-down list box in ClassWizard.

Step 3: Adding a Second Recordset

Here you will add a second recordset that uses the columns of three tables found in the stored procedure. The stored procedure uses joins on common columns in the tables to obtain a list of titles by the author. When you use Class-Wizard, qualifiers are added automatically to distinguish between the common columns in each table. Add the recordset first; then add the dialog box.

1. Choose ClassWizard from the View menu.

2. Click Add Class, and select New. Fill in the class name as *CShowTitle-Set*. Then choose *CRecordset* as the base class. Click OK to add the class.

3. Choose ODBC from the Database Options dialog box, and select the data source name for the PUBS database from the list. Supply the necessary login information in the Server Login dialog box. Then click OK.

4. From the Select Database Tables dialog box, select the dbo.Authors, dbo.Titleauthor, and dbo.Titles tables. Then click OK.

5. Click the Member Variables tab, and select the *CShowTitleSet* class. Then delete the member variables for the unneeded columns, leaving only the member variables for the following columns:

   ❑ Author's First Name from the Authors table (m_au_fname)

   ❑ Author's Last Name from the Authors table (m_au_lname)

   ❑ Author's ID from the Authors table (m_authors_au_id)

   ❑ Title ID from the Titleauthor table (m_titleauthor_title_id)

   ❑ Title from the Titles table (m_titles_title)

   ❑ Notes from the Titles table (m_notes)

   It's essential that you select the correct columns, but the member variable names might differ slightly from those shown above.

6. Click OK to add the class, and save your work.

Step 4: Adding to the *GetDefaultConnect* String for the Recordsets

AppWizard and ClassWizard both supply a partial connect string for ODBC data sources. If you follow the instructions below for adding to the recordset connect string for both types of recordset classes, you won't have to supply connection information each time you run the application.

1. In the ClassView pane, select the *GetDefaultConnect* member function for each recordset class. AppWizard supplies part of the login information for the application ("ODBC;*<your DSN here>*").

2. Add the UID and PWD parameters to the string. For the SQL Server PUBS database, this is the final result:

```
return _T("ODBC;DSN=SQLServerPubs;UID=sa;PWD=;");
```

Be sure you adjust this code if your DSN differs from the string shown here. Notice that there are no spaces around any of the parameters; if you leave spaces, MFC throws an exception.

Step 5: Adding Data Members for the Stored Procedure Parameters

The stored procedure that creates the second recordset needs two parameters supplied to it before it runs the query: the author's first name and last name. You need to add the parameters to the *CShowTitleSet* recordset class.

1. Double-click the *CShowTitleSet* node in the ClassView pane to open the header file.

2. Just outside the //Field/Param Data section, add the following lines of code (below the //}}AFX_FIELD comment block) to define the parameter data members:

```
CString m_strAuLN;
CString m_strAuFN;
```

3. Next double-click the constructor in the ClassView pane, and add the following lines of code just below the *m_nDefaultType* data member (*snapshot*) to initialize the parameter data members.

```
m_nParams = 2;
m_strAuLN = _T("");
m_strAuFN = _T("");
```

Parameter data members are added manually. You must also initialize the *m_nParams* data member so that the *DoFieldExchange* function knows how many parameters to expect.

4. Now double-click the *DoFieldExchange* member function in the ClassView pane, and add the field exchange information for the parameter data member.

```
pFX->SetFieldType(CFieldExchange::param);
RFX_Text(pFX, _T("auLN"), m_strAuLN);
RFX_Text(pFX, _T("auFN"), m_strAuFN);
```

This *SetFieldType* call tells *DoFieldExchange* that there are two parameter data members, and it provides the mapping from the parameters in the stored procedure to the data members.

Step 6: Adding the Show Titles Dialog Box

The second dialog box displays the records from the second recordset based on the stored procedure. The parameter data member you added in step 5 is used in the stored procedure to select the records. At this time, you only have to add the Title ID, Title, and Notes fields to the second dialog box. The code that you'll add later in step 9 uses the author's first name and last name from the current record to select the titles.

1. Right-click the Dialog node in the ResourceView pane, and choose Insert Dialog.

2. Add static controls for labels, and then add edit controls for the Title ID, Title, and Notes fields. Add two buttons for Previous and Next so that you can scroll through the records. To save space, I deleted the Cancel button and changed the caption of the IDOK button to Close.

3. Double-click the dialog box. ClassWizard displays the Adding A Class dialog box, which tells you that you have to create a class for this dialog box.

4. Select Create A New Class, and name it *CSTDlg*. The base class *CDialog* and the dialog resource ID are already displayed, so click OK to accept the defaults.

5. Click the Class Info tab in ClassWizard. Under Advanced Options, select *CShowTitleSet* from the Foreign Variable drop-down list box. For the foreign variable, enter *m_pSet2*, and then click OK.

Step 7: Adding the Handlers for the Previous and Next Buttons

To be able to navigate among the titles for each author in the Show Titles dialog box, you have to override the default implementation of MovePrev and MoveNext.

1. Select the Show Titles dialog box in the ResourceView pane.

2. Hold down Ctrl and double-click Previous to create a message handler for the button. Add the following code to the body of the handler:

```
CRecordset* pSet = m_pSet2;
if (pSet->IsBOF())
    return;

pSet->MovePrev();
if (pSet->IsBOF())
    pSet->MoveFirst();

// Show results of move operation
UpdateData(FALSE);
```

3. Hold down Ctrl and double-click Next to create a message handler for the button. Add the following code to the body of the handler:

```
CRecordset* pSet = m_pSet2;
if (pSet->IsEOF())
    return;

pSet->MoveNext();
if (pSet->IsEOF())
    pSet->MoveLast();

// Show results of move operation
UpdateData(FALSE);
```

The code shown above for the Previous and Next buttons does not include code for enabling or disabling buttons on the basis of the total number of records retrieved, but you can certainly add such code later if you like.

Step 8: Adding the Directives for the Show Titles Dialog Box

Although ClassWizard knows about your dialog box, you have to add a forward declaration to the dialog box header file and a #include to the implementation file for the view.

To add a second recordset to the dialog box header file, double-click the *CSTDlg* node in the ClassView pane to open the header file. Just above the declaration for the class, add the following line of code:

```
class CShowTitleSet;
```

This forward declaration enables the dialog box class to handle the routing of field data from the recordset class to the controls on the dialog box.

To add the second recordset to the view's header file, double-click the view class node in the ClassView pane to open the header file. Just above the declaration for the class, add the following line of code:

```
class CShowTitleSet;
```

This forward declaration makes the view class aware of the second recordset class so that you can obtain the author's first name and last name from the primary recordset.

To add the directives to the application object's header file, double-click the constructor for the application object in the ClassView pane, and navigate to the top of the file. Just below the #include for the primary record-set, add the following line of code:

```
#include "ShowTitleSet.h"
```

To add the directives to the document's implementation file, double-click the constructor for the document in the ClassView pane, and navigate to the top of the file. Just below the #include for the primary recordset, add the following lines of code:

```
#include "ShowTitleSet.h"
#include "STDlg.h"
```

To add the directives to the view's implementation file, follow the procedure described below:

1. Double-click the constructor for the view object in the ClassView pane, and navigate to the top of the file.

2. Just below the #include for the primary recordset, add the following line of code:

   ```
   #include "ShowTitleSet.h"
   ```

3. Below the #include for the view's header file, add the following line of code:

   ```
   #include "stdlg.h"
   ```

   The view now knows about the second dialog box and will react appropriately.

4. In the section under //Attributes, add a data member for the second recordset:

   ```
   CShowTitleSet m_showTitleSet;
   ```

To add the directives to the second dialog's implementation file, double-click the constructor for the dialog object in the ClassView pane, and navigate to the top of the file. Just below #include for the application object, add the following line of code:

```
#include "ShowTitleSet.h"
```

Step 9: Adding the Handler for the Show Titles Dialog Box

To add the handler for the Show Titles dialog box, follow the procedure described below.

1. Switch to the record view in the Resource editor, and add a button that will launch the second dialog box. Give the button the resource ID IDC_SHOWTITLES.

2. Hold down Ctrl and double-click the button to add the message handler for the button.

   ```
   CString strSQL = _T("{CALL au_titles (?,?)}");

   CSTDlg dlg;
   dlg.m_pSet2 = &GetDocument()->m_sSTSet;

   dlg.m_pSet2->m_strAuLN = m_pSet->m_au_lname;
   dlg.m_pSet2->m_strAuFN = m_pSet->m_au_fname;
   dlg.m_pSet2->Open(CRecordset::snapshot, strSQL,
       CRecordset::readOnly);

   dlg.DoModal();
   dlg.m_pSet2->Close();
   ```

   This code creates a dialog box object, initializes the SQL string using the author's first name and last name from the current record, creates a recordset, and opens the recordset that is based on the stored procedure call. The *DoModal* call opens the dialog box and populates it with the fields from the recordset.

Step 10: Adding the Stored Procedure to the SQL Server PUBS Database

You're now ready to add the stored procedure to the PUBS database. If you are not using the Enterprise Edition of Visual C++ 5.x, you can load the AU_TITLES.SQL file from the companion CD-ROM into the SQL Server client utility ISQL_W and run the script there. If you do not have SQL Server utilities on your computer, ask your database administrator to load the script for you. If you are using the Enterprise Edition of Visual C++ 5.x, you can insert a database project into your workspace and create a stored procedure within your project.

Add the stored procedure as described below.

1. Choose New Database Project from the File menu. Give the subproject a name, and click Add To Current Workspace.

2. In the Select Data Source dialog box that appears, select the DSN for SQL Server's PUBS database from the Machine Data Sources tab. Then click OK. Supply the necessary login information; the database subproject will appear in both the ClassView and DataView panes that you added to the project.

3. In the DataView pane, expand the Stored Procedures node. You'll see several stored procedures that are included in the PUBS database. Right-click the Stored Procedures node, and select New Stored Procedure.

4. Insert the following code into the body of the stored procedure:

```
CREATE PROCEDURE au_titles @auLN varchar(20),
    @auFN varchar(40) AS

SELECT authors.au_id, authors.au_lname, authors.au_fname,
titleauthor.title_id, titles.title, titles.notes
FROM authors, titleauthor, titles
WHERE authors.au_lname = @auLN
and authors.au_fname = @auFN
and authors.au_id = titleauthor.au_id
and titleauthor.title_id = titles.title_id
order by titleauthor.title_id
```

Remove the default line below:

```
return (0)
```

This stored procedure declares the variables supplied by the current record and then creates a join between three tables to create the recordset for the class *CShowTitleSet*. You use only the last three fields in the secondary dialog box.

Step 11: Compiling and Running the Application

Now that you've added all of the code and laid out the record view and dialog box controls, compile and run the application.

- The record view loads the primary recordset; now you can scroll through the records as much as you like.

■ Click Show Titles to display the secondary dialog box. The stored procedure AU_TITLES runs and returns a recordset that is based on the parameters (in this case, the first name and last name of the author). You can use the Previous and Next buttons to scroll through the records. (There are usually only one or two records per author.)

Additional Information

Parameters for any recordset must be listed in the same order in which the recordset is retrieved. For more information, see the following topics in the Visual C++ online help:

■ Recordset: Declaring a Class for a Predefined Query (ODBC)

■ Recordset: Parameterizing a Recordset (ODBC)

These Microsoft Knowledge Base articles also have excellent information:

■ How to Use Dynasets with Microsoft SQL Server Version 6.*x*: Q136994

■ MFC ODBC Classes and Parameterized Pre-Defined Queries: Q137814

■ SAMPLE: DLGDB32 CDialog Sharing a CRecordset Object: Q141445

■ PRB: Opening a Dynaset on a SQL Server Stored Procedure: Q152520

Using Output Parameters with the ODBC API and ODBC Database Classes

The purpose of this task is to demonstrate how results from a stored procedure can be obtained and displayed using ODBC API calls. It is a continuation of the previous task, "Opening a Recordset on a Stored Procedure Using ODBC Database Classes," and it uses the same project code base—*SPROC.* Here you'll add another button to the record view for running a second stored procedure that is based on the *CShowTitleSet* recordset. This stored procedure calculates the total number of units sold for each author in the database by joining three tables and calculating a result.

A SQL SELECT statement based on a join is costly in terms of the total processing time required, which means it makes sense to run this kind of stored procedure only on demand rather than recalculating the value each time a user scrolls through a record. Although it's possible to use an existing *CDatabase::m_hdbc* connection and *CRecordset::m_hstmt* statement to run stored procedures, the recordset you use must already be open. You also can't use the existing connection because you're not creating a recordset; rather, you're merely calculating a result.

The task consists of five steps:

1. Adding a button for the stored procedure

2. Preparing a message handler for the button

3. Adding a message handler for the button

4. Adding the stored procedure to the SQL Server PUBS database

5. Compiling and running the application

Step 1: Adding a Button for the Stored Procedure

If you don't want to repeat all the work you did in the previous task, just copy the files from the companion CD-ROM and use them as a starting point for this task.

1. Open the Resource editor, and add another button to the record view.

2. Right-click the button, and select Properties. Give the control the resource ID IDC_SUMSOLD. Then change the caption to Calculate Units Sold.

3. Hold down Ctrl and double-click the button to create a message handler for it.

Step 2: Preparing a Message Handler for the Button

The next few steps will describe the process of making a direct ODBC call to a stored procedure and capturing its output to display to the user. You'll begin by adding data members to the view class.

1. Double-click the *CSProcView* class node in the ClassView pane to open the header file.

2. Add the following lines of code to reserve storage for information that will be reused when the button is clicked:

```
HENV henvHndl;      // Environment handle for ODBC direct calls
HDBC hdbcConn;      // Connection handle for ODBC direct calls
HSTMT hstmtStmt;    // Statement handle for ODBC direct calls
RETCODE retCode;    // Return code for ODBC functions
```

Each time you use the ODBC API, you must allocate and deallocate an environment handle, a connection handle, and a statement handle. Each call returns a return code for which you also need storage. These members will be statically allocated in the body of the function so that they need be stored only once and are retrievable each time the connection is made.

Next add a parsing member function to the view class. Use the ODBC API *SQLError* function, which returns the result code SQL_SUCCESS_WITH-_INFO and a corresponding message string. During debug operations, it's useful to have the entire message string because if there is an error, the state and native error code information is included. However, you don't need to display that information to the user. Add a member function to parse the message string, and then remove the information that precedes the results you want to display. In the header file for the view, add the following code for the message parser in the //Operations section under "public:".

```
UCHAR* ParseMsg(UCHAR* pstrMsg);
```

Now add the parsing message function to the view class implementation file. This code looks for the third right bracket (]) and returns the starting point of the remainder of the message that is to be displayed in the message box.

```
UCHAR* CSProcView::ParseMsg(UCHAR* szErrMsg)
{
    int cnt = 0;
    while(*szErrMsg != '\0')
    {
        if (*szErrMsg == ']')
        {
            cnt ++;
            if (cnt == 3)
                return szErrMsg+1;
        }
        szErrMsg++;
    }
    return NULL;
}
```

Step 3: Adding a Message Handler for the Button

The body of the message handler is somewhat lengthy because you'll be using direct ODBC API calls to establish a connection and retrieve results from the stored procedure.

Copy the following code into the message handler *OnSumSold* (or whatever name you've given it):

```
CWaitCursor wait;

CString strAuID = m_pSet->m_au_id;

static UCHAR szDSN[] = "SQLServerPubs";
static UCHAR szUID[] = "sa";
static UCHAR szPWD[] = "";

// Allocate a connection handle
retCode = SQLAllocEnv(&henvHndl);

// Allocate environment handle and connection handle
retCode = SQLAllocConnect(henvHndl, &hdbcConn);

// Connect to the data source
retCode = SQLConnect(hdbcConn,
    szDSN, SQL_NTS,  // Data source & length
    szUID, SQL_NTS,  // User ID & length
    szPWD, SQL_NTS); // Password & length

// Allocate the hstmtStmt & its storage
retCode = SQLAllocStmt(hdbcConn, &hstmtStmt);

// Construct the string from edit box input, and add single quotes
CString strSum_Sold;
strSum_Sold = _T("sum_sold @auID='");
strSum_Sold += strAuID;
strSum_Sold += _T("'");

// Execute Sum_Sold. This message returns SQL_SUCCESS_WITH_INFO
// We need a couple of casts of the string to arrive at a UCHAR*
retCode = SQLExecDirect(hstmtStmt,
    (UCHAR*)(LPSTR)(LPCTSTR)strSum_Sold, SQL_NTS);

// Allocate some storage for the returned message
UCHAR szSqlSt[6];
UCHAR szErrMsg[SQL_MAX_MESSAGE_LENGTH];
SDWORD pfNativeErr;
SWORD pcbErrMsg;

// Now get the Sum_Sold PRINT message
retCode = SQLError(henvHndl, hdbcConn, hstmtStmt, szSqlSt,
```

(continued)

317

```
&pfNativeErr, szErrMsg, (SQL_MAX_MESSAGE_LENGTH - 1),
&pcbErrMsg);

// Get rid of the header info in the message
UCHAR* pszMsg;
pszMsg = ParseMsg(szErrMsg);

// Display PRINT message
if (pszMsg == NULL)
    AfxMessageBox("Author has not sold any books.");
else
    AfxMessageBox((char*)pszMsg, MB_OK | MB_ICONINFORMATION);

// Close the connection
retCode = SQLFreeStmt(hstmtStmt, SQL_DROP);
retCode = SQLDisconnect(hdbcConn);
retCode = SQLFreeConnect(hdbcConn);
retCode = SQLFreeEnv(&henvHndl);
```

Now let's review the code. The first line of code starts a "wait cursor" that is automatically destroyed when the function ends. Whenever I have an operation that might take more than a second or two, I change the cursor to let the user know that processing is taking place. You need only one line of code for this:

```
CWaitCursor wait;
```

The next line of code initializes a variable by obtaining the current value in the Author ID field.

```
CString strAuID = m_pSet->m_au_id;
```

When establishing the connection to the data source, I allocate storage for the DSN, the user ID, and the password using the *static* keyword. This makes the storage available the next time the function executes.

```
static UCHAR szDSN[] = "SQLServerPubs";
static UCHAR szUID[] = "sa";
static UCHAR szPWD[] = "";
```

Next I allocate the handles to the environment, the connection, and the statement for the ODBC call. The values for *retCode* should be either 0 for SQL_SUCCESS or 1 for SQL_SUCCESS_WITH_INFO. These values are defined in the ODBC header file SQL.H. As I step through the code in Debug mode, I can check these values.

```
// Allocate a connection handle
retCode = SQLAllocEnv(&henvHndl);
```

```
// Allocate environment handle and connection handle
retCode = SQLAllocConnect(henvHndl, &hdbcConn);

// Connect to the data source
retCode = SQLConnect(hdbcConn,
    szDSN, SQL_NTS,        // Data source and length
    szUID, SQL_NTS,        // User ID and length
    szPWD, SQL_NTS);       // Password and length

// Allocate the hstmtStmt and its storage
retCode = SQLAllocStmt(hdbcConn, &hstmtStmt);
```

To run the stored procedure, I assemble the string from the *CString* that I allocated earlier. I build up the *strSumSold* and then add apostrophes around the value.

```
// Construct the string from edit box input, and add single quotes
CString strSum_Sold;
strSum_Sold = _T("sum_sold @auID='");
strSum_Sold += strAuID;
strSum_Sold += _T("'");
```

Then I run the SUM_SOLD stored procedure using *SQLExecuteDirect*. The return code for this should be a *1* for SQL_SUCCESS_WITH_INFO. It is that "info" that I want to capture and display to the user.

```
// Execute Sum_Sold. This message returns SQL_SUCCESS_WITH_INFO
// We need a couple of casts of the string to arrive at a UCHAR*
retCode = SQLExecDirect(hstmtStmt,
    (UCHAR*)(LPSTR)(LPCTSTR)strSum_Sold, SQL_NTS);
```

To retrieve the results of the stored procedure, I allocate some storage for the parameters of the *SQLError* call and then retrieve the PRINT message from the stored procedure. The PRINT message is found in the *szErrMsg* parameter below.

```
// Allocate some storage for the returned message
UCHAR szSqlSt[6];
UCHAR szErrMsg[SQL_MAX_MESSAGE_LENGTH];
SDWORD pfNativeErr;
SWORD pcbErrMsg;

// Now get the Sum_Sold PRINT message
retCode = SQLError(henvHndl, hdbcConn, hstmtStmt, szSqlSt,
    &pfNativeErr, szErrMsg, (SQL_MAX_MESSAGE_LENGTH - 1),
    &pcbErrMsg);
```

To remove header information, I parse the message using the function I added earlier and display the results—in this case, a number returned as a string. If the string is null, I provide an alternative message box stating that the author hasn't sold any books.

```
// Get rid of the header info in the message
UCHAR* pszMsg;
pszMsg = ParseMsg(szErrMsg);

// Display PRINT message
if (pszMsg == NULL)
    AfxMessageBox("Author has not sold any books.");
else
    AfxMessageBox((char*)pszMsg, MB_OK | MB_ICONINFORMATION);
```

The connection is closed after the user acknowledges the message box.

```
// Close the connection
retCode = SQLFreeStmt(hstmtStmt, SQL_DROP);
retCode = SQLDisconnect(hdbcConn);
retCode = SQLFreeConnect(hdbcConn);
retCode = SQLFreeEnv(&henvHndl);
```

Step 4: Adding the Stored Procedure to the SQL Server PUBS Database

Now you add the stored procedure to your SQL Server PUBS database.

- If you are not using Visual C++ Enterprise Edition, you can also load the SUM_SOLD.SQL file from the companion CD-ROM into the SQL Server client utility ISQL_W and run the script there.

- If you do not have SQL Server utilities on your computer, ask your database administrator to load the script for you.

- If you are using Visual C++ Enterprise Edition, you can insert a database project into your workspace and create the new stored procedure from within your project.

Follow the procedure described below.

1. Choose New Database Project from the File menu. Give the subproject a name, and click Add To Current Workspace.

2. In the Select Data Source dialog box, select the correct DSN for SQL Server's PUBS database from the Machine Data Sources tab. Then click OK.

Supply the necessary login information; the database subproject will appear in both the ClassView and DataView panes that you added to the project.

3. In the DataView pane, expand the Stored Procedures node. You'll see several stored procedures that are included in the PUBS database. Right-click the Stored Procedures node, and select New Stored Procedure.

4. Insert the following code into the body of the stored procedure:

```
CREATE PROCEDURE sum_sold @auID varchar(11),
    @retval int = 0 OUTPUT AS

SELECT @retval = SUM(DISTINCT sales.qty)
FROM authors, titleauthor, titles, sales
WHERE authors.au_id LIKE @auID
and authors.au_id = titleauthor.au_id
and titleauthor.title_id = sales.title_id

DECLARE @convertval char(7)
SELECT @convertval = CONVERT(char(7),@retval)
PRINT @convertval

RETURN
```

Remove this default line

```
return (0)
```

The stored procedure SUM_SOLD needs values from three tables to calculate the total number of units sold by this author's work. The variable used to select the records is the author's ID. It's relatively easy to calculate the value, but you have to use a PRINT message to return the result—and the PRINT message takes only strings. The CONVERT function takes care of that problem; it is the converted string that appears in AfxMessageBox.

Step 5: Compiling and Running the Application

You're now ready to compile and run the application. Start by compiling for Debug mode; put breakpoints in the *OnSumSold* member function to observe the process. Scroll through the records. Click Calculate Units Sold to display either the number of units sold or the "no units sold" message box.

Additional Information

Because opening and closing separate connections to a data source results in extra overhead, use this capability sparingly. It can be an effective method for retrieving information you need only occasionally.

As of MFC version 4.2, output parameters are supported, so it's possible to accomplish this task without the ODBC API calls. I decided, however, to use them in this example to demonstrate the minimum number of calls that are required to establish a connection with a data source using the ODBC API.

Normally, you wouldn't use *SQLError* to retrieve results from a stored procedure either, but *SQLError* is an API function that is used frequently. So this is an example you can copy and use in your own code. The calls you typically would use for retrieving results from a stored procedure using the ODBC API would look like this:

```
{
    // ...login, password, and so on...
    SQLAllocStmt(...)
    SQLExecDirect(...)
    SQLBindCol(...)
    SQLFetch(...)
    SQLFreeStmt(...)
    // ...free the handles, and so on...
}
```

Consult the ODBC Programmer's Reference if you would like more information about these APIs. Be sure you read the following topics in the Visual C++ online help.

- SQL: Making Direct SQL Calls (ODBC)
- SQL: Customizing Your Recordset's SQL Statement (ODBC)
- Data Source: Programmatically Creating a Table in an ODBC Data Source
- Recordset: How Recordsets Select Records (ODBC)

The following Knowledge Base article is also useful:

- How to Detect an Empty Recordset Object: Q121950

PART II

REFERENCE
SECTION

Knowledge Base Articles

In Part I of this book, several references were made to articles found in the Microsoft Knowledge Base. The Knowledge Base is a database of technical support articles about Microsoft products, which usually fall into two categories: how-to articles and bug-related articles. For the most part, the Knowledge Base articles referenced in this book fell into the second category.

The main reason for using these existing Knowledge Base articles is a product of the structure of the book. Before writing up each task, I used a set of criteria to determine what information would be needed in the task. One of the main criteria used was this: Is the information absolutely needed to complete the task or improve the usability of the feature? I wanted to be rigorous in task focus and clarity because there is nothing I hate more than wading through ten pages of story about a hypothetical parts store of electronic widgets, when all I wanted to know was how information is being passed between two discrete objects! This kept the tasks tightly focused and concise. But occasionally, there would be a cool Knowledge Base article that discussed an alternate approach or presented related information that also would be useful to read. Therefore, instead of trying to include the information in the article in the task, I referenced the article.

To save you the time and effort of searching for a referenced article in the Knowledge Base itself, I collected the articles referenced in the text in a separate part of the book. However, keep the following in mind when referencing these articles:

- Every effort was made to include the latest version of the Knowledge Base articles. However, due to the "dynamic" nature of the Knowledge Base (and the not so dynamic nature of a book), the content of the referenced articles is subject to change. For the latest version of an article, please check the online version in the Knowledge Base, which can be found at the Microsoft World Wide Web site, **http://microsoft.com/kb**.

- Each article has a query number ("Q" number) as part of its title. This query number can be used to quickly access the article when searching on line. Sometimes an article is referenced in two different chapters. Because of this, the articles are listed here by their query number in ascending order, not by the chapter in which they were referenced.

Using *CFormView* in SDI and MDI Applications

(Q98598)

The information in this article applies to the Microsoft Foundation Classes (MFC) included with:

- Microsoft Visual C++ for Windows, versions 1.0, 1.5, 1.51, and 1.52

- Microsoft Visual C++ 32-bit edition, versions 1.0, 2.0, 2.1, 4.0, 4.1, 4.2, and 5.0

Summary

The *CFormView* class provides a convenient method to place controls into a view that is based on a dialog box template. The general procedure to use a *CFormView* is described in the documentation for the class and is illustrated in the VIEWEX and CHKBOOK sample applications provided with Microsoft Foundation Classes (MFC) versions 2.*x* and above. However, these applications do not demonstrate making the initial size of the frame window to be the same as the initial size of the form.

The following section lists the steps required to support creating a single document interface (SDI) or multiple document interface (MDI) application based on a *CFormView,* sizing the initial frame window around the form, changing the style of the frame, and closing an MDI document using a button in the form.

More Information

The following four steps describe how to create an AppWizard generated application using the *CFormView* as the default view.

1. Use AppWizard to generate an SDI or MDI application skeleton, stopping at step six of AppWizard.

2. At step six of AppWizard, select the view class and specify *CFormView* as the base class using the Base class combo box. This will insert a dialog box template with the proper styles set for your project's resource file.

3. Override the *OnUpdate* member function and call *UpdateData* as documented in the *CFormView* documentation to update the member variables with the current document data and to perform dialog data exchange (DDX). Note: *UpdateData* is not virtual and calling the base class ensures that the derived class *DoDataExchange* is called through

standard polymorphism. The *CFormView* documentation states to call, not to override *UpdateData*.

4. If you would like to set the initial size of the form view, override the *OnInitialUpdate* function. The text below provides additional information about this step, which is slightly different in an SDI or MDI application.

Changing the Size of an SDI Main Frame Around a *CFormView*

To change the size of the main frame of an SDI application (that uses *CFormView* as its view class) to be the appropriate size for the form you designed in App Studio, override the *OnInitialUpdate* function in your class derived from *CFormView*, as follows:

```
void CMyFormView::OnInitialUpdate()
{
    CFormView::OnInitialUpdate();
    GetParentFrame()->RecalcLayout();
    ResizeParentToFit(); // default argument is TRUE
}
```

The *ResizeParentToFit* function does not prevent the form from changing size when the user changes the size of the application main frame. (Scroll bars are added automatically if needed.) To modify the style of the frame window that is the parent of a form view, you can override the *PreCreateWindow* function in the *CMainFrame* class generated by AppWizard. For example, to remove the WS_THICKFRAME style and prevent the user from changing the size of the window, declare *PreCreateWindow* in MAINFRM.H and add the following code to MAINFRM.CPP:

```
BOOL CMainFrame::PreCreateWindow(CREATESTRUCT &cs)
{
    cs.style &= ~WS_THICKFRAME;
    return CFrameWnd::PreCreateWindow(cs);
}
```

Changing the Size of an MDI Child Frame Around a *CFormView*

The process of changing the size of an MDI child frame is similar to changing the size of a main frame for an SDI application, as explained above. However, the *RecalcLayout* call is not required.

To change the size of an MDI child frame around a form view, override the *OnInitialUpdate* function in your class derived from *CFormView* as follows:

```
void CMDIFormView::OnInitialUpdate()
{
    CFormView::OnInitialUpdate();
    ResizeParentToFit(); // Default argument is TRUE.
}
```

If the application overrides the default argument to the *ResizeParent-ToFit* function, essentially the same consequences occur as for an SDI application, as explained above. In addition, the child window may be too large for the enclosing MDI main frame or for the entire screen.

To change the style of the MDI child frame (for example, to remove the WS_THICKFRAME style so the user cannot change the size of the window), derive an MDI child window class and override the *PreCreateWindow* function as demonstrated in the SDI example above.

Closing an MDI Form with a Button

To create a button on a form that closes the document, use ClassWizard to add a message handler for the BN_CLICKED message to the *CFormView* class. Make sure that the buttons in *CFormView* do not have the default IDOK or ID-CANCEL identifiers. If they do, ClassWizard creates incorrect entries in the message map and incorrect functions for the buttons.

Once the message handler is in place, you can simulate the Close command on the File menu with the following code:

```
void CMyForm::OnClickedButton1()
{
    PostMessage(WM_COMMAND, ID_FILE_CLOSE);
}
```

This method to close a form prompts the user to save the file if the *IsModified* member function associated with the document returns TRUE.

Additional reference words: kbinf 1.00 1.50 1.51 1.52 2.00 2.10 4.00 4.10 4.20 5.00

KBCategory: kbprg fasttip

KBSubcategory: MfcUI

How to Change an MFC-Based MDI Child Window's Frame Text

(Q99182)

The information in this article applies to the Microsoft Foundation Classes (MFC) included with:

- Microsoft Visual C++ for Windows, versions 1.0, 1.5, 1.51, and 1.52

- Microsoft Visual C++ 32-bit Edition, versions 1.0, 2.0, 2.1, 4.0, 4.1, 4.2, and 5.0

Summary

A user may find it desirable to change the title of an MFC-based child window. To do this, *PreCreateWindow* must be overridden for the child frame, and *OnInitialUpdate* must be overridden for the view.

More Information

These are the steps necessary to change the title of a multiple document interface (MDI) child window frame. When doing this, follow the rules of "The Windows Interface: An Application Design Guide" for child frame titles, which states the following: "A document window title bar should contain a caption that displays the name of the document in the window." Add your customized information in addition to that.

1. Create an MDI application from AppWizard.

2. Using ClassWizard, create a new class based on *CMDIChildWnd*. These steps assume the class is named *CMyChildFrame*.

3. Choose Project. Scan All Dependencies. This step is not necessary with Visual C++ version 4.*x* or 5.0.

4. Choose the project's main .CPP file and replace the *CMDIChildWnd* class in the call to the *AddDocTemplate* function to the new class you created.

5. Include the newly created .H file at the top of the project's main .CPP file.

6. Choose the .H file from the project list for the newly created class and add the following line to the protected implementation section:

```
virtual BOOL PreCreateWindow(CREATESTRUCT &cs);
```

N O T E : With Visual C++ version 4.*x* or 5.0, you may use Class-Wizard to do the above.

7. Choose the .CPP file from the project list for the newly created class and add the following to the end of the file:

```
BOOL CMyChildFrame::PreCreateWindow(CREATESTRUCT &cs)
{
    // Do default processing.
    if (CMDIChildWnd::PreCreateWindow(cs)==0) return
        FALSE;
    return TRUE;
}
```

where *CMyChildFrame* is the class name of your newly created class. This function calls the base class's version for the *PreCreateWindow* function.

8. Add the following code line to the newly created *PreCreateWindow* function immediately following the default call to *CMDIChild-Wnd::PreCreateWindow*:

```
cs.style &= ~(LONG)FWS_ADDTOTITLE;
```

9. Choose the .H file corresponding to your application's view window and add the following code to the public implementation section:

```
virtual void OnInitialUpdate();
```

N O T E : With Visual C++ version 4.*x* or 5.0, you may use Class-Wizard to do the above.

10. Choose the .CPP file corresponding to your application's view window and add the following code to the end of the file:

```
void CMyAppView::OnInitialUpdate()
{
    // Do default processing.
    CView::OnInitialUpdate();
}
```

where *CMyAppView* is the view class for the application.

11. Add your customization code. Remember to follow the rules of "The Windows Interface: An Application Design Guide" for child frame titles.

Then add your customized information, in addition to that, immediately following the default call to *CView::OnInitialUpdate*. An example of this is:

```
GetParent()->SetWindowText(GetDocument()->GetTitle()+
        " - This is a test!");
```

12. Build the program.

13. Run it and you will see the change implemented. In this example, the first view will display "Myapp1 - this is a test!". Additional views will be identical except for the document name (Myapp1).

N O T E : It is necessary to override *OnInitialUpdate* instead of *OnCreate* because the document has not been instantiated, and therefore calling *GetTitle* would return an empty string.

N O T E : It may also be necessary to override *CDocument::CanCloseFrame* if multiple views of the same document are open. This is because the *CMDIChildWnd* member *m_nWindow* is not updated if FWS_ADDTOTITLE is not set for the MDI Child frame. This prevents the "Save File" dialog from coming up when any view other than the last view open for the document is closed.

This does NOT apply to Visual C++ for Windows, version 1.52, and Visual C++ 32-bit Edition, versions 2.10 and above. The behavior of *m_nWindows* was modified in these versions to handle this scenario properly. The overridden function would look something like this:

```
BOOL CMyDoc::CanCloseFrame(CFrameWnd* pFrameArg)
{
    ASSERT_VALID(pFrameArg);
    UINT iCount = 0;

    POSITION pos = GetFirstViewPosition();
    while (pos != NULL)
    {
        CView* pView = GetNextView(pos);
        ASSERT_VALID(pView);
        CFrameWnd* pFrame = pView->GetParentFrame();
        // assume frameless views are ok to close
        if (pFrame != NULL)
        {
```

(continued)

```
        // assumes 1 document per frame
        ASSERT_VALID(pFrame);
        iCount++;
    }
}

if ( iCount > 1 )
    return TRUE;

// otherwise only one frame that we know about
return SaveModified();
}
```

Additional reference words: kbinf 1.00 1.50 2.00 2.10 2.50 2.51 2.52 3.00
3.10 4.00 4.10 4.20 5.00

KBCategory: kbprg kbfasttip

KBSubcategory: MfcUI

Displaying the Current Time in a *CStatusBar* Pane

(Q99198)

The information in this article applies to the Microsoft Foundation Classes
(MFC) included with:

- Microsoft Visual C++ for Windows, versions 1.0, 1.5, 1.51, and 1.52

- Microsoft Visual C++, 32-bit Edition, versions 2.0, 2.1, 4.0, and 5.0

Summary

The text below describes a process by which an MFC AppWizard application
can be designed to display the current time on its status bar.

1. Use App Studio, or the Resource View in Visual C++ versions later than
   4.0, to edit the application's string tables. Add a new string in the seg-
   ment that defines ID_INDICATOR_NUM and so on; for example, create a new string with the ID ID_INDICATOR_TIME. Specify a caption
   like 00:00. The status bar uses the specified initial value to calculate
   the size of the pane. An application can dynamically change the size
   of the pane using the *CStatusBar::SetPaneInfo* function. With Visual
   C++ versions prior to 4.0 or later, close App Studio to save the .RC file.
   With Visual C++ version 4.0, use the File menu to Save and Close the
   string table resource.

2. Edit the MAINFRM.CPP file. The *CStatusBar* object builds the status
   bar using the data in the *indicators[ ]* array in sequential order. Insert
   the ID_INDICATOR_TIME indicator into the array at the desired position. If you compiled the program at this stage, you would see a new
   pane in the status bar but it would not contain any text.

3. Edit the message map for the *CMainFrame* object to add the following
   line (add the line outside the AFX_MSG_MAP comments):

   ```
   ON_UPDATE_COMMAND_UI(ID_INDICATOR_TIME, OnUpdateTime)
   ```

   Because ID_INDICATOR_TIME is an ID, and not an object, you cannot use Class Wizard to make this addition.

4. Edit the MAINFRM.CPP file and create a function similar to the
   following:

```
void CMainFrame::OnUpdateTime(CCmdUI *pCmdUI)
{
    CTime t = CTime::GetCurrentTime();
    char szTime[6];
    int nHour = t.GetHour();
    int nMinute = t.GetMinute();

    // Base hours on 12 instead of 24
    if (nHour > 12)
        nHour = nHour - 12;

    wsprintf(szTime, "%i:%02i", nHour, nMinute);

    // Now set the text of the pane.
    m_wndStatusBar.SetPaneText(
        m_wndStatusBar.CommandToIndex(ID_INDICATOR_TIME),
        LPCSTR(szTime));
    pCmdUI->Enable();
}
```

The application calls this function once when it has idle time. Each time the application empties its message queue, it sends a WM_IDLE-UPDATECMDUI message (new idle time). For more information on idle time, please refer to Technical Note #24 in the online help or to the documentation of the *CWinApp::OnIdle* function. The application must call the *pCmdUI->Enable* function to enable the user-interface item for this command. If the application doesn't enable the user-interface item, the pane appears in the status bar, but it does not display any text.

If you compiled the program at this point, the status bar would display the current time in one of its panes. However, one implementation problem would remain. Because the application calls the UI command handler only once each time the system becomes idle, what happens if the application runs and the user does not interact with it? The application does not reset the time until it receives one or more messages and empties its queue (new idle time). The code in step 5 addresses this situation.

5. Even though there are several methods to accomplish this, the simplest method takes advantage of the fact that the application calls the UI command handler only once when the application's message queue is emptied. Add the following statement to the *CMainFrame::OnCreate* member function:

```
m_wndStatusBar.SetTimer(1, 1000, NULL);
```

The *CWnd::SetTimer* event generates a message in the application's queue every second. Even if the user does not interact with the application, the queue empties after processing the timer event, new idle time is available, and the application updates the time pane in its status bar. Be sure to call *KillTimer* when the window is destroyed.

More Information

When a modal dialog box is up, the dialog manager manages the application's message queue. Since the dialog manager's message loop does not include calls to do idle time processing, the above mentioned *OnUpdateTime* function never gets called. If you would like to use a modal dialog box, yet still have the time on the status bar updated, you will have to avoid using the message queue. The following procedure demonstrates this.

1. Start with the code above.

2. In MAINFRM.H, add the following to the *CMainFrame* class definition.

```
UINT m_nIDTimer;
static VOID __export CALLBACK TimerProc(HWND hwnd, UINT uMsg,
    UINT uIDEvent, DWORD dwTime);
```

N O T E : In Win32, the "__export" keyword is obsolete and will cause the compiler to generate a C4236 warning in Visual C++ version 4.0 or later. To correct, simply remove the keyword.

3. In MAINFRM.CPP, change the *SetTimer* call in *CMainFrame::OnCreate* to:

```
m_nIDTimer = ::SetTimer(NULL, 0, 1000, TimerProc);
```

4. Add a timer procedure:

```
VOID __export CALLBACK CMainFrame::TimerProc(HWND hwnd,
UINT uMsg, UINT uIDEvent, DWORD dwTime)
{
    CMainFrame *pMainWnd =
        (CMainFrame *)AfxGetApp()->m_pMainWnd;
    ASSERT(uIDEvent == pMainWnd->m_nIDTimer);

    CCmdUI cui;
    cui.m_nID = ID_INDICATOR_TIME;
    cui.m_nIndex = 4;
    cui.m_pMenu = NULL;
```

(continued)

```
        cui.m_pOther = &pMainWnd->m_wndStatusBar;

        pMainWnd->OnUpdateTime(&cui);
    }
```

5. In the destructor, use

```
    ::KillTimer(NULL, m_nIDTimer);
```

Additional reference words: kbinf 1.00 1.50 2.00 2.50 2.51 2.52 3.00 3.10 4.00 5.00

KBCategory: kbprg

KBSubcategory: MfcUI

Switching Views in a Single Document Interface Program

(Q99562)

The information in this article applies to the Microsoft Foundation Classes (MFC) included with:

- Microsoft Visual C++ for Windows, versions 1.0, 1.5, 1.51, and 1.52
- Microsoft Visual C++, 32-bit Edition, versions 1.0, 2.0, 2.1, 4.0, and 5.0

Summary

In a single document interface (SDI) application, created with the Microsoft Foundation Class library, to create an alternate *CView* and use both the *CView* specified in the *CDocumentTemplate* and the alternate view in the application, perform the steps listed below.

N O T E :   These steps assume that the name of the *CWinApp*-derived object is *CMyWinApp*; that *CMyWinApp* is declared and defined in MYWINAPP.H and MYWINAPP.CPP, respectively; that *CNewView* is the name of the new, *CView*-derived object; and that *CNewView* is declared and defined in NEWVIEW.H and NEWVIEW.CPP, respectively. Substitute these with your own class and file names as needed.

1. Add the following members to the declaration of *CMyWinApp* in MY-WINAPP.H:

```
CView* m_pOldView;
CView* m_pNewView;
CView* SwitchView(CView* pNewView);
```

2. If *CNewView* was created with ClassWizard, modify the CNEWVIEW.H to change the access specifier for the constructor, destructor, and *OnInitialUpdate* function from protected to public.

3. Add "#include <AFXPRIV.H>" (without the quotation marks) to the include section of MYWINAPP.CPP. This is required to define the WM_INITIALUPDATE message to be added in step 4.

4. Create a new view and attach it to the document. The following code fragment creates a new view in the *InitInstance* member of the *CMyWinApp* object. In this way, both new and existing views persist for the life-

time of the application; however, the application could just as easily create the new view dynamically.

This code requires the main frame window, document, and default view to exist already. In Visual C++ for Windows and Visual C++ 32-bit Edition, versions 1.0 through 2.*x*, insert the following code into *CMyWinApp::InitInstance* after the call to *OnFileNew*, as *OnFileNew* creates each of these elements. In Visual C++ 32-bit Edition, versions 4.0 or later, insert this code after the call to *ProcessShellCommand*.

```
⋮
CView* pActiveView = ((CFrameWnd*)
    m_pMainWnd)->GetActiveView();
m_pOldView = pActiveView;
m_pNewView = (CView*) new CNewView;

CDocument* pCurrentDoc = ((CFrameWnd*)
    m_pMainWnd)->GetActiveDocument();

// Initialize a CCreateContext to point to the active document.
// With this context, the new view is added to the document
// when the view is created in CView::OnCreate().
CCreateContext newContext;
newContext.m_pNewViewClass = NULL;
newContext.m_pNewDocTemplate = NULL;
newContext.m_pLastView = NULL;
newContext.m_pCurrentFrame = NULL;
newContext.m_pCurrentDoc = pCurrentDoc;

// The ID of the initial active view is AFX_IDW_PANE_FIRST.
// Incrementing this value by one for additional views works
// in the standard document/view case but the technique cannot
// be extended for the CSplitterWnd case.
UINT viewID = AFX_IDW_PANE_FIRST + 1;
CRect rect(0, 0, 0, 0); // gets resized later

// Create the new view. In this example, the view persists for
// the life of the application. The application automatically
// deletes the view when the application is closed.
m_pNewView->Create(NULL, "AnyWindowName", WS_CHILD, rect,
    m_pMainWnd, viewID, &newContext);

// When a document template creates a view, the
// WM_INITIALUPDATE message is sent automatically.
// However, this code must explicitly send the message,
// as follows.
m_pNewView->SendMessage(WM_INITIALUPDATE, 0, 0);
⋮
```

5. Define the *CMyApp::SwitchView* function. (Alternatively, *SwitchView* could be declared and defined as a member of the main frame class.)

```
CView* CMyWinApp::SwitchView(CView* pNewView)
{
    CView* pActiveView =
        ((CFrameWnd*) m_pMainWnd)->GetActiveView();

    // Exchange view window ID's so RecalcLayout() works.
    #ifndef _WIN32
    UINT temp = ::GetWindowWord(pActiveView->m_hWnd, GWW_ID);
    ::SetWindowWord(pActiveView->m_hWnd, GWW_ID,
        ::GetWindowWord(pNewView->m_hWnd, GWW_ID));
    ::SetWindowWord(pNewView->m_hWnd, GWW_ID, temp);
    #else
    UINT temp = ::GetWindowLong(pActiveView->m_hWnd, GWL_ID);
    ::SetWindowLong(pActiveView->m_hWnd, GWL_ID,
        ::GetWindowLong(pNewView->m_hWnd, GWL_ID));
    ::SetWindowLong(pNewView->m_hWnd, GWL_ID, temp);
    #endif

    pActiveView->ShowWindow(SW_HIDE);
    pNewView->ShowWindow(SW_SHOW);
    ((CFrameWnd*) m_pMainWnd)->SetActiveView(pNewView);
    ((CFrameWnd*) m_pMainWnd)->RecalcLayout();
    pNewView->Invalidate();
    return pActiveView;
}
```

N O T E : This function returns a pointer to the old view so that the old view can be destroyed if desired. Before destroying the view though, *CDocument::RemoveView* should be called so the association between the view and the document is removed.

6. Add command handlers or other code to call the *SwitchView* function when the application needs to switch between views.

Additional reference words: kbinf 1.00 1.50 2.00 2.10 2.50 3.00 3.10 4.00 5.00 constructor destructor multiple

KBCategory: kbprg

KBSubcategory: MfcDocView

Create Additional Views with *CreateNewFrame* Function

(Q100993)

The information in this article applies to the Microsoft Foundation Classes (MFC) included with:

■ Microsoft Visual C++ for Windows, versions 1.0, 1.5, 1.51, and 1.52

■ Microsoft Visual C++ 32-bit Edition, versions 1.0, 2.0, 2.1, 4.0, 4.1, and 5.0

Summary

The *CDocTemplate::CreateNewFrame* function creates additional views of a document in a multiple document interface (MDI) application written using the Microsoft Foundation Class library. The prototype of the *CreateNewFrame* function is as follows:

```
CFrameWnd * CDocTemplate::CreateNewFrame(CDocument *,
    CFrameWnd *)
```

To call this function, specify a pointer to a *CDocument* object (the document for which the function will create a view) and a pointer to a frame window that has properties to duplicate. Typically, the second parameter of the function is NULL.

When an application calls *CreateNewFrame*, the function creates a new frame window and a view in the frame window. The frame window type and view type depend on the document template (*CDocTemplate*) associated with the document specified in the *CreateNewFrame* call.

More Information

To better understand how to use *CreateNewFrame*, it might be useful to review two examples. The first example is the WINMDI.CPP file in the Microsoft Foundation Class library source code. WINMDI.CPP defines the function *CMDIFrameWnd::OnWindowNew* that calls *CreateNewFrame* to add an additional frame and view for a specified document. The application calls *OnWindowNew* each time the user selects New from the MDI application's Windows menu.

The *OnWindowNew* function contains two significant lines of code, as follows:

```
CFrameWnd * pFrame = pTemplate->CreateNewFrame(pDocument,
    pActiveChild);
pTemplate->InitialUpdateFrame(pFrame, pDocument);
```

This code creates and displays the new frame window and document view.

The other example is the DOCMULTI.CPP file, also in the Microsoft Foundation Class library source code. The *CMultiDocTemplate::OpenDocument-File* function includes the following code:

```
CFrameWnd * pFrame = CreateNewFrame(pDocument, NULL);
```

Note that the second parameter is NULL because the design of the *OpenDocumentFile* function assumes that the programmer is not interested in duplicating any of the other frames that contain views of this document.

The CHKBOOK sample also demonstrates creating additional frames and views for documents. In CHKBOOK.CPP, the *CChkBookApp::OpenDocumentFile* function includes the following code:

```
CChkBookDoc* pDoc =
    (CChkBookDoc *)CWinApp::OpenDocumentFile(lpszFileName);
if (pDoc == NULL)
    return NULL;

CMDIChildWnd* pframe = ((CMDIFrameWnd *)
    AfxGetApp()->m_pMainWnd)->MDIGetActive();
CFrameWnd* pNewFrame =
    m_pCheckViewTemplate->CreateNewFrame(pDoc, NULL);
if (pNewFrame == NULL)
    return pDoc;
m_pCheckViewTemplate->InitialUpdateFrame(pNewFrame, pDoc);
```

Here are two points to consider when you use the *CreateNewFrame*.

■ The source code for *CDocTemplate::CreateNewFrame* is in DOC-TEMPL.CPP. It includes the following code:

```
if (!pFrame->LoadFrame(m_nIDResource, WS_OVERLAPPEDWINDOW |
    FWS_ADDTOTITLE, // default frame styles
    NULL, &context)
```

Because this code creates the frame window with a NULL parent window, the Microsoft Foundation Class library uses the application's main window as the parent window.

■ *CreateNewFrame* creates both a frame and a view, not only a view.

If, for some reason, *CreateNewFrame* does not quite address your situation, the source code for *CreateNewFrame* is quite useful to demonstrate the steps required to create frames and views.

Additional reference words: Kbinf 1.00 1.50 2.00 2.10 2.50 2.51 3.00 3.10 4.00 4.10 5.00 change view

KBCategory: kbprg

KBSubcategory: MfcDocView

Setting First Pane of *CStatusBar*

(Q110505)

The information in this article applies to the Microsoft Foundation Classes (MFC) included with:

- Microsoft Visual C++ for Windows, versions 1.0, 1.5, 1.51, and 1.52

- Microsoft Visual C++ 32-bit Edition, versions 1.0, 2.0, 2.1, 4.0, 4.1, 4.2, and 5.0

Symptoms

If the text in the first pane of a *CStatusBar* window is changed using *SetPaneText* and a menu is selected, the text is overwritten by the help prompts for the menu.

Cause

Setting any but the first pane of the status bar is relatively simple. You just need to set the pane using *SetPaneText* and make sure you have added in an ON_UPDATE_COMMAND_UI handler for the ID of that pane (set in your MAINFRAME.CPP as an element of an *indicators[ ]* array). This handler should call *Enable* in the following manner to make sure that the pane is not erased.

```
void CMainFrame::OnUpdateMystat(CCmdUI* pCmdUI)
{
    pCmdUI->Enable();
}
```

However, setting the FIRST pane of a status bar using *SetPaneText* or calling *SetWindowText* on the status bar is a bit more difficult. The problem is that the framework itself is changing the first pane using some special techniques. Basically, the framework is passing a WM_SETTEXT command directly to the status bar, from a number of places within its own code.

Adding ON_UPDATE_COMMAND_UI handlers or calling *SetPaneText* for the first pane of the status bar does not permanently set it. The framework eventually sends a WM_SETTEXT message directly to the status bar, changing the text from what was set.

Resolution

One way of setting the first pane yourself and keeping it set to what you want is to derive your own class from *CStatusBar* (for example *CMyStat*) and to give it a WM_SETTEXT handler. (Adding the WM_SETTEXT handler cannot be done using ClassWizard, so the handler must be added by hand.) The steps to do this are as follows:

1. Use ClassWizard to add a new class, derived from a generic *CWnd*. Now edit the .H and .CPP files to change the two references to *CWnd* to *CStatusBar*.

2. Add a protected member function of *CMyStat*:

   ```
   afx_msg LRESULT OnSetText(WPARAM, LPARAM);
   ```

3. Add a message map entry for the function in the .CPP file, as follows:

   ```
   BEGIN_MESSAGE_MAP(CMyStat, CStatusBar)
       //{{AFX_MSG_MAP(CMyStat)
       // NOTE: ClassWizard will add and remove mapping
       macros here.
       //}}AFX_MSG_MAP
       ON_MESSAGE( WM_SETTEXT, OnSetText )
   END_MESSAGE_MAP()
   ```

4. Now implement the function as follows:

   ```
   LRESULT CMyStat::OnSetText(WPARAM wParam, LPARAM lParam)
       {
           if ( !bIgnoreSetText )
               return CStatusBar::OnSetText( wParam, lParam );
           return 0;  // Same as CStatusBar::OnSetText success
       }
   ```

   where *bIgnoreSetText* is true only if you have set your own text in the status bar with a *SetPaneText* call.

5. Now just include *CMyStat* class header file in your MAINFRM.H file and replace:

   ```
   CStatusBar m_wndStatusBar;
   ```

   with the following:

   ```
   CMyStat     m_wndStatusBar;
   ```

Now, whenever *bIgnoreSetText* is true, the first pane of the status bar will be updated only when you update it with *SetPaneText*. The frameworks

WM_SETTEXT messages will be blocked when you have this flag set to a non-zero value. Note that this blocking affects only the first pane of the status bar.

You could also add member functions to your status bar class that both set the text of the status bar and set the *bIgnoreSetText* flag to lock or unlock the status bar in one step. You might call them *SetPaneOneAndLock* and *SetPaneOneAndUnlock*.

Additional references: 1.00 1.50 1.51 1.52 2.00 2.10 2.50 2.51 2.52 3.00 3.10 4.00 4.10 4.20 5.00

KBCategory: kbprg kbprb

KBSubcategory: MfcUI

How to Create New Documents Without *CWinApp::OnFileNew*

(Q113257) _____

The information in this article applies to the Microsoft Foundation Classes (MFC) included with:

■ Microsoft Visual C++ for Windows, versions 1.0, 1.5, 1.51, and 1.52

■ Microsoft Visual C++ 32-bit Edition, versions 1.0, 2.0, 2.1, 4.0, 4.1, 4.2, and 5.0

Summary

It is sometimes desirable to create a *CMultiDocTemplate* based window (in other words, a *CFrameWnd/CDocument/CView* combination) without using the mechanism provided by *CWinApp::OnFileNew.* For example, if the program has multiple document templates, *CWinApp::OnFileNew* will prompt the user with a dialog box asking which type of document to open. The programmer may already know which type of *CMultiDocTemplate* to use, and therefore may not want to prompt the user because it would be inappropriate in the given context of the application.

More Information

Assuming the application was originally created with AppWizard, the undocumented *CMultiDocTemplate::OpenDocumentFile* function can be used to create a new *CMultiDocTemplate* based window. There are several steps involved:

1. Add a *CMultiDocTemplate* pointer to your *CWinApp* derived class:

```
class CMyApp : public CWinApp
{
    ⋮

    public:
        CMultiDocTemplate* m_pDocTemplate;

    ⋮

}
```

N O T E : If you plan to use multiple document types, you must create a *CMultiDocTemplate* pointer member variable for each document type.

2. In the call to *CWinApp::InitInstance,* remove the creation of the *CMulti-DocTemplate* from the call to *AddDocTemplate.* Set the pointer to point to the new *CMultiDocTemplate.* Use the pointer to call *AddDocTemplate*:

```
BOOL CMyApp::InitInstance()
{
    ⋮

    m_pDocTemplate = new CMultiDocTemplate(IDR_TEXTTYPE,
        RUNTIME_CLASS(CMyDoc),
        RUNTIME_CLASS(CMDIChildWnd),
        RUNTIME_CLASS(CMyView));

    AddDocTemplate(m_pDocTemplate);

    ⋮

}
```

3. Use the pointer to call *CMultiDocTemplate::OpenDocumentFile* with a NULL parameter to create the new window. For this example, assume there is a button in a *CView* window. In the BN_CLICKED handler for the button, we want to create a window based on *m_pDocTemplate*:

```
void CMyView::OnNewWindowButtonClicked()
{
    CMyApp* pApp = (CMyApp*)AfxGetApp();
    pApp->m_pDocTemplate->OpenDocumentFile(NULL);
}
```

This same technique could be used to create a *CSingleDocTemplate* based window in a single document interface (SDI) application. However, it is not necessary. Because there is only one document template for the application, calling *OnFileNew* will create the new window without prompting the user for the type of document.

Additional reference words: kbinf 1.00 1.50 2.00 2.10 2.50 2.51 2.52 3.00 3.10 4.00 4.10 4.20 5.00

KBCategory: kbprg

KBSubcategory: MfcDocView

Changing the Background Color of an MFC Edit Control

(Q117778)

The information in this article applies to the Microsoft Foundation Classes (MFC) included with:

- Microsoft Visual C++ for Windows, versions 1.0, 1.5, 1.51, and 1.52

- Microsoft Visual C++ 32-bit Edition, versions 1.0, 2.0, 2.1, 4.0, 4.1, 4.2, and 5.0

Summary

To change the background color of an edit control in an MFC application, you must override the *OnCtlColor* message-handling function of the window containing the edit control.

In the new *OnCtlColor* function, set the background color and return a handle to a brush that will be used for painting the background. This must be done in response to receiving both the CTLCOLOR_EDIT and CTLCOLOR-_MSGBOX messages in the *OnCtlColor* function.

This is also documented in the Visual C++ online documentation, under *CWnd::OnCtlColor.*

More Information

The sample code below uses a *CDialog*-derived class (*CEditDialog*) to demonstrate the process. Class Wizard was used to generate message-handling functions for the WM_CTLCOLOR and WM_DESTROY messages. These functions are called *CEditDialog::OnCtlColor* and *CEditDialog::OnDestroy*, respectively.

```
// editdlg.h : header file
//

///////////////////////////////////////////////////////////////

// CEditDialog dialog

class CEditDialog : public CDialog
{
// Construction
public:
    CEditDialog(CWnd* pParent = NULL);
```

```
    // standard constructor

    // Add a CBrush* to store the new background brush for edit
    // controls.
        CBrush* m_pEditBkBrush;

    // Dialog Data
        //{{AFX_DATA(CEditDialog)
        enum { IDD = IDD_EDITDIALOG };
            // NOTE: The ClassWizard will add data members here.
        //}}AFX_DATA
    // Overrides
        // ClassWizard generated virtual function overrides
        //{{AFX_VIRTUAL(CEditDialog)
        protected:
        virtual void DoDataExchange(CDataExchange* pDX); // DDX/DDV
                                                         // support
        //}}AFX_VIRTUAL
    // Implementation
    protected:

        // Generated message map functions
        //{{AFX_MSG(CEditDialog)
        afx_msg HBRUSH OnCtlColor(CDC* pDC, CWnd* pWnd,
            UINT nCtlColor);
        afx_msg void OnDestroy();
        //}}AFX_MSG
        DECLARE_MESSAGE_MAP()
};

// editdlg.cpp : implementation file
//
#include "stdafx.h"
#include "mdi.h"
#include "editdlg.h"

#ifdef _DEBUG
#undef THIS_FILE
static char BASED_CODE THIS_FILE[] = __FILE__;
#endif

/////////////////////////////////////////////////////////////////
// CEditDialog dialog
```

(continued)

```
CEditDialog::CEditDialog(CWnd* pParent /*=NULL*/)
    : CDialog(CEditDialog::IDD, pParent)
{
    //{{AFX_DATA_INIT(CEditDialog)
        // NOTE: The ClassWizard will add member initialization
        // here.
    //}}AFX_DATA_INIT

    // Instantiate and initialize the background brush to
    // black.
    m_pEditBkBrush = new CBrush(RGB(0, 0, 0));
}

void CEditDialog::DoDataExchange(CDataExchange* pDX)
{
    CDialog::DoDataExchange(pDX);
    //{{AFX_DATA_MAP(CEditDialog)
        // NOTE: The ClassWizard will add DDX and DDV calls
        // here.
    //}}AFX_DATA_MAP
}

BEGIN_MESSAGE_MAP(CEditDialog, CDialog)
    //{{AFX_MSG_MAP(CEditDialog)
    ON_WM_CTLCOLOR()
    ON_WM_DESTROY()
    //}}AFX_MSG_MAP
END_MESSAGE_MAP()

/////////////////////////////////////////////////////////////
// CEditDialog message handlers

HBRUSH CEditDialog::OnCtlColor(CDC* pDC, CWnd* pWnd, UINT nCtlColor)
{
    switch (nCtlColor) {

    case CTLCOLOR_EDIT:
    case CTLCOLOR_MSGBOX:
        // Set color to green on black and return the
        // background brush.
        pDC->SetTextColor(RGB(0, 255, 0));
        pDC->SetBkColor(RGB(0, 0, 0));
        return (HBRUSH)(m_pEditBkBrush->GetSafeHandle());

    default:
        return CDialog::OnCtlColor(pDC, pWnd, nCtlColor);
    }
}
```

```
void CEditDialog::OnDestroy()
{
    CDialog::OnDestroy();

    // Free the space allocated for the background brush
    delete m_pEditBkBrush;
}
```

Additional reference words: kbinf 1.00 1.50 1.51 1.52 2.00 2.10 2.50 2.51 2.52 3.00 2.10 3.10 4.00 4.10 4.20 5.00 CEdit

KBCategory: kbprg

KBSubcategory: MfcUI

How to Detect an Empty *CRecordset* Object

(Q121950)

The information in this article applies to the Microsoft Foundation Classes (MFC) included with:

- Microsoft Visual C++ for Windows, versions 1.5 and 1.51
- Microsoft Visual C++, 32-bit Edition, versions 2.0, 4.0, 4.1, 4.2, and 5.0

Summary

The *CRecordset* represents a set of records obtained from a data source through a query. If no records from the data source match the query, there will be no records in the record set object, so *CRecordset::IsEOF* and *CRecordset::IsBOF* both return a nonzero value. A query is executed during calls to *CRecordset::- Open* and *CRecordset::Requery*, so empty record sets can be detected calling *CRecordset::IsEOF* and/or *CRecordset::IsBOF* after executing a query. This behavior is described in the documentation for *CRecordset::IsEOF* and *CRecordset::IsBOF*.

> **Additional reference words:** kbinf empty recordset 1.50 2.00 2.50 2.51 3.00 4.00 4.10 4.20 5.00
>
> **KBCategory:** kbprg
>
> **KBSubcategory:** MfcDatabase

Format of the Document Template String

(Q129095)

The information in this article applies to the Microsoft Foundation Classes (MFC) included with:

- Microsoft Visual C++ for Windows, versions 1.0, 1.5, 1.51, and 1.52

- Microsoft Visual C++ 32-bit Edition, versions 1.0, 2.0, 2.1, 4.0, 4.1, 4.2, and 5.0

Summary

This article explains the format of the document template string.

More Information

The document template string is a string resource consisting of up to nine substrings separated by the \n character. Each substring contains information specific to the document template. The document template string is contained in the document template and can be edited by the Resource editor (App Studio).

Format of the Document Template String

N O T E :   If a substring is not wanted and therefore not included in the complete document template string, you must still use the \n character as a delimiter. However, trailing \n characters are not necessary.

```
IDR_MAINFRAME <windowTitle>\n<docName>\n<fileNewName>\n<filterName>\n
    <filterExt>\n<regFileTypeID>\n<regFileTypeName>\n
    <filterMacExt(filterWinExt)>\n
    <filterMacName(filterWinName)>
```

The table on the following page defines each of the substrings.

The final two substrings are defined conditionally. When _MAC is defined, the substrings are assigned to <filterName> and <filterExt>, while the two substrings that normally have these names are defined as <filterWinName> and <filterWinExt>. When _MAC is not defined, the two new substrings are assigned the names <filterMacName> and <filterMacExt>. These last two substrings allow references to filename extensions to be removed from filterName and allow the four-character Macintosh file type for your application to be specified in filterExt.

Substring	Definition
<windowTitle>	Name that appears in the application window's title bar (for example, "Microsoft Excel"). Present only in the document template for SDI applications.
<docName>	Root for the default document name (for example, "Sheet"). This root plus a number is used for the default name of a new document of this type whenever the user chooses the New command from the File menu (for example, "Sheet1" or "Sheet2"). If not specified, "Untitled" is used as the default.
<fileNewName>	Name of this document type. If the application supports more than one type of document, this string is displayed in the File New dialog box (for example, "Worksheet"). If not specified, the document type is inaccessible using the File New command.
<filterName>	Description of the document type and a wildcard filter matching documents of this type. This string is displayed in the List Files Of Type drop-down list in the File Open dialog box (for example, "Worksheets (*.XLS)"). If not specified, the document type is inaccessible using the File Open command.
<filterExt>	Extension for documents of this type (for example, ".XLS"). If not specified, the document type is inaccessible using the File Open command.
<regFileTypeId>	Identifier for the document type to be stored in the registration database maintained by Windows. This string is for internal use only (for example, "ExcelWorksheet"). If not specified, the document type cannot be registered with the Windows File Manager.
<regFileTypeName>	Name of the document type to be stored in the registration database. This string may be displayed in dialog boxes of applications that access the registration database (for example, "Microsoft Excel Worksheet").

Example

This example is the document template string used in the Scribble step 4 example provided with Visual C++ version 2.1.

> **N O T E :** _MAC is not defined. Also, the first substring is not used in MDI applications. Therefore a document template string for an MDI application begins with the \n character.

```
IDR_SCRIBTYPE \nScrib\nScrib\nScrib Files (*.scr)\n.SCR
    \nScribble.Document.1\nScrib Document
    \nSCRI\nscri Files
```

<windowTitle>	Not used due to MDI application
<docName>	Scrib
<fileNewName>	Scrib
<filterName>	Scrib Files (*.scr)
<filterExt>	.SCR
<regFileTypeId>	Scribble.Document.1
<regFileTypeName>	Scrib Document
<filterMacExt>	SCRI
<filterMacName>	scri Files

Platform Differences

The string resource is parsed into the following substrings based on the platform:

Win16

windowTitle	default window title
docName	user visible name for default document
fileNewName	user visible name for FileNew
filterName	user visible name for FileOpen
filterExt	user visible extension for FileOpen
regFileTypeId	REGEDIT visible registered file type identifier
regFileTypeName	Shell visible registered file type name

Win32

windowTitle	default window title
docName	user visible name for default document
fileNewName	user visible name for FileNew
filterName	user visible name for FileOpen
filterExt	user visible extension for FileOpen
regFileTypeId	REGEDIT visible registered file type identifier
regFileTypeName	Shell visible registered file type name
filterMacExt[1]	Macintosh file type for FileOpen
filterMacName[1]	user visible name for Macintosh FileOpen

---

1. Not documented in VC 5.00.

Win32 Mac

windowTitle	default window title
docName	user visible name for default document
fileNewName	user visible name for FileNew
filterWinName	user visible name for FileOpen
filterWinExt	user visible extension for FileOpen
regFileTypeId	REGEDIT visible registered file type identifier
regFileTypeName	Shell visible registered file type name
filterExt	Macintosh file type for FileOpen
filterName	user visible name for Macintosh FileOpen

References

Search in the Visual C++ online documentation for the following topics:

- Doc Template Files
- Resource Editors
  - ❑ *CDocTemplate::GetDocString*
  - ❑ *CSingleDocTemplate::CSingleDocTemplate*
  - ❑ *CMultiDocTemplate::CMultiDocTemplate*

Additional reference words: appstudio resource 1.00 1.50 1.51 1.52 2.00 2.10 2.50 2.51 2.52 3.00 3.10 4.00 4.10 4.20 5.00

KBCategory: kbusage kbprg

KBSubcategory: MfcDocView

How to Remove the System Menu from an Iconized Application

(Q129224) _____

The information in this article applies to the Microsoft Foundation Classes (MFC) included with:

- ■ Microsoft Visual C++ for Windows, versions 1.0, 1.5, 1.51, and 1.52
- ■ Microsoft Visual C++ 32-bit Edition, versions 2.0, 2.1, 4.0, and 5.0

Summary

There are two ways to remove the system menu of an application when a user clicks an iconized application:

- ■ Override the main frame window's *PreCreateWindow* function to remove the WS_SYSMENU from the window's style field. However, this method removes the system menu altogether from the application.

- ■ Override the main frame window's *OnSize* method, and change the window style of the mainframe to either include or exclude the WS_SYSMENU style bit depending on user action. Use this technique if the user wants to remove the system menu when the application is iconized and add the system menu back to the application when the application is restored.

More Information

Method One

To remove the system menu completely from the application, override the main frame window's *PreCreateWindow* method as follows:

```
BOOL CMainFrame::PreCreateWindow(CREATESTRUCT & cs)
{
// Call the base class version of PreCreateWindow, replace
// CMDIFrameWnd with CFrameWnd in the following line
// for an SDI application

    if (!CMDIFrameWnd::PreCreateWindow(cs))
        return FALSE;
```

(continued)

357

```
// Remove the system menu style bit from the window

    cs.style &= ~WS_SYSMENU;
    return TRUE;
}
```

Method Two

The following steps and code fragments show how to remove the system menu when a user clicks an iconized application. The system menu is restored when the application is not iconized.

1. Declare a BOOL public data member in the class declaration of *CMainFrame*. This data member determines if the system menu is enabled or not.

```
// In an SDI application CMainFrame will be derived from
CFrameWnd

class CMainFrame : public CMDIFrameWnd
{
public:
    BOOL sys_menu_enabled;

        .
        .  // Existing class declarations
        .

}
```

2. Modify the *CMainFrame* constructor to initialize the *sys_menu_enabled* data member function to TRUE.

```
CMainFrame::CMainFrame()
{
    //default the system menu to be enabled
    sys_menu_enabled = TRUE;


        .
        .  // Continue with normal constructor code, if any
        .

}
```

3. Use the Class Wizard to create a message handler for the WM_SIZE message for the *CMainFrame* class, and add the following code to the *CMainFrame::OnSize* message handler.

```
void CMainFrame::OnSize(UINT nType, int cx, int cy)
{
```

```
// declare a local variable to hold the window style

    long window_style;

//call base class's OnSize function,
//If SDI application call CFrameWnd::OnSize()

CMDIFrameWnd::OnSize(nType, cx, cy);

//if user is minimizing or iconizing the application

if (nType == SIZE_MINIMIZED)
{
    // Get the main frame window's style
    window_style = GetWindowLong(m_hWnd, GWL_STYLE);

    //Remove the system menu from the window's style
    window_style &= ~WS_SYSMENU;

    //toggle the boolean data member to show sys menu
    //disabled
    sys_menu_enabled = FALSE;

    //set the style attribute of the main frame window
    SetWindowLong(m_hWnd, GWL_STYLE, window_style);
}
else
{
    //if user is restoring the application and his system
    //menu
    //is disabled,
    if ((nType == SIZE_RESTORED) && (!sys_menu_enabled))
    {
        window_style = GetWindowLong(m_hWnd, GWL_STYLE);

        //Add the system menu to the window's style
        window_style |= WS_SYSMENU;

        //toggle the boolean data member to show sys menu
        //enabled
        sys_menu_enabled = TRUE;

        SetWindowLong(m_hWnd, GWL_STYLE, window_style);
        SendMessage(WM_NCACTIVATE,TRUE);
    }
}
}
```

Additional reference words: kbinf 1.00 1.50 1.51 1.52 2.00 2.10 2.00 2.50 2.51 2.52 3.00 3.10 4.00 5.00

KBCategory: kbprg kbcode

KBSubcategory: MfcUI

How to Subclass the MDIClient by Using MFC

(Q129471)

The information in this article applies to the Microsoft Foundation Classes (MFC) included with:

- Microsoft Visual C++ for Windows, versions 1.0, 1.5, 1.51, and 1.52

- Microsoft Visual C++, 32-bit Edition, versions 1.0, 2.0, 2.1, 4.0, 4.1, 4.2, and 5.0

Summary

In MFC, the MDICLIENT window is stored in a public HWND member variable (*m_hwndMDIClient*) within the *CMDIFrameWnd* class. *CMDIFrameWnd* is the base class of the *CMainFrame* class in an AppWizard-generated MDI application. There are three steps required to subclass the MDICLIENT window:

1. Use ClassWizard to derive a class from *CWnd* called *CMDIClientWnd*.

2. Add the function, *GetSuperWndProcAddr*, to *CMDIClientWnd*.

3. Use *CMDIClientWnd* to subclass the MDICLIENT window.

Once the MDICLIENT window has been subclassed with *CMDIClientWnd*, message handlers and other functions can be placed in the *CMDIClientWnd* class.

More Information

Here is more detailed information about each of the steps:

1. Use ClassWizard to derive a class from *CWnd* called *CMDIClientWnd*. For details on how to derive a class using ClassWizard, please see the User's Guide documentation on ClassWizard, specifically the "Adding a New Class" section.

2. Add the function *GetSuperWndProcAddr* to *CMDIClientWnd*.

NOTE: This step need only be performed if you are using 16-bit versions of Visual C++, not 32-bit. The 32-bit versions of Visual C++ implement this functionality for you.

Add the following prototype to the header file, once the class has been created:

```
public:
    WNDPROC* GetSuperWndProcAddr();
```

Add the following function to the .CPP file:

```
WNDPROC* CMDIClientWnd::GetSuperWndProcAddr() {
    static WNDPROC NEAR pfnSuper = NULL;
    return &pfnSuper;
}
```

3. Use *CMDIClientWnd* to subclass the MDICLIENT window in the *CMDIFrameWnd* class (usually *CMainFrame*).

To the *CMainFrame* class, add a public variable of type *CMDIClientWnd* called *m_wndMDIClient*. Modify *OnCreate* for *CMainFrame* as follows:

```
int CMainFrame::OnCreate(LPCREATESTRUCT lpCreateStruct)
{
    if (CMDIFrameWnd::OnCreate(lpCreateStruct) == -1)
        return -1;

// Add
    if (!m_wndMDIClient.SubclassWindow (m_hWndMDIClient)) {
// Add
TRACE ("Failed to subclass MDI client window\n");
// Add
        return (-1);
// Add
    }
    ⋮
}
```

After completing these three steps, you can use ClassWizard to add message handlers to *CMDIClientWnd* similar to the one below, which changes the MDICLIENT's background color.

```
BOOL CMDIClientWnd::OnEraseBkgnd(CDC* pDC)
{
    // Set brush to desired background color
    CBrush backBrush(RGB(255, 128, 128));

    // Save old brush
    CBrush* pOldBrush = pDC->SelectObject(&backBrush);
```

```
CRect rect;
pDC->GetClipBox(&rect);        // Erase the area needed

pDC->PatBlt(rect.left, rect.top, rect.Width(), rect.Height(),
    PATCOPY);
pDC->SelectObject(pOldBrush);
return TRUE;
}
```

Additional reference words: kbinf 1.00 2.00 1.50 2.50 1.51 2.51 1.52 2.52 2.10 3.00 3.10 4.00 4.10 4.20 5.00

KBCategory: kbprg kbcode

KBSubcategory: MfcMisc

Avoiding Error LNK2001
Unresolved External Using DEFINE_GUID

(Q130869)

The information in this article applies to the Microsoft Foundation Classes (MFC) included with:

- Microsoft Visual C++ 32-bit Edition, versions 2.0, 2.1, 4.0, 4.1, 4.2, and 5.0

Summary

A GUID must be initialized exactly once. For this reason, there are two different versions of the DEFINE_GUID macro. One version just declares an external reference to the symbol name. The other version actually initializes the symbol name to the value of the GUID. If you receive an LNK2001 error for the symbol name of the GUID, the GUID was not initialized. You can make sure your GUID gets initialized in one of two ways:

- If you are using precompiled header files, include the INITGUID.H header file before defining the GUID in the implementation file where it should be initialized. (AppWizard-generated MFC projects use precompiled headers by default.)

- If you are not using precompiled headers, define INITGUID before including OBJBASE.H. (OBJBASE.H is included by OLE2.H.)

More Information

Here is the definition of DEFINE_GUID as it appears in OBJBASE.H:

```
#ifndef INITGUID
#define DEFINE_GUID(name, 1, w1, w2, b1, b2, b3, b4, b5, b6, \
    b7, b8) \
    EXTERN_C const GUID FAR name
#else

#define DEFINE_GUID(name, 1, w1, w2, b1, b2, b3, b4, b5, b6, \
    b7, b8) \
    EXTERN_C const GUID name \
    = { 1, w1, w2, { b1, b2, b3, b4, b5, b6, b7, b8 } }
#endif // INITGUID
```

Note that if the symbol INITGUID is not defined, DEFINE_GUID simply defines an external reference to the name.

In INITGUID.H, you find (among other things):

```
#undef DEFINE_GUID

// Other code

⋮

#define DEFINE_GUID(name, l, w1, w2, b1, b2, b3, b4, b5, b6, b7, b8) \
    EXTERN_C const GUID __based(__segname("_CODE")) name \
    = { l, w1, w2, { b1, b2,  b3,  b4,  b5,  b6,  b7,  b8 } }
```

By including INITGUID.H after OBJBASE.H, DEFINE_GUID is modified to actually initialize the GUID.

> **N O T E :** It is important to make sure that this is done exactly once for each DLL or EXE. If you try to initialize the GUID in two different implementation files and then link them together, you get this error: LNK2005 <symbol> already defined.

Additional reference words: kbinf 2.00 2.10 4.00 4.10 4.20 5.00

KBCategory: kbole kberrmsg

KBSubcategory: VCGenIss

How to Create MFC Applications That Do Not Have a Menu Bar

(Q131368)

The information in this article applies to the Microsoft Foundation Classes (MFC) included with:

- Microsoft Visual C++ for Windows, versions 1.5, 1.51, and 1.52
- Microsoft Visual C++ 32-bit Edition, versions 1.0, 2.0, 2.1, 4.0, 4.1, 4.2, and 5.0

Summary

For most Windows-based applications, a menu bar is a part of the user interface. The menu bar provides a functionality summary for the person using the program. However, it is not required that every Windows-based application must contain a menu bar. This article describes how to create an MFC application that does not have a menu bar.

For Windows-based applications generated by AppWizard, the IDR_MAINFRAME menu resource is the standard menu resource for both SDI and MDI applications. It is the only menu resource for an SDI application. MDI applications contain additional menus for each type of MDI child window they support. Those menu resources are usually named IDR_xxxTYPE, where xxx is related to the name of the corresponding document type. Thus, creating an application with no menus is not as easy for an MDI application as for an SDI application. You basically have to modify all functions related to loading and switching menus.

More Information

Steps to Create SDI Application That Has No Menu Bar

1. Generate an SDI application with AppWizard. Do not delete the IDR_MAINFRAME menu resource. If you have an application that was not generated with AppWizard, do not delete the corresponding main menu resource. Leaving the menu resource is required to avoid assertion failures in the MFC code.

2. To prevent the main application window from having a menu bar, delete the already loaded menu, and set the *hMenu* field of the

CREATESTRUCT structure to NULL in the *CFrameWnd::PreCreateWindow* function:

```
BOOL CMainFrame::PreCreateWindow(CREATESTRUCT& cs)
{
    if (cs.hMenu!=NULL)
    {
        ::DestroyMenu(cs.hMenu);    // delete menu if loaded
        cs.hMenu = NULL;            // no menu for this window
    }

    return CFrameWnd::PreCreateWindow(cs);
}
```

Steps to Create MDI Application That Has No Menu Bar

1. Generate an MDI application with AppWizard. Do not delete the IDR_MAINFRAME menu resource. If you have an application that was not generated with AppWizard, do not delete the corresponding main menu resource. Leaving the menu resource is required to avoid assertion failures in the MFC code.

2. Delete menu resources associated with MDI child windows (IDR-_xxxTYPE). They are not used. By deleting them, you avoid a resource (memory) leak.

3. Override the *PreCreateWindow* function for the *CMainFrame* class:

```
BOOL CMainFrame::PreCreateWindow(CREATESTRUCT& cs)
{
    if (cs.hMenu!=NULL)
    {
        ::DestroyMenu(cs.hMenu);    // delete menu if loaded
        cs.hMenu = NULL;            // no menu for this window
    }

    return CMDIFrameWnd::PreCreateWindow(cs);
}
```

4. Modify the code responsible for switching menus by overriding the *LoadFrame* and *OnCreateClient* methods of *CMainFrame*. This is necessary because MFC has already loaded and switched menus automatically. The following shows what must be done:

```
// Overridden method declarations for CMainFrame
BOOL LoadFrame( UINT nIDResource,
```

(continued)

```
        DWORD dwDefaultStyle = WS_OVERLAPPEDWINDOW |
        FWS_ADDTOTITLE, CWnd* pParentWnd = NULL,
        CCreateContext* pContext = NULL);
    BOOL CMainFrame::OnCreateClient(LPCREATESTRUCT lpcs,
        CCreateContext* /*pContext*/);

    // Overridden method declarations for CMainFrame
    BOOL CMainFrame::LoadFrame(UINT nIDResource, DWORD
        dwDefaultStyle,
        CWnd* pParentWnd, CCreateContext* pContext)
    {
        return CFrameWnd::LoadFrame(nIDResource,dwDefaultStyle,
            pParentWnd,pContext);
    }

        BOOL CMainFrame::OnCreateClient(LPCREATESTRUCT lpcs,
            CCreateContext* /*pContext*/)
        {
            return CreateClient(lpcs,NULL);
        }
```

N O T E :   Instead of calling the base class (*CMDIFrameWnd*) in the override of *LoadFrame*, you call its base class, *CFrameWnd*, instead. That way you can avoid the code that deals with MDI menus.

Additional reference words: kbinf 1.50 1.51 1.52 1.00 2.00 2.10 2.5 2.50 2.51 2.52 2.10 3.00 3.10 4.00 4.10 4.20 5.00

KBCategory: kbprg

KBSubcategory: MfcUI

How to Change the Mouse Pointer for a Window in MFC

(Q131991) _____

The information in this article applies to the Microsoft Foundation Classes (MFC) included with:

- Microsoft Visual C++ for Windows, versions 1.5, 1.51, and 1.52
- Microsoft Visual C++, 32-bit Edition, versions 1.0, 2.0, 2.1, 4.0, and 5.0

Summary

In a Windows-based application, a window is always created based on a window class. The window class identifies several characteristics of the windows based on it, including the default mouse pointer (cursor). In some cases, an application may want to change the pointer associated with certain windows that it creates. This article describes three methods an MFC application can use to display different pointers at different times.

More Information

Here are some situations when you might want an MFC application to display different pointers at different times:

- When the default pointer isn't a good user-interface object for a particular application. For example, an I-beam pointer is more suitable than the arrow for a text editor window in NotePad. This could involve changing the pointer for the entire run of the application.

- When an application performs a lengthy operation, such as disk I/O, an hourglass pointer is more appropriate than the arrow. By changing the pointer to an hourglass, you provide good visual feedback to the user. This could involve changing the pointer for a limited period of time.

Three Methods

Here are three ways an application can change the mouse pointer in a window:

- Override the _CWnd::OnSetCursor_ function. Call the Windows API _SetCursor_ function to change the pointer.

■ Register your own window class with the desired mouse pointer, override the *CWnd::PreCreateWindow* function, and use the newly registered window class to create the window.

■ To show the standard hourglass pointer, an application can call the *CCmdTarget::BeginWaitCursor*, which displays the hourglass, and call *CmdTarget::EndWaitCursor* to revert back to the default pointer. This scheme works only for the duration of a single message. If the mouse is moved before a call to *EndWaitCursor* is made, Windows sends a WM_SETCURSOR message to the window underneath the pointer. The default handling of this message resets the pointer to the default type, the one registered with the class, so you need to override *CWnd::OnSetCursor* for that window, and reset the pointer back to the hourglass.

Code to Illustrate the Three Methods

The following code shows by example how to change the mouse pointer of a *CView* derived class window by using the three methods. *m_ChangeCursor* is a member variable of *CMyView* class and is of type BOOL. It indicates whether a different pointer type needs to be displayed.

Method One

Change the mouse pointer for the *CMyView* object by overriding *CWnd::OnSetCursor* function. Use ClassWizard to establish the message map function *CMyView::OnSetCursor* for Windows message WM_SETCURSOR and supply the body of the function as follows:

```
BOOL CMyView::OnSetCursor(CWnd* pWnd, UINT nHitTest, UINT
    message)
{
    if ( m_ChangeCursor )
    {
        ::SetCursor(AfxGetApp()->LoadStandardCursor(IDC_WAIT));
        return TRUE;
    }

    return CView::OnSetCursor(pWnd, nHitTest, message);
}
```

Method Two

Register your own window class containing the desired mouse pointer using either the *AfxRegisterClass* or *AfxRegisterWndClass* function. Then create the view window based on the registered window class. For more information on registering window classes in MFC, please see MFC Tech Note 1, "Window Class Registration."

```
BOOL CMyView::PreCreateWindow(CREATESTRUCT& cs)
{
    cs.lpszClass = AfxRegisterWndClass(CS_DBLCLKS |
        CS_HREDRAW | CS_VREDRAW, // use any window styles
        AfxGetApp()->LoadStandardCursor(IDC_WAIT),
        (HBRUSH) (COLOR_WINDOW + 1));          // background brush

    return CView::PreCreateWindow(cs)
}
```

Method Three

Call the *BeginWaitCursor* and *EndWaitCursor* functions to change the mouse pointer.

> N O T E : *CWinApp::DoWaitCursor(1)* and *CWinApp::DoWaitCursor(-1)* work similarly to *BeginWaitCursor* and *EndWaitCursor*, respectively.

```
void CMyView::PerformLengthyOperation()
{
    BeginWaitCursor();  // or AfxGetApp()->DoWaitCursor(1)

    //...

    EndWaitCursor();     // or AfxGetApp()->DoWaitCursor(-1)
}
```

If calls to *BeginWaitCursor* and *EndWaitCursor* are not in the same handler, you must override *OnSetCursor* as follows:

```
BOOL CMyView::OnSetCursor(CWnd* pWnd, UINT nHitTest, UINT
    message)
{
    if (m_ChangeCursor)
    {
        RestoreWaitCursor();
        return TRUE;
    }

    return CView::OnSetCursor(pWnd, nHitTest, message);
}
```

In this example, set *m_ChangeCursor* to TRUE just before the call to *BeginWaitCursor*, and set it back to FALSE after the call to *EndWaitCursor*.

Additional reference words: kbinf 1.52 2.00 2.10 2.52 3.00 3.10 4.00 5.00

KBCategory: kbprg kbui kbcode

KBSubcategory: MfcUI

How to Customize the Common Print Dialog

(Q132909)

The information in this article applies to the Microsoft Foundation Classes (MFC) included with:

- Microsoft Visual C++ for Windows, versions 1.0, 1.5, 1.51, and 1.52

- Microsoft Visual C++, 32-bit Edition, versions 2.0, 2.1, 2.2, 4.0, 4.1, 4.2 and 5.0

Summary

This article explains how the standard print dialog box can be modified and used in a typical MFC application. Customizing the print dialog involves modifying Window's default common print dialog box template. When customizing the common print dialog box, you can add new controls and/or remove existing controls.

More Information

In some situations, you may find it necessary to customize the standard print dialog box. This involves modifying the existing print dialog box template and modifying the views implementation of printing to use this customized template.

Step-by-Step Procedure

Use this method to implement a customized print dialog box:

1. Copy the PRINTDLGORD dialog box template from COMMDLG.RC to the application's .RC file. (In Visual C++ 4.x and 5.0, this dialog box template resides in the \MSDEV\INCLUDE\PRNSETUP.DLG file.) To do this:

   ❑ Open MSVC\MFC\SAMPLES\APSTUDIO\COMMDLG.RC and your application's resource file by using App Studio (the Resource editor). This file is in \msdev\samples\mfc\general\clipart under 32-bit Visual C++. If you are using Visual C++ 4.x or 5.0, add the line

   ```
   #include "windows.h"
   ```

   to the top of the file \MSDEV\INCLUDE\PRNSETUP.DLG. Save and close this file. Reopen it as 'Resources'. (See the 'Open As' combo box in the File Open dialog box.)

❑ In the resource browser window of the "from" file, select the PRINTDLGORD (id 1528) dialog box resource.

❑ As you hold down the Ctrl key, drag the resource to the resource browser window of the "to" file.

N O T E : Dragging the resource without holding the Ctrl key moves the resource rather than copies it.

2. Make the necessary changes to the copied dialog template.

N O T E : None of the controls present in the original dialog template should be deleted. Deleting the controls will cause a problems in the *DoDataExchange* function of *CPrintDialog*. Instead, the unwanted controls should be disabled and/or hidden in an overridden *OnInitDialog* member function of your *CPrintDialog*-derived class.

3. Use ClassWizard to add a C++ class (say, *CMyPrintDialog*) for this dialog box template. Derive this new class from *CDialog* with PRINTDLGORD as the dialog ID. (Note: In Visual C++ 4.*x* and 5.0 this class can be derived directly from *CPrintDialog*.)

4. Change all references from *CDialog* to *CPrintDialog* in both the header and implementation file of the newly created class. (This step is not necessary if you have derived your class directly from *CPrintDialog*.)

5. Because the constructor of *CPrintDialog* differs from *CDialog*, modify the constructor of *CMyPrintDialog* using this code (this step is not necessary if you have derived your class directly from *CPrintDialog*):

```
// Header file of CMyPrintDialog
class CMyPrintDialog : public CPrintDialog
{
// Construction
public:

    // The arguments to the following constructor closely match
    // CPrintDialog. Note the difference in the second argument.
    CMyPrintDialog(BOOL bPrintSetupOnly,
    // TRUE for Print Setup, FALSE for Print Dialog
    DWORD dwFlags = PD_ALLPAGES | PD_USEDEVMODECOPIES |
      PD_HIDEPRINTTOFILE,
    // Combination of flags. Refer to the Windows SDK
    // documentation for PRINTDLG structure for a
    // description of all the flags that can be used.
```

```
        CWnd* pParentWnd = NULL);

        // Rest of the class declaration
        ⋮

DECLARE_MESSAGE_MAP()
};

// Implementation file of CMyPrintDialog
CMyPrintDialog::CMyPrintDialog(BOOL bPrintSetupOnly,
    DWORD dwFlags /* = PD_ALLPAGES | PD_USEDEVMODECOPIES |
    PD_HIDEPRINTTOFILE */, CWnd* pParentWnd /* = NULL */)
    : CPrintDialog(bPrintSetupOnly, dwFlags, pParentWnd)
{
    //{{AFX_DATA_INIT(CMyPrintDialog)
    // NOTE: the ClassWizard will add member initialization here
    //}}AFX_DATA_INIT
}
```

6 Modify the *CView*-derived class (say, *CMyView*) to use the customized print dialog by using this code:

```
//   Implementation file of the view (say, in myview.cpp)
⋮
#include "myprintd.h"  // Include the CMyPrintDialog header
                       // file
⋮

// Override OnPreparePrinting of the CView-derived class as
// below:
BOOL CMyView::OnPreparePrinting(CPrintInfo* pInfo)
{
    // Delete the CPrintDialog object created in the CPrintInfo
    // constructor, and substitute with customized print
    // dialog.
    delete pInfo->m_pPD;

    // Construct and substitute with customized print dialog.
    pInfo->m_pPD = new CMyPrintDialog(FALSE);

    // Set the page range.
    pInfo->m_pPD->m_pd.nMinPage = 1;        // one based page
                                            // numbers
    pInfo->m_pPD->m_pd.nMaxPage = 0xffff; // how many pages is
                                            // unknown
```

(continued)

```
// Change the PRINTDLG struct so that the custom print
// dialog will be used.
pInfo->m_pPD->m_pd.hInstance = AfxGetInstanceHandle();
pInfo->m_pPD->m_pd.lpPrintTemplateName =
    MAKEINTRESOURCE(PRINTDLGORD);

// Set the Flags of the PRINTDLG structure as shown, else
// the changes will have no effect
pInfo->m_pPD->m_pd.Flags |= PD_ENABLEPRINTTEMPLATE;

// For details about these flags, refer to the SDK
// documentation on the PRINTDLG structure.

return DoPreparePrinting(pInfo);
}
```

References

For more information, please see the PRINTDLG structure in Windows SDK documentation and *OnPreparePrinting* and *CPrintDialog* in Microsoft Foundation Class documentation.

Additional reference words: 1.00 1.50 2.00 2.10 2.51 2.52 3.00 3.10 4.00 4.10 5.00 CFileDialog

KBCategory: kbprg kbprint kbcode

KBSubcategory: MfcPrinting

How to Detect Mouse Clicks on Client Area of MDI Frame Windows

(Q133716)

The information in this article applies to the Microsoft Foundation Classes (MFC) included with:

- Microsoft Visual C++ for Windows, versions 1.5, 1.51, and 1.52

- Microsoft Visual C++, 32-bit Edition, versions 1.0, 2.0, 2.1, 2.2, 4.0, 4.1, 4.2 and 5.0

Summary

You can detect when a user clicks the mouse while the pointer is over the client area of your main MDI frame window (the area of the client not covered by any open MDI child windows). To do so, you must first subclass the MDIClient so you can intercept the mouse messages being sent to it. This article shows by example how to do it using MFC. You can extend the method outlined here to handle any messages sent to the MDIClient.

More Information

To manage its MDI child windows, the *CMDIFrameWnd* class creates a window of the class "mdiclient" to cover its entire client area (also referred to as the Application Workspace). MFC stores a handle to this MDIClient window in a public member variable, *m_hWndMDIClient*, of the *CMDIFrameWnd* class.

The MDIClient is a standard Windows window, not an MFC object. However, subclassing it allows you to treat it just as you would any other *CWnd*, taking advantage of standard MFC features like message maps. For example, you could use this technique to provide a context menu when the user clicks the right mouse button. Or, as the Windows 95 desktop does, you could use it to provide an easy means of selecting a group of iconized MDI child windows, enclosing them within a tracker rectangle as the user drags with the left mouse button held down.

Subclassing the MDIClient

Subclassing the MDIClient is actually quite easy as summarized in the following three steps. For more detailed information about this process, please see the following article in the Knowledge Base: "How to Subclass the MDIClient by Using MFC," Q129471.

1. Derive a class from *CWnd*, called *CMyMDIClient* for example, and add it to your project. You can use ClassWizard to help you do this.

2. If you are creating a 16-bit application, you need to add a public function called *GetSuperWndProcAddr* to your new *CMyMDIClient* class. Do not do this step when building applications with 32-bit versions of Visual C++.

```
WNDPROC* CMyMDIClient::GetSuperWndProcAddr()
{
    static WNDPROC NEAR pfnSuper = NULL;
    return &pfnSuper;
}
```

3. Include your class header file in MAINFRM.H. Embed a public member object of your new class in your *CMainFrame* class, for example *CMyMDIClient m_MyMDIClient*. If you have not already done so, override *CMDIFrameWnd::OnCreate*. In your *CMainFrame::OnCreate*, first call the base class implementation, *CMDIFrameWnd::OnCreate*, which creates the MDIClient window itself and stores the handle in *m_hWndMDIClient*. Then subclass that window to your embedded member object:

```
int CMainFrame::OnCreate(LPCREATESTRUCT lpCreateStruct)
{
    // Call the base class implementation to create the
    // MDIClient window.
    if (CMDIFrameWnd::OnCreate(lpCreateStruct) == -1)
        return -1;

    // Subclass the MDIClient window.
    if (!m_MyMDIClient.SubclassWindow(m_hWndMDIClient))
    {
        TRACE ("Failed to subclass MDI client window\n");
        return (-1);
    }

    ⋮
}
```

Code Sample

Once you subclass the MDIClient in this way, you can add any needed message handlers directly to your *CMyMDIClient* class. To illustrate, the following code displays your application's File menu as a context menu when the user clicks the MDIClient using the right mouse button.

```
void CMyMDIClient::OnRButtonDown(UINT nFlags, CPoint point)
{
    POINT ScreenPoint = point;
    CMenu* pMenuTrackPopup;

    // Get a pointer to the app's File menu popup.
    // AfxGetMainWnd() returns a pointer to the main frame
    // window,
    // GetMenu() returns a pointer to the main menu of the
    // application,
    // and GetSubMenu(0) retrieves the submenu at position 0
    // (here the File menu).
    pMenuTrackPopup = ((AfxGetMainWnd())->GetMenu())
        ->GetSubMenu(0);

    // Convert the mouse point to screen coordinates since that
    // is what TrackPopupMenu() expects.
    ClientToScreen(&ScreenPoint);

    // Draw and track the "floating" popup
    pMenuTrackPopup->TrackPopupMenu(TPM_RIGHTBUTTON,
        ScreenPoint.x, ScreenPoint.y,
        AfxGetMainWnd(),    // Use the 'this' pointer if you
    // want commands to be handled in your CMyMDIClient class
    // instead
        NULL);

    // NOTE: Do not destroy this menu here!

    // Call the base class
    CWnd::OnRButtonDown(nFlags, point);
}
```

Additional reference words: kbinf 1.50 1.51 1.52 1.00 2.00 2.10 2.50 2.51 2.52 2.10 2.20 3.00 3.10 4.00 4.10 4.20 5.0

KBCategory: kbprg kbcode

KBSubcategory: MfcUI

SAMPLE: Using MFC OLE Drag & Drop to Drag Text Between Windows

(Q135299)

The information in this article applies to the Microsoft Foundation Classes (MFC) included with:

- Microsoft Visual C++ for Windows, versions 1.50, 1.51, 1.52, and 1.52b

- Microsoft Visual C++, 32-bit Edition, versions 2.0, 2.10, 2.2, 4.0, 4.1, 4.2, and 5.0

Summary

In a Microsoft Foundation Classes (MFC) application, you may want to enable the user to drag text between various windows, including those in *CWnd*-derived objects as well as standard control windows in *CListBox* and *CEdit*-derived objects. A sample (LSTDRG) is available that demonstrates how to add OLE drag-and-drop functionality to a pre-existing MFC application. This sample demonstrates using OLE drag-and drop functionality to drag text between two list boxes, an edit control, and a *CWnd*-derived object's window. You can also use any other application with OLE text drag-and-drop functionality enabled as a drag source or a drop target (Word for Windows 6.*x* is one such application).

Download LSTDRG.EXE, a self-extracting file, from the Microsoft Software Library (MSL) on the following services:

- Microsoft Download Service (MSDL)
  Dial (206) 936-6735 to connect to MSDL
  Download LSTDRG.EXE

- Internet (anonymous FTP)
  ftp ftp.microsoft.com
  Change to the SOFTLIB\MSLFILES directory
  Get LSTDRG.EXE

More Information

To enable OLE for a pre-existing MFC application, you must initialize the OLE DLLs. This is done in the InitInstance() of your application object by calling *AfxOleInit()*. The LSTDRG sample was first created with no OLE support using AppWizard. The code that calls *AfxOleInit()* was then cut-and-pasted from *InitInstance()* of the OCLIENT MFC sample application that is supplied with the above-mentioned products.

OLE drag-and-drop functionality was enabled for each window by following the procedure outlined in the MFC version 2.5 OLE 2 Classes documentation. Sections of interest are listed below. You will also want to review the MFC Classes *COleDataSource* and *COleDropTarget*.

- ■ "Drag and Drop: Implementing a Drop Source"
- ■ "Drag and Drop: Implementing a Drop Target"
- ■ "Data Objects and Data Sources: Creation and Destruction"
- ■ "Data Objects and Data Sources: Manipulation"

To turn a *CWnd*-derived object into a drop source, you must instantiate a *COleDataSource* object in your *CWnd*-derived object. You can then call *COleDataSource::CacheGlobalData()* to cache the data (text) that you are going to drag. Then call *COleDataSource::DoDragDrop()* to actually initiate the drag drop. The return value from *DoDragDrop()* gives you the result of the drag drop operation. The DROPEFFECT return value from *DoDragDrop()* is a bit field, so you have to test specific bits of the return value to determine the drag drop results.

Turning a *CWnd*-derived object into a drop target is a bit more complicated. You must derive your own class from *COleDropTarget*, and instantiate a member of your *COleDropTarget*-derived object in the *CWnd*-derived class. In your *COleDropTarget* object you have to, at a minimum, override these four member functions:

- ■ *COleDropTarget::OnDragEnter()*
- ■ *COleDropTarget::OnDragLeave()*
- ■ *COleDropTarget::OnDragOver()*
- ■ *COleDropTarget::OnDrop()*

You must also initialize the *COleDropTarget* derived object as a drop target with the OLE DLLs by calling *COleDropTarget::Register()*. This would normally be done in the *OnCreate* member function of a *CWnd*-derived object (see the *CDDWnd::OnCreate* method in LSTDRG).

A problem in dialog box template created classes (*CListBox*, *CEdit*, and so on created by App Studio) is that *OnCreate* is not called. This is because control windows associated with the dialog box template are created during the dialog box creation process before their actual *CWnd*-derived C++ objects are created. These windows are then attached by using *Attached()* to the C++ *CWnd*-derived objects once they are created. To work around this, an *Initialize()* method was created for the *CListBox* and *CEdit*-derived classes where *COleDropTarget::Register()* is called. This *Initialize()* method is then called for each template-created control in the *CFormView*-derived classes *OnInitialUpdate()* method (see *CListdragView::OnInitialUpdate()* and *CDDListBox::Initialize()*).

Another interesting aspect of the LSTDRG application is the use of a burning trash can animation when text is dropped on a window. This animation uses a single bitmap composed of multiple 'cells' or images. The use of a single bitmap as opposed to multiple bitmaps conserves GDI resources and is more efficient to paint. It also turns off the mouse pointer (cursor) by loading an empty pointer during painting to eliminate pointer flicker on Windows version 3.*x* computers.

References

"MFC 2.5 OLE 2 Classes" reference book, available in the Books Online of Visual C++ version 1.5. See sections on Drag and Drop beginning with the section titled "Drag and Drop." Also review the *COleDataSource* class and the *COleDataTarget* class in the same reference book.

For good background information on how OLE handles drag and drop, please see *Inside OLE 2* by Kraig Brockschmidt, published by Microsoft Press.

Additional reference words: 1.50, 1.51 1.52 1.52b 2.00 2.10 2.20 2.50 2.51 2.52 2.52b 3.00 3.10 3.20 4.00 4.10 4.20 5.00

KBCategory: kbprg kbfile kbcode

KBSubCategory: MfcOLE

How to Use Dynasets with Microsoft SQL Server Version 6.x

(Q136994)

The information in this article applies to the Microsoft Foundation Classes (MFC) included with:

- Microsoft Visual C++, 16-bit Edition, versions 1.51, and 1.52
- Microsoft Visual C++, 32-bit Edition, versions 2.0, 2.1, 2.2, 4.0, 4.1, 4.2, and 5.0

Summary

Microsoft SQL Server versions 6.0 and 6.5 support dynasets. To use an updatable dynaset, you must have a unique index on one or more field(s) in the table. If there is no such index, the recordset will be read only.

More Information

If you create a dynaset without specifying a unique index on one or more field(s) in the table and then try to update or add a record, MFC will throw an exception that says the cursor is read only. Additionally, you will see the following errors in the MFC Trace output:

In Visual C++ version 1.5x:

Cursor is read only
State:S1009[Microsoft][ODBC SQL Server Driver][SQL Server]

Warning: 0 rows affected by update operation (expected 1).
No rows were affected by the update or delete operation.

In Visual C++ versions 2.x and 4.x:

Error: failure updating record.
Cursor is read only
State:S1009,Native:16929,Origin:[Microsoft][ODBC SQL Server Driver]
[SQL Server]

In Visual C++ 5.0:

Cursor concurrency changed

State:01S02, Native:0, Origin: [Microsoft] [ODBC SQL Server Driver]

Warning: Concurrency changed by the driver.

Marking CRecordset as not updatable.

Recordset is read-only.

Note that if you use the PRIMARY KEY specification new to SQL Server version 6.0 when creating your tables, you will automatically generate a unique index on the primary key. Here is an example of this syntax:

```
CREATE TABLE Table1
    (cola CHAR(8) PRIMARY KEY NOT NULL,
    colb CHAR(8))
```

If you are using the Microsoft SQL Server ODBC driver, version 2.65.0201, which comes with SQL Server version 6.5, MFC will throw an exception that says "Invalid argument value." Additionally, you will see the following errors in the MFC Trace output:

Error: failure updating record

Invalid argument value

State:S1009,Native:0,Origin:[Microsoft] [ODBC SQL Server Driver]

Additional reference words: kbinf 1.51 1.52 2.00 2.10 2.20 3.00 3.10 3.20 4.00 4.10 4.20 5.00

KBCategory: kbusage

KBSubcategory: MfcDatabase

MFC ODBC Classes and Parameterized Pre-Defined Queries

(Q137814)

The information in this article applies to the Microsoft Foundation Classes (MFC) included with:

- Microsoft Visual C++ for Windows, versions 1.5, 1.51, and 1.52
- Microsoft Visual C++, 32-bit Edition, versions 2.0, 2.1, 2.2, 4.0, 4.1, 4.2, and 5.0

Summary

The MFC Encyclopedia article "Recordset: Declaring a Class for a Predefined Query" describes how to invoke a predefined query that takes parameters and returns a result set. The instructions in that article will not work for pre-defined queries that take parameters and do not return a result set. Some possible error messages you may receive when attempting to do this are:

No columns were bound prior to calling SQLExtendedFetch
State:SL009:, NATIVE:0, Origin: [Microsoft][ODBC Cursor Library]

Invalid cursor state
State:24000, Native:24, Origin:[Microsoft][ODBC Microsoft Access Driver]

There are two ways that you can use predefined queries that take parameters and don't return a result set with the MFC ODBC classes:

1. You can execute the query from the *CRecordset::Open* member function. If you do this, you will have to override the *Open* function to not try to move to the first record and also not call any recordset member functions that expect a result set to be present.

2. You can execute the query using direct ODBC API calls. In this case, you will have to bind the parameters yourself rather than letting the RFX functions do this for you.

More Information

If your SQL command returns a result set, it is preferable to use a *CRecordset*-derived class, and pass the SQL to the recordset *Open* member function. Using

CRecordset is preferable when a result set is returned because the database classes do most of the work of binding the returned data to variables in your program. The *CRecordset* class will also do most of the work of binding parameters as well.

If you have a predefined query that takes parameters, you have a choice between using a *CRecordset*-derived class to take advantage of its support for binding the parameters or using the *CDatabase::m_hdbc* member variable and doing the binding yourself.

Using a *CRecordset*-Derived Class

In the first case, you can use the technique that is shown in the encyclopedia article "Recordset: Declaring a Class for a Predefined Query." You just have to make sure that you don't try to manipulate the result set, because there isn't one. The mandatory step is to override *CRecordset::Open* to prevent calling the code that moves to the first record once the recordset is opened. This is accomplished by copying the code from *CRecordset::Open* (in DBCORE.CPP) and commenting out the code that tries to move to the first record. For example, in MFC 3.2, you would comment out the *MoveFirst* call at the end of the *Open* function:

```
BOOL CMyRecordset::Open( … )
{
    ⋮

    // MoveFirst();   <<<< comment this line out!
}
```

In addition, you should also not call any function that assumes a result set is present.

Then, set up the predefined query as mentioned in the encyclopedia article. To actually invoke the query, you would do something like this:

```
CMyRecordset rs;
rs.m_Param = someValue    // value for parameter
rs.Open(CRecordset::snapshot,"{CALL MyQuery (?)}",
    CRecordset::readOnly);
rs.Close();
```

However, in Visual C++ 4.0 and 4.1, the implementation of *CRecordset* was changed and, as a result, requires four additional steps to be taken to make this first approach work:

1. You need to use a database object derived from *CDatabase* that contains an accessor function that returns a reference (or pointer) to its

m_listRecordsets member. Your *CRecordset*-derived class needs to use this reference to add itself to the *m_listRecordsets*. Here is how you can define the *CDatabase*-derived class (you can place this declaration at the top of your *CRecordset*-derived class's header file):

```
class CMyDatabase : public CDatabase
{
public:
    CPtrList& GetRecordsetList() { return m_listRecordsets; }
};
```

In order to use this function to add your recordset to the database's list of recordsets, you must construct your *CRecordset*-derived class off of a *MyDatabase* (or whatever you called the derived class) and replace the following lines in the copy of the *CRecordset::Open*:

```
// Add to list of CRecordsets with allocated hstmts
m_pDatabase->m_listRecordsets.AddHead(this);
```

with this:

```
// Add to list of CRecordsets with allocated hstmts
CPtrList& listRecordsets =
    ((CMyDatabase*)m_pDatabase)->GetRecordsetList();
listRecordsets.AddHead(this);
```

The reason for this step is that MFC 4.0 and 4.1 declare *CRecordset* to be a friend of *CDatabase* which allows it to directly manipulate the protected *m_listRecordsets* member. Friendship is not inherited, however, so other measures must be taken to allow the recordset to add itself to the database's list of recordsets.

2. #include <afxpriv.h> at the top of your *CRecordset*-derived class's .CPP file. This is necessary because *CRecordset::Open* that you copied into your recordset class makes use of the USES_CONVERSION and T2A macros.

3. Remove the following line from *Open*:

```
NO_CPP_EXCEPTION(strDefaultConnect.Empty());
```

This line is only needed if you are building MFC.

4. Add the following line at the top of your *CRecordset*-derived class's .CPP file:

```
static const TCHAR szDriverNotCapable[] = _T("State:S1C00");
```

387

This line is present in DBCORE.CPP and *szDriverNotCapable* is used in *CRecordset::Open.* Since it is static, it is not visible outside of DB-CORE.CPP, so we must provide it in order to use the code for *Open.*

Using *CDatabase::m_hdbc* and Doing Your Own Binding

Another possibility is to execute the predefined query using the *m_hdbc* member of *CDatabase.* If you choose this method, you will have to do the parameter binding yourself using ODBC API calls:

```
CDatabase*    pDb;
RETCODE       nRetCode;
HSTMT         hstmt;
SDWORD        cBytes;
SDWORD        nParamValue;

// Construct and open the database object
pDb = new CDatabase;
pDb->Open("My_Datasource");

// allocate the hstmt
AFX_SQL_SYNC(::SQLAllocStmt(pDb->m_hdbc,&hstmt));
if (!pDb->Check(nRetCode))
    AfxThrowDBException(nRetCode,pDb,hstmt);

// bind the parameter
AFX_SQL_SYNC(::SQLBindParameter(hstmt,1,SQL_PARAM_INPUT,
    SQL_C_LONG,SQL_INTEGER,10,0,&nParamValue,4,&cBytes));
if (nRetCode != SQL_SUCCESS)
    AfxThrowDBException(nRetCode,pDb,hstmt);

// set the parameter value
nParamValue = 3;

// execute the query
AFX_SQL_ASYNC(pDb,::SQLExecDirect(hstmt,
    (UCHAR FAR*)"{CALL MyQuery (?)}",SQL_NTS));
if (nRetCode != SQL_SUCCESS && nRetCode !=
    SQL_SUCCESS_WITH_INFO)
    AfxThrowDBException(nRetCode,pDb,hstmt);

// free the hstmt
AFX_SQL_SYNC(::SQLFreeStmt(hstmt,SQL_DROP));

// Close and destruct the database object
pDb->Close();
delete pDb;
```

References

MFC Encyclopedia Article: "Recordset: Declaring a Class for a Predefined Query."

Additional reference words: kbinf 1.50 2.00 2.10 2.20 2.50 2.51 2.52 2.52a 2.52b 3.00 3.10 3.20 4.00 4.10 5.00

KBCategory: kbusage kbdocerr kbcode

KBSubcategory: MfcDatabase

SAMPLE: VSWAP32 Demos Multiple-View Switching in SDI

(Q141334)

The information in this article applies to the Microsoft Foundation Classes (MFC) included with:

■ Microsoft Visual C++, 32-bit Edition, versions 4.0, 4.1, 4.2, and 5.0

Summary

VSWAP32 demonstrates methods of switching between multiple views on a single document in a single-document interface (SDI) application. VSWAP32 displays two form views and a normal view that displays the list of data collected in the two form views.

N O T E :   This is the 32-bit version of this sample. There is also a 16-bit version available called VSWAP.EXE.

This sample application demonstrates using DDX/DDV (dialog data exchange/dialog data validation), with correct document updating and data validation when switching between views. It also correctly catches unsaved/unvalidated data when the application is closed.

Download VSWAP32.EXE, a self-extracting file, from the Microsoft Software Library (MSL) on the following services:

■ Microsoft Download Service (MSDL)
    Dial (206) 936-6735 to connect to MSDL. Download VSWAP32.EXE.

■ Microsoft's World Wide Web site on the Internet
    On the www.microsoft.com home page, click the Support icon. In the Microsoft Knowledge Base, search for VSWAP32.EXE. Open the article, and click the button to download the file.

■ Internet (anonymous FTP)
    ftp ftp.microsoft.com: Change to the SOFTLIB\MSLFILES directory. Get VSWAP32.EXE. After downloading the file, use the following command to extract the sample and build the appropriate directory structure:

    VSWAP32.EXE -d

More Information

The most important implementations of this are in:

```
CVswapApp::InitInstance
CVswapApp::SwitchView
CVswapApp::SaveActiveViewsData
```

The standard InitInstance code creates an initial document template, document, and view during the call to *ProcessShellCommand*. The code added to the end of *InitInstance* creates the view objects for the extra views used in this application and stores their pointers in a *CVswapApp* member array. It then cycles through a loop which creates the windows for the view objects. Each view window is created with a unique child window ID and a *CCreateContext* object that associates each view with the same *CDocument* object, which was created by *ProcessShellCommand*. Finally, the sample code triggers the *OnInitialUpdate* for the extra views. In this sample, both views persist for the lifetime of the application; however, the application could create the new view dynamically.

The *SwitchView* function created in this sample swaps the current view with a previously hidden view. It accomplishes this by first switching their child window IDs. This step is necessary because MFC relies on the standard view pane having the child window ID of AFX_IDW_PANE_FIRST. The rest of the code hides the current view and tells MFC to repaint and begin using the new view.

The *SaveActiveViewsData* is used to save the information from the active view to the document object. It is called by SwitchView whenever a view is switched. *SaveActiveViewsData* subsequently calls *SetToDoc*, which actually updates the data from the form view to the document by using MFC's DDX/DDV mechanisms in *DoDataExchange*.

Sample Code

The *SwitchView* function is included here as a reference.

```
CView* CVswapApp::SwitchView( UINT nIndex )
{
    ASSERT( nIndex >=0 && nIndex < NUMVIEWS );

    CView* pNewView = m_pViews[nIndex];

    CView* pActiveView =
        ((CFrameWnd*) m_pMainWnd)->GetActiveView();
```

(continued)

```
if ( !pActiveView )     // No currently active view
    return NULL;

if ( pNewView == pActiveView )     // Already there
    return pActiveView;

// Update Doc's data if needed
// Don't change view if data valiation fails
if ( ! SaveActiveViewsData() )
{
    return pActiveView;
}

m_nCurView = nIndex;     // Store the new current view's index

// exchange view window ID's so RecalcLayout() works
UINT temp = ::GetWindowLong(pActiveView->m_hWnd, GWL_ID);
::SetWindowLong(pActiveView->m_hWnd, GWL_ID,
    ::GetWindowLong(pNewView->m_hWnd, GWL_ID));
::SetWindowLong(pNewView->m_hWnd, GWL_ID, temp);

// Display and update the new current view - hide the old one
pActiveView->ShowWindow(SW_HIDE);
pNewView->ShowWindow(SW_SHOW);
((CFrameWnd*) m_pMainWnd)->SetActiveView(pNewView);
((CFrameWnd*) m_pMainWnd)->RecalcLayout();
pNewView->Invalidate();
return pActiveView;
}
```

References

For other examples of applications that switch views, please refer to the following samples:

- COLLECT (SDI)
- ENROLL (SDI)
- VWRPLC32 (MDI)
- SPLIT32 (Splitter)

For more information on DDX and DDV routines, please see Technical Note 26: "DDX and DDV Routines" in the Visual C++ online documentation.

Additional reference words: 4.00 4.10 4.20 5.00 VSWAP32 Q99562

KBCategory: kbprg kbfile

KBSubcategory: MfcDocView

SAMPLE: DLGDB32 *CDialog* Sharing a *CRecordset* Object

(Q141445)

The information in this article applies to the Microsoft Foundation Classes (MFC) included with:

- Microsoft Visual C++, 32-bit Edition, versions 4.0, 4.1, 4.2, and 5.0

This is the 32-bit version of this sample. The DLGDB32 code sample demonstrates how to have a *CDialog*-derived class share a *CRecordset* object that a *CRecordView* is already using. In addition, when used by itself, the code sample also demonstrates how to select *CRecordset* object from a *CDocument* without having a *CRecordView.*

N O T E :   This sample assumes that ODBC has been installed and that the Student Registration data source has been configured.

Download DLGDB32.EXE, a self-extracting file, from the Microsoft Software Library (MSL) on the services shown below. (The file must be decompressed by typing *DLGDB32 -d.*)

- The Microsoft Network
    On the Edit menu, click Go To, and then click Other Location.
    Type mssupport.
    Double-click the MS Software Library icon.
    Find the appropriate product area.
    Download DLGDB32.EXE.

- Microsoft Download Service (MSDL)
    Dial (206) 936-6735 to connect to MSDL.
    Download DLGDB32.EXE.

- Internet (anonymous FTP)
    ftp ftp.microsoft.com.
    Change to the SOFTLIB\MSLFILES directory.
    Get DLGDB32.EXE.

Additional reference words: 4.00 4.10 4.20 5.00

KBCategory: kbprg kbcode kbhowto kbfile

KBSubcategory: MfcDatabase

SAMPLE: VWRPLC32, Replacing a View in a *CMDIChildWnd* Window

(Q141499)

The information in this article applies to the Microsoft Foundation Classes (MFC) included with:

■ Microsoft Visual C++, 32-bit Edition, versions 4.0, 4.1, 4.2, and 5.0

Summary

The VWRPLC32 sample demonstrates how, in a Multiple Document Interface (MDI) application, a programmer can write a *ReplaceView* member function for a *CMDIChildWnd*-derived class. The following samples, which also replace various views, exist:

■ SPLIT32 (SDI)

■ COLLECT (MDI)

■ ENROLL (SDI)

■ VSWAP32 (SDI)

VWRPLC32 can be found in the Microsoft Software Library (MSL). Download VWRPLC32.EXE, a self-extracting file, from MSL on the following services:

■ Microsoft's World Wide Web site on the Internet
    On the www.microsoft.com home page, click the Support icon. In the Microsoft Knowledge Base, search for VWRPLC32.EXE. Open the article, and click the button to download the file.

■ Microsoft Download Service (MSDL)
    Dial (206) 936-6735 to connect to MSDL. Download VWRPLC32.EXE.

■ Internet (anonymous FTP)
    ftp ftp.microsoft.com: Change to the SOFTLIB\MSLFILES directory. Get VWRPLC32.EXE.

N O T E : Use the -d option when running VWRPLC32.EXE to decompress the file and re-create the proper directory structure.

More Information

The core of the sample can be found in FRAME.CPP. You will see the following function:

```
BOOL CFrame::ReplaceView(CRuntimeClass* pViewClass)
{
    CCreateContext context;
    CView * pCurrentView;

    // If no active view for the frame, return FALSE because this
    // function retrieves the current document from the active view.
    if ((pCurrentView=GetActiveView()) == NULL)
        return FALSE;

    // If we're already displaying this kind of view, no need to go
    // further.
    if ((pCurrentView->IsKindOf(pViewClass))==TRUE)
        return TRUE;

    // Get pointer to CDocument object so that it can be used in the
    // creation process of the new view.
    CDocument * pDoc= pCurrentView->GetDocument();

    // Set flag so that document will not be deleted when view is
    // destroyed.
    BOOL bAutoDelete=pDoc->m_bAutoDelete;
    pDoc->m_bAutoDelete=FALSE;
    // Delete existing view
    pCurrentView->DestroyWindow();
    // restore flag
    pDoc->m_bAutoDelete=bAutoDelete;

    // Create new view and redraw.
    context.m_pNewViewClass = pViewClass;
    context.m_pCurrentDoc = pDoc;
    context.m_pNewDocTemplate = NULL;
    context.m_pLastView = NULL;
    context.m_pCurrentFrame = this;

    CView* pNewView = (CView*) pViewClass->CreateObject();

    if (pNewView == NULL)
```

(continued)

395

```
{
    TRACE1("Warning: Dynamic create of view type %Fs failed\n",
        pViewClass->m_lpszClassName);
    return FALSE;
}

if (!pNewView->Create(NULL, NULL, AFX_WS_DEFAULT_VIEW,
    CRect(0,0,0,0), this, AFX_IDW_PANE_FIRST, &context))
{
    TRACE0("Warning: couldn't create view for frame\n");
    return FALSE; // Programmer can assume FALSE return value
                  // from this function means that there
                  // isn't a view.
}


// WM_INITIALUPDATE is define in AFXPRIV.H.
pNewView->SendMessage(WM_INITIALUPDATE, 0, 0);

 RecalcLayout();

pNewView->UpdateWindow();

SetActiveView(pNewView);

return TRUE;
}
```

The function receives a pointer to *CRuntimeClass* object for the new view that is desired. It destroys the old view and replaces it with a new view of the same *CDocument*. When *DestroyWindow* is called for the old view, this causes a "delete this" in the *CView::PostNcDestroy* function. Also, the *CView::~CView* destructor calls *CView::RemoveView*, which removes the view from the document's view list.

Additional reference words: kbinf 4.00 4.10 4.20 5.00 Q102829 MDI
  CMDIChildWnd

KBCategory: kbprg kbfile kbcode

KBSubcategory: MfcDocView

SAMPLE: Adding Control Bars to Dialog Boxes in MFC

(Q141751)

The information in this article applies to the Microsoft Foundation Classes (MFC) included with:

- Microsoft Visual C++, 32-bit Edition, versions 4.0, 4.1, 4.2, and 5.0

Summary

In a Microsoft Foundation Class (MFC) application, you can attach control bars such as status bars and toolbars to a frame window. However, for many applications a simple dialog box–based user interface is sufficient. MFC does not provide built-in support for adding control bars to dialog boxes.

DLGCBR32 is a sample application that demonstrates how to add a status bar and toolbar to a dialog box. In addition, it demonstrates a number of techniques related to using a modeless dialog box as the main window of an MFC application.

Download DLGCBR32.EXE, a self-extracting file, from the Microsoft Software Library (MSL) on the following services:

- Microsoft Download Service (MSDL)
  Dial (206) 936-6735 to connect to MSDL. Download DLGCBR32.EXE.

- Internet (anonymous FTP)
  ftp ftp.microsoft.com: Change to the SOFTLIB\MSLFILES directory. Get DLGCBR32.EXE.

More Information

To add a control bar to a dialog box, you must create the control bar as usual, and then make room for the control bar within the client area of the dialog box. For the control bar to function properly, the dialog box must duplicate some of the functionality of frame windows. If you want ON_UPDATE_COMMAND_UI handlers to work for the control bars, you also need to derive new control bar classes, and handle the WM_IDLEUPDATECMDUI message. If your dialog box is not the main window of your application, you will also need to modify its parent frame window to pass the WM_IDLEUPDATECMDUI message on to the dialog box's control bars.

To make room for a control bar within the client area of the dialog box, follow these steps in your dialog box's *OnInitDialog* function.

1. Create the control bars.

2. Figure out how much room the control bars will take by using the reposQuery option of *RepositionBars:*

```
CRect rcClientStart;
CRect rcClientNow;
GetClientRect(rcClientStart);
RepositionBars(AFX_IDW_CONTROLBAR_FIRST,
    AFX_IDW_CONTROLBAR_LAST,
    0, reposQuery, rcClientNow);
```

3. Move all the controls in your dialog box to account for space used by control bars at the top or left of the client area. If your dialog box contains a menu, you also need to account for the space used by the menu:

```
CPoint ptOffset(rcClientNow.left - rcClientStart.left,
    rcClientNow.top - rcClientStart.top);

CRect  rcChild;
CWnd* pwndChild = GetWindow(GW_CHILD);
while (pwndChild)
{
    pwndChild->GetWindowRect(rcChild);
    ScreenToClient(rcChild);
    rcChild.OffsetRect(ptOffset);
    pwndChild->MoveWindow(rcChild, FALSE);
    pwndChild = pwndChild->GetNextWindow();
}
```

4. Increase the dialog box window dimensions by the amount of space used by the control bars:

```
CRect rcWindow;
GetWindowRect(rcWindow);
rcWindow.right += rcClientStart.Width() - rcClientNow.Width();
rcWindow.bottom += rcClientStart.Height() -      rcClient-
Now.Height();
MoveWindow(rcWindow, FALSE);
```

5. Position the control bars using *RepositionBars*.

To update the first pane of a status bar with menu item text, you must handle WM_MENUSELECT, WM_ENTERIDLE, and WM_SETMESSAGE-STRING in your dialog box class. You need to duplicate the functionality of the *CFrameWnd* handlers for these messages. See the *CModelessMain* class in the sample program for examples of these message handlers.

To allow ON_UPDATE_COMMAND_UI handlers to work for other status bar panes and for toolbar buttons, you must derive new control bar classes and implement a message handler for WM_IDLEUPDATECMDUI. This is necessary because the default control bar implementations of *OnUpdateCmdUI* assume the parent window is a frame window. However, it doesn't do anything but pass the parent window pointer on to a function which only requires a *CCmdTarget* pointer. Therefore, you can temporarily tell *OnUpdateCmdUI* that the parent window pointer you are giving it is a *CFrameWnd* pointer to meet the compiler requirements. Here's an example:

```
LRESULT CDlgToolBar::OnIdleUpdateCmdUI(WPARAM wParam,
    LPARAM lParam)
{
    if (IsWindowVisible())
    {
        CFrameWnd* pParent = (CFrameWnd*)GetParent();
        if (pParent)
            OnUpdateCmdUI(pParent, (BOOL)wParam);
    }
    return 0L;
}
```

To pass WM_IDLEUPDATECMDUI messages on to dialog boxes other than the main window, save dialog pointers in your frame window class and create a WM_IDLEUPDATECMDUI handler in that class. The handler should send the WM_IDLEUPDATECMDUI message on to the dialog child windows by using *CWnd::SendMessageToDescendants*. Then perform default processing for the message within the frame window.

Additional reference words: kbinf 1.00 1.50 2.00 2.50 2.51 3.00 4.00 4.10 4.20 5.00 CDialog CStatusBar CToolBar

KBCategory: kbprg

KBSubcategory: MfcUI

How to Add Tooltips to OLE Controls

(Q141871)

The information in this article applies to the Microsoft Foundation Classes (MFC) included with:

■ Microsoft Visual C++, 32-bit Edition, versions 4.0, 4.2, and 5.0

Summary

This article demonstrates how to add a tooltip to an OLE Control.

More Information

By default, OLE controls do not support tooltips. The following steps, however, demonstrate how to modify a basic OLE control generated using the OLE Control Wizard to add this support.

1. Use the MFC ActiveX Control Wizard to generate a basic control named Basic.

2. Open the Stdafx.h file associated with the project and add the following line:

```
#include <afxcmn.h>
```

The header file Afxcmn.h contains declarations for MFC classes that serve as wrappers to Windows common controls including *CToolTipCtrl*.

3. Add the following lines to *COleControl*-derived class *CBasicCtrl* located in Basicctl.h:

```
CToolTipCtrl m_ttip;
void RelayEvent(UINT message, WPARAM wParam, LPARAM lParam);
```

The *RelayEvent* method will be used by the mouse message handlers to relay those messages to the tooltip control.

4. Use ClassWizard to add an *OnCreate* handler to the message map. It is in this routine that the tooltip control will be created. Add the following code to this handler:

```
if (!m_ttip.Create(this))
    TRACE0("Unable to create tip window.");
else
```

```
        if (!m_ttip.AddTool(this, LPCTSTR(m_toolTipText)))
            TRACE0("Unable to add tip for the control window.");
        else
            m_ttip.Activate(m_showToolTip);
```

5. To relay appropriate messages to the tooltip control, add handlers
   for WM_LBUTTONDOWN, WM_LBUTTONUP, and
   WM_MOUSEMOVE to the control's message map. The message map
   and code for these handlers follows:

```
// Message maps
//{{AFX_MSG(CTestpropCtrl)
    afx_msg int OnCreate(LPCREATESTRUCT lpCreateStruct);
    afx_msg void OnLButtonDown(UINT nFlags, CPoint point);
    afx_msg void OnLButtonUp(UINT nFlags, CPoint point);
    afx_msg void OnMouseMove(UINT nFlags, CPoint point);
//}}AFX_MSG
DECLARE_MESSAGE_MAP()

void CBasicCtrl::OnLButtonDown(UINT nFlags, CPoint point)
{
    RelayEvent(WM_LBUTTONDOWN, (WPARAM)nFlags,
        MAKELPARAM(LOWORD(point.x), LOWORD(point.y)));

    COleControl:: OnLButtonDown(nFlags, point);
}


void CBasicCtrl::OnLButtonUp(UINT nFlags, CPoint point)
{
    RelayEvent(WM_LBUTTONUP, (WPARAM)nFlags,
        MAKELPARAM(LOWORD(point.x), LOWORD(point.y)));

    COleControl::OnLButtonUp(nFlags, point);
}


void CBasicCtrl::OnMouseMove(UINT nFlags, CPoint point)
{
    RelayEvent(WM_MOUSEMOVE, (WPARAM)nFlags,
        MAKELPARAM(LOWORD(point.x), LOWORD(point.y)));

    COleControl::OnMouseMove(nFlags, point);
}

// implementation of the CBasicCtrl::RelayEvent method:
```

(continued)

```
void CBasicCtrl::RelayEvent(UINT message, WPARAM wParam,
    LPARAM lParam)
{
    if (NULL != m_ttip.m_hWnd) {
        MSG msg;

        msg.hwnd = m_hWnd;
        msg.message = message;
        msg.wParam = wParam;
        msg.lParam = lParam;
        msg.time = 0;
        msg.pt.x = LOWORD (lParam);
        msg.pt.y = HIWORD (lParam);

        m_ttip.RelayEvent(&msg);
    }
}
```

While it might seem reasonable to call *CWnd::GetCurrentMessage* instead of manually building a message, the value of the point that is returned is expressed in screen coordinates. When the tooltip performs a hit test to determine if the point of the relayed message falls within the boundary of the client rectangle of any associated tools, the test will fail, and the tooltip will not be displayed.

6. Alter *CBasicCtrl::DoPropExchange* by adding code to initialize the *m_toolTipText* and *m_showToolTip* properties:

```
PX_Bool(pPX, _T("ShowToolTip"), m_showToolTip, FALSE);
PX_String(pPX, _T("ToolTipText"), m_toolTipText, _T(""));
```

7. To allow the user of the control some control over the tooltip functionality, use ClassWizard to add the following OLE automation properties to the *CBasicCtrl* class:

External Name:	ShowToolTip	ToolTipText
Type:	BOOL	CString
Variable name:	m_showToolTip	m_toolTipText
Notification function:	OnShowToolTipChanged	OnToolTipTextChanged

ShowToolTip will allow the user to suppress the display of the tooltip, and ToolTipText will track the text that is to be displayed when the tooltip is visible.

8. Modify the property change notification functions for these properties in the following manner:

```
void CBasicCtrl::OnToolTipTextChanged()
{
    if (m_ttip.m_hWnd && AmbientUserMode()) {
        m_ttip.UpdateTipText(LPCTSTR(m_toolTipText), this);
        SetModifiedFlag();
    }
}

void CBaseCtrl::OnShowToolTipChanged()
{
    if (m_ttip.m_hWnd && AmbientUserMode()) {
        m_ttip.Activate(m_showToolTip);
        SetModifiedFlag();
    }
}
```

Test the Control

To test the control, build it, launch the ActiveX Control Test Container and insert the control into the Test Container. Then follow these steps:

1. On the View menu, click Properties.

2. Pull down the Property combo, set the ShowToolTip property to −1, and choose Apply.

3. Pull down the Property combo, set the ToolTipText property to SomeTip, and choose Apply.

4. Move the pointer over the client area of the control. A tooltip containing the text "Some Tip" should be displayed over the client area of the control.

REFERENCES

Microsoft Visual C++ version 4.0 Books Online: Cluts, Nancy, "Programming the Windows 95 User Interface," Microsoft Press, 1995, Pages 26-28.

Additional reference words: kbinf 4.00 4.10 4.20 5.00

KBCategory: kbprg kbhowto kbcode

KBSubcategory: MfcOLE

How to Handle OCM_CTLCOLORxxx Reflected Messages

(Q148242)

The information in this article applies to the Microsoft Foundation Classes (MFC) included with:

■ Microsoft Visual C++, 32-bit Edition, versions 4.0, 4.1, 4.2, and 5.0

Summary

This article shows you how to change the background color of an OLE control that subclasses a Windows control, with sample code for an Edit control. This article should apply to Button, Static, ListBox, and ComboBox controls as well.

More Information

Please refer to the following article in the Knowledge Base, "WM_CTL-COLORxxx Message Changes for Windows 95" (Q130952) for more about the exact WM_CTLCOLORxxx message sent by each control. If a control sends the WM_CTLCOLORSTATIC, you have to handle the OCM_CTL-COLORSTATIC message in the OCX and so on.

To change the background color of an OLE control that subclasses an Edit control, you must handle the OCM_CTLCOLOREDIT (32-bit) messages. These messages are intercepted by the "reflector window" (created for an OLE control that subclasses a Windows control) that reflects them back to the OLE control itself. In response to these reflected messages, you must set the background color (and optionally the foreground color) and return a handle to a brush initialized with the background color.

Step-by-Step Example

The sample code in this example illustrates how to handle OCM_CTL-COLOREDIT in order to change the background color of an OLE control that subclasses an Edit control.

1. Generate an MFC ActiveX Control Wizard application, and select the option that allows you to subclass an Edit control.

2. To handle an OCM_CTLCOLOREDIT reflected window message, declare the following handler function in the .H file of your control's class:

```
LRESULT OnOcmCtlColor(WPARAM wParam, LPARAM lParam);
```

3. In the .CPP file of your control's class, add an ON_MESSAGE entry to the message map:

```
ON_MESSAGE(OCM_CTLCOLOREDIT, OnOcmCtlColor)
```

4. Also in the .CPP file, implement the *OnOcmCtlColor* member function to process the reflected message:

```
//Assuming CEdtclrCtrl is the class for this control
LRESULT CEdtclrCtrl::OnOcmCtlColor(WPARAM wParam, LPARAM
    lParam)
{
    //Declare CBrush* m_pBackBrush in your control's .h file
    if (m_pBackBrush == NULL)
        m_pBackBrush = new CBrush(RGB(0,0,0));
    CDC* pdc = CDC::FromHandle((HDC)wParam);
    pdc->SetBkMode(TRANSPARENT);
    pdc->SetBkColor(RGB(0,0,0));
    pdc->SetTextColor(RGB(0,255,0));
    HBRUSH far* hbr = (HBRUSH far*)m_pBackBrush->GetSafeHandle();
    return ((DWORD)hbr);
}
```

N O T E :   In your control's constructor, set *m_pBackBrush* = NULL, and in your control's destructor, delete *m_pBackBrush*.

5. Build and register your control.

6. Insert this control into the ActiveX Control Test Container. Notice that the background color of your OLE control is changed.

References

Refer to technical article Technical Note 062: "Message Reflection for Windows Controls" and the article "ActiveX Controls: Subclassing a Windows Control in Visual C++ Programmer's Guide."

Additional reference words: 4.00 4.10 4.20 5.00

KBCategory: kbprg kbole kbhowto kbcode

KBSubcategory: MfcOLE

PRB: MFC Loads Wrong Resource in Extension DLL

(Q150121)

The information in this article applies to the Microsoft Foundation Classes (MFC) included with:

- Microsoft Visual C++ for Windows, versions 1.0, 1.5, 1.51, and 1.52
- Microsoft Visual C++, 32-bit Edition, versions 2.0, 2.1, 2.2, 4.0, 4.1, 4.2, and 5.0

Symptoms

The wrong resource is loaded when *CBitmap::LoadBitmap, CMenu::LoadMenu, CString::LoadString* or any other MFC resource-loading function is called in an MFC extension DLL (AFXDLL). In some cases, a resource in the application is loaded instead of the appropriate resource in the extension DLL.

Cause

When a resource in the application or another extension DLL gets loaded instead of a resource in the current extension DLL, the cause is usually improper resource management. An MFC application and all of its extension DLLs are one global chain of resources. If there are multiple resources with the same ID value in any of the modules in the chain, MFC uses the first resource it finds with the desired ID value. The first resource is often found in the application, which is searched before any of the extension DLLs.

Resolution

Change the ID values of any resources that conflict so they are unique in both the application and any extension DLL that the application uses. These values are stored in the RESOURCE.H file for each project and can be modified in the Resource editor or Developer Studio with the Resource Symbols command.

To ensure that modules do not use conflicting symbol values, reserve different ranges of ID values for each module in the 1 through 0x6FFFF range. Set the _APS_NEXT_RESOURCE_VALUE definition in the RESOURCE.H file for each module to the low end of that module's range before creating any resources. The Resource Editor uses this symbol to determine the ID value of the next resource created. This technique is documented in

MFC Technical Note 35 and in the DLLHUSK sample included with Visual C++.

More Information

In .EXE or .DLL files that link to MFC dynamically, MFC resource-loading functions call *AfxFindResourceHandle* to obtain the handle of the module where a resource is located. *AfxFindResourceHandle* searches for resources by type and symbol value in:

- The module returned by *AfxGetResourceHandle*. This is usually the application.

- The extension DLLs through the chain of *CDynLinkLibrary* objects.

- Any language-specific resource DLLs.

- Any attached MFC system DLLs (MFCxx.DLL, for example).

N O T E : Some 16-bit MFC resource loading functions do not call *AfxFindResourceHandle*, but instead use the value returned from *AfxCurrentResourceHandle*.

Each extension DLL creates, initializes, and then passes a *CDynLinkLibrary* object to *AfxInitExtensionModule* that places the DLL in the resource chain. *AfxTermExtensionModule* removes the DLL from the chain when the DLL is detached from the application.

A benefit of this design is that MFC automatically locates a resource for an application or extension DLL, even if that resource is located in a distant extension DLL or the application itself. All resources in the process are chained, so ID values are passed between DLLs and the application and the proper resources are loaded. A disadvantage is that there are no duplicate ID values between any of the extension DLLs or the application that uses them.

To set the default location where *AfxFindResourceHandle* first checks for a resource, use *AfxSetResourceHandle*. Because *AfxFindResourceHandle* first checks the handle set by *AfxSetResourceHandle*, it can be used to circumvent the chain and load a resource from one particular DLL or application. The resource handle is restored to its original value immediately after loading the resources. The current default resource handle is found with *AfxGetResourceHandle*. The DLLHUSK sample included with Visual C++ also illustrates this technique. In TESTDLL2.CPP, *CListOutputFrame::Create* sets the resource handle to the module handle stored in the AFX_EXTENSION_MODULE structure extension DLL. This structure is initialized with the module handle when it is passed to the *CDynLinkLibrary* constructor in *InitTestDLL2*.

Status

This behavior is by design.

References

For information on:

- Extension DLLs, see the MFC Technical Note 33 and the DLLHUSK sample.

- Resource management in projects, see Technical Note 35.

Additional reference words: 1.00 1.50 1.51 1.52 2.00 2.10 2.20 4.00 4.10 4.20 5.00

KBCategory: kbprg kbprb

KBSubcategory: MfcDLL

DRAGD95.EXE:SAMPLE:OLE
Drag/Drop in Windows 95 Common Controls

(Q152092)

The information in this article applies to the Microsoft Foundation Classes (MFC) included with:

- Microsoft Visual C++, 32-bit Edition, versions 4.0, 4.1, 4.2, and 5.0

Summary

This sample demonstrates implementing OLE drag and drop in Windows 95 common controls. It also demonstrates how the drag image functionality can be preserved while dragging within the application that is the source of the data.

You can find DRAGD95.EXE, a self-extracting file, on these services:

- Microsoft's World Wide Web site on the Internet
  On the www.microsoft.com home page, click the Support icon. In the Microsoft Knowledge Base search for DRAGD95.EXE. Open the article, and click the button to download the file.

- Internet (anonymous FTP)
  ftp ftp.microsoft.com: Change to the SOFTLIB/MSLFILES folder. Get DRAGD95.EXE.

- Microsoft Download Service (MSDL)
  Dial (206) 936-6735 to connect to MSDL. Download DRAGD95.EXE.

N O T E : Use the -d option when running DRAGD95.EXE to de-compress the file and re-create the proper directory structure. If you are using Visual C++ 5.0 you may get a message "This project was generated by a previous version of Developer Studio. Continuing will convert it to the new format. Do you want to convert the project ?" Accept this by clicking "Yes."

More Information

Windows 95 common controls implement their own style of drag and drop. However, this style of drag and drop does not support dragging to other applications. To enable this functionality, it is possible to implement OLE drag and drop using the common controls. Unfortunately, when OLE drag and drop is implemented, the common control drag image is lost.

It is possible, when implementing OLE drag and drop, to preserve the common control drag image. However, this image will only be displayed when the pointer is over the application that is the source of the data. This is because the image is not a system-wide resource and belongs to the application that is the source of the data. This behavior is consistent with that of the shell in Windows 95. In Windows 95, you will notice that the drag image is lost over applications other than the Windows Explorer or the Windows shell. The shell and any instances of the Explorer that are running are a single instance of the same application.

OLE drag and drop as implemented by this sample is straightforward. When a drag is started, a *COleDataSource* object is loaded with data and *COleDataSource::DoDragDrop* is called. The data source is loaded with a CF_TEXT format and a private clipboard format that has been registered. Applications that understand CF_TEXT, such as Microsoft Word, can be a drop target for the data. You can also implement a *COleDropTarget* object so that you can be a drop target for your own custom clipboard format.

Common controls normally begin a drag operation in response to the LVN_BEGINDRAG message. You can also take advantage of this message to begin the drag operation. This is where the similarity with common control drag and drop ends. Common control drag and drop uses mouse messages to control tracking the drag image and processing the drop. You will not be able to use mouse messages because, after you begin the drag operation, control is passed to OLE's *DoDragDrop* function.

To control the tracking and display of the common control drag image, you will implement a *COleDropSource* object and pass it to the *DoDragDrop* function. *COleDropSource* implements a *GiveFeedback* function that is called to give feedback about the effect of a drop at the current mouse position as the mouse is moved over a drop target. Overriding the *GiveFeedback* function and obtaining the position of the mouse gives you a chance to control tracking and display of the drag image.

References

Programming with MFC Encyclopedia - Drag and Drop (OLE)

Additional reference words: 4.00 4.10 4.20 5.00

KBCategory: kbole kbfile

KBSubcategory: MfcOLE

PRB: Opening a Dynaset on a SQL Server Stored Procedure

(Q152520)

The information in this article applies to the Microsoft Foundation Classes (MFC) included with:

- Microsoft Visual C++, 32-bit Edition, versions 2.0, 2.1, 2.2, 4.0, 4.1, 4.2, and 5.0

Symptoms

An attempt to call a SQL Server 6.*x* stored procedure from a dynaset-type *CRecordset* throws a *CDBException* if the procedure has any additional SELECT, INSERT, UPDATE or DELETE statement other than a single SELECT statement. You will see the following error message on recordset Open (DB Tracing enabled):

Cannot open a cursor on a stored procedure that has anything other than a single select statement in it

State:37000,Native:16937,Origin:[Microsoft][ODBC SQL Server Driver][SQL Server]

Cause

Calling the following stored procedure from a dynaset-type recordset will cause the error described above:

```
CREATE PROCEDURE twosel AS
    BEGIN

    select * from myTable
    select * from myTable

    End
```

This is by design as documented in the Help file for SQL Server ODBC driver version 2.5. You can navigate the Help file in the following way to get to the description:

What's New
   Server Cursors
     Using ODBC Cursors
      Creating Cursors

"You will get a cursor on SQLExecDirect (Exec procedure_name or{Call procedure_name}) only if the procedure contains one SELECTstatement and nothing else. Otherwise, SQL Server generates an error message. Because of this restriction, you cannot use server cursors with the ODBC catalog functions (which use stored procedures that contain multiple SELECT statements)."

You will also get the same error message when using dynaset if your stored procedure has a RETURN statement in addition to a SELECT statement.

Resolution

Use a snapshot or readOnly forwardOnly type recordset when the stored procedure has more data manipulation statements other than a single SELECT statement.

Status

This behavior is by design.

References

MFC Encyclopedia article: "Recordset: Declaring a Class for a Predefined Query."

Additional reference words: 2.00 2.10 2.20 3.00 3.10 3.20 4.00 4.10 4.20 5.00

KBCategory: kbprg kberrmsg kbusage kbprb

KBSubcategory: MfcDatabase

A P P E N D I X

Searching for Articles in the Microsoft Knowledge Base

Keywords are the means used to locate articles in the Microsoft Knowledge Base. In this appendix, I list the keywords that are specific to articles in the Languages collection of the Knowledge Base, which includes most of the articles pertaining to Microsoft Visual C++.

Major and Minor Keywords in the Languages Collection

Each Knowledge Base article in the Languages collection can contain one or more product-specific subcategory keywords that place the article in an appropriate category within this collection. Some of these keywords (called KB-Subcategory keywords) are a concatenation of major topic keyword and minor topic keyword. For example, you can find all MFC ODBC database-related articles by using *MfcDatabase* as the keyword when you query the Knowledge Base. In some cases, you can use the asterisk (*) wildcard to find articles that fall into a general subcategory. For example, to find all articles that apply to MFC issues, query on *Mfc**. An article usually has only one subcategory keyword, but in some cases, it has more.

The topics and corresponding KBSubcategory keywords for the Languages collection are listed on the following pages. The minor topics are indented under each major topic.

Languages Collection Topics and Keywords

Topics	KBSubcategory Keywords
Setup/Install	
Visual C++ 1.0 32-bit install	vc10setup
Visual C++ 1.5x install	vc15setup
Visual C++ 2.x 32-bit install	vc20setup
Visual C++ Mac-side install issues	vcMacSetup
Tools	
DEVELOPMENT ENVIRONMENT TOOLS:	
AppStudio/Resource editor	AppStudioIss
AppWizard or ClassWizard	WizardIss
Visual Workbench/IDE	VWBIss
Integrated debugger	WBDebug
COMPILER-SPECIFIC:	
Non-MASM assembler issues such as in-line assembler issues	InlineAsmIss
C/C++ compilers	CLIss
C++ compiler (not C compiler)	CPPIss
Bad-code generation	CodeGen
MACINTOSH TOOLS:	
MFILE - File Transfer Utility	MFILEIss
MPROF - Profiler	MPROFIss
MRC	MRCIss
MPW2LIB	MPW2LIBIss
Macintosh Help compiler	MHELPIss
PRODUCT-INDEPENDENT TOOLS:	
CodeView debugger	CVWIss
NMAKE	NmakeIss
Linker	LinkIss
Librarian	LibIss

Topics	KBSubcategory Keywords
MISC TOOLS ISSUES:	
Product sample code	CodeSam
Phar Lap DOSXNT extender	DOSXNTIss
All other tools	TlsMisc
Programming	
C language	CLngIss
C++ language	CPPLngIss
C Run Time	CRTIss
Differences between Mac and Windows	MacPrgIss
Standard template library issues	STLIss
MFC Programming	
MFC ODBC/database	MfcDatabase
MFC DLLs	MfcDLL
MFC document/view	MfcDocView
MFC file I/O	MfcFileIO
MFC Macintosh	MfcMac
MFC OLE	MfcOLE
MFC printing	MfcPrinting
MFC multi-threaded	MfcThreadIss
MFC user interface development	MfcUI
MFC VBX	MfcVBX
MFC Sockets issues	MfcSockets
MFC context-sensitive Help issues	MfcHelp
All other MFC issues	MfcMisc
Add-ons	
OLE control development kit	CDKIss

(continued)

Languages Collection Topics and Keywords *continued*

Topics	KBSubcategory Keywords
General	
General Visual C++ product info	VCGenIss
Online Doc tools issues	OLDocIss
Issue doesn't apply to all platforms	
Applies to Visual C++ for Alpha	VCAlpha
Applies to Visual C++ for Macintosh	VCMac
Applies to Visual C++ for MIPS	VCMips
Applies to Visual C++ for x86	VCx86
Applies to Win32s	Win32s
Buglist Keywords	
On the VC++ 4.00	buglist vcbuglist400
New bug in VC++ 4.10	vcbuglist410
New bug in VC++ 4.20	vcbuglist420
Fixed bug in VC++ 4.1	vcfixlist410
Fixed bug in VC++ 4.2	vcfixlist420

The following table shows examples of several types of queries using the keywords listed above.

Information Type	Query Syntax
All bugs in VC++ 4.0	vcbuglist400
All bugs in VC++ 4.1	(vcbuglist410 and vcbuglist400) not vcfixlist410
All bugs in VC++ 4.2	(vcbuglist420 and vcbuglist410 and vcbuglist400) not (vcfixlist410 or vcfixlist420)
Fixed bug in VC++ 4.1	vcfixlist410
Fixed bug in VC++ 4.2	vcfixlist420

Product-Specific Keywords

You can use KBSubcategory keywords to organize Languages articles or to search for specific groups of Languages articles. For information about KB-Subcategory keywords for other Microsoft developer products, please query the Knowledge Base using the keywords *dskbguide* and *kbkeyword*.

Knowledge Base–Wide Keywords

Each article in the Languages collection also contains at least one generic, Knowledge Base–wide keyword (called a KBCategory keyword). The KBCategory keywords are standard throughout the Knowledge Base and appear in all Knowledge Base articles, regardless of the type of product. You can use KBCategory keywords to organize all Knowledge Base articles for viewing or to search for articles across several Microsoft products. For more information about these KBCategory keywords, please see the following Knowledge Base article on line: "Categories and Keywords for All Knowledge Base Articles": Q94671.

INDEX

Page numbers in italics refer to tables, figures, or illustrations.

Symbols and Numbers

'' (apostophes) in SQL data strings, 319
* (asterisk) wildcard in Knowledge Base searches, 413
16-color bitmaps, 133

A

About dialog box, 48
About Ellipse menu command, 157
About Rect menu command, 157
About SysMenu command, checking for, 52
accelerator table of an ActiveX control, 216–20
ACCEL project, 217–20
Access database
  attaching DBF tables to, 281
  attaching FoxPro to, 271, 287–93
  attaching Oracle to, 271, 299
  attaching SQL Server to, 271, 293–98
  linking DBF tables to, 273–74
AccessPict control, adding, 276
AccessPict OLE control project, building a Release version of, 274
access points, 75, 78
ACCFOXDLG1.CPP file, 292
ACCFOXDLG.OGX Developer Studio component (on the companion CD-ROM), 289
ACCFOX.H file, 291
ACCSPICT control, inserting, 302
ACCSPICT OLE control, building, 300
ACCSQLDLG1.CPP file, 297
ACCSQLDLG.OGX Developer Studio component (on the companion CD-ROM), 295
ACCSQL.H file, 297
ActivateFrame function, 86
  implementing for child frame windows, 262
  overriding, 55
active frame window in MDI applications, 40
active view in SDI vs. MDI applications, 41–42

ActiveX control class, adding data members and functions to, 197–98
ActiveX controls
  checking for unsafe areas, 192
  guidelines for scripting or initializing safety, 190
  interaction with Internet Explorer, *182*
  loading properties asynchronously, 193–201
  making safe for scripting and initializing, 182–93
  overriding the *COleControl::OnGetControlInfo* function, 217
AddDBDlg component, inserting, 290, 295–96
AddDocTemplate function, 77, 81, 90
Add method, adding to the collection class, 229
AddRef function, 186–87, 208, 209
Afxcmn.h header file, 400
AFXCORE.RTF source file, 126
AfxCurrentResourceHandle function, 407
AFXDISP.H, 249
AfxFindResourceHandle function, 407
AfxGetApp function, 94
AfxGetResourceHandle function, 407
AFXOLE.H file, 205, 240
AfxOleInit function, 240, 380–81
AFXPRINT.RC resource file, 25
AfxSetResourceHandle function, 407
AfxTermExtensionModule function, 407
Alt-M key combination, 219
ANIMBAR project, 66–73
apostrophes in SQL data strings, 319
application attributes, saving the state of, 233, 253–64
application class, modifying, 64–65, 154–56
application element, 4–5
application layers in MFC
  primary, 4–7, *6*
  secondary, 7, *8*
  tertiary, 7–8, *9*
application object, 45
application-related functions, 79–81

COM
without the
complexity.

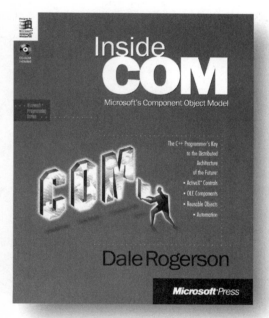

Inside COM
Microsoft's Component Object Model

The C++ Programmer's Key
to the Distributed
Architecture
of the Future:
• ActiveX Controls
• OLE Components
• Reusable Objects
• Automation

Dale Rogerson

Microsoft Press

U.S.A.	**$34.99**
U.K.	£32.99 [V.A.T. included]
Canada	$46.99
ISBN 1-57231-349-8	

The Component Object Model (COM) isn't just another standard. It's the basis of Microsoft's approach to distributed computing. It's also the method for customizing Microsoft® applications, present and future. And it's the foundation of OLE and ActiveX™. In short, COM is a major key to the future of development. And this is the book that unlocks COM. In it, you'll discover:

- A clear and simple, practical guide to building elegant, robust, portable COM components
- An eye-opening presentation of how accessible COM can be—especially for those already familiar with C++
- An insightful, progressive view of COM design
- Plenty of illustrations in the form of code samples

INSIDE COM is for intermediate to advanced C++ programmers; beginning to advanced COM, ActiveX, and OLE programmers; academics with an interest in component design; and even programmers who want to use COM when it's ported to UNIX, MVS, and other environments. To put it simply, if you work with COM, then INSIDE COM was written for you.

Microsoft ®*Press*

Harness
the power of
ActiveX™ *controls.*

ActiveX controls are an important ingredient in Microsoft's emerging "object model" approach to the Internet, applications, development tools, and operating systems. Written by a former data management consultant and current program manager at Microsoft in the Visual Languages group, ACTIVEX CONTROLS INSIDE OUT is an in-depth guide for C++ and Microsoft® Visual Basic® programmers who want to build powerful custom controls and "componentware" using Microsoft's new tools and revolutionary COM (Component Object Model) technology. A comprehensive update to the successful first edition, *OLE Controls Inside Out,* this book contains the latest on MFC, changes to OLE, and Visual Basic and Microsoft Internet Explorer support for hosting ActiveX controls. It is an indispensable resource for all those programming for Windows® and the Internet.

U.S.A.	**$39.95**
U.K.	£37.49 [V.A.T. included]
Canada	$54.95
ISBN 1-57231-350-1	

Microsoft®*Press*

IMPORTANT—READ CAREFULLY BEFORE OPENING SOFTWARE PACKET(S). By opening the sealed packet(s) containing the software, you indicate your acceptance of the following Microsoft License Agreement.

MICROSOFT LICENSE AGREEMENT

(Book Companion CD)

This is a legal agreement between you (either an individual or an entity) and Microsoft Corporation. By opening the sealed software packet(s) you are agreeing to be bound by the terms of this agreement. If you do not agree to the terms of this agreement, promptly return the unopened software packet(s) and any accompanying written materials to the place you obtained them for a full refund.

MICROSOFT SOFTWARE LICENSE

1. GRANT OF LICENSE. Microsoft grants to you the right to use one copy of the Microsoft software program included with this book (the "SOFTWARE") on a single terminal connected to a single computer. The SOFTWARE is in "use" on a computer when it is loaded into the temporary memory (i.e., RAM) or installed into the permanent memory (e.g., hard disk, CD-ROM, or other storage device) of that computer. You may not network the SOFTWARE or otherwise use it on more than one computer or computer terminal at the same time.

2. COPYRIGHT. The SOFTWARE is owned by Microsoft or its suppliers and is protected by United States copyright laws and international treaty provisions. Therefore, you must treat the SOFTWARE like any other copyrighted material (e.g., a book or musical recording) except that you may either (a) make one copy of the SOFTWARE solely for backup or archival purposes, or (b) transfer the SOFTWARE to a single hard disk provided you keep the original solely for backup or archival purposes. You may not copy the written materials accompanying the SOFTWARE.

3. OTHER RESTRICTIONS. You may not rent or lease the SOFTWARE, but you may transfer the SOFTWARE and accompanying written materials on a permanent basis provided you retain no copies and the recipient agrees to the terms of this Agreement. You may not reverse engineer, decompile, or disassemble the SOFTWARE. If the SOFTWARE is an update or has been updated, any transfer must include the most recent update and all prior versions.

4. DUAL MEDIA SOFTWARE. If the SOFTWARE package contains more than one kind of disk (3.5", 5.25", and CD-ROM), then you may use only the disks appropriate for your single-user computer. You may not use the other disks on another computer or loan, rent, lease, or transfer them to another user except as part of the permanent transfer (as provided above) of all SOFTWARE and written materials.

5. SAMPLE CODE. If the SOFTWARE includes Sample Code, then Microsoft grants you a royalty-free right to reproduce and distribute the sample code of the SOFTWARE provided that you: (a) distribute the sample code only in conjunction with and as a part of your software product; (b) do not use Microsoft's or its authors' names, logos, or trademarks to market your software product; (c) include the copyright notice that appears on the SOFTWARE on your product label and as a part of the sign-on message for your software product; and (d) agree to indemnify, hold harmless, and defend Microsoft and its authors from and against any claims or lawsuits, including attorneys' fees, that arise or result from the use or distribution of your software product.

DISCLAIMER OF WARRANTY

The SOFTWARE (including instructions for its use) is provided "AS IS" WITHOUT WARRANTY OF ANY KIND. MICROSOFT FURTHER DISCLAIMS ALL IMPLIED WARRANTIES INCLUDING WITHOUT LIMITATION ANY IMPLIED WARRANTIES OF MERCHANTABILITY OR OF FITNESS FOR A PARTICULAR PURPOSE. THE ENTIRE RISK ARISING OUT OF THE USE OR PERFORMANCE OF THE SOFTWARE AND DOCUMENTATION REMAINS WITH YOU.

IN NO EVENT SHALL MICROSOFT, ITS AUTHORS, OR ANYONE ELSE INVOLVED IN THE CREATION, PRODUCTION, OR DELIVERY OF THE SOFTWARE BE LIABLE FOR ANY DAMAGES WHATSOEVER (INCLUDING, WITHOUT LIMITATION, DAMAGES FOR LOSS OF BUSINESS PROFITS, BUSINESS INTERRUPTION, LOSS OF BUSINESS INFORMATION, OR OTHER PECUNIARY LOSS) ARISING OUT OF THE USE OF OR INABILITY TO USE THE SOFTWARE OR DOCUMENTATION, EVEN IF MICROSOFT HAS BEEN ADVISED OF THE POSSIBILITY OF SUCH DAMAGES. BECAUSE SOME STATES/COUNTRIES DO NOT ALLOW THE EXCLUSION OR LIMITATION OF LIABILITY FOR CONSEQUENTIAL OR INCIDENTAL DAMAGES, THE ABOVE LIMITATION MAY NOT APPLY TO YOU.

U.S. GOVERNMENT RESTRICTED RIGHTS

The SOFTWARE and documentation are provided with RESTRICTED RIGHTS. Use, duplication, or disclosure by the Government is subject to restrictions as set forth in subparagraph (c)(1)(ii) of The Rights in Technical Data and Computer Software clause at DFARS 252.227-7013 or subparagraphs (c)(1) and (2) of the Commercial Computer Software — Restricted Rights 48 CFR 52.227-19, as applicable. Manufacturer is Microsoft Corporation, One Microsoft Way, Redmond, WA 98052-6399.

If you acquired this product in the United States, this Agreement is governed by the laws of the State of Washington. Should you have any questions concerning this Agreement, or if you desire to contact Microsoft Press for any reason, please write: Microsoft Press, One Microsoft Way, Redmond, WA 98052-6399.